THE METROPOLITAN ENIGMA

Inquiries into the Nature and Dimensions
of America's "Urban Crisis"

Edited by James Q. Wilson

ANCHOR BOOKS

DOUBLEDAY & COMPANY, INC.
GARDEN CITY, NEW YORK

The Metropolitan Enigma was originally published in hardcover by the Harvard University Press in 1968. The Anchor Books edition is published by arrangement with the Harvard University Press.

Anchor Books edition: 1970

CONTENTS

PREFACE

This is a revised and expanded version of a book that was first published, in a softcover edition, by the Task Force on Economic Growth and Opportunity of the United States Chamber of Commerce. In 1966, the Task Force asked the Joint Center for Urban Studies of M.I.T. and Harvard to prepare a set of background papers on urban issues with the understanding that while the Task Force would pay the bill and print the results, the Joint Center would have complete freedom in selecting the topics and authors and editing the papers. The agreement was carefully respected and this book is the result.

Subsequently, the Harvard University Press decided to publish the volume under its own imprint in a hardcover edition. The authors were given an opportunity to revise their papers and the editor took the opportunity to commission an additional paper. Minor editorial changes were made in all the papers and those by Professors Kain, Meyer, and Sizer were substantially rewritten and new material added. That by Professor Banfield appeared for the first time in the hardcover edition. Minor revisions in some of the essays were made for the Anchor edition of 1970.

The contents of the papers are in every case the responsibility of the authors. The Joint Center attempted to find the ablest scholars to write them but it allowed each to develop his topic in his own way. No effort was made to produce a unified work or one animated by a single point of view. This is true also of the editor's paper at the end—though intended as a kind of summing up, it represents his own views and not necessarily those of the other authors, the Joint Center, or the Task Force.

The editor would like to thank Dr. Carl Madden, Director of Research for the Task Force, and Erwin D. Canham, Chairman of the Task Force, for their interest and support; Mrs. Janet Eckstein and Miss Karla Weatherall for their assistance in seeing the manuscript through the hardcover edition; and Professor Daniel Patrick Moynihan, then Director of the Joint Center for Urban Studies, for his encouragement and counsel.

JAMES Q. WILSON

FOREWORD

Carl H. Madden

Director of Research
The Task Force on Economic Growth and Opportunity

The Task Force on Economic Growth and Opportunity, a special purpose group sponsored by the Chamber of Commerce of the United States, is composed of over one hundred leaders of American industry, business, and finance. Membership is personal, and the reports of the Task Force represent the views of its members, not necessarily those of the Chamber of Commerce.

The Task Force attempts to link research and action by business leaders on selected national social and economic questions in an environment of independent thinking. It attempts to contribute to the public dialogue by making available both its own views and the findings of research. It believes that business leaders need to apply to their thinking about social and economic issues the same careful analysis that is already employed in our most progressive industry in order that the needed will and action be illuminated by knowledge and understanding.

The Task Force thus brings to bear on broad social and economic problems the independent, objective analysis and planning of some of the nation's best business, academic, and professional leaders. It does so by carefully selecting the problems to be studied, designing comprehensive study plans, and following a research strategy that draws upon a wide variety of experts from independent groups. Task Force studies lead to recommendations reported to the public and the Chamber of Commerce of the United States, aimed at practical and effective private and public policies to help resolve national problems.

Since its creation in 1964, the Task Force has studied the problem of poverty in the United States. Several reports are available on this subject, including in each report the background papers of independent scholars. The Task Force is also studying the complex problems and potential of metropolitan America: "The Potential for America's Cities."

To provide part of the background research being developed to support its study, the Task Force in January 1966 asked the Joint Center for Urban Studies of Harvard and M.I.T. to prepare a series of papers on urban problems. The Joint Center had complete freedom in selecting topics, choosing authors, and editing the papers. The Task Force paid for the articles and published the collection in a special volume entitled, *The Metropolitan Enigma: Inquiries into the Nature and Dimensions of America's "Urban Crisis."* This arrangement assures the freedom and independence of the authors; it also means, of course, that their opinions do not necessarily reflect the views of the Task Force, the Chamber of Commerce of the United States, or the Joint Center for Urban Studies.

The association of a national organization of business and professional executives with a leading academic institution, for the purpose of pooling their respective talents and resources in a free exploration of issues of urbanism, has proved to be a mutually rewarding experience. Business leaders have grown to understand better the complexity and magnitude of urban issues. Some member organizations of the Chamber of Commerce have employed this report as the basis for intensive study of their own cities, and others are likely to do so. Indeed, from this beginning the Chamber of Commerce, with the cooperation of faculty members at the Harvard Business School and employing case material developed by the School, have developed a program, "Continuing Education in Managing Urban Problems," which will be offered to business leaders and others in major cities throughout the country. Meanwhile, scholars have come to appreciate better the business community's respect for and interest in serious and scholarly analysis into urban issues. And both businessmen and scholars are coming to recognize more clearly the need for social innovation consistent with the values of our American system to achieve the pace of social and economic advance that is promised by our potential for scientific and technological gains in the future.

THE DISTRIBUTION AND MOVEMENT OF
JOBS AND INDUSTRY

John F. Kain

By any measure metropolitan growth, since World War II, has been rapid but unevenly distributed. Outlying portions of metropolitan areas have been growing quickly, while the central areas have been growing very little and, in an increasing number of instances, have actually declined. During this period, what began as a *relative* decline became an *absolute* decline for a lengthening list of central cities. Losses in retail sales and property values, declining profits for central city merchants, and falling tax bases have usually followed from these employment and population declines. Moreover, depopulation was selective; the young, employed, well-to-do, and white moved to suburban areas leaving behind the aged, the unemployed, the poor, and the Negro. This selective depopu-

I wish to thank my research assistants Molly R. Mayo and Randall Weiss for their invaluable assistance in the preparation of this paper. Of the many persons who gave advice and criticism, I am particularly in debt to John R. Meyer, James Q. Wilson, Eric A. Hanushek, and Joseph J. Persky. Any errors that remain are, of course, my own responsibility.

lation and employment decline aggravated old problems and created new ones for central city governments.

These trends did not pass unnoticed or unchallenged. Demands that public policy do something to halt the "decay" of our central cities were and are still frequently heard and much legislation directed to this end has been enacted. Some persons even argue that this decay is in large part the result of direct subsidies, such as FHA-insured loans for low density suburban housing, indirect federal subsidies to suburban communities, and services provided to the suburbanite (especially the commuter) but paid for by the central cities. Indeed, a slavish worship of the private automobile is regarded by many as the sole, or at least primary, cause of the "undesirable" pattern of postwar metropolitan development.

Proposals to solve the "problem" are even more numerous and include: central city residential and industrial renewal, increased taxation of private automobiles, a moratorium on expressway construction, the abolition of federal income tax credits for interest and real estate taxes paid by homeowners, and subsidization of public transit and construction of new high-speed rail rapid transit systems.

However, among scholars who have investigated these questions, there is general agreement that central city decline is nothing new—that only perception and concern about it are new—and that there is no or little reason to expect a reversal of these trends in the foreseeable future, given current and proposed policies. And there is an equal measure of agreement about the principal causes of these declines.[1]

[1] These studies include: Raymond Vernon, *The Changing Economic Function of the Central City* (Area Development Committee of the Committee for Economic Development, New York, January 1959); Edgar M. Hoover and Raymond Vernon, *Anatomy of a Metropolis* (Cambridge: Harvard University Press, 1959); John H. Niedercorn and John F. Kain, "An Econometric Model of Metropolitan Development," *Papers and Proceedings of the Regional Science Association,* 1962; John H. Niedercorn and John F. Kain, "Suburbanization and Population, 1948–1975," *Proceedings of the Highway Research Board,* 1963; John R. Meyer, John F. Kain, and Martin Wohl, *The Urban Transportation Problem* (Cambridge: Harvard University Press, 1965).

The relative and absolute decline of central cities, and their downtown areas in particular, is the result of several important technological and economic changes that have made decentralization a more feasible, more economic, or more desirable choice for increasing numbers of households and businesses. Developments in transportation and communication have made different parcels of land increasingly interchangeable for most manufacturing, retailing, wholesaling, residential, and other uses. Many activities once willing to pay the higher costs of central locations no longer find it to their advantage to do so. Firms previously restricted to a fairly limited number of central locations by their need to be near ports, freight and passenger terminals, rail lines, and the like now depend to an ever increasing extent on trucks. Transport costs for these firms may be lower at an outlying site near an interchange on the burgeoning metropolitan expressway system. This is particularly true of the growing fraction of wholesaling and manufacturing firms that rely mainly on truck transport. Similarly, rapid increases in automobile ownership have released many firms from their need to be located convenient to mass transit facilities in order to attract a labor force. Though experiences are somewhat mixed, firms relocating to outlying areas, with abundant free parking, often find they have an easier time attracting a labor force than they once did at their central city locations. The transportation and communications savings that caused many firms to choose central locations have become smaller or disappeared entirely.

Still other forces are affecting the location of wholesaling and manufacturing. Changes in production methods, which increasingly require spacious, single-story plants, are among the most important of these. Such plants are difficult and enormously expensive to construct in built-up central city areas but easy to build on large vacant sites in outlying areas. In addition, rapid technological changes in communications and data processing appear to be reducing the need for armies of white collar workers employed in central city offices, or at least allowing them to be located in less expensive space in outlying areas. The growth in white collar employment has for the time being offset these forces in many instances, but

the impact of the communications revolution is only beginning to be felt.

Trends Prior to 1945

Interpreting these postwar changes in metropolitan structure
and the spatial distribution of jobs is made difficult by the fact
that they follow fifteen years of "abnormal" development.
Metropolitan growth and development was twice disrupted—
first by the sharp reduction of employment and investment
during the great depression, and then by the rapid expansion
of employment during World War II. Wartime expansion was
accompanied by government controls on materials, construction, and investment in plant and equipment. These controls
affected the level and spatial distribution of economic activity
both within and among metropolitan areas.

One leading interpretation of the impact of World War II
on the spatial distribution of economic activity within and
among metropolitan areas was advanced by Woodbury (1953)
and Creamer (1963).[2] Both studies are limited to manufacturing. Their arguments about the effect of World War II on the
location of manufacturing activity may be summarized as
follows:

1. World War II caused a huge increase in U.S. manufacturing employment from a prewar (1939) level of approximately
9.6 million workers (nearly identical to the level in 1929)
to a postwar (1947) level of 14.4 million. (By comparison,
total U.S. employment in manufacturing increased by only
one million more between 1947 and 1954, reaching a level
of 15.4 million workers in 1954, and by 1958 had declined
slightly to 15.2 million workers.)

[2] Coleman Woodbury, with the assistance of Frank Cliffe, "Industrial Location and Urban Redevelopment," in Coleman Woodbury, ed., *The Future of Cities and Urban Redevelopment* (Chicago: The University of Chicago Press, 1953), pp. 103–286; and
Daniel Creamer, *Changing Location of Manufacturing Employment*, Part I: *Changes by Type of Location, 1947–1961* (New
York: National Industrial Conference Board, 1963).

2. Because of controls, most of this wartime increase in manufacturing employment had to be accommodated at existing manufacturing plants and was achieved principally by means of a more intensive use of facilities existing at the beginning of the war.

3. Because the big central cities were the primary recipients of this captive increase in manufacturing employment, wartime expansion reversed a long-term trend toward employment dispersal within metropolitan areas.

4. Were it not for wartime controls, most of this increased manufacturing employment would have located at newer plants at less central locations and in newer metropolitan areas. The removal of controls at the end of World War II was followed by rapid dispersal.

5. Thus, much of the postwar dispersal of manufacturing (and probably by extension many other kinds of employment) was simply a delayed redistribution. It follows that employment dispersal should slow down as this backlog of relocations is worked off.

Thus, Woodbury and Creamer conclude that the principal effect of World War II was to halt or reverse long-standing and well-documented trends toward suburbanization within, and diffusion among, metropolitan areas. They argue that prior to World War II manufacturing employment was becoming more evenly distributed among U.S. metropolitan areas with the smaller, more rapidly growing, and less industrialized metropolitan areas of the South and the West increasing their share of manufacturing employment at the expense of the older, more mature manufacturing centers of the North and Northeast.

An Alternate View

But there is an alternative interpretation of these trends, which could lead to substantially different forecasts of metropolitan spatial structure. The key element in the Woodbury and Creamer interpretation is the assumed limitations on the construction of new plant and equipment. For example, Creamer cites data on the amount of *private* investment in

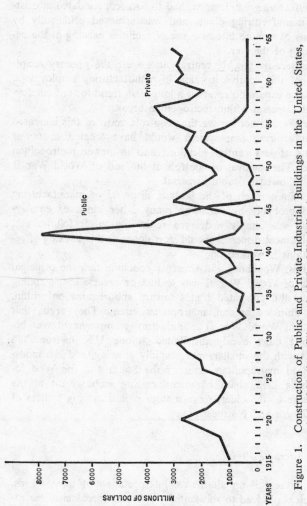

Figure 1. Construction of Public and Private Industrial Buildings in the United States, 1915-1965 (in millions of 1957-1959 dollars)

industrial plant and equipment during and immediately following World War II: "The real net value of privately owned structures and equipment was expanded by less than 10%, from $51.5 billion in 1954 prices in 1939 to $55.7 billion in 1945 . . . By the end of 1947, the real net stock of fixed capital was about 25% larger than in 1939 and 15% above the 1945 figure."[3] However, Creamer overlooks the fact that most of the wartime investment in plant and equipment was provided by the federal government. The *Quarterly Progress Report* of the Surplus Property Administration notes: "The total government investment in war plants and equipment was more than 18 billion dollars of which 17 billion dollars was for manufacturing facilities—a staggering figure, for the entire cost of construction of all the manufacturing facilities in the United States before the war was only 40 billion dollars."[4]

Yearly data are available on the level of private and public outlays for industrial buildings and these are plotted in Figure 1. Government construction of industrial buildings exceeded private outlays for the same purpose by a wide margin during 1941–1944. Construction of privately owned industrial buildings had declined to $351 million by 1943, but during the same year $4.2 billion worth of publicly financed industrial buildings were completed. Outlays for public industrial buildings were even larger in the previous year ($8 billion), but those for privately owned industrial buildings were only about one tenth as large ($829 million). By comparison, new construction of privately owned industrial buildings amounted to $3.1 billion in 1946, and that of publicly owned industrial buildings was only $209 million.[5]

Data presented in Table 1 on the mean yearly construction expenditures by use suggest a significantly different interpretation of the impact of World War II on metropolitan development. The time periods in Table 1 correspond to the dates of

[3] Creamer, *Changing Location*, pp. 37–38.

[4] Surplus Property Administration, *The Liquidation of War Surpluses, Quarterly Progress Report to the Congress*, Fourth Quarter, 1945, p. 18.

[5] U.S. Department of Commerce, *Construction Statistics 1915–1964: A Supplement to Construction Review*, January 1966.

Table 1. Mean yearly value of construction put in place, by period (millions of constant 1957–1959 dollars).

Type of construction	1918–1928	1928–1938	1938–1946	1946–1953	1953–1957	1957–1962
Private residential	9,807	3,539	4,527	14,503	17,012	16,606
Public residential	14	59	736	491	371	832
Total residential	9,821	3,598	5,264	14,994	17,383	17,438
Private office buildings	914	602	220	713	1,600	2,062
Private stores, restaurants, etc.	1,569	744	625	1,069	1,847	1,936
Public other nonresidential	155	193	137	319	436	524
Private industrial buildings	1,895	1,112	1,303	2,173	3,026	2,564
Public industrial buildings	–	11	2,631	875	898	409
Total industrial buildings	1,895	1,123	3,928	3,057	3,924	2,973

Source: U.S. Department of Commerce, Construction Statistics 1915–1964: A Supplement to Construction Review, January 1966.

the censuses of manufacturing moved forward one year because employment at a new plant usually would lag behind its construction. The impact of both the depression and World War II are clearly evident in the statistics in Table 1. Yearly outlays for the new construction of residential structures during 1938–1946 were only 35 percent of expenditures during the immediate postwar period, and the ratio for the depression period (1929–1938) was even more unfavorable. Similarly, yearly outlays for the construction of stores and restaurants during 1938–1946 amounted to only 58 percent of those during 1946–1953. A far different situation characterized the industrial buildings category. New construction of industrial buildings during 1938–1946 was 128 percent of that for 1946–1953. Outlays for privately constructed industrial buildings were only 60 percent of 1946–1953 levels, but those for publicly financed structures were 351 percent of 1946–1953 levels.

These data indicate that whereas the construction of new

residences, stores, office buildings, restaurants, and the like was severely restricted by wartime controls, a great deal of investment in industrial plant took place. Following World War II nearly all this new industrial plant was transferred to private ownership, often at nominal cost. The spatial distribution of this new investment is crucial to an analysis of metropolitan development. Further investigations of this question are planned by the author. As yet no definitive answer can be given, but some hypotheses can be advanced.

It appears that Creamer and Woodbury were right to an important degree. A significant amount of new manufacturing employment probably did occur in the way they suggest. However, a significant portion also was accommodated by means of new plant and equipment investment. Also, much of this new investment occurred within large central cities. No data are available (or at least obtainable at reasonable cost) that describe investment in plant construction by city. However, yearly data on the value of construction and number of new structures for all nonresidential uses are available for a large number of cities. Table 2 lists the investment and number of new nonresidential buildings constructed in the twenty largest cities during 1939–1946. By any criterion the amount of construction during the period is very large, and in some cities phenomenal. For example, in Los Angeles alone more than half a billion dollars of new nonresidential construction and 94,346 new nonresidential structures were put in place during 1939–1946. The outlays for new construction were even larger in Chicago, even though only about a third as many new nonresidential structures were built.

In interpreting the construction data in Table 2 it should be recalled that central cities are large and heterogeneous. If a substantial part of the new investment took place in a different spatial pattern than existing employment, the impact on metropolitan structure might be quite large. In fact there are good *a priori* reasons for believing this was the case, and the data for the New York City boroughs in Table 2 provide some support for this view. It seems very likely that a disproportionate amount of the new industrial plant built during World War II was located at the periphery of central cities,

Table 2. Value of new nonresidential construction and number of
new nonresidential structures during 1939–1946:
20 largest cities, 1960 population
(thousands of constant 1947–1949 dollars).

City	1939–1946	
	Value	Number
New York City		
Bronx	40,382	1,414
Brooklyn	261,934	3,912
Manhattan	92,384	930
Queens	142,072	9,276
Chicago	539,134	17,364
Los Angeles	515,369	94,396
Philadelphia	305,742	3,786
Detroit	275,368	36,289
Baltimore	176,699	13,600
Houston	176,835	6,831
Cleveland	215,600	14,064
Washington, D.C.	269,715	4,518
St. Louis	165,496	10,893
Milwaukee	72,644	8,853
San Francisco	212,200	2,089
Boston	134,204	2,209
Dallas	64,278	9,219
New Orleans	129,078	1,240
Pittsburgh	56,313	2,863
San Antonio	43,336	4,436
San Diego	198,855	16,459
Seattle	150,661	9,704
Cincinnati	46,015	3,322

Source: U.S. Department of Labor, Bureau of Labor Statistics,
Bulletin 693, Building Construction 1940; Bulletin 713, Building
Construction 1941; Bulletin 786, Construction Industry in the
United States 1942; Bulletin 918, Construction in the War Years
1942–1945; Bulletin 941, Construction and Housing 1946–1947.

but within their legal boundaries. At the start of World War
II most central cities contained large amounts of usable
vacant land. Industry by itself is a small user of urban land
and the large-scale housebuilding that invariably accompanied
new plants in the postwar period was constrained by wartime

controls on homebuilding.[6] Still more plants might have been constructed outside of their boundaries and then quickly annexed to the central city.

If this hypothesis about the wartime expansion of manufacturing employment within central cities is in part, or substantially, correct, it implies a far different interpretation of postwar metropolitan development than is usually advanced. It suggests a great deal of largely unnoticed employment dispersal (and, more important, nonpopulation-serving employment) took place *during World War II*. If so, this *wartime* dispersal of *jobs* would provide a powerful force for *postwar* dispersal of *housing* and population-serving employment.[7] The argument is that a fundamental redistribution of employment took place during World War II within central city boundaries (or what were central city boundaries by 1947). This employment redistribution set the stage for the rapid dispersal of population and population-serving employment as soon as wartime controls on homebuilding and noncritical nonresidential construction were removed. Though there is a fair amount of evidence that would seem to support this hypothesis, its final acceptance or rejection must await better

[6] Niedercorn and Hearle determined that industry used only 9 percent of all land within 48 large American cities and only 11 percent of all developed land. These data were obtained from land-use surveys conducted at various dates since 1945 within the 48 cities. By comparison, residential uses account for 30 percent of developed land. Even following the postwar expansion, central cities contained substantial amounts of vacant land. The Niedercorn-Hearle survey reports that 21 percent of all land in the 48 cities included in their survey was vacant. John H. Niedercorn and Edward F. R. Hearle, *Recent Land Use Trends in Forty-Eight Central Cities*, RAND Corporation, Memorandum RM-3663-FF, June 1963, p. 4.

[7] If true, the author's own earlier studies would understate the effect of employment redistribution in causing population suburbanization. Meyer, Kain, and Wohl, *The Urban Transportation Problem;* Niedercorn and Kain, "An Econometric Model of Metropolitan Development"; Niedercorn and Kain, "Suburbanization and Population, 1948–1975"; Vernon, *The Changing Economic Function.*

documentation of the changes in the geographic location of metropolitan employment during and prior to World War II.

If correct, this alternative view of the process of metropolitan dispersal could have substantial effect on many existing forecasts of metropolitan structure and on our perception of many metropolitan problems. For example, since most projections of employment and population dispersal are based on extrapolations of historical trends, it is conceivable that we are currently overestimating the rate and extent of population and employment dispersal. Much of the rapid postwar suburbanization of population and dispersal of employment, other than manufacturing, may be due to restraints on new construction during World War II and thereby be temporary. If so, many current forecasts of land use based on this experience may be erroneous.

Postwar Trends in the Location of Jobs[8]

At the end of World War II, the average metropolitan area—based on the data in Table 3 for 40 large areas—had an

---

[8] The analyses of postwar trends in the location of employment and population presented in this section rely heavily on analyses presented in Chapter 3 of Meyer, Kain, and Wohl, *The Urban Transportation Problem*, pp. 25–56. In fact, they might be viewed as an updating and extension of the analyses presented there.

Analyses of postwar changes in spatial distributions of employment are seriously handicapped by the lack of consistent and comprehensive data. The best over-all view of recent changes in employment locations is found in the Census of Business and Manufactures. However, these data are available for only a limited number of years, are not always consistent, provide very little information on changes within large and heterogeneous central cities, and account for only about 60 percent of all metropolitan employment. Still they are the best data we have. The 1948, 1954, 1958, and 1963 Censuses of Business present data on total employment in retailing, selected services, and wholesaling for central cities and standard metropolitan statistical areas (SMSA's). Figures on total employment in manufacturing in SMSA's and central cities are available from the 1947, 1954, and 1958 Censuses of

Table 3. Mean SMSA, central city, and ring employment and
population in 1948 and central city and ring shares:
40 large central cities.

Item	Central city Number	Per- cent	Ring Number	Per- cent	SMSA Number	Per- cent
Employment						
Manufacturing[a]	118,652	66.9	58,805	33.1	177,457	100
Wholesaling[b]	33,124	91.8	2,959	8.2	36,083	100
Retailing	61,048	75.3	19,992	24.7	81,040	100
Services	23,654	84.8	4,240	15.2	27,894	100
Population[c]	899,625	64.1	504,790	36.0	1,404,415	100

Source: See note 9.

[a] Data pertain to 1947–1954.

[b] Wholesaling data available for 39 SMSA's only.

[c] Obtained by interpolation of 1940, 1950, and 1960 data.

Manufactures and for a limited number of cities from the 1963
Census of Manufactures. Suburban ring employment may be obtained by subtracting central city employment from SMSA employment. This geographic division of metropolitan areas is crude, but
it provides at least somewhat meaningful descriptions of postwar
trends in urban development.

Most of the analyses of postwar changes in the spatial distribution of employment and population that appear in this paper are
based on the experience of 40 large metropolitan areas. In earlier
versions of this paper, they were referred to as the 40 largest metropolitan areas. This latter description is somewhat misleading, since
a few metropolitan areas with larger populations in 1960 were not
included in the analysis. The criteria for inclusion in the sample
took into account central city size in 1950 and 1960 as well as
metropolitan area population. Thus, the list consists of the 40
largest only if a fairly complex criteria of "largest" is employed.
(The 40 largest SMSA's are: Akron, Atlanta, Baltimore, Boston,
Buffalo, Chicago, Cincinnati, Cleveland, Columbus, Dallas, Dayton, Denver, Detroit, Fort Worth, Houston, Indianapolis, Jersey
City, Kansas City, Los Angeles–Long Beach, Louisville, Memphis,
Miami, Milwaukee, Minneapolis–St. Paul, New Orleans, New York,
Newark, Oklahoma City, Philadelphia, Phoenix, Pittsburgh, Port-
land, Rochester, St. Louis, San Antonio, San Diego, San Francisco–
Oakland, Seattle, Tampa–St. Petersburg, and Washington, D.C.).

estimated population of 1.4 million.[9] About 64 percent of these people lived within the central city and about 36 percent lived in the suburban or metropolitan ring. Manufacturing was clearly the most important of the four industry categories analyzed. The average metropolitan area had about 177,000 manufacturing workers distributed between its central city and ring in nearly the same proportions as the population. Retailing accounts for the next largest number of employees and except for manufacturing was least concentrated in the central city. Even so, at the beginning of the period an average

---

Most of the trends observable in the central cities in these larger metropolitan areas have been occurring in smaller centers as well. However, because the central cities of these smaller areas more often have room for expansion inside their political boundaries or can more often annex outlying areas (are less often hemmed in by existing political subdivisions), these redistributions of employment are harder to identify from published data.

[9] Statistics presented in Tables 3 to 8 and 10 were calculated from published data obtained from the following publications of the U.S. Department of Commerce, Bureau of the Census: *Census of Manufactures: 1947, Vol. III, Area Statistics; Census of Manufactures: 1954, Vol. III, Area Statistics; Census of Manufactures: 1958, Vol. III, Area Statistics; Census of Manufactures: 1963, Vol. III, Area Statistics; Census of Business: 1948, Vol. III, Retail Trade-Area Statistics; Census of Business: 1948, Vol. V, Wholesale Trade-Area Statistics; Census of Business: 1948, Vol. VII, Selected Services-Area Statistics; Census of Business: 1954, Vol. II, Retail Trade-Area Statistics; Census of Business: 1954, Vol. IV, Wholesale Trade-Area Statistics; Census of Business: 1958, Vol. VI, Selected Services-Area Statistics; Census of Business: 1958, Vol. II, Retail Trade-Area Statistics; Census of Business: 1958, Vol. IV, Wholesale Trade-Area Statistics; Census of Business: 1958, Vol. VI, Selected Services-Area Statistics; Census of Business: 1963, Vol. II, Retail Trade-Area Statistics; Census of Business: 1963, Vol. V, Wholesale Trade-Area Statistics; Census of Business: 1963, Vol. VII, Selected Services-Area Statistics; Census of Population: 1940, Vol. II, Characteristics of the Population; Census of Population: 1950, Vol. II, Characteristics of the Population; Census of Population: 1960, Vol. I, Characteristics of the Population; Current Population Reports* Series P-25, no. 371, "Estimates of the Population of Standard Metropolitan Statistical Areas: July 1, 1965."

of only 25 percent of the 81,000 employees of retailing firms worked in the ring. Wholesaling was the most centralized industry, with nearly 92 percent of its labor force employed in the central city. Selected services were nearly as concentrated as wholesaling, with 85 percent of its workers employed in the central city. The four categories of employment for which data are available account for roughly two thirds of total employment in the average metropolitan area.

It is not surprising to find, as Table 4 shows, that suburban

Table 4. Estimated mean annual percentage changes[a] in population and employment for the central cities and suburban rings of 40 large SMSA's
(1950 central city boundaries).

	Central city			Ring		
Item	1948–1954	1954–1958	1958–1963	1948–1954	1954–1958	1958–1963
Employment						
Manufacturing[b]	1.9	−1.7	−0.4	13.2	6.9	6.0
Wholesaling[c]	0.8	0.2	−0.2	24.9	16.6	15.1
Retailing	−0.6	0.1	−2.0	11.3	13.5	13.4
Services	1.6	3.9	0.9	18.0	16.6	13.5
Population[d]	0.2	0.1	−0.5	8.7	6.4	5.5

Source: See note 9.

[a] Simple, unweighted averages of individual city percentage changes.

[b] Data pertain to 1947–1954.

[c] Wholesaling data available for 39 SMSA's only.

[d] Obtained by interpolation and extrapolation of 1940, 1950, 1960, and 1965 data.

rings grew faster than central cities in the postwar period.[10] Even so, the yearly percentage growth in ring population and

[10] Some of the statistics presented in Tables 4, 5, 6, 7, 8, and 10 differ slightly from those found in the earlier version of this paper published in: *The Metropolitan Enigma* (U.S., Chamber of Commerce, Task Force on Economic Growth and Opportunity, 1967). The tables presented here rely on more recent Census publications and "presumably" are based on more accurate data.

all categories of employment is rather remarkable. Except for manufacturing during 1954–1958 and 1958–1963, the average yearly percentage increases in employment exceeded 10 percent for all four employment categories and three time periods. Wholesaling employment exhibits the most rapid suburban growth, amounting to 25 percent a year during the six-year period immediately following the war. This rapid suburban growth of wholesaling is all the more remarkable given its extreme centralization at the beginning of the period. (Of course, this growth took place on a small base, a fact that may explain in part why its *rate* of growth declined during the postwar period.) Suburban wholesaling grew at an average yearly rate of 15 percent during 1958–1963. It should be emphasized that the employment data in Tables 4 to 6 have been "corrected" for annexations. Thus, the employment data refer to changes in employment within the boundaries of the central cities and suburban rings as defined in 1950.[11]

[11] The 1960 Census of Population provides the 1960 population within the central city boundaries of 1950; data on population annexations by the 40 central cities are obtainable from the Municipal Year Books 1949–1965. The International City Managers Association, *The Municipal Year Book* (1949–1965), Chicago, Illinois.

Table 4 lists the mean annual percentage changes in population and in manufacturing, wholesaling, retailing, and selected services employment in the central cities and metropolitan rings of these same 40 SMSA's during three postwar periods, 1948 (1947)–1954, 1954–1958, and 1958–1963. Employment and population data in Table 4 are corrected for annexations to the central city. Use of uncorrected data systematically, and on occasion hugely, overstates central city growth. No information is available on the amount of employment annexed to central cities. Thus, employment data used in this paper are corrected for annexations by assuming that the percentage of employment annexed in each category was the same as the percentage of population annexed. It is believed this yields a conservative estimate of employment annexations. Meyer, Kain, Wohl, *The Urban Transportation Problem*, p. 27. The annexation corrections for 1958–1963 are somewhat different from those used for 1948 (1947)–1954 and 1954–1958 because of differences in data availability.

It is contended that for most analytical purposes, estimates of employment and population change within constant areas are more

Manufacturing and retailing grew least rapidly in the suburban rings, a fact that may be related to their greater suburbanization at the beginning of the period. Even so, suburban retailing employment increased by 11 percent a year during its period of slowest growth (1948–1954) and averaged 13 percent a year during both 1954–1958 and 1958–1963. Suburban manufacturing employment experienced the least growth in both of the two most recent periods. This lower suburban growth rate in manufacturing is consistent with the lesser restrictions on manufacturing investment during World War II and a greater wartime dispersal than other employment categories. Even so its growth rate during the most recent, and most slowly growing, period amounted to a healthy 6.0 percent a year. Data on changes in manufacturing employment must be interpreted carefully, since they are particularly sensitive to the business cycle. Of the years studied, cyclical effects were particularly important in the recession year of 1958, although 1954 was also a year of mild recession. By comparison, manufacturing employment in 1963, buoyed by the Vietnam build up, was unusually high. (Nationally, manufacturing employment declined by 0.2 percent a year during the four year period 1954–1958, while it increased by approximately 1.2 percent a year during the five year period 1958–1963.) Yearly percentage increases in suburban population, though considerable, are only about half as large as the increases in suburban employment. This permits a guarded conclusion that these jobs, at least, were moving to the suburbs at a faster rate than people.

In contrast to the marked uniformity of suburban growth rates, changes in central city employment and population

---

useful than ones that are not "corrected" for annexations. This is particularly true for those aspects of public policy that are related to the pattern of urban development. The emphasis of this paper is on attempting to describe, explain, and project changes in urban form or structure. However, there are some uses, for example, questions of central city finance, for which employment and population within legal boundaries may be the crucial variables. Obviously central city declines would be fewer and on average smaller if legal boundaries were used.

were highly irregular. Central city manufacturing employment grew at an average rate of 1.9 percent during 1947–1954. But during the next four years it declined at an average rate of 1.7 percent a year. Central cities also lost manufacturing jobs during the most recent period, but at a reduced rate, 0.4 percent a year. The previous comments about cyclical variability of manufacturing employment apply here. During slack periods multi-plant firms generally reduce production most in their older and less efficient plants. It is likely that central cities contain a disproportionate amount of this older and less efficient capacity. Thus, cyclical effects might be especially pronounced in central cities. This suggests that the very large central decline in manufacturing employment during 1954–1958 may be somewhat overstated by the recession year of 1958. By the same logic, the much smaller 1958–1963 decline may be relatively understated. Regardless of how much weight is given to the impacts of the business cycle, the nearly 2 percent decline during 1954–1958 and the 0.4 percent decline during 1958–1963 compare unfavorably with the substantial suburban growth rates during both periods.

Central city wholesaling employment exhibits only a small percentage increase in each of the first two periods. Moreover, there is a suggestive decline in the yearly rate of growth until the final period (1958–1963), when central city wholesaling employment actually decreased slightly (minus 0.2 percent per year). By contrast, ring wholesaling increased by 15.1 percent during 1958–1963. Even central city service employment shows some tendency toward decline in the later period. Central city employment in selected services increased during every time period. Its growth during 1954–1958 was especially rapid, averaging nearly 4 percent a year. However, an undetermined share of this rapid growth in central city services employment during 1954–1958 was "statistical" and resulted from the addition of establishments not previously included. During 1958–1963 the growth rate of central city employment in selected services amounted to a more modest 0.9 percent per year. Suburban growth of selected services employment exceeded 13 percent in all three periods, declining somewhat over the fifteen years.

Percentage growth rates are but one way of examining changes in employment and population levels. If used alone, they give an incomplete, and perhaps even misleading, description of urban change. Where the base is very small, an employment category may have a very high mean percentage rate of growth, but a very small absolute change. Therefore, mean annual absolute changes in employment for the population for the same 40 metropolitan areas are presented in Table 5.

The marked importance for urban development trends of changes in the level and spatial distribution of manufacturing employment is evident from the data presented in Table 5. During the period 1954–1958 central cities lost an average of 2,122 manufacturing jobs each year. The yearly loss during the most recent period was even larger, averaging 3,462 jobs per year. Thus, during the nine year period 1954–1963, the central cities of these 40 large metropolitan areas lost an average of 25,798 manufacturing jobs. This loss in central city manu-

Table 5. Estimated mean annual absolute changes in population and employment for central cities and suburban rings of 40 large SMSA's (1950 central city boundaries).

	Central city			Ring		
Item	1948–1954	1954–1958	1958–1963	1948–1954	1954–1958	1958–1963
Employment						
Manufacturing[a]	218	−2,122	−3,462	2,396	1,262	4,180
Wholesaling[b]	−85	55	−198	425	767	831
Retailing	−588	188	−985	896	2,263	1,931
Services	479	1,011	294	510	874	756
Population[c]	464	25	−4,595	31,491	36,722	41,000
Population annexations	4,180	5,532	2,610	−4,180	−5,532	−2,610

Source: See note 9.

[a] Data pertain to 1947–1954.

[b] Wholesaling data available for 39 SMSA's only.

[c] Obtained by interpolation and extrapolation of 1940, 1950, 1960, and 1965 data.

facturing employment was almost exactly offset by a growth of manufacturing employment in suburban areas, which averaged 25,948 jobs during the same period.

The much more unfavorable performance of central city manufacturing employment when absolute changes are used as the measure is due to the greater weight given to large cities and particularly those with disproportionate amounts of manufacturing. This is consistent with other information that suggests the most rapid declines are being experienced by the older, dense manufacturing centers of the North and East. By comparison, the newer, less dense cities of the South, West, and Southwest have suffered smaller declines and in many instances have grown.

As noted above, the location of manufacturing is especially critical in determining metropolitan spatial structure, since the locational decisions of most manufacturing firms are largely unaffected by the distribution of metropolitan population. Manufacturing determines the locational decisions of urban households, not vice versa.

Smaller, but persistent, declines occurred throughout the period in central city wholesaling and retailing employment as well. In both industry groups employment increased during 1954–1958 after declining during the period immediately following World War II. This improvement was short lived, however, as larger employment declines were experienced by both industry groups during the most recent period. During 1958–1963 the average absolute decline in central city wholesaling employment increased to an average yearly loss of 198 jobs. Changes in central city retailing employment, after becoming slightly positive during 1954–1958, are heavily negative during the 1958–1963 period, when central cities lost an average of 985 jobs per year. As was true of the percentage growth rates, the absolute growth of central city services is significantly less during 1958–1963 than during 1954–1958.

Large yearly absolute increases occurred in every category of suburban ring employment during every time period. During the 1958–1963 period, suburban rings of the 40 large metropolitan areas included in Table 5 gained an average of 831 wholesaling, 1,931 retailing, and 756 selected services jobs each year. Suburban manufacturing employment posted especially large gains during the period with an average absolute increase of 4,180 per year, almost twice that experienced during either of the two previous postwar periods.

The pervasiveness of postwar declines in central city population and employment during the postwar period is shown even more clearly by data presented in Table 6, which contains a tabulation of the number of declining central cities and suburban rings in each employment and population classification during each of the three postwar periods. During the first period retailing employment declined in 27, manufacturing employment in 15, and wholesaling employment in 16 of the central cities. During the second period central city manufacturing employment declines were still more frequent, occurring in 30 of the 40 central cities. (The previously noted cyclical impacts should be kept in mind in evaluating these data.) Central city wholesaling employment declines were also more frequent during the second period, occurring in 18

Table 6. Estimated number of central city and suburban rings (out of 40) having employment and population declines (1950 central city boundaries).

Item	Central city			Ring		
	1948–1954	1954–1958	1958–1963	1948–1954	1954–1958	1958–1963
Employment						
Manufacturing[a]	15	30	28	6	9	11
Wholesaling[b]	16	18	21	4	0	1
Retailing	27	17	37	4	0	0
Services	7	4	15	2	1	0
Population[c] (legal boundaries)	17	16	18	1	2	0
Population (1950 central city boundaries)	21	22	24	1	1	0

Source: See note 9.

[a] Data pertain to 1947–1954.

[b] Wholesaling data available for 39 SMSA's only.

[c] Obtained by interpolation and extrapolation of 1940, 1950, 1960, and 1965 data.

cities. City retailing employment rebounded somewhat, with only 17 out of 40 metropolitan areas recording central city declines. However, during 1958–1963, the number of central cities experiencing a decline in employment in wholesaling, retailing, and selected services was again greater than in the earlier two periods. Central city employment declines were the rule. Wholesaling employment declined in 21 central cities, retailing in 37 central cities, and selected services, which showed considerable resistance to decline in the decade following the war, in 15 central cities. Even with the national growth in manufacturing employment during 1958–1963, manufacturing employment declined in all but 12 of the 40 central cities. These data even more clearly than those presented previously suggest an *acceleration* of postwar trends toward metropolitan dispersal.

Metropolitan and Central City Growth

There is of course a great deal of variation among different metropolitan areas. The forty metropolitan areas analyzed above range in population (1960) from a low of 514,000 (Akron, Ohio) to a high of 10,695,000 (New York). Similarly, central city populations vary from 262,000 (Dayton, Ohio) to 7,782,000 (New York). Central city and metropolitan area age and densities are also quite varied. For example, central city population densities were, in 1960, approximately 25,000 persons per square mile in New York City and more than 14,000 per square mile in Boston, Chicago, and Philadelphia, but less than 3,000 persons per square mile in San Diego, Houston, Dallas, and several other central cities. Even more important in terms of the central city and suburban employment and population growth rates presented above, the 40 areas experienced very different growth rates during the period. Between 1950 and 1960 changes in metropolitan population varied from a 6 percent decline (Jersey City) to a 100 percent increase (Phoenix).

These variations in metropolitan growth rates are of particular importance because changes in metropolitan structure are strongly affected by metropolitan growth.[12] Since the 40 areas in Tables 3 to 6 have widely varying rates of growth, statistical averages disguise a great deal of variation in central city and ring growth. To evaluate the impact of over-all metropolitan growth on central city and ring growth, these 40 areas are divided by the rate of metropolitan growth during the decade 1950–1960. Specifically, three subgroups are defined (for the 40 areas analyzed): the 13 areas with the highest percentage rate of population growth for 1950–1960, the 13 with the second highest, and the 14 with the lowest.[13] Over-all metropolitan growth strongly affects employment growth in both the central city and the suburban ring. Percentage changes in employment and population by these population growth categories are shown in Table 7. With a few exceptions, the areas with the highest population growth have the greatest change in employment, in both the central city and ring, and the areas with the least population growth show the least employment growth.

The absolute changes in employment and population by subgroups are similar to those for percentage changes, as shown in Table 8. Central city declines are somewhat more prevalent, suggesting that the larger central cities within each population growth category are the slowest growing. Services are the only central city employment or population group

[12] For a more explicit statement of the relationship between metropolitan and central city growth, see John H. Niedercorn and John F. Kain, "An Econometric Model of Metropolitan Development," and "Suburbanization and Population, 1948–1975."

[13] The 13 SMSA's with the highest percentage rate of population growth for 1950–1960 were Atlanta, Columbus, Dallas, Denver, Fort Worth, Houston, Los Angeles–Long Beach, Miami, Phoenix, San Antonio, San Diego, Tampa–St. Petersburg, and Washington, D.C. The 13 SMSA's with the second highest percentage change were Baltimore, Dayton, Detroit, Indianapolis, Kansas City, Louisville, Memphis, Milwaukee, Minneapolis–St. Paul, New Orleans, Oklahoma City, San Francisco–Oakland, and Seattle. The 14 SMSA's with the lowest percentage change were Akron, Boston, Buffalo, Chicago, Cincinnati, Cleveland, Jersey City, New York, Newark, Philadelphia, Pittsburgh, Portland, Rochester, and St. Louis.

Table 7. Estimated mean annual percentage changes in employment
and population for the central cities and rings of 40 large
SMSA's by the SMSA growth rate
(1950 central city boundaries).

	Central city			Ring		
Item	1948–1954	1954–1958	1958–1963	1948–1954	1954–1958	1958–1963
Employment						
Manufacturing[a]						
Highest	6.0	0.3	0.2	27.5	15.7	9.0
Medium	0.1	−1.9	0.5	9.0	3.6	6.0
Lowest	−0.4	−3.5	−2.0	3.6	1.8	4.0
Wholesaling[b]						
Highest	1.2	2.0	1.1	35.4	21.8	15.1
Medium	0.5	−0.2	−0.02	33.0	16.8	16.6
Lowest	0.8	−0.2	−1.5	8.2	11.9	13.7
Retailing						
Highest	0.2	0.6	−1.3	19.2	20.2	13.6
Medium	−0.8	−0.1	−2.2	13.0	14.4	17.6
Lowest	−1.2	−0.02	−2.4	2.1	6.6	9.3
Services						
Highest	2.4	4.1	2.3	25.5	25.4	14.9
Medium	1.4	4.1	−0.1	22.2	17.3	16.6
Lowest	1.1	3.5	0.5	7.2	7.6	9.3
Population[c]						
(1950 boundaries)						
Highest	1.3	1.0	0.7	12.5	9.2	6.0
Medium	−0.2	−0.2	−0.8	9.5	6.6	6.2
Lowest	−0.5	−0.6	−1.5	4.4	3.5	4.2

Source: See note 9. The SMSA's included in each population
change group are listed in note 13.

[a] Data pertain to 1947–1954.

[b] Wholesaling data available for 39 SMSA's only.

[c] Obtained by interpolation and extrapolation of 1940, 1950,
1960, and 1965 data.

for which there were consistent increases for both the medium
and lowest population growth categories, and even they recorded declines during 1958–1963 in the medium growth
category. Between 1948 and 1963, the central cities in the
14 areas with the lowest growth rate lost on the average

117,000 people, 66,705 manufacturing jobs, 14,358 retailing jobs, and 6,493 wholesaling jobs. Offsetting these losses since the war are only 11,458 services jobs. Central cities in the 13 areas having intermediate rates of growth fared somewhat better. During the fifteen years 1948–1963, they lost on the

Table 8. Estimated mean annual absolute changes in employment and population for the central cities and suburban rings of 40 large SMSA's, by the SMSA growth rate (1950 central city boundaries).

Item	Central city			Ring		
	1948–1954	1954–1958	1958–1963	1948–1954	1954–1958	1958–1963
Employment						
Manufacturing[a]						
Highest	2,332	294	−222	2,860	2,992	2,222
Medium	−549	−2,784	−630	1,945	26	2,100
Lowest	−1,035	−3,750	−9,099	2,384	806	7,929
Wholesaling[b]						
Highest	245	226	284	447	1,006	649
Medium	7	−7	−73	325	440	525
Lowest	−453	−35	−727	473	813	1,272
Retailing						
Highest	91	−312	−372	1,197	2,872	1,576
Medium	−446	−198	−1,115	898	1,628	1,657
Lowest	−1,352	227	−1,431	617	2,285	2,516
Services						
Highest	587	826	501	703	1,417	759
Medium	209	771	−43	304	513	557
Lowest	628	1,405	414	521	705	937
Population[c]						
Highest	8,000	7,000	7,000	33,000	44,000	37,000
Medium	−2,000	−2,000	−8,000	30,000	32,000	35,000
Lowest	−4,000	−4,500	−15,000	34,000	38,000	50,000

Source: See note 9. The SMSA's included in each population change group are listed in note 13.

[a] Data pertain to 1947–1954.

[b] Wholesaling data available for 39 SMSA's only.

[c] Obtained by interpolation and extrapolation of 1940, 1950, 1960, and 1965 data.

average 60,000 people (within 1950 boundaries), 17,580 manufacturing jobs, 9,043 retailing jobs, 351 wholesaling jobs, and gained 4,123 selected services jobs.

During the same period in which the 14 central cities of the slowest growing areas lost 66,705 manufacturing jobs, their suburban rings gained 58,785 manufacturing jobs. Likewise, while these same cities lost an average of 14,359 retailing jobs, employment in their suburban rings increased by 25,422. Wholesaling employment in these central cities declined on the average by 6,493, while ring employment in wholesaling increased on the average by 12,450. On the other hand, the central city gain in services for these areas was actually greater (11,458) than in the ring (10,131).

Trends Within Central Cities

The gravest weakness of the employment statistics presented thus far is that they cover such large areas. Central city statistics, in particular, may hide very diverse and critical differences in employment and population growth within central city boundaries. For example, they may mask large increases in employment within central business districts (CBD's). This is especially worrisome because data presented thus far are especially deficient in the coverage of such important CBD employment activities as central office employment, banking, finance, and business services. Unfortunately, few employment data have been collected that would permit a definite answer about changes in employment levels within CBD's and other points of the central city. The fragmentary data available, however, fail to support the belief (or hope) that despite central city employment and population losses, sizable increases in CBD employment levels have occurred.[14]

For 39 of the 40 metropolitan areas discussed previously, data are available on changes in CBD retail employment levels during 1958–1963. CBD retailing employment in these areas declined by 4.2 percent a year during 1958–1963. The

[14] For a summary of some of these data, see Meyer, Kain, and Wohl, *The Urban Transportation Problem*, pp. 35–39.

corresponding average absolute decline is 636 jobs per year. Thus, it appears that the losses in retailing jobs were *greatest* in the CBD.

Some data are available that provide a more complete description of changes in the spatial distribution of employment within particular central cities. In every instance there are serious problems of completeness, accuracy, and unknown bias. One such source provides statistics on workers covered by unemployment compensation by postal zones within the city of Chicago.[15] For the period 1958–1963, postal zones within the city of Chicago are aggregated into seven larger areas roughly corresponding to concentric distance rings (or parts of rings) surrounding the CBD as illustrated in Figure 2. During the five year period 1958–1963, the central city lost each year roughly 20,042 jobs covered by unemployment insurance, or in excess of 100,000 jobs over the entire period. In percentage terms the decline amounts to about 1.5 percent a year, a figure that is reasonably consistent with other statistics on Chicago employment.

In general the data in Table 9 bear out our previous speculations about the geographic distribution of employment growth and decline within central city boundaries. Significantly, the most rapid growth (4.9 percent and 4,538 jobs per year) is taking place to the northwest near O'Hare International Airport (area 5N). This finding will come as no

[15] There are numerous problems associated with these data. The most serious is significant variations in coverage by industry. In the Chicago SMSA an estimated 77 percent of all wage and salaried workers were covered by unemployment insurance in March 1954. However, the percentage of workers varies considerably as between manufacturing and nonmanufacturing, being nearly 100 percent in the former, but only 64.9 percent in the latter. No government employees are covered. Even so, if the ratio of covered to noncovered workers remained relatively constant as between areas, analysis of changes in covered employment would provide a reasonably accurate index of changes in the distribution of total employment over time. An assumption of stability seems plausible for relatively short time periods. Also, because coverage tends to increase over time, these data, if anything, would probably understate employment declines.

Table 9. Annual absolute and percentage change in
employment by subarea: Chicago 1958–1963.

Area	Number	Percent
CBD	−2,120	−1.0
2	−5,065	−1.7
3	−6,889	−3.2
4	−4,903	−1.5
5N	4,538	4.9
5S	−3,922	−3.1
6S	304	1.1
Unclassified	−1,983	−2.4
Total	−20,042	−1.5

Source: Illinois State Employment Service, "Employed Workers
Covered by the Illinois Unemployment Compensation Act, 1955–
1964: Chicago Standard Metropolitan Statistical Area." Chicago:
Chicago Research and Statistics Units, ISES, 1965.

great surprise to regular air travelers, since rapid employment
growth is occurring around every major airport. The far south
(areas 6S) is the only other area posting a gain. Of the five
remaining areas, the central business district (area 1) shows
the greatest stability, with its losses being held to 1 percent
and 2,120 jobs a year. The outer business ring (area 2), with
a decline of 1.7 percent and 5,065 jobs a year, exhibits somewhat less resistance, and the two remaining areas (area 3 and
area 5S) did most poorly (−3.2 and −3.1 percent a year).
Two facts emerge from these data. Central city declines are
much greater in central (except for the CBD) than outlying
areas. Employment growth in the northern parts of the city,
and especially near the airport, is much greater than in the
south, especially near the Negro ghetto. Whether employers
are being attracted by the airport or are fleeing the ghetto is
an interesting question and an important issue for public
policy.

In summary, neither the evidence presented here nor that
published elsewhere suggests that the fairly general declines
in central city employment levels conceal any large-scale increases in employment within the most central parts of central cities. Rather, the opposite is probably the case. The

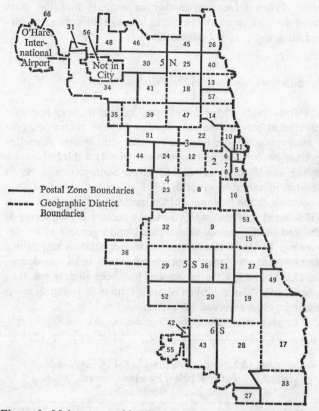

Figure 2. Major geographic districts of the city of Chicago by postal zone

Source: Illinois State Employment Service, "Employed Workers Covered by the Illinois Unemployment Compensation Act, 1955–1964: Chicago Standard Metropolitan Statistical Area." Chicago: Chicago Research and Statistics Units, ISES, 1965.

evidence regarding CBD employment levels is far from clear cut; even so, it suggests that CBD declines are somewhat smaller than in the immediately surrounding areas. This is consistent with the views of those who emphasize the importance of increased employment in central office employment. In an increasing number of central cities the most rapid declines appear to be taking place in the core areas surrounding the central business districts.

Metropolitan Structure After Fifteen Years

Fifteen years of rapid metropolitan growth, very unevenly distributed between the central cities and suburban rings, profoundly affected the level and spatial distribution of metropolitan employment and populations. Nearly a third of wholesaling employment in the 40 large metropolitan areas is located in suburban rings in 1963 as compared to less than one tenth at the beginning of the postwar period (Table 10). Of selected services employment, 31 percent is in the ring at the end of the period, as compared to 15 percent at the beginning. By 1963 nearly half of metropolitan area retailing employment was located outside of central cities (as defined in 1950); in 1948 the proportion had been slightly less than one fourth. The suburban share of manufacturing employment in 1963 exceeded 50 percent.

The proportion of metropolitan population residing in suburban areas increased during the period as well. By 1958 al-

Table 10. Suburban ring share of SMSA employment
and population, by selected years
(1950 central city boundaries).

Item	1948	1954	1958	1963
Employment				
Manufacturing[a]	33.1	38.6	42.0	51.8
Wholesaling[b]	8.2	14.5	20.7	28.6
Retailing	24.7	30.6	37.2	45.4
Services	15.2	21.6	26.1	31.3
Population[c]	36.0	43.5	48.2	54.3

Source: See note 9.

[a] Data pertain to 1947–1954.

[b] Wholesaling data available for 39 SMSA's only.

[c] Obtained by interpolation and extrapolation of 1940, 1950, 1960, and 1965 data.

most half of the population of these 40 large metropolitan areas resided outside of 1950 central city boundaries. In 1963 the percentage had reached 54 percent. Even so, the data in Table 10 suggest employment may be shifting toward suburban areas at a *more* rapid rate than population.

Future Urban Form

Projecting future metropolitan employment patterns is a difficult and uncertain exercise, but such projections are needed for a wide range of urban public investment and policy decisions. The above analyses of historical trends have strong implications for forecasting. Granted the difficulties of projection, it is useful to risk some speculation about future urban form.

First, despite the many objections that might be raised about the quality and meaning of the data presented above, it is impossible not to conclude that the most central parts of metropolitan areas are losing employment to outlying areas and that this process is, if anything, accelerating. Slow growth and not infrequent decline of central areas have accumulated to the point where absolute declines in central city employment are now commonplace.

Second, metropolitan spatial structures are undergoing rapid change. If historical trends continue, future central cities will have substantially smaller populations and employment levels. As employment is becoming more evenly dispersed over the surface of the metropolitan regions, metropolitan centers are becoming less dense. The large concentrations of employment that characterized the historic central city appear to be becoming less pronounced. Perhaps the most common visual conception of the distribution of metropolitan employment is a tent with its highest point at the center. Metropolitan growth and the agglomeration of numerous formerly independent cities into a metropolitan region meant that smaller peaks—outlying employment and commercial centers—had to be added to the traditional visualization. Figure 3, which shows the number of daily person-trip destinations by quarter-mile area in Chicago, illustrates the complex, many-peaked surface of this kind. Even so, the cone or tent-like surface remains the basic spatial structure. The outlying subcenters are merely an elaboration of the historic central city model.

However, if the changes in employment distributions identified above continue, they will bring about even more changes in the shape of the metropolitan area. The extreme peaks will steadily erode away. City and suburb are already becoming similar. Over the long haul, these processes could result in a relatively "flat" distribution of employment and population that is sharply different from what we know today and even less like what we remember of the historic city.

Third, though gaps in the available data make it impossible to be certain, it appears that employment is dispersing even more rapidly than the metropolitan population. However, since the population of the rapidly growing suburban areas includes disproportionate numbers of persons who do not belong to the labor force (housewives and children), more careful analysis might disprove this hypothesis. Even so, one may conjecture that the doughnut may be the model of the future—that is, employment opportunities will be located around the periphery and workers' homes in the central city. This image of metropolitan structure is far different from that more commonly held. Obviously, such a radical redistribution of jobs would profoundly affect many urban problems, of which transportation is only the most obvious.

Some Contrary Evidence on Future Urban Form

Land-use forecasts have been prepared for nearly every U.S. metropolitan area. Almost without exception these depict a much different picture of probable future developments in land use than that presented in this paper. Forecasts of employment and population for Philadelphia over a 25 year period, 1960–1985, prepared by the Delaware Valley Regional Planning Commission (the follow-up agency to the Penn-Jersey Transportation Study), are typical of these projections of urban development. For the Philadelphia Central Business District (CBD) they show "a substantial growth in office employment, modest retail growth, a stability or decline

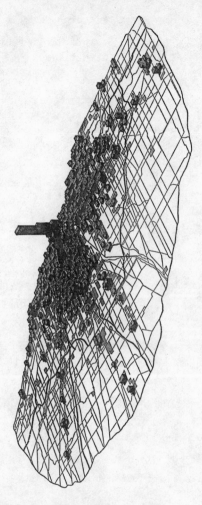

Figure 3. Total person-trip destinations: Chicago

The destinations of 10,212,000 person-trips on the average week-day, are distributed throughout the study area as shown in this model. The highest blocks represent 144,000 trip destinations per quarter square mile grid, the lowest blocks 5,000. The flat shaded areas represent less than 5,000 but more than 2,500.

Source: Chicago Area Transportation Study, Vol. 1 Fig. 7, p. 25.

Figure. Total relationship in metropolitan Chicago

The locations of 10,313 destinations on the morning week. Gas, gas distributed throughout the entire area as shown in the figure. The placed blocks represent 14,000. The destinations per square mile, with each the lower blocks 2,000. The flat shaded areas represent less than 3000 but more than 2500.

Source: Chicago Area Transportation Study, vol. I, fig. 2, p. 28.

in other employment groups and little change in households."[16] Moreover, the study concludes that the city of Philadelphia will lose 3 percent of its households and 21 percent of its manufacturing jobs. However, an expected 52 percent increase in nonmanufacturing employment leads to an over-all employment increase of 29 percent or 1.2 percent a year. These projections of population and employment lead the authors to conclude that: "The continued effect of these two trends—dispersed residences and relatively centralized economic activity—will be a marked spatial separation of residences from employment, which in the past led to large volumes of long, peak hour radial trips. The region's transportation need apparent in 1960 will, therefore, not only continue into the future but will increase in intensity."[17]

These conclusions are diametrically opposed to those presented in this paper. Since both views cannot be correct, the obvious question is which one is? It is possible that this paper's speculations about future urban form are true for some metropolitan areas but that Philadelphia is an exception. Only the future can determine which view is more accurate. Meanwhile, it is useful to examine the postwar experience of Philadelphia and the available data underlying these two very different forecasts. Table 11 summarizes the "historical" census data for Philadelphia and the forecasts prepared by the Delaware Valley Regional Planning Commission. These census employment data for Philadelphia differ from those for the 40 SMSA's in the earlier analyses in that active proprietors are aggregated with paid employees to obtain employment. Projected levels of employment growth from the Delaware Valley study have been converted to simple yearly averages to simplify their comparison with the census data presented in Table 11 and in previous sections.

Several observations can be made about the data in Table 11. As noted previously, the census data categories provide

16 Delaware Valley Regional Planning Commission, 1985 Regional Projections for the Delaware Valley, DVRPC Planning Report no. 1, 1967, p. 3.
17 Ibid., p. 3.

Table 11. Yearly percentage and absolute changes in central city and suburban employment (paid employees plus proprietors): Philadelphia.

Type of employment	Central city				Ring			
	48–54	54–58	58–63	60–85	48–54	54–58	58–63	60–85
Retailing	−3,046	−1,171	−3,588	2,440	2,398	3,815	3,261	4,005
Selected services	529	1,843	245		534	1,978	1,660	
Wholesaling	−284	−562	−992		1,094	1,146	1,720	2,012
Manufacturing	−2,648	−2,818	−6,726	−1,357	4,824	285	6,505	
Office work				5,698				4,121
Education, institutions, and communications				3,689				2,758
Total				11,307				14,177
Percent growth per year								
Retailing	−1.9	−0.8	−2.6	1.8	3.1	4.1	3.0	3.4
Selected services	1.0	3.2	0.4		2.7	8.6	5.4	
Wholesaling	−0.4	−0.8	−1.5		11.9	7.3	8.5	0.7
Manufacturing	−0.8	−0.9	−2.2	−0.3	2.4	0.1	2.7	
Office work				3.1				2.2
Education, institutions, and communications				4.4				5.2
Total				1.2				2.3

Source: See notes 9 and 16.

incomplete employment coverage. Indeed, they account for only about 60 percent of all employment in the Philadelphia SMSA. By comparison, the Delaware Valley forecasts include all categories of employment. Thus, the census data presented in Table 11 and earlier sections of this paper may be providing a misleading picture of employment changes by focusing on those employment categories that are decentralizing most rapidly.[18]

As shown in Table 11, the largest forecast growth rates are for the "education, institutions, and communications" and "office" employment categories. Office employment is projected to have a growth of 3.1 percent per year in the central city. Central city employment in the education, institutions, and communications category has an even higher growth rate amounting to 4.4 percent per year. It could be argued on this basis that employment in central areas will increase and that increases in central office and other activities will more than offset declines in the categories for which historical data are available.[19]

[18] Some time series data on "education, institutions, and communications" and "office" employment can be obtained from the U.S. Bureau of the Census, *U.S. Census of Governments: 1957,* vol. II, no. 3, "Local Government in Standard Metropolitan Areas" and *U.S. Census of Governments: 1962,* vol. V, "Local Government in Metropolitan Areas." In 1962, the Census of Government accounted for over 45,000 full-time jobs in education and $46,000 "other" government jobs in the Philadelphia metropolitan area. The experiences of these two categories differ significantly. Between 1957 and 1962 education employment in the central city grew by 990 jobs, nearly 10 percent a year, while education employment in the suburbs grew by 3,120 jobs, 22 percent a year. "Other" government employment in the central city declined by 426 jobs, 1.3 percent a year, while suburban "other" government employment grew by 100 jobs, only 0.6 of 1 percent a year. These limited historical data on education and other government employment, which represent 26.9 percent and 17.6 percent of the 1960 employment in "office" and "education, institution, and communications" categories, do not present a markedly different picture from employment data for the four census categories.

[19] Because the city of Philadelphia is coexistensive with Philadelphia County, additional historical data from *County Business*

It is difficult to compare the data shown in Table 11 since the aggregated categories used for the Delaware Valley forecasts are not precisely the same as for the census categories. Still it is impossible to avoid the impression that the forecasts are optimistic in terms of available historical information. While the authors of the Delaware Valley forecasts project a decline of 0.3 percent and 1,357 jobs in wholesaling and manufacturing combined, they report that the declines are limited to manufacturing. This is in contrast to the postwar experience of small, but persistent, declines in central city wholesaling employment between 1948 and 1963. Similarly, the decline in central city wholesaling and manufacturing employment between 1960–1985 forecasted by the Delaware Valley report amounts to only 34,000 jobs. Yet the decline estimated from census data in these two employment groups between 1960 and 1963, amounted to over 23,000 jobs, despite a rapid expansion of economic activity on the national

Patterns, Pennsylvania, 1946, 1947, 1948, 1949, 1950, 1951, 1953, 1956, 1959, 1962, 1964, 1965, and 1966, provide some further insights about postwar changes in the location of covered employment in the metropolitan area. Despite the probable definitional growth of the central city labor force, resulting from increased Social Security coverage and more complete assignment of employment to counties, covered employment in the city of Philadelphia declined from 774,000 in 1951, to 744,000 in 1956, to 732,000 in 1962, to a low of 708,000 in 1964, before it rose to 724,000 in 1965. Even so the decline in "covered" employment between 1951 and 1965 was 50,000. The over-all decrease in covered employment masks a complex pattern of growth and decline. Between the initial (1951) and terminal year (1965) manufacturing employment declined by 90,000 jobs; transportation and public utilities, by over 10,000 jobs; retailing, by nearly 15,000 jobs; and wholesaling, by nearly 4,000 jobs. Partially offsetting these declines were increases in finance, real estate, and insurance of 8,000 jobs and increases in services of 69,000 jobs. Closer examination of these changes suggest that much of the increases in central city "covered" employment, especially services, are probably due to extension in coverage. These statistics for additional categories of employment, as those for government and education, do not depict a significantly different pattern of historical changes in central city employment from that indicated by the four census categories.

level. Thus, according to census data, the rate of decline of manufacturing and wholesaling employment in Philadelphia's central city appears to have accelerated in the recent 1958–1963 period, with most of the loss being offset by increases in suburban area manufacturing and wholesaling employment.

The Delaware Valley forecasts also include a retail trade and services category which, though it includes about 60,000 fewer workers, corresponds roughly to the combined census categories of selected services and retail trade. According to census data for the 1958–1963 period, the increase in selected services jobs of 245 per year fell far short of offsetting a yearly decline of 3,588 retailing jobs. Yet the Delaware Valley report forecasts a yearly growth of 2,440 jobs in retailing and service trades between 1960–1985.

Clearly, discrepancies exist between the projections of future urban form presented earlier in this paper and those developed by the Delaware Valley Planning Commission and similar groups preparing forecasts for specific metropolitan areas. The forecasts for individual metropolitan areas are almost always much more favorable than those suggested by the analyses presented here. A significant part of these optimistic projections result from reversals of the declines noted for employment groups for which census data are available. Yet neither the Delaware Valley study, nor others of its type, present these census data or identify the forces that are to "cause" these changes. This optimism may be due in part to the fact that these projections are often conditional and assume some favorable changes in government policy that will improve the prospects of central cities. However, I suspect that there is a more fundamental explanation.

The Delaware Valley Planning Commission forecasts central city declines in employment for only one category, manufacturing. Therefore, it is important that the manufacturing employment location model is the only one of those developed by the study that is based on historical data, for the period 1950–1960. The remaining models were estimated from data for a single year, 1960. It seems possible that the land-use forecasting models estimated by the study from cross section data fail to capture some important dynamic elements underlying employment dispersal. From this point of view, the uniform historical experience of widely different metropolitan areas presented previously may provide a sounder basis for forecasting changes in metropolitan structure, despite its partial character.

It would seem prudent to give more attention to the experience of central office employment about which so little is known and on which so many hopes for central cities and central business districts depend. In their discussion of methods used in forecasting future spatial distributions of office employment, the authors of the Delaware Valley Planning Commission report appear to be arguing that: (1) they have no information on changes in employment levels over time for office employment and a number of other categories of employment; (2) these activities are rather highly concentrated during the one year for which the data are available; and (3) it is reasonable that they will remain highly concentrated. The employment location model developed by the study from 1960 data allocates about the same proportion of employment in these categories to the central city in 1985. Since a large proportion of these activities were located in the central city in 1960 and since they are expected to grow rapidly, the model projects a large increase in central city employment. The remaining allocation models appear to have similar biases. Thus, during the entire 25 year period the projected growth of central city employment outstrips the growth of suburban employment by approximately 3,000 jobs a year. Yet all the historical evidence points to a much more rapid employment growth in suburban areas and the possibility of significant central area employment decline trends, if the postwar trends were to accelerate.

The weakness of the logic used by the Delaware Valley planners and the model based on it can be illustrated by reference to wholesaling employment for which historical data are available. In 1948 roughly 91 percent of wholesaling employment in 39 metropolitan areas was concentrated in the central city. If this fraction were used to project the central city growth of these 39 cities, wholesaling employment would increase by 1,280 jobs between 1948 and 1963. In fact, central city wholesaling employment declined by 6,003 jobs during this period.

It seems entirely possible that the Delaware Valley projections, and others obtained using similar methods, may have grossly underestimated the strength of the economic and technological forces leading to employment dispersal and as a result may have grossly overestimated future levels of employment in the central portions of U.S. metropolitan areas.[20]

Very little systematic time series information is available on employment in central city offices. One of the few sources is a "directory study" of changes in the location of a sample of the central offices of large corporations between 1950 and 1960.[21] Table 12 summarizes the 1950 and 1960 locations of "mover" firms located in the 40 SMSA's used in the earlier analyses. Because of the importance of New York City as a central office location, data for it are presented separately; data for Philadelphia are also listed separately.

There are a number of difficulties with the study summarized in Table 12 and its findings must be interpreted carefully. Nevertheless, its results are highly pertinent to this discussion. The central business districts (CBD's) of the 39

[20] See Real Estate Research Corporation, *Economic Survey and Market Analysis of Downtown Denver,* prepared for the Downtown Denver Master Plan Committee, Denver, Colorado, September 1962, pp. 77–83. The Denver projections which are based on a single year's information, predict an increase of 26,000 jobs between 1962 and 1974, 54 percent in the central business district, with 93 percent of this increase accounted for by office employment. In 1962 only 9.5 percent of the SMSA's office employment was located in the CBD. These optimistic employment projections for Denver's CBD assume the proportion will increase to 16.1 for the period 1962–1968 and to 18.9 for the period of 1968–1974.

[21] In this study addresses published in the *1960 Dun and Bradstreet Million Dollar Directory* were matched with listings in the *1950 MacRae's Blue Book* and the *1950 Standard and Poor's Directory.* About 6,000 firms were located in both years, of which 2,000 had different street addresses in 1960. These 6,000 sample firms and 2,000 movers were coded by 1950 and 1960 locations. For a more detailed discussion of this study see, Meyer, Kain, and Wohl, *The Urban Transportation Problem,* pp. 40 and 41.

Table 12. Central office "mover firms" locating in
new geographic areas, 1950 and 1960.

Area	1950	1960	Difference	Percentage change
39 Large SMSA's (excluding New York)				
CBD	530	404	−126	−23.8
CC	394	392	−2	−0.5
Ring	102	235	133	130.4
New York SMSA				
CBD	314	300	−14	−4.4
CC	31	12	−19	−61.3
Ring	20	45	25	125.0
Philadelphia				
CBD	36	36	0	−
CC	44	22	−22	−50.0
Ring	4	28	24	500.0

Source: Meyer, Kain, and Wohl, The Urban Transportation Problem, p. 41.

SMSA's lost 126 mover firms over the decade, while their central cities (outside the CBD) lost two. By comparison, their suburban rings gained 133 mover firms. In New York, the CBD lost 14, and the central city 19, mover firms, while the suburban ring gained 25. Philadelphia's CBD had 36 mover firms in both 1950 and 1960, but its central city lost 22 between 1950 and 1960. By comparison, the suburban ring which had only 4 mover firms in 1950, had 28 in 1960.

Though these data are incomplete, they do raise the possibility of central office dispersal. In the past few decades, any tendency toward dispersal of central office activities has been offset by a rapid increase in employment in these activities. As a result, the growth of employment in central office and other "control" activities in CBD's has been rapid in most instances. Though these increases have offset some of the CBD's declines in wholesaling, retailing, and manufacturing employment, they have not been large enough to cause increases in the levels of CBD employment. The fragmentary evidence on CBD employment levels indicates that employment declines have been the general rule in American cities.

Some observers argue that the declining employment sectors in the CBD's have run their course and that the postwar employment declines will be reversed by continued rapid growth of office employment. The location decisions of central office activities, thus, are especially critical to the future levels of employment in the CBD. It is difficult to be as optimistic about central city employment increases since the central city still contains a great deal of the kinds of employment that historically are dispersing rapidly. For example, the city of Philadelphia lost over 63,000 manufacturing jobs between 1947 and 1963, a major component of its overall employment decline. Yet in 1963 it still contained an estimated 285,000 manufacturing jobs, a number representing more than one third of central city employment that year.

Given these observations, my prognosis remains that of a continued decline in employment within the central cities of U.S. metropolitan areas and further rapid growth in the suburban rings. However, because of the incompleteness of the data used in both this discussion and in the large number of planning studies within U.S. urban areas, I would emphasize the speculative nature of these predictions and the need for more research on the determinants of industry location within metropolitan areas.

Questions of Public Policy

We are constantly told that public policy should do something to halt or reverse these trends. Several proposals directed to this end have been mentioned. Nonresidential urban renewal is the most direct attack on employment dispersal; it is a way of reducing the difficulty and cost of assembling the large tracts of unencumbered land needed for the construction of modern plants and warehouses. Another proposal is to subsidize the location of plants within central city ghettos. This is justified, in the view of some, by the high unemployment rates among Negroes trapped in central city ghettos, made worse by the steady and frequently rapid movement of jobs away from these centrally located residential neighborhoods.

No detailed discussion of these two programs is attempted here, but I can offer a few general observations about their underlying rationale. First, I know of no good statement of why these trends *should* be reversed. It is not obvious that a reduction in central area employment and population densities is detrimental. The argument most frequently used against it holds that such dispersal jeopardizes the tax base of central cities; though true, there are many straightforward, and more efficient, ways of solving the admittedly difficult fiscal problems of central cities than by redirecting metropolitan growth. Attempting to reverse a massive, nationwide social and economic movement (that is, suburbanization) strikes me as the most costly method—and the one least likely to succeed—of helping pay for needed central city services.

Central city nonresidential renewal is frequently justified on the grounds that the market for urban land is imperfect and that these imperfections sharply increase the cost of acquiring and assembling the large tracts needed for modern industrial plants. Nonresidential renewal is simply a means of overcoming these imperfections and providing a locational pattern more like that which would occur in a perfect market. Far more analysis is needed, but it appears that the high costs of nonresidential renewal in central cities are due more to a need to acquire and destroy many still useful residential and nonresidential structures than to market imperfections. At a minimum it would appear that nonresidential urban renewal should be subjected to careful scrutiny to determine whether its supposed benefits are commensurate with its costs.

Ghetto job creation is a far more difficult question. Negro Americans appear severely limited in their housing choices by collusive behavior on the part of whites. If high Negro unemployment rates in central city ghettos are due in part to these housing restrictions (and perhaps, even if they are not), there would appear to be a fairly strong justification for public action.[22] But there are several serious questions

[22] For a paper that provides some indication that housing segregation may affect Negro employment, see John F. Kain, "Housing Segregation, Negro Employment, and Metropolitan Decentralization," *Quarterly Journal of Economics* (May 1968), also available

that need to be raised about ghetto job creation schemes. Job creation in central city ghettos would be very expensive. The subsidy per job would almost certainly be very large. Such programs might reduce pressures for residential integration and would tend to perpetuate existing patterns of racial segregation.[23] But the most telling objection is that such policies might well fail altogether. There are strong linkages between northern ghettos and the still vast pools of rural, southern Negroes. Ghetto improvement and particularly ghetto job creation programs might well have as their principal result increased migration of southern Negroes to northern metropolitan areas. The growth rates of northern ghettos might increase several-fold, greatly aggravating the already serious problems there, while leaving the existing adverse levels of income and unemployment unchanged. Undoubtedly the well-being of many southern Negroes might be increased, but just as assuredly the distortions of metropolitan growth would be magnified, and the goal of assimilating and integrating the Negro into the urban society made far more difficult. Moreover, as with the central city public finance issue, better and more direct means exist for improving the conditions of southern Negroes.

---

as: Harvard Program on Regional and Urban Economics, Discussion Paper no. 14, revised July 1967.

[23] See John F. Kain, "The Big Cities' Big Problem," *Challenge,* vol. 15, no. 1 (September/October 1966), pp. 4–8, and John F. Kain and Joseph J. Persky, "Alternatives to the Gilded Ghetto," paper prepared for the Economic Development Administration Research Conference, U.S. Department of Commerce, Washington, D.C., February 1968. Also available as: Harvard Program on Regional and Urban Economics, Discussion Paper no. 21, September 1967.

URBAN TRANSPORTATION

John R. Meyer

Definition

Urban transportation can be viewed from many perspectives. For the city planner, urban transportation is a tool for shaping or creating a city with certain desired characteristics. For local businessmen and property owners, urban transportation is a force that creates or modifies real estate values and business potentials. For the engineer, urban transportation is a challenge to design facilities to meet the needs of the community while remaining within budgetary constraints. For the economist, it is a bit of all of these plus a problem in public finance.

To the consumer, however, urban transportation is something rather different. Users, naturally enough, are interested in getting to and from work or school, to and from shopping, to and from homes of friends and family, and to and from the locations of recreational activities—as economically and expeditiously as possible. To the consumer, moreover, satisfactory transportation implies not only economy and speed, but also such factors as comfort, privacy, protection from bad weather, schedule frequency and flexibility, and a host of other considerations. In short, urban transportation is a consumer good and, like others, is purchased because of intangible as well as tangible considerations. One of the least understood aspects of urban transportation is exactly what value consumers place on each of these considerations in making their choices.[1]

Clearly, then, many different objectives might be served by urban transportation plans or, at least, many people *think* that different urban transportation plans might serve a variety of objectives. From the standpoint of analyzing urban transportation problems objectively this impression creates certain difficulties—specifically, that of discerning which goals (or which compromise between different objectives) are to be observed.

For present purposes, let us take the consumer point of view and accept as given present governmental arrangements. This assumption is not to say that this point of view or these arrangements are necessarily optimal.[2] Rather, it is simply

[1] Among the better of the few studies available are W. Y. Oi and P. W. Shuldiner, *An Analysis of Urban Travel Demands* (Evanston: Northwestern University Press, 1962); S. L. Warner, *Stochastic Choice of Mode in Urban Travel: A Study in Binary Choice* (Evanston: Northwestern University Press, 1962); and L. N. Moses and H. F. Williamson, Jr., "Value of Time, Choice of Mode, and the Subsidy Issue in Urban Transportation," *Journal of Political Economy*, 71 (June 1963), 247–264. Other sources of detailed information are area transportation studies performed for specific cities or municipalities, e.g., Chicago, Pittsburgh, and Philadelphia. For some suggestive questionnaire information on public attitudes toward different transport modes see the editors of *Fortune, The Exploding Metropolis* (Garden City, N.J.: Doubleday & Company, Inc., 1958), and John B. Lansing, *Residential Location and Urban Mobility: The Second Wave of Interviews* (Ann Arbor: Survey Research Center, University of Michigan, January 1960), as well as two earlier reports in the same series involving the same author.

[2] As Senator Claiborne Pell has aptly put it in *Megalopolis Unbound: The Supercity and the Transportation of Tomorrow* (New York, 1966, p. 88): "We must debate our intentions and preferences and, within the limits of our constitutional, democratic system, devise at least a philosophical plan for a future growth on a regional

an assertion that there seems to be no clearly obvious and feasible alternative. As a corollary, this acceptance of present institutional arrangements also means a heavy emphasis upon quantifiably measuring what current behavioral choices actually are.

The Setting and Trends[3]

One of the more striking facts about urban transportation in the United States today is the extent to which it is dominated by the highway. It is reasonably clear that, like it or not, the automobile is here to stay, at least for a while. According to the 1960 Census of Population, about 64 percent of all work trips in United States urban areas were made by auto. Only about 20 percent of all urban area work trips are made by public transit; if one looks only at the central city portions of these urban areas, the public transit figure increases, but only to 26 percent. Indeed, almost half as many people walk to work as use public transit in urban areas.

Of course, the level of public transit usage for work trips varies widely among urban areas. It is less than 2 percent in some of our smaller cities (for example, Eugene, Oregon, or Bay City, Michigan), well over half in New York City (61 percent), and between one third and one half in several other cities (for example, Chicago, Boston, Washington, New Orleans, and Philadelphia). Thus, transit is also here to stay, at least in our largest cities.

More significantly, approximately 70 percent of all public transit work trips in the United States are made entirely on local streets or highways (mainly using buses but also involving some streetcars). In addition, a third or so of those using rail transit on reserved rights-of-way also use bus or

---

national basis. Only then will the specific local plans for municipal development have coherence and integrity."

[3] Documentation and more detailed presentation of the materials presented in this section can be found in J. Meyer, J. Kain, and M. Wohl, *The Urban Transportation Problem* (Cambridge, Mass.: Harvard University Press, 1965), chaps. 3, 4, and 5.

other local street transit for some portion of their work trips. It would appear that well over 70 percent of all public transit used for getting to and from work occurs on urban streets or highways and an even higher portion of public transit usage for all purposes is probably on such facilities (because rail transit is more highly specialized in serving work trips than other transit modes). Rail transit is not only a small fraction of all public transit, it is concentrated in a few areas: roughly one third or a bit more of all rail commuting is done in New York City and environs.

The obvious implication of all this is that popular discussion that assumes that the fundamental urban transportation problem is one of choosing between private auto or rail rapid transit is badly misdirected, especially for cities other than New York City and, possibly, Chicago. At a minimum, such an assumption diverts attention from ways of improving the performance of those modes that account for the vast majority of all transit.

Nor is there any reason to believe that rail transit will become much more widely used in the near future. In large measure the attractiveness of rail as compared to other modes of transit depends on the number of persons demanding transit service in a particular urban corridor during the rush hours; this, in turn, depends on where people work and how densely populated are their residential neighborhoods. As illustrated by the comparative costs shown in Figures 1 and 2, the greater the demand volume and urban density, the lower the cost per passenger trip of transit. Even so, only where there are high-density residential areas (Figure 2) is the cost of rail transit lower than other forms; where densities are medium (Figure 1), buses are generally cheaper. These costs are also dependent on the means employed to get rail commuters to and from their homes and whether subways are used in central business areas. Rail transit improves if subways are used but is disadvantaged if people must drive and park their own cars at the rail station. As for the primary condition necessary to make rail transit economical, high hourly passenger transit volumes per corridor, only Chicago and New York have corridor flows exceeding 25,000 per hour in the United States today. Very few urban corridors in the

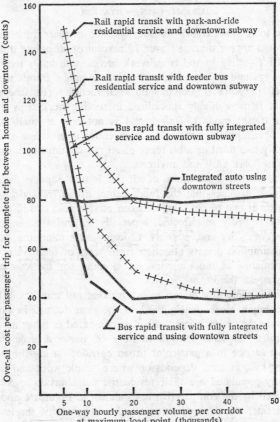

Figure 1. Over-all home-downtown passenger-trip costs for medium residential density along corridor (for example, as in Pittsburgh), hourly downtown passenger-trip originations of ten per block at the home end, 10-mile line-haul facility, and 2-mile downtown distribution system route length.

"Park-and-ride" denotes use of a private auto for the trip from home to the railroad station, with the car parked at the station during the day. "Integrated service" indicates that the same vehicle is used for residential or downtown service as for the line haul between residential areas and downtown.

(Reprinted from Meyer, Kain, and Wohl, *The Urban Transportation Problem*, Cambridge, Mass.: Harvard University Press, 1965. Copyright 1965 by the RAND Corporation.)

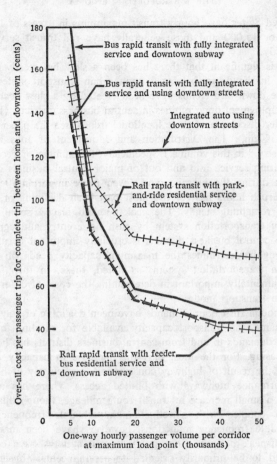

Figure 2. Over-all home-downtown passenger-trip costs for higher residential density along corridor (for example, as in Chicago), hourly downtown passenger-trip originations of ten per block at the home end, 10-mile line-haul facility, and 2-mile downtown distribution system route length.

(Reprinted from Meyer, Kain, and Wohl, *The Urban Transportation Problem*, Cambridge, Mass.: Harvard University Press, 1965. Copyright 1965 by the RAND Corporation.)

United States have hourly transit maximums in excess of 10,-000 or 15,000 and those generally have rail transit service already.

It is significant that there has been a slow but steady decline in the demands placed upon urban transport systems. These downward trends have been created by a slow decline in employment opportunities in central business districts. (For further discussion of these locational trends, see the paper by John Kain, "The Distribution and Movement of Jobs and Industry," in this volume.) Specifically, the number of people requiring service into and out of major central business districts during the morning and (even more important) evening rush hours has for the most part been declining or, at best, remaining steady. The peak demand placed upon the urban transportation system by rush hour entry and egress from central business districts is crucially important because it roughly determines the maximum capacity needs of the urban transportation system; as noted, these, in turn, are fundamentally important in determining the costs of different urban transport modes.

Though rush hour demands have been declining or staying the same, the transport capacity available for meeting these peak demands to and from central business districts has been increasing. For the most part this increase in capacity has been the result of highway construction, particularly of high performance highways with limited access. There has also been a small increase in transit route mileage, though this is often coupled with a reduction in schedule frequencies. Schedule frequency reductions, however, have been mainly in off-peak periods. Since public transit systems have continued to be primarily oriented to serving central business districts, the public transit capacity available for meeting peak hour central business district requirements has tended to remain constant or, in a few cases, to have increased somewhat.

Given this combination of a slowly declining or steady level of peak hour demands plus an increase in available capacity, some slow improvement in the over-all performance of urban transportation systems has taken place. Contrary to popular impression, it does not typically take the average commuter longer to travel the same distance in the city today as formerly. On the contrary, the point to point travel times required between various centrally located workplaces and residential sites has, on the whole, been reduced in most United States cities in the last ten or fifteen years. During the rush hours, though, these improvements have been relatively small. An urban commuter trip that might have taken twenty-five minutes ten or fifteen years ago probably takes some twenty minutes or so today. The improvement, moreover, is likely to be shared by public transit systems as well as by private automobiles. Better expressways, for example, usually mean that fewer cars use local streets on which the buses operate, so that the buses (as well as the cars that remain on the local streets) usually experience a three to seven mile per hour improvement in speed whenever a parallel urban expressway is completed nearby. Similarly, any reduction in demands on a rail transit system (caused, say, by the greater attractiveness of private automobiles on improved highways) usually means that the rail transit system is somewhat less congested during rush hours and can therefore reduce waiting times at major downtown stations and thereby marginally improve its performance speed.

Needless to say, faster rush hour speeds resulting from major improvements in the highway system are only a fraction of the higher speeds now possible during off-peak or non-rush hours. Average speeds of 50 or 60 miles an hour or more are not uncommon experiences on urban expressways during off-peak periods today. These are to be contrasted with speeds rarely in excess of 35 or 40 miles an hour during rush periods today, which, while an improvement on the 30 miles or less speeds of a decade or so ago, are still not fast by modern standards.

Perhaps an even more relevant measure of performance for an urban transportation system is the time required to "decongest" or evacuate central business districts in the evening rush hours. (The evening rush seems more pertinent than the morning, since a higher level of demand is placed upon the system in the evening, apparently because of the addition of shoppers and other travelers to normal commuter demands.) A major problem with this measure is that it is somewhat difficult to define objectively. Roughly speaking, however, it can be represented as the time period during which the capacity of the central portion of the urban transportation system is more or less fully utilized because of outgoing commuters and other travelers. As an approximation, it seems that in most major cities this period has shortened by about 30 to 40 percent in recent years, say, from approximately an hour or so in the late 1940's to approximately 40 minutes today. (These numbers will vary, of course, from city to city.)

Evacuation times for central business districts also make evident another important aspect of urban transportation. It is simply quite unrealistic to speak about the "elimination of congestion" as a major goal for urban transportation planning, at least so long as most businesses choose to close shop at approximately the same hour of the day. To speak of eliminating most congestion in or around major central business districts during the evening rush hour under such circumstances is very much like speaking of eliminating congestion in or around a major football stadium just after the final whistle. To do so would require an inordinately large transport capacity—inordinately large in the sense that the cost of completely eliminating congestion under such circumstances probably would be considered outrageous by most consumers.

The Problem

If there has been a slow but steady improvement in the performance of urban transportation systems, why do we hear so much discussion of a so-called "urban transportation crisis"? The answer lies in a complex set of considerations of which probably the most important is what might be termed "a failure of anticipations."

This failure of anticipations is in great part a consequence of the uneven rates of improvement in off-peak and peak performances of urban transport systems. Traveling across densely populated urban areas at 50 or 60 miles an hour on a high-performance highway during an off-peak period seems to be an exhilarating experience, and urban commuters, quite humanly, would like to duplicate the experience during the rush hours. The difficulty, of course, is that too many of them wish to do so at one time and thus it becomes impossible without a vast increase in capacity. Whether or not they would be willing to pay the high price is open to debate. There is considerable evidence, though, that if we had a free market in the provision of urban highway commuter facilities, some considerable expansion of such facilities would probably take place.[4]

To put it another way, in our modern affluent society an improvement from 25 to 30 or 35 miles an hour or so in the average performance speed of private transport systems during the rush hours has not satisfied some commuters. This is particularly true since many of them have chosen to give up the improved transport time by living further away from their workplaces. Thus, the average time required to commute from home to workplace and return has remained more or less constant. People have apparently been willing to incur higher transportation costs in order to achieve a lower cost for a certain quality of housing or yard space. Possibly, too, as one social psychologist has hypothesized, the typical male wage earner considers the time it takes to get between work and home as the only time that is truly his own, without interruption by foreman or wife. It is possible (no one knows) that some commuters are reluctant to reduce this time.

At any rate, more and better public transit seems to have a considerable attraction for many commuters, *not* because they want to use the transit themselves, but because they hope that it will attract *other* auto drivers off the roads. Those remaining could then realize faster speeds and less congestion on the highways. The alternative of trying to provide sufficient highway capacity so that they can commute at 50 miles an hour or so even during the rush hours is likely to be expensive both in terms of direct dollar outlays and in terms of property displacement. Indeed, if we were to go down this "road,"

---

[4] H. Mohring, "Urban Highway Investments," in R. Dorfman, ed., *Measuring Benefits of Government Investments* (Washington, D.C.: The Brookings Institution, 1965).

some of the wilder claims about paving over our urban areas might actually be realized!

Another sense in which anticipations may have been frustrated is because of different rates of increase in urban real estate prices between central and peripheral locations. Though it is difficult to find good evidence, the common belief is that central business district property values have not grown at as high a rate as suburban commercial properties. The extent to which such differential property value increases have occurred is apparently due to a complex set of influences that can best be summarized as a reduction in the demand for the services of central city property. Changes in manufacturing, transportation, communication, and bookkeeping technologies seem to have made many businesses more independent of central locations. In short, there are not as many good reasons today for businesses to put up with the congestion and other high costs of central locations. (For documentation on these trends, again see the paper by John Kain in this volume.)

Historically, the creation of high property values in downtown areas has occurred because such sites are at the point where major transport networks, both inter-city and intra-city, converge. Many owners of central business properties have therefore looked on expansion of the transport system—in particular, increasing the extent to which the transit network is centered on their properties—as a means of producing an increase, or a greater increase, in property values. This is especially true if the cost of providing such transport improvements does not fall upon the owners of central properties. Then they can hardly lose. Such owners naturally become strong advocates of government subsidies to improve downtown transportation facilities, particularly when the tax base used to supply such subsidies is statewide or nationwide. However, if urban property values today are less dependent on public transit service than they were under more primitive technological conditions, then it is not clear that improved transit access will confer major benefits upon centrally located properties.

In general, there is little evidence that the provision of public transit greatly modifies locational choices, at least in the aggregate. This raises questions about the feasibility of using urban transport policy as a tool for achieving a particular urban physical form. Specifically, the number of people desiring to live at higher residential densities (that is, in apartment houses or multiple-dwelling units) seems to be mainly dependent upon age composition of the population, the number of families with two or more wage earners, per capita income levels, and the relative costs of single family dwellings and apartments. Similarly, a businessman's choice of site will depend as much upon his need for land (say, to achieve an economical one-story layout of his production line) or the extent to which he is dependent or not dependent upon heavy rail or water transport as upon accessibility to urban public transit. In particular, as buses and private automobiles have become available, the need to be near an urban rail rapid transit facility has been considerably reduced for virtually all classes of employers, even those heavily reliant upon female secretarial or clerical work forces (for example, insurance companies). As a consequence of these related trends, the patterns of decentralization or industrial relocation being experienced by American cities seem little different for those with well-developed or highly utilized public transit systems as for those without such a "public transit tradition."

However, though public transit is apparently not sufficient to create any gross increase in urban residential or workplace densities, the availability of high-performance public transit along a particular corridor may concentrate whatever demand for high-density living or work locations may exist in the community. Stated another way, the availability of high-performance public transit may relocate or concentrate dense activities but there is no evidence that it creates a new demand for such density. As a corollary, to justify extensive expenditure on high-performance public transit because it creates higher land values and property taxes on adjacent properties is a rather dubious procedure. Whatever increase occurs may only be the result of a transfer of values from one place to another rather than an increase in the total property tax base of the community. Of course, to the extent future high-density residential development is concentrated along a new public transit facility, that facility's basic economic prospects will be improved.

Another source of much of the public talk about an urban transportation crisis may result from a confusion of other urban problems with transport problems. For a variety of reasons (see the paper by Dick Netzer, "Financing Urban Government," in this volume) our major cities have faced increasing financial difficulties throughout the postwar period. The creation of express highways in central urban areas often seems, at least superficially, to accentuate these financial problems. Expressway construction removes property from the tax rolls; highway competition reduces the demand for public transit and thereby increases the transit deficits normally borne by city governments; expressways make it easier for middle-class people employed in central business districts to live in suburban residential locations, so that they can more easily "escape" their fiscal responsibilities in the city. There are at least partial answers to each of these arguments: without improved highway access urban properties generally might be reduced in value (for example, by a more rapid exodus of manufacturing and other employment to suburban locations); improved urban highways should reduce the operating costs of urban bus transit (because of reduced congestion and improved operating times); without the expressways, the middle classes might remove their places of employment as well as their places of residence from central urban areas. Exactly what is the net result of these opposing considerations is difficult to determine.

Furthermore, the argument may be more or less beside the point. The financial problems of city governments are almost certainly more attributable to over-reliance on property taxes and, at least in some states, to inadequate urban representation in state legislatures than to urban transportation choices. Similarly, making the central city a more attractive place for the middle classes almost surely depends on solving the problems of urban Negro ghettos as much as it does on transport policy. An interesting question is this: How many more middle-class whites employed in central business districts would choose to live closer to their places of work, rather than in remote suburbs, if the price of urban residences near central business districts were not in some cases artificially inflated or otherwise made less attractive by the existence of a captive Negro market for central locations?

Another source of confusion is the complex interdependency that exists between transport choices and the physical adequacy of our older central business districts. Manufacturing lofts, narrow streets and sidewalks, and other physical characteristics of older central business districts were determined by and suitable for a different set of technologies than seems optimal today. The creation of improved highway access to the fringes of these older business districts without taking compensating action in the physical design and layout of the districts themselves can lead to very difficult congestion and other transport problems. Under the circumstances, it is obviously quite tempting to seek at least a short-run solution or amelioration of the problem by attempting to reduce the pace of modernization in transport technologies.

A better longer-term solution may lie, however, in adjusting the physical layouts of these older business areas to modern technological circumstances, at least to the extent that doing so is not prohibitively expensive. The major public policy for facilitating such changes has been, of course, urban renewal. Whether or not one agrees with the methods or objectives of that program, it is reasonably clear that renewal does make a major contribution toward adjusting the physical characteristics of central urban areas so as to make them more compatible with modern transport and other technologies. Rarely, though, have urban renewal planners gone as far or been as imaginative as they might in making these accommodations. For example, many urban renewal plans have not separated different classes of vehicular and pedestrian traffic.

Urban transportation planning problems have also arisen in recent years because of special modal (or technological) preoccupations and considerable fragmentation of decision making. New highway planning, for example, has been devoted to a considerable extent to the immediate task of simply providing highway capacity at lowest possible cost, with costs sometimes construed narrowly as those of acquiring right of way and constructing facilities. This has given rise to a number of complaints that insufficient account has been taken of the consequences for community values, neighborhood characteristics, the needs of the community for recreational and other public land uses, and so forth.

Highway planning also has been more oriented to serving private vehicular traffic than public transit. There has, of course, been some considerable justification for this emphasis in that private vehicular traffic has been growing much more rapidly than public transit demands. Nevertheless, there are reasons for believing that somewhat more imaginative use of modern highway facilities for public transit needs might heighten the attractiveness of public services.

Myopia has also characterized much public transit management in recent years. Indeed, such management has on the whole been singularly unimaginative. Bus routes in most major cities today follow to a remarkable degree the routes of the streetcars they replaced—despite the obvious fact that the bus is a considerably more geographically mobile (if not almost ubiquitous) vehicle than the streetcar. Transit planners have also displayed a remarkable technological naïveté in generally equating rapid transit to rail transit and, in fact, using the two terms more or less interchangeably. With modern technology it is at least conceivable that one can design a high performance rapid-transit system using buses or hydrofoils or other vehicles.

Growing cognizance of these problems has led to a fairly widespread movement to broaden the basis on which urban transportation decisions are made. In particular, there is growing pressure to take into account the many externalities, both positive and negative, normally involved in urban transportation developments. With regard to highway development, there is an increasing demand that esthetics, neighborhood effects, and the impact on existing uses be evaluated as well as the direct costs of constructing a facility. Actually, more or less the same problems are generally encountered when developing a new rail transit facility. Public recognition and concern, however, have been considerably less due to the obvious fact that highway construction has quantitatively dominated urban transportation development over the past decade.

Organizational issues thus arise over the problem of how to formulate political processes to better reflect social valuations on such less directly quantifiable effects as esthetics, neighborhood characteristics, and so forth. For example, what improvements in existing government institutions might be introduced to better take into account or represent differing points of views on these matters? Similarly, is it possible to refine the tools of program budgeting or social accounting to arrive at technically better measures of these effects? Also, how might government institutions be improved so that the communication of technical findings to political decision makers is improved, both with respect to quantity and clarity?

There are also unresolved issues with regard to the level of government at which such decision making is best placed. Would it be better, for example, to place it within existing municipal or state governmental institutions or, alternatively, would a preferable solution lie in the development of new regional or metropolitan agencies? Some important unresolved issues are also to be found with regard to how the federal government might (or might not) participate in these decisions. Furthermore, since much urban public transit is still made available by private business organizations, there are also some classic problems of government-business relationships and regulation to be resolved.

Some highly controversial financial issues can also be injected. For example, rather remarkable vehemence can be generated about the question of whether general tax funds should be used to support urban transportation functions. Also, even the suggestion that gasoline-user taxes now earmarked and placed in highway trust funds might be used for purposes other than simply constructing highways generally encounters very vocal opposition from highway user groups, highway contractors, and automobile manufacturers.

Considerable disagreement also exists as to how the burden of highway development and construction should be divided between federal, state, and local government. A consensus is emerging, though, that urban highway users generally tend to contribute more in the way of user taxes than the cost of the facilities that they use. However, some redistribution in favor of rural areas is also generally justified on the grounds of systems effects, that is, of achieving an integrated and balanced system connecting different major population centers. Still, there are many reasons for wondering today if the highway program, with its roots deep in the movement to provide better access of farms to markets, is not perpetuating a division of funds between urban and rural needs that is out of keeping with today's population trends and requirements.

A question may also be raised as to what role special toll facilities might properly play in urban transportation development. Even with the Interstate Highway Program, some important toll facilities, such as tunnels and bridges and even a few urban expressways, have been constructed in American cities in the last decade. With a few notable exceptions (the Calumet Skyway and the Massachusetts Turnpike extension into Boston) most of these urban toll facilities have been remarkably successful from a financial standpoint. This, in turn, has given rise to a number of proposals to use the "profits" of these facilities to subsidize public transit. As will be discussed below, proposals have also been made to extend the principal of special tolls or tariffs for urban facilities to help alleviate the peak-hour congestion that is customarily experienced on almost all urban transportation facilities, whether public or private.

Organizational questions can also interact importantly with financial arrangements, especially when considering various federal-state-local sharing formulas. For example, it is often suggested that the federal government's support of 90 percent of the cost of Interstate Highway development, with only 10 percent falling on state government, has biased local and state governments toward accepting highway solutions to their urban transportation problems. By contrast, federal support for public transit, when available, has at its most generous been on a two thirds federal and a one third local basis. Of course, 10 percent of a highway development program may be a much larger figure than one third of an "equivalent" public transit program. Also, federal support for highways other than Interstate is usually on a fifty-fifty basis. From the standpoint of economic efficiency, moreover, there may be an offset to any bias introduced by the sharing formulas in that the highway funds are provided almost entirely from user charges, but the public transit subsidies are taken from general tax funds; thus, to some extent, the *total* level of available highway funds reflects reported demands for highway use, albeit highly imperfect and with many potential distortions.

Indeed, a curious anomaly has emerged in the federal approach to providing funds for public transit and highway developments. By law, the 90 percent federal portion of Interstate Highway development must be financed from user charges; federal gasoline taxes, in fact, have been twice revised upward in recent years in order to cover unexpected increases in the costs of the Interstate program. Federal support of public transit, on the other hand, not only comes from general tax funds, but local governments are usually prohibited from using charges at the fare box to cover their one third (or more) of matching funds. Transit matching funds largely come from new general tax sources. The irony, of course, is that as a practical matter this means that most of the local costs have to be pushed back on the property tax, one of the most regressive of taxes and one of the most overextended sources of support for local government programs.

Policy Alternatives

The public policy aspects of urban transportation can be classified under three categories. The first is achievement of certain broad social welfare goals through improvement of public transportation facilities, for example, better access to jobs and other opportunities for ghetto dwellers and greater mobility for children, the aged, the infirm, or others who for one reason or another cannot drive their own vehicles. The second is finding means to recapitalize dilapidated but nevertheless reasonably essential public transport services in and around some of our larger and older cities, for example, the New Haven, the Long Island Railroad, the New York subway, the Reading Railroad, and similar installations. The third is creation of *new* public transportation facilities to meet the growing needs of some of our most rapidly growing cities of medium to large size, such as Atlanta, Los Angeles, San Francisco, and Houston.

Clearly, then, when discussing urban transportation policies it is necessary to distinguish sharply between the situation in large cities, particularly those that are older, and that in newer or smaller cities. From the economic and engineering viewpoint, these distinctions are important if for no other reason than that residential and workplace densities are crucial in determining the relative cost of different modes of urban transportation. As noted, the greater the density of residences and workplaces, the easier it is to design a reasonably inexpensive and relatively high quality public transit service. Similarly, the layout and width of existing streets in central areas can have an important impact on the relative costs of different urban transportation modes. Older cities with crooked or narrow streets almost certainly will have greater difficulty accommodating automobile traffic than newer cities with wide avenues and gridiron street layouts. Furthermore, the desirability of exploring the "third dimension" for expansion of urban transportation facilities—be it either tunneling or the use of elevated structures—is likely to be greater when street space is limited. The greatest single advantage of rail transport over other forms of urban transportation is its lower cost for accommodating large volumes of traffic in tunnels or on elevated structures.

Under the circumstances, therefore, the older and larger cities that already have extensive rail rapid transit systems are almost certainly well advised to keep these facilities operational. Furthermore, on the grounds that investments in right-of-way and many other facilities used in rail transit are sunk (that is, have low salvage or alternative opportunity value) and therefore are best ignored, rail transit when already in place can be an exceedingly inexpensive means of serving high density urban corridors. In some cases, moreover, further investment in central portions of these systems, so as to improve their service characteristics or reduce costs, might be quite attractive on economic or marketing considerations.

Somewhat the same propositions apply to railroad commuter services. Railroad commuter services also face the special difficulty of being unable to properly maintain and reequip their operations. This inability, in turn, is often quite directly traceable to rather misguided, short-run, politically motivated regulatory policies that have prevented the relevant operating agencies (usually private railroads) from earning a reasonable rate of return on their commuter operations. The natural re-action of private managements in such circumstances is sim-ply to systematically depreciate the quality of the service, to better align short-run costs with revenues. In the long run, however, such policies can lead to an unfortunate spiral of increased operating costs, reduced patronage, reduced reve-nues, and an inability to recapitalize and reequip that, in turn, push operating costs up further and make it even more diffi-cult to render a reasonable quality of service. In short, the regulatory agencies that have imposed barriers to upward rate adjustments may have been bestowing a short-run benefit upon commuters while in the long run creating problems of a very substantial magnitude.

In such circumstances, the policy problem reduces to find-ing ways to inject needed capital while rationalizing the rate structure. In particular, it is not obvious that suburban rail commuters, usually among the higher income brackets of our society, should receive massive public subsidy of their trans-portation needs. However, any rationalization of commuter rate structures probably should not be done in a fashion that imposes a difficult *immediate* adjustment upon those who have chosen the "suburban way of life." Many people may have quite innocently committed savings and bought houses in the suburbs on the premise that they would have a certain level of transportation service available at certain stipulated prices. Only belatedly do they come to recognize these rates as artificially low. To alleviate the adjustment, low-interest loans to operators or loan guarantees might be the best solution, with bestowal of these loans contingent upon an acceptance by operators and regulatory agencies of a systematic scheme to rationalize tariffs.

It should also be noted that it may be highly inefficient to maintain rail commuter services that serve only very small daily or hourly volumes. Even with right-of-way and road-bed maintenance costs ignored, suburban commuter rail lines serving fewer than a thousand or two commuters per day are likely to be exceedingly expensive. (In Boston, for example, about $300 to $500 per year per passenger is required in pub-lic subsidy to maintain existing suburban rail commuter services.)

Lengthy extensions of existing rail rapid transit systems into low-density residential areas face many of the same economic difficulties as small-scale suburban rail commuter operations. The additional revenues will usually be less than the additional costs. And, of course, the capital costs are likely to be high; such costs are not sunk and are quite certainly avoidable. The only major exception to this rule will occur when the extension represents a revival of a previous rail transit type of service and therefore can be made at relatively low costs (as in the case of the Skokie shuttle in Chicago).

The provision of parking lots near suburban rail stations is not likely to improve matters in any large measure. Parking lots, even in suburban locations, do involve some expense (though this fact may be disguised by an implicit subsidy). Even more important, by the time the suburban resident has driven his car to the railroad station he has incurred a substantial proportion of the total costs involved in using his automobile as a commuter vehicle. Specifically, the additional cost of continuing in the car to the work location will not be very large unless the workplace is in a very dense central business district. Obviously, too, completing the commuter trip in the automobile has the additional advantage of eliminating a transfer with all that may imply about loss of time and exposure to bad weather.

For the smaller and newer cities the major policy problem is likely to be how to increase highway capacity effectively without a major restructuring of the existing urban areas. The newer and smaller cities not only have lower residential and workplace densities (making highway transport, either by private auto or bus, less costly and better able to render integrated no-transfer service than rail) but they also have fewer opportunities for perpetuating or converting existing rail facilities into public transit.

Most of these newer and smaller cities already have or shortly will have extensive limited-access, high-performance highway systems coming to the very edge or even penetrating their central business districts. This capacity is likely to be quite sufficient to meet all demands placed upon it except during the rush hours. On the presumption that expansion of capacity to a level sufficient to accommodate rush-hour traffic with only limited congestion is too expensive, the solution for these cities is one of achieving better utilization of high-performance highways during peak periods. Special tolls or license fees for use of centrally located highways during rush hours would be one means of achieving such discipline. Another would be to apply more physical controls by, for example, improving traffic signals, restricting access to high-performance facilities (so as to avoid extreme congestion that chokes highways and actually reduces peak-hour capacity), or reserving lanes or otherwise giving priority to public transit buses during the rush hours. The physical control of access to high-performance urban expressways may provide a particularly simple means of creating inexpensive high-performance transit. Specifically, if access to the expressways is limited so as to maintain high performance capability (for example, 50 miles an hour or so) and if buses are given priority access to these facilities during the rush hours, it should be possible to design high-performance express bus services between central workplaces and suburban residential locations at relatively low cost. Ultimately, better utilization of urban highways might also be achieved by automation, which would permit closer spacing of vehicles on expressways (as well as improve safety).

To determine which of these solutions should be preferred involves several difficult evaluations. Special tolls or license fees normally encounter a number of political objections: they seem to give the "rich" preferential access to what is commonly considered to be a public good. A more serious objection from the economic standpoint is the fact that implementing a useful toll system on urban highways is likely to be quite expensive, especially on a per mile basis, since urban trips are rather short. Furthermore, unless implemented on a fairly wide scale and with sophisticated differentiation between different classes of facilities, the application of the pricing techniques may do as much harm as good. Specifically, selective application of tolls to only a few urban facilities during the rush hours can have adverse repercussions on other facilities because of the high degree of substitutability between different portions of the system; for example, the gain through reducing congestion on the highway to which the tolls are applied may be more than offset by displacement of vehicles to untolled facilities, thereby creating congestion and accompanying losses on these facilities.[5]

Physical controls (for example, restricting access to high-speed highways) usually are less expensive to implement (though still far from free). They will not differentiate as well as a good pricing or toll system, however, between different classes of users and the intensity of different groups' desire to use urban highways. Physical controls, incidentally, may create spillover effects on other facilities in much the same fashion as price rationing. The congestion created or added to facilities receiving diverted traffic may offset the improvement achieved by imposition of the controls on a high performance facility. In general, physical controls represent a somewhat gross approach to achieving the same ends as price rationing. There is superficial evidence, though, that physical controls are somewhat more politically acceptable than tolls or special license fees.

The major disadvantage of automation as a means of increasing urban highway capacity during peak periods is that it is likely to be quite expensive. Though the technology is relatively simple conceptually, the costs could run as high as $500 or $600 per vehicle. In addition, some investment would be required in electronic devices as part of the highway, but these should be relatively inexpensive, at least as compared with the costs of automating the vehicle itself. Automation also requires close cooperation between public highway authorities and the vehicle manufacturers, something which has not been easy to achieve in the past.

Still another policy alternative for improving the performance of urban transport systems is, as implied previously, to restructure older central business districts to better suit them to modern technologies. In this connection, one can imagine elevated sidewalks, malls, or plazas for exclusive pedestrian use, better facilities for loading freight vehicles so as to remove such operations from major arterials or streets, and so forth. These measures, quite obviously, can be expensive. However,

[5] M. Wohl, "The Short-Run Congestion Cost and Pricing Dilemma," *Traffic Quarterly* (January 1966).

if incorporated into an urban renewal project, undertaken for other reasons as well, the costs may not be prohibitive.

As for government efforts to organize better to meet urban transportation development needs, one can detect different prototype solutions emerging. These prototypes differ in about four important dimensions: (1) orientation to public as against private solutions to urban transportation problems; (2) the degree to which control primarily resides in existing city or state as against new regional governmental institutions; (3) reliance upon general funds as against specific user taxes or toll financing; and (4) centralization of decision making, both within the civil service and between governmental administrative procedures and representative processes. Generally speaking (but with important exceptions), those who emphasize private transportation also tend to prefer that the principal decision-making power reside at the state level, that user-tax financing be employed and earmarked for specific uses, and that the decision-making process be at least somewhat decentralized, particularly with respect to modes (so that, in particular, highway development decisions are made independently of decisions about public transit). On the other hand, those favoring public transit development tend to prefer municipal or city government control and to favor use of general tax funds for transport development; to some extent these same people also favor some centralization of decision making, but attitudes on this issue can vary from group to group and place to place.

State highway officials, for example, favor maintenance of separate state highway organizations and like existing arrangements for earmarking gasoline and other vehicle excise taxes for exclusive use on highway development. They also seem reasonably well satisfied with the present arrangements for coordinating highway development between the states, mainly through the Federal Bureau of Public Roads. To some extent, in fact, their strong preference for existing arrangements probably stems from unfortunate historical experiences when it was difficult to coordinate highway development so that each state's programs meshed to create a comprehensive nationwide network or system. There is also little doubt that the status quo is one in which state highway officials wield considerable power, having by far the largest single share of government development funds devoted to transportation promotion and development.

City planners, by contrast, have recently advocated creation of special panels at the municipal level to review and possibly participate directly in the preliminary planning of urban highways. They suggest that these review panels include not only civil engineers, who currently dominate highway planning within the state highway agencies, but also architects, city planners, real estate economists, representatives of public transit agencies, and so forth. In essence, this proposal would modify present practice in two important ways: first, it would greatly broaden the representation or the number of the parties participating in urban highway design and planning and, second, it would tend to shift the locus of decision making on urban highways closer to the municipal government and away from state government. Also implicit in the proposal is the view that increased consideration be given to public transit needs when doing urban highway planning. Finally, one might expect that by broadening the number of groups and viewpoints represented in urban highway planning, there might be some tendency for highway financial practices to become somewhat less narrow in orientation; specifically, under such a scheme one might anticipate pressures to build somewhat more expensive but more esthetically attractive highways or to use highway trust funds to compensate those who are harmed by highway building.

Another increasingly popular organizational device is that of the single centralized state transportation agency. It is usually suggested that such agencies would have responsibility for virtually all transportation developments in their state, of highways, airports, public transit, and so forth. To some extent creation of such state agencies would mirror what has been happening at the federal level with the creation of a Department of Transportation. Such agencies should at least pose the possibility of better *coordinating* public and private transportation developments to a somewhat greater extent than in the past. On the other hand, the comprehensive agency would tend, if anything, to strengthen the state government's role in transport development, sometimes at the expense of municipal responsibilities. Multi-modal state transportation agencies should also have within them the seeds of more cross-subsidization between different modes, thereby reducing the likelihood that highway user taxes will be exclusively used for highway development. The comprehensive agency could also result in more centralization in the decision-making process and quite probably allow less scope for "citizen participation" than is the case today. Specifically, some of the problems of social evaluation of esthetic and noneconomic goals that play such a prominent role in the planners' proposals would not seem facilitated by creation of a comprehensive state agency. On the other hand, an advisory committee structured along lines advocated by the planners might be built into a comprehensive state agency's review procedures without too much difficulty.

Another organizational concept attracting increasing attention in public transportation circles is that of the specialized regional authority. Specifically, some experimentation is now under way with the creation of regional bodies that have responsibilities for transport development in large metropolitan areas and environs. Theoretically at least, these agencies are often expected to become concerned with comprehensive planning of all modal development within their areas. In practice, however, they usually become relatively specialized because of difficulties of acquiring authority from already established agencies. Perhaps the most important experience with this kind of agency today is that which is represented by the Massachusetts Bay Transportation Authority (created for the greater Boston area); somewhat similar experiments, however, have been mounted elsewhere. Like the comprehensive state agency, these regional authorities very often create a framework that makes it possible to cross-subsidize or provide special help from other tax funds in support of transport development. In the case of the Masschusetts Bay Authority, for example, two cents on every package of cigarettes sold in the entire state of Massachusetts is earmarked for support of the Authority.

Regional authorities tend to compromise the question of whether prime responsibility should reside with state or local government. In the case of the Massachusetts Bay Authority, for example, the governor appoints the commissioners but their actions are subject to review and veto by an advisory council composed of mayors and other representatives of local communities. It would also seem conceivable that by simple adaptation these regional authorities could be reconciled with the concept of broader citizen participation and consultation on esthetic and social objectives.

One major omission from the preceding discussion of organizational matters is the development of better decision-making procedures for planning transportation facilities to serve new urban areas as these emerge. In particular, unless something unexpected happens, most of the urban population growth in our society will occur in the next two or three decades, as it has in the recent past, in suburban rings around our major metropolitan areas. To the extent that this is true, a major objective of good planning in transportation should be to anticipate these developments and, specifically, to minimize the dislocations of people, businesses, and communities so often created when transport developments take place in already developed urban environments.

For example, one possibility worth scrutiny is advanced acquisition of rights-of-way for future transport requirements in and around major urban areas before the fact of actual development. Advance acquisition might be particularly advantageous if coupled with better land-use planning than has characterized American community development in the past. Some important exploratory work toward strengthening these planning institutions, and specifically providing for the possibility of advanced acquisition of lands for public purposes, has already been launched under sponsorship of the Department of Housing and Urban Development and the Department of Transportation. Thus far these efforts have not included integration of highway engineering and development planning with general land-use planning.

Evaluation

The best urban transportation policy and organization for any particular city quite obviously will depend on its physical characteristics, political inclinations, history, and traditions. As a corollary, policies based solely on such simple slogans as "achieving balanced transportation" are quite likely to be deficient. There is no reason to believe that every mode of urban transportation has to be developed in every city and that every urbanite must be given a choice between several different modes. To pursue such a policy is almost certain to be prohibitively expensive. Given the many demands placed upon the limited financial resources of city governments, it would seem wise to pursue somewhat less extravagant or ambitious programs.

To the extent that there is some truth in the notion of balance in urban transportation programs it would seem, rather, to lie in the fact that the different policy alternatives outlined in the previous section are not mutually exclusive. Restructuring older central business districts to better suit modern transport technologies is likely to be a reasonably wise policy whether a community continues, say, to place heavy reliance on rail rapid transit or becomes increasingly oriented to highway modes. Similarly, disciplining the use of central urban highway facilities during rush hours is likely to be productive whether or not public or private transportation is emphasized. Finally, even if a high-performance rail rapid transit system is to be continued, development of better express bus services between various parts of the city may still be attractive.

In general, four basically different transportation systems seem to be emerging in most of our metropolitan areas. The demands placed upon these four systems are, in turn, very much a function of the changing industrial and residential location patterns discussed earlier.

The first of these systems might be described as *traditional public transit*. This system serves people employed in central business districts who also reside reasonably close by. In smaller and less dense cities this system's functions are customarily performed by buses, while in our larger, denser, and older cities they may be performed by rail transit. Costs per trip on these systems are customarily quite low. The typical trip is relatively short and takes approximately 15 or 20 minutes to complete. The clientele will be secretaries and other clerical workers employed in banks, offices, stores, and similar activities as well as service workers, very often from minority groups, with jobs in hotels, restaurants, and related activities.

The second system is *long distance commutation*. Its main function is to move people from relatively distant suburban residential locations to workplaces at the heart of the central business district. The typical trip is a good deal longer than that performed by traditional public transit. The clientele usually has a much higher average income and comes from management or the professions. These systems tend to have very high performance characteristics, so that even though the typical trip is considerably longer than that by traditional transit, the travel time required does not rise proportionally. The costs per trip for these systems also tend to be high, commonly being over one dollar per trip and sometimes as high as three dollars per trip or more. (It should be emphasized that these costs are very often *not* fully paid by the users in the form of assessed charges.) Rail commutation is a very common mode for these trips, especially in our larger and older cities. Operation of a private automobile over high-speed urban expressways is another popular choice for these trips. Occasionally, high-speed express buses may be used.

The third system pertains to *cross-commutation*, designed for commuters who find both their employment and residences in suburban areas. An almost complete cross-section of urban America—blue-collar, clerical, managerial, and professional— is likely to be involved. For the most part these trips are made today by private automobile, although occasionally the bus is used. (Better marketing and design of bus transit might well increase the percentage using public transit for these trips, but the poor finances and, possibly, the traditional conservatism of transit management have tended to prohibit experimentation with new transit services aimed at capturing more of this market.) An important feature of this type of commuter trip is that the demand for it is growing very rapidly and there is every reason to expect that it will continue to grow.

The fourth type of basic urban transportation system might be described as an *inside-out system*. It serves work-trips made by people living in relatively central locations and working in the suburbs. The Negro female domestic working in a suburban home and living in a centrally located ghetto is the archetype; today, however, she is probably increasingly joined by male Negroes because employment opportunities in manufacturing, inter-city transportation, and even wholesaling and retailing are increasingly found at suburban locations, whereas housing opportunities remain restricted to the central ghetto. Furthermore, many white families with two or more workers, at least one of whom is employed in the central business district and one in a suburban workplace, have often found central city residential locations convenient.

The usual technical description of these outbound commuter trips is "reverse commutation," but this suggests that the central city systems described above can adequately serve these outbound commuter trips on their "empty backhauls." However, this is an oversimplification because the origination and destination patterns required for these inside-out trips is often very different from that of downtown-oriented transit. For example, it is unlikely that a Negro male employed in a suburban industry will be adequately served by a simple reversal of a downtown system. The chances of these systems serving the outbound white commuter well are also remote, since he normally does not live as close to the central business district as the minority groups.

The fact that conventional public transit or commuter systems have not served these inside-out trips well has been documented recently by Negro complaints about difficulties in reaching certain employment opportunities. Such complaints were recognized in the McCone report on the Watts riots. These inside-out trips are very often performed by private automobiles, with the cost of the trips being reduced by carpooling. Some recent public transit experiments financed by the Department of Housing and Urban Development (as in Watts, for example) may eventually reduce this reliance upon private automobiles.

It should be quite clear that since the groups served by these four different basic urban transportation systems are rather different, the incidence of benefits derived from improvements in these systems will vary considerably. For example, improvement of the long-distance, high performance suburb to downtown systems will tend primarily to benefit higher income groups. To the extent that development of these systems is subsidized from public funds, the implicit income transfer probably would be regressive. By contrast, expenditures aimed at improving conventional short-haul central city transit will almost certainly benefit mostly low- to middle-income groups.

It is also clear that future demands placed upon these different systems may vary widely. The need for cross-haul services between suburban residences and workplaces seems to be growing most rapidly, while the demand for conventional public transit seems to be declining. Demands for long-distance commutation seem to be more or less constant or slowly increasing, depending upon the extent to which a particular downtown area houses office and related service activities. Finally, as long as housing opportunities for minority groups are primarily limited to the centrally located ghetto, the demand for "inside-out" commutation is likely to grow.

Thus, in light of anticipated future needs, public policy might well focus attention on the development of cross-haul and inside-out systems. Any such emphasis would depart, of course, from that implicit in the development or subsidization of long-distance rail commuter lines, an all too characteristic emphasis in recent urban transportation planning.

The most neglected aspect of urban transportation planning would seem to be devising means to meet cross-haul or reverse commuter trips via public transit. The need is for experimentation with new and more flexible forms of public transit and the establishment of more public transit routes that traverse *only* suburban and non-central locations. In particular, many cross-haul and reverse commuter trips are almost certainly better served by public transit that does *not* become involved in downtown congestion with all that implies in time losses and increased operating costs. More intensive analysis of basic urban commuter markets and a concomitant improvement in marketing strategies employed by public transit managements would greatly facilitate these developments.[6]

---

[6] Lewis M. Schneider, *Marketing Urban Mass Transit: A Comparative Study of Management Strategies* (Boston, 1965), presents

In summary, it must be recognized that cities are constantly undergoing change. There are many reasons for believing that the changes in workplace and residential location being induced by ever-changing manufacturing, bookkeeping, transportation, and communication technologies may result in radically different urban transportation patterns in the near future. Indeed, one of the major failures of many urban public transit systems has been their failure to serve new workplaces in suburban or metropolitan ring locations. If present trends in residential and workplace locations continue, the major unmet urban transportation needs ten or twenty years from now may well be between, within, and across the outer portions of our large metropolitan areas rather than to and from the core.

That future, however, is still some time away. The most urgent policy question seems to be whether cities will choose to solve any short-run transportation problems they face by using rather blunt and unsophisticated methods (in the form of heavy capital investments in immobile and inflexible rail transit used on a standby or part-time basis for a few hours a day) or whether the self-discipline can be mustered to organize the extensive urban street and highway capacity already in place to better serve today's needs. Remembering that over 70 percent of public transit is now performed on highways, the possibilities for immediate gain from such discipline would appear quite promising. Perhaps the money saved might be better spent on educational, recreational, and rehabilitation programs more directly related to making the central city a better place to live.

---

several interesting ideas on how these improvements migh~ implemented.

FINANCING URBAN GOVERNMENT

Dick Netzer

Few state or local governments are without fiscal problems. The rapid and virtually universal increase in public expenditures in the past two decades and the frequency and ubiquity of tax rate increases afford ample evidence of this. But the problems seem most severe for local governments serving the larger and older metropolitan areas of the country—say, the two dozen or so metropolitan areas with populations of more than one million and central city populations (usually) of more than 500,000, located mostly but not entirely in the northeast and midwest.

Their problems are more severe, despite the fact that much of the country's income and wealth is concentrated in such areas, in part because they operate with diverse and fragmented structures of local government. In part, their difficulties reflect the concentration of the urban poverty and race problems in the large old central cities. Also, the very fact of age creates problems associated with physical and functional obsolescence. In addition, there are difficulties stemming from extremely rapid growth rates on their urbanizing fringes.

The existence of these difficulties and the national interest in solving them have been recognized in various pieces of Great Society legislation enacted or proposed in the past few years. But these federal actions by no means solve all the local fiscal problems (nor should they be expected to). This analysis is addressed to the fiscal problems of the larger, older metropolitan areas, especially their central cities. It is not universal coverage, but it does encompass quite a large segment of our urban population and it does suggest something about the future prospects for some of the smaller and newer urban areas.

Some Recent Trends

In recent years, as throughout the twenty years following World War II, local (and state government) public expenditures have been increasing substantially more rapidly than has the nation's total output and income (see table).[1] Public expenditures in urban areas have always been significantly higher, in relative terms, than those in nonurban areas and recently have been increasing slightly faster, in dollar terms, within the urban areas. This difference is to be expected, since nearly all the nation's population growth has been occurring in urban areas. But urban population growth alone does not explain the rate of increase in public spending. Indeed, the increase in *per capita* local government expenditures in metropolitan areas has been more rapid than the increase in *aggregate* gross national product.

What is perhaps most striking, public expenditures in the larger central cities have been climbing steeply, despite their losses or slow growth in population. In the most recent seven-year period for which data are available, expenditures of municipal governments in the larger cities rose by 45 percent (see table), about two thirds as rapidly as expenditures of all other local governments combined. Consider the twelve

[1] The dates used here are related to data availability. A Census of Governments was conducted in 1962 and in 1957; the preceding Census of Governments occurred in 1942.

Percentage increases in nonfederal public expenditures,
1957–1962 and 1957–1963/64.

Expenditure item	Percentage increase	
	1957–1962	1957–1963/64
Gross national product[a]	27	43
Total expenditures		
All state and local governments	48	70
All local governments	46	65
Local governments in metropolitan areas[b]	47	–
Central city governments in large cities[c]	31	45
Per capita expenditures[d]		
All state and local governments	36	51
All local governments	34	47
Local governments in metropolitan areas	30	–

Source: Adapted from various publications of the U.S. Bureau of the Census, Governments Division.

[a] For calendar years 1957–1962 and 1957–1964.

[b] For identical collections of metropolitan areas in 1957 and 1962.

[c] Includes only the municipal governments per se (that is, excluding overlapping but separate county, school district, and special district governments); for the 42 cities with a 1960 population of more than 300,000, excluding Honolulu.

[d] Based on estimated 1957, 1962, and 1964 populations.

largest metropolitan areas (1964 population over 1.8 million). In the eight-year period, 1957 to 1965, property tax revenues (used here as a partial proxy for local expenditures) rose by 86 percent for these entire areas. In their central portions, property tax revenues rose by 69 percent.[2] But there has been little population growth in the central portions—less than half the rate of the entire areas between 1960 and 1964.

[2] "Central portions" are the counties that include the central cities. In five of the twelve areas, the "central portions" and central cities are substantially identical. In 1960, the central cities' population was 74 percent of that of the "central portions."

To be sure, substantially more external aid to central cities in the provision of public services has been forthcoming in recent years. State and federal aid to central city governments has risen considerably more rapidly than have central city expenditures. Also, the *direct* role of state governments in the provision of public services in and for the central cities has expanded considerably. Since the passage of the Interstate Highway Act in 1956, the states have been far more active in the construction of central city highways than previously. In a growing number of states, the state government is directly involved in urban mass transportation, in park and open space activities, and in housing programs. In some states in the northeast, expansion of state higher education programs has had an important effect on central city populations. But despite all this, the taxes imposed by central city governments, collected from static populations and slowly growing central city economies, continue to rise sharply.

The Purposes of Urban Government

The explanation for rising public expenditures in urban areas is not hard to find. In the central cities, local-tax-financed outlays for services directly linked to poverty (in the health and welfare fields) have not been static; the central cities of the twelve largest metropolitan areas account for an eighth of the country's population, but nearly 40 percent of health and welfare outlays financed from local taxes. For central city governments, the problems associated with poverty and race are by far the most urgent of public problems.

Neither poverty nor racial disabilities can be eliminated solely by governmental action, and still less by action by local or state and local governments combined (that is, governments other than the federal government). But local governments do have a major responsibility to grapple with these problems and can make a major contribution toward their alleviation. In the American system of government, it is local governments that are responsible for providing educational services that over time will have a major bearing on the chances of the poor and racially disadvantaged to overcome their disadvantages. Local governments are also responsible for a wide range of health and welfare services, which are almost entirely oriented toward the poor in American cities. They have had, since the late forties, major responsibilities in connection with the housing of the poor. And, as far as the poor are concerned, local government recreational facilities are about the only recreational facilities available.

A second major set of problems confronting the older central cities lies in the fact that they have a huge legacy of obsolescence. Their stock of housing and other social capital —that is, public and quasi-public facilities of all kinds—is old, often physically deteriorated, and generally far from competitive with the newer parts of the same urban areas. It may be, as some have argued, that the best national policy would be to allow this obsolescence to continue and allow further deterioration of the older parts of the older cities. In this case, population would decline in these sections and, presumably at some stage, values would be so low that private renewal of such areas would become possible. Or, if desirable, public renewal could be undertaken, but on the basis of exceedingly low values.

Developments in recent years suggest that this obsolescence policy is hardly a likely course of action. For one thing, there is the plight of those who, because they are poor, or Negro, or both, have little chance to escape the deteriorating areas. Amelioration, for these hundreds of thousands of people, is both politically and morally necessary. Quite apart from moral issues, most cities and the federal government appear to have decided that it is necessary to replace obsolete social capital and to compete for residents and businesses in an atmosphere of rising expectations. That is, the cities feel they must offer an environment of public facilities services that, together with other attractions that the central locations may have, will offset the blandishments of the newer and presumably more modern sections of the metropolitan areas where standards of public services and amenity are high indeed.

In the newer sections of metropolitan areas—the new portions of central cities as well as the urbanizing fringes of the metropolitan area—the main governmental problem is the provision of the new social capital needed by a rising population, and a population that has peculiarly heavy demands for public services and facilities, notably schools.

In the aggregate, these urban problems have resulted in a diversion of resources from private to public uses via tax increases. But this relative expansion of the public sector is costly in another way. If local governments are to command resources, they must pay prices for these resources that are competitive with those prevailing in the economy, notably salaries of public employees. If they are to expand *more rapidly* than the private sector, they must bid away resources by paying even more, which largely explains the rapid increase in urban government salary levels, especially for occupational groups whose talents are in heavy demand in the private sector.

Ideal Solutions

This catalog of governmental problems suggests something about the nature of the solutions. Assume for the moment that we are free to devise a structure of local government that is ideal from both an administrative and a financial standpoint.

First, consider the governmental fiscal problems associated with poverty and race. It seems clear that, in an ideal world, the financial burden of public services that exist primarily to cope with these problems would not rest on particular local governments with small geographic coverage. Poor people tend to be concentrated in the central cities of metropolitan areas for good reasons. The supply of housing that they can afford is in such places, the kinds of jobs to which their skills give them access tend also to be located in these sections, and the variety of social services they require tend to be available only in central cities. Indeed, it is probably in the national interest that the poor be concentrated in central cities, for it is rather unlikely that their needs would ever be sufficiently attended to were they not so conspicuous.

Another factor in the geographic location of the poor, and even more in the geographic location of those in racial minority groups, is national in character. This society is a very mobile one and over the years it has undergone rapid economic changes. There have been, in response to these economic changes, massive migrations of people from rural areas to urban areas, from central cities of urban areas to the suburbs, from the urban areas of the north and midwest to the southwest and west. No individual central city has been known to put up billboards advertising its attractions for the poor, trying to recruit them from other parts of the country. They have migrated to the cities in response to pressures in their older locations and attractions in the newer locations, but all these have been essentially national economic and social forces. Such being the case, it seems appropriate that the costs of attending to the needs of such people should be spread over a fairly wide geographic area. And because it is the economies or, rather, the economic prosperity of the larger metropolitan areas that have been the attraction for the poor and the disadvantaged, it could be argued that the metropolitan areas as a whole ought to finance the poverty-linked social services.

There is a good case for this argument because the great bulk of the wealth and income of the country is concentrated in metropolitan areas. But almost nowhere is there a governmental structure such that taxes can be levied throughout the metropolitan area on the economic base of the entire metropolitan area for the support of such services. In some places, in states that are overwhelmingly urban and metropolitan in character, the state government may be a reasonable substitute for metropolitan area government. But this is not true of all states, and, moreover, some metropolitan areas straddle state boundary lines. Also, the migration of the poor among the states has not been an even, proportional movement; some states, like New York, have been the recipients of very large numbers of poor in-migrants because of accidents of geography (access to Puerto Rico) rather than economic strength. All this suggests that the national government is the proper source of support for the bulk of poverty-linked services provided in urban areas.

In addition, it could be argued that some of the poverty-linked services actually provided by urban local governments should be directly *provided* as well as *financed* by governments covering a wider area. One example of this is the suggested negative income tax, which would supplant state and local public assistance expenditures.

What about the rebuilding of the central cities and the provision of adequate amenities in the form of public services? In a broad sense, if a central city has sensible redevelopment policies and strategies, ones that actually provide a good payoff in social terms relative to the funds invested, the cities themselves should be able to finance the costs fairly readily. That is, the additional public expenditures in time will improve the environment of the city sufficiently so that its tax base —broadly defined—will be enhanced considerably.

There are some exceptions to this. First, there is need for outside help to offset some biases and imperfections in present arrangements. For example, recent heavy investment in urban highway facilities, based on outside financial support, may make it rather difficult to finance investment in public transportation facilities from local resources. A second qualification is that the particular local tax devices used to finance these socially self-liquidating investments have side effects. High central city taxes on business activity may make the central cities much less attractive locations for businesses capable of operating elsewhere. Equally important, high taxes based on the value of real property can discourage private investment which raises real property values. In old cities full of obsolete private structures, an ideal fiscal solution would avoid taxes that defer private rebuilding. Instead, such a solution would involve taxes that either encourage the needed rebuilding or are neutral in their effect. And the most nearly neutral kind of tax that is widely used and produces much revenue at any level of government is the tax on individual income.

The newer parts of metropolitan areas in general are characterized by relatively high levels of personal income and wealth. This suggests that they should be able to finance themselves with a minimum of outside help, provided they have boundaries that make some sense from the standpoint of the nature of the services provided and that do not fragment the potential tax base into wildly unequal portions. Also, because a good part of the problem in the newer areas is provision for new public investment, the outer areas would be able to finance themselves adequately only if they are free to meet the bunched-up (in time) needs they now face. That is, they should be able to borrow rather freely to meet current needs for capital outlays and repay this over the useful lives of the facilities. At a later stage, their capital needs will be much lower.

The poverty-linked services aside, many of the public services provided by local governments are in many ways like those provided by public utility companies. That is, they are not provided uniformly to the entire population, but rather in distinguishable quantities and qualities to individual families in the population, who consume them in accord with their personal preferences. For example, not all families use the same amount of water, not all use the same amount of highway transportation, and so on. There is a strong case for financing such services in the same way public utility services are financed—that is, via user charges, which are like prices, rather than through general taxes.

If the purpose of providing the public service is to offer different consumers the services they want, and place some value on, then they ought to pay for such services in proportion to the costs. Otherwise, governments will be called upon to provide a great deal more of the service than people would be willing to consume if they did have to pay for it—a wasteful use of resources; or the service will be in such short supply that a form of non-price rationing will be employed to allocate the service among consumers. The outstanding example is street congestion in cities: users pay for highways in the aggregate but not for specific individual uses of the streets and therefore, not surprisingly, treat highways as a free good. The only deterrent to use of the streets at the most crowded times and in the most crowded places is the value one places on time; the rationing in effect then results in those who place a low value on time preempting the street space from those who place a high value on time. Ordinarily, in our society, rationing is on the basis of price. Somebody who values a service highly bids it away from someone who places a lower value on that service and would rather use his income for alternative kinds of consumption.

This has relevance for public services in both the newly developing parts of urban areas and the older cities themselves. To the extent that pricelike mechanisms are employed, there is likely to be a more sensible allocation of resources in urban areas. Moreover, prices are by definition neutral in their economic effects. People do not exchange money for services or goods unless they consider the value of the services or goods they receive at least equal to the money they surrender. Substituting neutral prices for unneutral taxes has much to commend it. Of course, there is a limit to the extent to which pricing devices can be used, but the general principle remains: where prices make sense at all, they should be utilized and not rejected simply because the services are organized under public rather than private auspices.

There is a further extension of the market analogy to urban government. People do differ in their preferences for various kinds of public and private goods and services. For some people, locally available recreational facilities—say, public parks and swimming pools—are exceedingly valuable services, but for others—those who prefer to travel long distances on vacation, for example—the value is much less. And such differences are not simply a matter of differences in income—people with similar incomes have different tastes.

Since tastes differ, it is entirely conceivable that one might find people of similar tastes—in this case similar preferences for public services—tending to move into particular sections of the metropolitan area. There are real advantages to such ordering of residential patterns based on differences in preferences for various kinds of public goods and services. Without this arrangement, some people would be taxed to provide services they do not desire, while others would find that there are services they desire and would be willing to pay more taxes for.

In an ideal urban governmental and fiscal structure, it would be desirable to try to provide some arrangements that foster this kind of expression of differences in tastes. One such arrangement would result in large numbers of small separate service areas for kinds of public services that are likely to have this character, such as recreational services.

Neither user-charge financing (as a principal source of support) nor individual-preference-oriented service areas are appropriate for welfare and health services or any other poverty-linked services, and user-charge financing is inappropriate for schools as well. All of these are services provided to the poorer members of the urban community despite their inability to pay for the services, indeed *because of* their inability to pay. The consensus is that the rest of the community is better off if the poor are not destitute (hence public assistance) and have some medical care (hence clinics and free hospital care), and if their children are educated. Indeed, we feel so strongly about education that we *require* people to send their children to schools and levy the taxes necessary to provide the school places. Such "meritorious wants" as minimal health and educational levels contrast sharply with society's indifference as to whether individual families own more or fewer water-using appliances or own one, two, or three cars.

This description of ideal solutions has not mentioned a frequent source of controversy: suburban exploitation of the central city or central city exploitation of commuters. The poverty-linked services, as noted, do present a problem. Putting them to one side, it is entirely possible to develop a system in which there is no significant degree of exploitation of either set of residents and to do this without setting up any sort of a massive metropolitan governmental structure.

The truly needed metropolitan-area-wide governmental machinery is related to the nature of certain kinds of public services. Transportation, planning, water pollution, air pollution, and water supply are all services that, for the most part, cannot effectively be provided by small local governments and require fairly large geographic service areas. Although cost is one consideration, yet another is the provision of reasonably adequate standards of service. Where technology and geography dictate metropolitan governmental arrangements, they would exist in an ideal situation. Where technology does not dictate such arrangements, the real *metropolitan* governmental need is to ensure a wide area for financing the poverty-linked services.

The Real World of Urban Public Finance

How do present arrangements for financing urban local governments compare with this ideal? First, there *is* a substantial local tax burden due to the financing of poverty-linked services, a burden that exists for many local governments but is especially important in the older central cities. Public assistance, for example, is the most obvious poverty-linked public service. The federal government provides substantial amounts of funds for this, roughly 55 percent of the total spent in 1964. In most states in the United States, the remaining funds are provided entirely from state government sources, and indeed the state government administers public assistance programs itself. However, there are urban states with large *local* public assistance expenditures. They include California, Ohio, Indiana, Minnesota, Wisconsin, New York, New Jersey, and Massachusetts. In fact, in all except six of the metropolitan areas with a population of over one million, there are significant locally financed outlays for public assistance. For the country as a whole, roughly one sixth of the funds are provided from local financial resources.

Similarly, there are significant health expenditures (which in cities are primarily directed to the poor) and hospital expenditures financed from local tax funds. In 1964, the locally financed total of welfare expenditures, current expenditures for health purposes, and current expenditures for hospitals (net of charges received from hospital patients) was about $2 billion. Some idea of the relative importance of this amount can be seen by comparing it with the total of $20 billion that local governments received in that year from the local property tax. For the governments of the largest American cities (those with populations over 300,000), the ratio is much higher. Locally financed services that are fairly directly linked to poverty absorbed nearly one fourth of the big-city property tax revenues in 1964, or one sixth of their collections of taxes of all types. In a number of the larger metropolitan areas, if the local tax drain due to central city financing of social services were equalized over the entire area, central city tax loads would be well below those elsewhere in the metropolitan areas, rather than well above, which is the more usual case.[3]

Another aspect of the poverty-linked services fiscal problem relates to the financing of schools in the older central cities. Most programs of state aid to the local school districts in a state appear to be fair; typically, state aid programs are based on the numbers of children and the local property tax base per pupil. Big cities tend to have fewer school children per family in public schools than in other parts of a given state and also tend to have relatively high business property values. As a result, they receive relatively small amounts of state school aid.

But this apparent equity is misleading, because the assumption underlying almost all state aid programs is that the cost of providing a given quality of education is uniform throughout a state. There is much evidence that it is not—to provide an education equivalent in quality to that received in the better suburban schools would cost enormously more in the slum schools in the big cities. One commentator, Christopher Jencks, recently estimated that this equivalent-quality education would cost approximately twice as much per pupil. The reason is obvious. The many disadvantages under which children in poverty and minority group families suffer at home and before they come to school mean that they require a great deal more in the way of special services, small classes, and the like to assure a performance in school equivalent to that of the suburban middle-class child. And state aid formulas generally do not recognize this.

The 1965 Federal Aid to Education Act is specifically addressed to the problem of children from poorer families. It thus provides a substantial aid for large central city schools and partially makes up for the inadequacies of the state aid

[3] Per capita property tax revenues are significantly higher in most large central cities than in their surrounding areas; see Dick Netzer, *Economics of the Property Tax* (Brookings, 1966), p. 118. Where they are not, it is usually because the central city relies heavily on local *nonproperty* taxes (New York, St. Louis, cities in Ohio, for example).

formulas. This is all to the good, but big-city school systems now spend, from their own resources, several hundred million dollars for programs related to poverty. The ideal solution would call for such expenditures to be *entirely* financed from external funds. Moreover, if the problems of poverty and race are really to be attacked, big-city school expenditures probably will need to be increased at a very rapid rate indeed. Under present arrangements, they will be increased at a much slower rate than they should be and, moreover, even that slower rate will be a severe economic burden on the big cities themselves.

There are serious problems with the existing arrangements for financing the rebuilding and improvement of central cities, aside from the poverty problem. The principal difficulty is the choice of tax instruments for local fiscal support. The main problem is the extremely heavy taxation of housing, which works at cross-purposes with the desire to rebuild and renew central cities. In the United States, local property taxes on housing equal roughly 20 percent of the rental value of housing. That is, they are equivalent to a 25 percent excise tax on housing expenditures. In the larger metropolitan areas, particularly in the northeastern part of the United States, the excise tax is more like 30 percent, and for some of the central cities well over 30 percent. There is no other type of consumer product, aside from liquor, tobacco, and gasoline, which is as heavily taxed in the United States today. The effect of this very heavy taxation, other things being equal, is to deter people from spending their incomes for better housing.

Note the "other things being equal" clause. In suburban communities, particularly bedroom suburbs, the public services that a family receives or has access to are very closely tied to the local taxes that the same family pays. Therefore, in a sense, the property tax in many suburbs is analogous to a general charge for the use of public services, or perhaps even to a local income tax. It is unlikely to be a deterrent to consumption of housing, that is, to the expenditure of consumer income for housing. For the central cities, this is not the case. Central cities provide a wide variety of services and tax a wide variety of property types. Individuals cannot reasonably assume that the prices of housing confronting them include an identifiable tax component that is in effect a charge for a preferred package of public services. What they do observe is that housing is expensive in the central city. It may not be any more expensive in the central city than in the suburbs. But an effective city-rebuilding strategy requires that the central cities encourage more private expenditure for housing, and this may in turn require that housing be much cheaper in the central city than in the suburbs.

It may be argued that any tax paid by individuals and families in a central city will have some discouraging effect on their choice of the central city as a residence. This is true, as is the argument that any tax that reduces incomes will have some bearing on housing expenditure. However, a tax specifically related to housing expenditure is much more a deterrent to the needed rebuilding of the central cities than a tax on income in general would be.

Another element in the choice of tax strategy for central city programs concerns the taxation of businesses by the central city. It is clear that many types of business activity have been decentralizing away from the central cities of the larger metropolitan areas. If, to all the other disadvantages of congestion and lack of adequate space, and so on, the central city adds business taxes higher than those elsewhere in the area, it may very well spur the further migration of businesses. No doubt this has *not* been a serious problem in many areas, although in a few cases property taxes on business may have had a discouraging effect on economic activity. More often, the over-all effect of taxation of business property in the cities at differentially heavier rates is to depress land values, which is not necessarily the worst thing in the world.

However, it is worth noting New York City's experience.[4] The city has had, for many years, exceptionally heavy taxes on business activity and real property, including a unique (and heavy) tax on gross receipts and a sales tax far higher

---

[4] See Graduate School of Public Administration, New York University, *Financing Government in New York City,* Final Research Report to the Temporary Commission on City Finances (April 1966).

than in surrounding areas. The gross receipts tax was exceptionally burdensome to manufacturing and wholesale trade activities, which would have been migrating away from the city in any case. But there is evidence that the tax accelerated the rate of decline in these economic sectors. Similarly, there is evidence that the decentralization of retail trade was substantially speeded by the sales tax differential. Fortunately, the city has now shifted to a less oppressive form of business taxation and the sales tax differential has also been reduced.

What about the newly developing parts of metropolitan areas? The major problem here is connected with boundary lines. The boundary lines of political subdivisions in the suburbs are those that have evolved over a long period. They have no necessary relationship to the natural areas for the performance of particular services or for grouping people of similar preferences, which is a less important consideration. Moreover, the tax base of the suburban areas tends to be so fragmented in some parts of the country that there are enormous disparities between needs and taxable resources, particularly in connection with financing the schools.

One consequence of this fragmentation has been what has been referred to as "fiscal zoning": controlling land use in newly developing areas in such a way as to minimize tax costs (have as few school children as possible) and maximize tax base (have non-residential or very high value residential property rather than ordinary houses). It is easy to think of organizational arrangements that can offset this problem: governmental reorganization, additional state aid for particular functions such as schools, or some kind of second-tier local governmental structure—that is, some form of fiscal federation within metropolitan areas. The idea is to offer common access to the tax base of large parts of the metropolitan area and reduce the incentive to plan land use primarily from the standpoint of fiscal considerations, rather than from the standpoint of larger notions of the suitability of functional patterns in metropolitan areas.

Real world solutions also fall short of the ideal in connection with the application of user charges to finance particular public services. They are frequently not used at all in cases where they *can* be sensibly employed. They are also frequently used in a most inept fashion. Air and water pollution is an excellent example of failure to apply user charges where they clearly make sense. By and large, the construction and operation of sewerage systems and sewage treatment facilities is financed in the United States by local property taxes. Some places have sewer service charges of one kind or another, but they are by no means the majority. Yet here is a case where it is rather easy to identify the specific people who give rise to public costs. The benefits of water pollution control or air pollution control may be very broad, but the sources of the public costs are highly individual. Moreover, it is not impractical to apply charges that have some relationship to the costs occasioned. This has been done in the Ruhr basin in Germany for many years; there is an elaborate system of pollution charges designed to apportion the costs of treatment facilities among the industrial establishments that actually occasion those costs and also to deter firms from polluting.

As noted earlier, conventional highway financing illustrates the inept use of user charges. Gasoline taxes and licenses have some relationship to the amount of use of the highways by all users as a group and by individual users over long periods of time. But flat charges of this kind cannot possibly discourage people from freely using the very high cost roads at the very high cost periods. There is no discrimination among the parts of the road system depending on the cost to the public of those road systems, including the costs of congestion.

Another example of inept use of user charges is in connection with the common structure of transit fares in cities. The flat fare is a time-hallowed principle, although the structure of costs would dictate a substantially higher fare in the peak hours than in the off-peak hours, differentials between predominant and reverse direction riding, and perhaps differentials based on distance in the larger cities. The use of parking meters as a user charge is also rather inept in most cases. Flat, low charges are the most commonly found kind of arrangement with relatively little discrimination among locations and times of day. As a result, in most places in central business districts metered curb space is cheaper but harder to find than less convenient off-street parking facilities.

Moreover, since many cities use parking meter revenues to subsidize their own off-street parking facilities, they are to some extent competing with themselves by inept parking meter charge policies.

Directions for Reform

This comparison of prevailing practice with one man's notions of what is ideal is, of course, not a practical program of reform. It suggests, for example, abolition of the property tax on housing in central cities, which is hardly an immediate possibility. But it does indicate one set of views as to the proper *directions* for reform—more outside aid for poverty-linked services (although 100 percent outside financing may be years off); refraining from increases in taxes on housing in the cities (although reduction may be even further off) and the substitution of other tax forms, preferably used on an area-wide basis; governmental structural improvements such as many have urged for years; and wider and more sophisticated applications of the price mechanism in local government.

What are the policy alternatives? One is to call for substantially increased federal (and in some cases, state) aid for a long list of urban, especially central city, activities. Federal assistance in the provision of urban services, either via aid to local and state governments or via direct federal performance (for example, expansion of social insurance, like Medicare), has increased sharply in the past few years. This assistance can be viewed as a belated recognition of the national interest in the resolution of certain urban problems, notably those related to poverty and those that leap geographic boundaries (for example, water pollution), with the increase in the federal role likely to level off at a new higher plateau, much as it did between the late 1930's and the late 1950's. Or it can be viewed as no more than the beginning of a continuously expanding federal role. The historical evidence suggests the former interpretation, but this is prophecy, not scholarship.

A second alternative is to reaffirm the received truth, discovered decades ago, that the property tax is inherently a good tax for local governments, which can be relied upon even more heavily, if only the abominations that characterize its administration are eliminated. This view has numerous proponents, but it is possible to entertain doubts as to whether a tax based on so ephemeral a standard as the "true value of property" can ever be equitably administered. Moreover, the persistence of bad administration over so many years makes one wonder whether good administration is publicly acceptable, even if attainable. It is worth noting that the advocates of a strengthened role for the property tax generally have little patience with those who propose to mitigate its effects on central city housing by special exemptions and abatements for administratively preferred types of housing investment.

The alternatives to the property tax are not easy ones. Proliferation of local nonproperty taxes imposed by existing local government units raises not only administrative problems but, more important, economic ones for central cities. If central cities are where the fiscal difficulties bind, they will be the heavy users of nonproperty taxes; differentially heavy taxation by central cities can surely affect their economic future, at the margin. The prospect of nonproperty taxes imposed on a metropolitan-area-wide basis, which would wash out competitive fears, is not promising, since there are few precedents in this country. But it remains an attractive concept. Finally, wider and more sophisticated applications of user charges demand local government imagination, administrative skill, and political courage. This course, more than any other, can run aground on the inherent conservatism of local government, a universal characteristic.

There is, perhaps, more knowledge concerning the mechanisms for financing urban public services than there is about the services themselves—consumer-voter preferences for public expenditures, cost functions for the major activities, alternative methods of achieving public *objectives* via differing public service *inputs,* and the like. The lack of knowledge on the expenditure side is considerable. There is, in addition, a special problem of uncertainty for central cities. We know very little indeed about the effects of differences in the supply of public services on locational choice within metropolitan areas—by businesses and households alike—and only slightly more about the effects of tax differentials on locational choice. But, in local finance as elsewhere, policy must be made daily, in the face of uncertainty. And the very fact that local finance has so many pressing problems has revived scholarly interest in the field, after a long lull, which ensures that the dimensions of uncertainty will be gradually narrowed in the years ahead.

POLLUTION AND CITIES

Roger Revelle

Pollution is the harmful alteration of our environment by our own actions. Pollutants are either unwanted by-products of our activities or the obnoxious residues of things we have made, used, and thrown away. Man has always produced pollutants, but until recently the natural processes in his environment were sufficient to change most of them into harmless or beneficial substances. In the modern world, however, pollutants are produced in such large quantities that the capacity of the environment to absorb them is often exceeded, and pollution results. Man is increasing in numbers, productivity, and technology, but the rest of nature remains fixed. As men clump themselves together in cities, the part of the environment that receives most of their pollutants is actually diminishing.

In 1890, some 22 million Americans were city and town dwellers. Today there are about 130 million, six times as many, and by the year 2000 the number may double again.

I am grateful to my colleague, Professor Harold A. Thomas, for several of the ideas and calculations in this paper.

With the growth of cities, we are placing ever heavier pollution pressure on a small fraction of our environment—about 2 percent of the area of our country. In the megalopolises of the future—the continuous strip cities like Philip Hauser's "Atlanticopolis" extending from Boston to Richmond—the problems of waste removal and avoidance of pollution will be on the same scale as the problems of water, air, and food supply, and of human transportation.

In many ways, the quality of our environment has deteriorated with each new advance of the gross national product. Increases in electric power production mean the burning of more coal and fuel oil, and hence the discharge of more sulphur dioxide into the air. The growth of the paper industry has brought a vast increase in trash. The production of new automobiles and the discard of old ones has resulted in unsightly piles of hulks. The growth of urban automobile transportation is choking both the mobility of the city and the lungs of the city dwellers.

Not only are we making and consuming more things, and consequently producing a larger quantity of residues, but our advancing technology is producing new kinds of poisons. President Johnson has said, "The uncontrolled waste products of our technology are menacing the world we live in, our enjoyment, and our health."[1] The marvelous advance of American agriculture has depended largely on chemical fertilizers and pesticides, substances that were never before present in nature and against which our fellow creatures, the birds and fishes, have no defense mechanism. Lead and other metallic additives in gasoline accumulate along our roadsides. New products of chemical industry poison our streams. Technological changes have reduced the kinds and amounts of materials that can be economically reused. Aluminum cans and plastic containers are worthless as salvage but virtually indestructible as litter.

In dealing with pollution, we must think about natural resources in two senses, both as raw materials or sources of energy, and as those parts of the environment that can be

[1] Natural Beauty Message to the Congress of President Lyndon B. Johnson, February 1965.

depleted or worsened by misuse. In our lifetimes and those of our children, the availability of energy and raw materials will not put any serious limits on American society, but we will be limited in human fulfillment—the quality of life will be lessened and dulled—by destructive changes in our environment. And future generations will suffer because of our prodigal methods of waste disposal. The phosphates we dump into streams and lakes are permanently lost to our farm lands; the rusting auto hulks in the countryside are a drain on our metal resources.

At the same time that we are producing more and worse pollutants, our aspirations for a better environment are rising. We now see pollution where before we were able to ignore it. As the national income increases, people are less willing to trade off environmental deterioration for lower costs of goods and services. The "third parties" who do not benefit from these trade-offs are more aware of their position and more impatient to see it remedied by the abatement or elimination of pollution.

In its report, "Restoring the Quality of Our Environment," the President's Science Advisory Committee has urged that "the public should come to recognize individual rights to quality of living, as expressed by the absence of pollution, just as it has come to recognize rights to education, to economic advance, and to public recreation . . . The responsibility of each pollutor for all forms of damage caused by his pollution should be effectively recognized and generally accepted. There should be no 'right' to pollute."[2]

Like education and economic opportunity, removing pollution is costly; we need to remember that the quality of life depends only in part on the quality of the environment.[3]

---

[2] *Restoring the Quality of Our Environment,* Report of the Environmental Pollution Panel of the President's Science Advisory Committee (Washington, D.C., November 1965), pp. i–xii and 1–317.

[3] *The Adequacy of Technology for Pollution Abatement,* Report of the Research Management Advisory Panel through the Subcommittee on Science, Research, and Development to the Committee on Science and Astronautics, U.S. House of Representatives (Washington, D.C., 1966), pp. i–ix and 1–17.

Economic abundance and civilized diversity are also ingredients. We must use our environment in a variety of ways, and limited environmental resources must be allocated optimally among different uses. Hence, the basic issue in considering problems of pollution is to define our goals.[4] In order to do this we need to find ways of balancing esthetic, recreational, and related aspects of the quality of human life against other values. Stated in economic terms, how much will people pay, and how much should they pay, for these intangibles?[5] How clean should this stream be, at what cost, for what purpose, and at what future time? It is meaningless simply to say that the stream should be "clean."

At present, we are unable to assess the full costs of pollution or the benefits from preventing it because we cannot measure adequately the psychic and physiological effects of a dirty environment. Consequently, our decisions are generally based on estimates of immediate monetary costs rather than on evaluations of the total benefits and costs of different courses of action.

Air Pollution

The problem

When I was a boy in Pasadena in the 1920's, we were always aware of the San Gabriel Mountains rising clear and steep, nearly a mile above our heads. The great line from "America the Beautiful," "For purple mountains' majesty above the fruited plain," was an ever present reality to us. Now when I return to Pasadena the mountains have disappeared. Of course, they are still there, but they are seldom seen; in their place is a grayish-brown haze.

One can be sure of seeing the mountains only from an airplane. When one flies into the Los Angeles International Airport, they are there, rising through a semitransparent brown

[4] *Ibid.*

[5] Alan Kneese, *The Economics of Regional Water Quality Management,* published for Resources for the Future by Johns Hopkins Press, Baltimore, Md., 1964.

Table 1. Emission of air pollutants in Los Angeles County (tons per day).

Source	Pollutants					Total
	Carbon monoxide	Sulphur dioxide	Hydrocarbons	Nitrogen oxide	Aerosols	
1950						
(1) Fuel combustion	1	350	8	140	35	534
(2) Petroleum	770	450	450	50	6	1,726
(3) Transportation	5,500	25	1,100	240	23	6,888
(4) Organic solvents	–	–	300	–	4	304
(5) Chemical industry	–	50	–	–	15	65
(6) Refuse incineration	130	12	95	18	90	345
(7) Miscellaneous	100	2	9	5	150	266
Total	6,501	889	1,962	453	323	10,128
1965						
(1) Fuel combustion						
(a) Electric power generation	–	270	8	145	25	448
(b) Domestic and commercial	1	–	6	55	9	65
(c) Industrial	–	1	6	25	2	34
(Subtotal)	(1)	(271)	(14)	(225)	(36)	(547)
(2) Petroleum						
(a) Production	–	–	60	10	–	70
(b) Refining	170	85	55	70	11	391

(c) Marketing	116	—	11	105	—	—
(Subtotal)	(577)	(11)	(91)	(220)	(85)	(170)
(3) Transportation						
(a) Gasoline powered motor vehicles	12,825	45	490	1,930	30	10,330
(b) All other	229	14	21	39	2	153
(Subtotal)	(13,054)	(59)	(511)	(1,969)	(32)	(10,483)
(4) Organic solvents	557	7	—	550	—	—
(5) Chemical industry	73	8	—	—	65	—
(6) Refuse incineration	2	—	1	—	1	—
(7) Miscellaneous	36	18	10	1	3	4
Total	14,846	139	838	2,754	456	10,659
1970 (projected)						
(1) Fuel combustion	1,002	35	450	16	500	1
(2) Petroleum	526	11	100	220	95	100
(3) Transportation	10,083	68	590	1,530	35	7,860
(4) Organic solvents	129	4	—	125	—	—
(5) Chemical industry	73	8	—	—	65	—
(6) Refuse incineration	2	—	1	—	—	1
(7) Miscellaneous	38	15	15	1	3	4
Total	11,853	141	1,156	1,892	698	7,966

Source: Summary of Total Air Pollution Data for Los Angeles County. A Report of the Engineering Division, Air Pollution Control District, County of Los Angeles, January 1965, pp. i–ii and 1–41.

blanket a thousand feet thick that stretches across the broad Los Angeles plain. As the aircraft loses altitude and dips into the blanket, distant objects disappear. When it lands, the passengers step out into a bright, diffuse light. Their eyes begin to smart and the air has an acrid smell. They are surrounded by the famous Los Angeles smog.

In December 1952 the city of London became enveloped in a fog that soon covered a large part of England. It was a black fog, visibility was extremely low, the air smelled of brimstone. The fog lasted a week, and during that time 4,000 people died who would otherwise have remained alive. Many of them were elderly; others had been ill with chronic heart or respiratory disease. They were the largest number of victims of a single episode of atmospheric poisoning ever recorded.

Both the mass tragedy in London and the unpleasant experience of travelers arriving in Los Angeles are examples of metropolitan air pollution, but of somewhat different kinds. So far as we know few people die directly from Los Angeles smog, although fatal accidents may be caused by the low visibility that accompanies it and by "freeway fatigue," which could be the initial stage of poisoning from the carbon monoxide in the air.[6] Its most evident ill effects are eye irritation, damage to orange and lemon trees and to vegetable crops and flowers, and the weathering and cracking of rubber. But it is also so unpleasant for so many people that Californians have been willing to spend half of all the money used for air pollution control in the United States[7] in an attempt to do something about it.

Pollutant emissions in Los Angeles from power plants, petroleum refineries, backyard trash burners, and many industrial sources have been greatly lowered since 1950. But the effluents from automobiles persist and now make up 88 percent by weight of the total of air contaminants (see Table 4

---

[6] *Waste Management and Control,* a Report to the Federal Council for Science and Technology by the Committee on Pollution of the National Academy of Sciences–National Research Council. Publication 1400, National Academy of Sciences–National Research Council, Washington, D.C., 1966, pp. i–vii and 1–257.

[7] *Ibid.,* p. 201.

below). The number of automobiles has doubled since 1950 (Table 2) and the amount of pollutants from automobiles has also just about doubled, even though the total weight of pollutants emitted each day from all sources has increased by less than 50 percent. Rush-hour traffic jams on Los Angeles' streets and freeways have become more than a frustrating

Table 2. Some statistics for Los Angeles County.

Category	1950	1965	1970 (projected)
Population (millions of persons)	4.3	6.82	7.75
Gasoline powered vehicles (millions)	1.7	3.45	4.00
Gasoline consumption (thousands of tons/day)	12.3	22.8	26.0

Source: See Table 1.

method of squandering commuters' time; they are also highly effective in multiplying atmospheric pollutants.

In a modern automobile more than three pounds of carbon monoxide and about two ounces of oxides of nitrogen are formed for every gallon of gasoline burned; in addition, a little over 8 percent of the hydrocarbons in the gasoline escapes without being oxidized, mostly through the exhaust but also through the crankcase vent, the carburetor, and the fuel tank. Together, the carbon monoxide and the unburned hydrocarbons represent a loss of fuel energy equivalent to about 15 percent of the total amount of gasoline consumed. Since each of the 3.5 million automobiles in Los Angeles uses, on the average, a little over two gallons per day, this loss corresponds to 400 million gallons a year for Los Angeles County alone, and for the nation as a whole it amounts to nearly 5 percent of the total consumption of liquid fuels.

The hydrocarbons emitted in automobile exhausts are those originally present in the fuel and new compounds formed by the high temperature of combustion. There are at least 200 different compounds. The nitrogen oxides are produced in the combustion chamber by the high temperature combination of oxygen and nitrogen from the intake air. In a sense, each automobile is a small nitrogen fertilizer plant. The total amount of nitrogen compounds produced by Los Angeles automobiles each year is enough to fertilize the entire county with 70 pounds of nitrogen per acre.

Nitrogen dioxide is a yellow-brown gas that absorbs the blue and ultraviolet rays of the sun and in doing so breaks down to nitrogen oxide and atomic oxygen. The latter combines with atmospheric oxygen molecules to form ozone. The ozone and the atomic oxygen attack the hydrocarbons in the air to produce a variety of highly reactive compounds. These in turn react with oxygen to form more ozone and other poisons such as formaldehyde, and with the nitrogen oxides to form plant-damaging peracyl nitrates (usually abbreviated to PAN).[8] Ultimately, as the end product of the chain of reactions, stable substances are formed, including carbon dioxide, which remains in the air, and compounds and particles that settle or are washed out of it.

Although the observed ozone concentrations near the ground in Los Angeles are often more than ten times the normal background concentration in rural areas, they are still only a few tenths of a part per million, and these low concentrations hold for all the reacting substances in the air (Table 3). PAN, for example, may be present in a few parts per billion.[9] Because of the extreme dilution, reactions that would proceed to completion in a second under ordinary laboratory concentrations take minutes or even hours in the atmosphere. This results in a complex of processes and a diversity of materials existing simultaneously, which are extremely difficult to study or to reproduce experimentally. Photochemical pollution of the Los Angeles type is probably self-limiting in intensity, because higher concentrations of the reacting substances would result in more rapid production of stable compounds. This is not true of carbon monoxide, most of which does not take part in the chain of photochemical reactions and instead slowly combines with atmospheric oxygen to form carbon dioxide.

Automobiles are everywhere one of the principal sources

[8] Seymour Tilson, "Air Pollution," *International Science and Technology*, June 1965, pp. 23–31.

[9] *Waste Management and Control*, p. 80.

Table 3. Daily maximum concentrations of air pollutants in
Los Angeles County.

Quantity	Pollutants (parts per million)				
	Carbon monoxide	Sulphur dioxide	Hydro-carbons	Nitrogen oxide	Ozone
Median value, May–October	20	0.10	0.60	0.30	0.25
Exceeded on 10 percent of days, May–October[a]	30	0.20	1.05	0.60	0.40
Median value, November–March	30	0.20	1.90	0.75	0.15
Exceeded on 10 percent of days, November–March[a]	45	0.40	2.55	1.25	0.25
Exceeded on 10 percent of days during highest month[a]	55	0.40	2.80	1.40	0.30
Highest observed	72	2.49	40	3.93	0.90
First "alert" stage[b]	100	3.00	–	3.00	0.50

Source: See Table 1.

[a] Maximum pollutant concentrations are higher than the indicated values on an average during three days per month.

[b] "Alerts" are called when a pollutant concentration reaches the indicated value. Certain industrial operations are curtailed during an alert stage, and other actions are taken to reduce emission of pollutants. All alerts called to date have been due to ozone.

of atmospheric pollutants, but their over-all importance in other United States cities is less than in Los Angeles. As Table 4 shows, transportation accounts for only about 60 percent of air pollution in the country as a whole, whereas pollutants from electric power generation and industry make up more than 30 percent. Sulphur dioxide and other odorous and corrosive sulphur compounds from the burning of sulphur-containing coal and fuel oils, together with ash and soot particles, are the principal pollutants produced by electric power utilities and industry. The 1952 tragedy in London, and similar catastrophes elsewhere, were the result of high and persistent concentrations of sulphur compounds and soot in

Table 4. Average proportion of different air pollutants in United States cities compared with Los Angeles County.

| | Percentage of total pollutants | | | | | | | | | | | |
| Source of pollution | Carbon monoxide | | Sulphur dioxide | | Hydrocarbons | | Nitrogen oxide | | Aerosols | | Total[a] | |
	U.S.	L.A.	U.S.	L.A.	U.S.	L.A.	U.S.	L.A.	U.S.	L.A.	U.S.	L.A.
Electric power generation	0.4	0.0	8.2	1.8	0.1	0.05	1.9	0.9	1.9	0.1	12.6	2.9
Industry	1.4	1.2	7.0	1.1	3.0	5.3	1.3	0.9	4.8	0.3	18.7	8.8
Space heating	1.4	0.01	2.7	–	0.4	–	0.6	0.06	1.0	0.4	6.2	0.5
Transportation	47.6	70.6	0.4	0.2	7.8	13.3	2.5	3.4	1.4	0.4	59.8	87.9
Refuse incineration	1.0	0.01	0.2	–	0.8	–	0.1	0.01	0.5	–	2.6	0.02
Total	51.9	71.8	18.4	3.1	12.1	18.5	6.4	5.7	9.6	0.9	99.9	100.1
Total pollutants (lbs./capita/day)[b]	2.74	3.12	0.97	0.13	0.63	0.81	0.34	0.24	0.51	0.04	5.23	4.35
Total pollutants (thousands of tons/day)	178	10.7	63	0.5	41	2.8	22	0.8	33	0.1	342.0	14.8

Sources: For the United States as a whole, *Waste Management and Control*, p. 128; for Los Angeles County, Table 1.
[a] "U.S." totals include a small percentage of "miscellaneous" pollutants not otherwise considered in this table.
[b] Assuming that "U.S." pollutants are emitted in metropolitan areas with a total population of 130 million people; population of Los Angeles County taken as 6.82 million from Table 2.

stagnant, foggy air. Los Angeles partly escapes these materials because natural gas, which is low in sulphur and produces no fly ash, is the major fuel for utilities and industry.

Next to water and air, fossil fuels make up the largest single weight of material used in our civilization. About a billion tons of coal and petroleum are consumed in the United States each year and 2 percent of this weight is sulphur dioxide, practically all of which is discharged into the atmosphere.[10]

Atmospheric pollutants reduce visibility and thus create hazards for airplanes. They damage crops, injure livestock, corrode metals, rot masonry, depress property values, and cost the community large cleaning bills for everything from dusty draperies to smoke blackened buildings. The growth of miniaturization in the electronics industry places increasing emphasis on the quality of the air. In many such plants elaborate air filtering systems, special clothing, and other procedures are required. These are much easier to use in areas that have clean outside air.

Common sense suggests that pollutants capable of darkening house paint, disintegrating stone statues, corroding metals, dissolving nylon stockings, and embrittling rubber must also be injurious to delicate bronchial and lung tissues, but there is little hard evidence at present. Acute exposures are clearly hazardous. Community catastrophes like the one in London in 1952 and previous incidents in Donora, Pennsylvania, in 1948 and in the Meuse Valley of Belgium in 1930 are grave warnings for the future. At lower concentrations, urban atmospheric pollution aggravates asthma and some other chronic respiratory illnesses and it can cause transient eye and respiratory tract irritations. The effects would undoubtedly be more serious if it were not for the fact that poisonous gases such as sulphur dioxide are largely absorbed in the nose and upper air passages, and only a small fraction of the amount in the air reaches the lungs.

The incidence of lung cancer is greater in cities than in the country. Urban air pollution may be a contributory factor, but its role is uncertain and cigarette smoking is apparently a greater hazard. In this connection, one little known atmos-

[10] *Ibid.*, p. 200.

pheric pollutant warrants special attention. This is asbestos, produced by the wear of automobile brake linings, and in other ways. Many city dwellers are now known to have asbestos fibers in their lungs. Industrial experience shows that some types of asbestos are strongly associated with lung cancer and other respiratory diseases.[11]

Large amounts of lead are discharged into the atmosphere from motor vehicle exhausts. This lead is widely dispersed—even the lead content of the surface waters of the ocean has doubled in the past thirty years—but it tends to concentrate in soils and plants located close to heavily traveled highways. Today every American citizen carries a burden of lead in his body, although the average levels are lower than those generally deemed hazardous. No one knows what the human body burdens were before the introduction of lead additives to gasoline. Phosphorus and boron are now being added to motor fuels, and nickel is beginning to appear. These may be hazards for human beings who have to breathe polluted city air.[12]

In general our knowledge of the effects of atmospheric pollutants on either human beings or animals is limited, particularly under conditions where preexisting disease may enhance the effects or increase susceptibility. Research is especially needed on the results of chronic exposures to comparatively low levels of lead, asbestos, nitrogen oxides, carbon monoxide, and sulphur compounds.

The atmosphere is not a sink for most of the pollutants it receives, but only a temporary reservoir that contains these substances until they become oxidized or are swept out by rain or snow. There is one pollutant, however, that is relatively inert chemically and tends to remain in the atmosphere for long periods. This is carbon dioxide. Because it is the ultimate product of combustion, carbon dioxide is produced by our worldwide industrial civilization in very large quantities—some 12 billion tons a year at the present time. Part of this "new" carbon dioxide, like that already in the air, is utilized in plant photosynthesis, and a fraction enters the ocean, but about half of it stays in the air. By the year 2000 the amount

[11] *Restoring the Quality of Our Environment,* pp. 99–100.
[12] *Ibid.,* p. 19.

of carbon dioxide in the atmosphere will probably have increased by 25 percent. Many people believe this will have a significant effect on the world's climate, but nobody has been able to make a convincing guess as to just what the effect will be. It probably will not be disastrous, but it will certainly represent an important geophysical experiment on an earthwide scale.[13]

There is some evidence that atmospheric pollution is also increasing the turbidity of the atmosphere, that is, the concentration of very small particles suspended in the air. Between 1961 and 1964, the atmospheric turbidity index in Boston rose from 0.06 to 0.17, in Chicago from 0.05 to 0.10, and in St. Cloud, Minnesota, from 0.05 to 0.09. Thus in all three cities the turbidity roughly doubled in four years. A 25 percent increase in atmospheric turbidity over the earth as a whole might result in a cooling of the air near the ground by several degrees Fahrenheit.[14]

Air pollution is a sickness of cities. The amount of air on earth is very large, a million and a half tons for every human being, and its total capacity for containing pollutants is great, but cities occupy only a small area—in the United States about 2 percent of the land—and the weight of air available to them at any instant is correspondingly small. At the same time most sources of pollution are concentrated in the cities. A single electric generating plant using fossil fuels may emit several hundred tons of sulphur dioxide per day. The weight of particles suspended in city air is commonly ten times higher than in rural areas.

Pollution of city air is by no means a new phenomenon. In the beginning of the nineteenth century Shelley wrote: "Hell is a city much like London, a populous and smoky city." Nearly 2,000 years earlier Seneca complained of the heavy air of Rome and the stench of its sooty chimneys. Drastic anti-pollution measures were taken in London in the Middle Ages; at least one man was hanged for burning coal.[15]

---

[13] *Ibid.*, pp. 111–133.

[14] *Waste Management and Control*, p. 53.

[15] C. W. Griggin, Jr., "America's Airborne Garbage," *Saturday Review*, May 22, 1965, pp. 32–34 and 95–96.

The modification of the air over an urban area is comparable to the effects of an active volcano. Pollutants tend to create their own climate. Over New York City, for example, atmospheric inversion layers a hundred feet or so thick, high in particles and sulphur dioxide, form and spread as a result of the absorption and reradiation of sunlight by the pollution particles themselves.[16]

A city affects the wind patterns in its vicinity. With high wind speeds it acts like a conical hill, but in light winds the excess heat produces a thermal circulation. Nevertheless, larger scale meteorological processes are the principal cause of variations in pollutant concentrations. These are the fluctuations in speed and direction of the winds related to barometric pressure variations that ventilate the city, and the naturally occurring thermal inversions—conditions in which the air aloft is warmer than at lower levels. The warm air forms an effective lid over the colder air beneath, and as a result pollutants are held close to the ground in relatively high concentrations. In much of the United States an inversion at heights of 500 to 1,500 feet occurs about half the time.

With an inversion at 1,000 feet over a crowded city, the weight of the column of air available at any given time near the ground is about a hundred tons per person. If the air is to remain breathable (carbon dioxide concentration less than 1 percent), the amount required each day for combustion of gasoline, fuel oil, diesel oil, coal, and natural gas at rates of use prevailing in 1965 is close to 6 tons per person. Thus, if the inversion persists, the city air needs to be completely changed at least once every 17 days. Periods of near stagnation lasting four or five days occur several times a year over large parts of the United States. It is clear that, even with present population densities and rates of use of fossil fuels, our cities are coming uncomfortably close to using up all their available air.

Some solutions

Under these circumstances, we can no longer think of urban air as a "free good." Instead, it must be thought of as

16 *Waste Management and Control,* p. 53.

a natural resource—that is, as part of the natural environment for which the demand is liable to outrun the supply, and to which a cost can be attached. It is not a resource in the older sense of a raw material for manufacturing but rather one of the "new" renewable resources we have become aware of only in recent years—a limited part of the environment whose quality has great economic and social importance. It is a common property resource which must be used by all the citizens, and, as such, it requires public regulation or management. Perloff[17] has pointed out that, "Invasion of the [common] domain [of city air] by polluters then may be regarded as trespass, and the cost of control assigned to the polluter."

Four ways of dealing with the principal source of metropolitan air pollution, the automobile, may be suggested: (1) control of emissions from present internal combustion engines; (2) lowering of the number of automobiles operating at any given time in the city; (3) treatment of the air into which the pollutants are emitted; and (4) a radical change in the kind of energy conversion used in automotive transport.

Both crankcase and exhaust emissions can be lowered by such devices as the direct-flame afterburner, which should remove 60 to 80 percent of the carbon monoxide and hydrocarbons, though it does not affect the emission of nitrogen oxides. The cost of these devices has been estimated at about $100 per vehicle, and their lifetime at five years. Annual maintenance costs should be about $5, and increased fuel requirements perhaps $10 per year.[18] Total costs for Los Angeles County with its present 3.5 million automobiles would be $350 million every five years for purchase and installation of the device, plus annual operating and excess fuel costs of approximately $50 million. These figures must be multiplied by about 20 to account for all the metropolitan areas of the country. In Table 1 it is assumed that half the automobiles operating in Los Angeles County in 1970 will be equipped with exhaust and crankcase emission control.

[17] Harvey S. Perloff, "New Resources in an Urban Age," paper presented at the ACTION Symposium on the Future American City, January 1966.

[18] *Waste Management and Control*, p. 240.

Because of the continuing increase in the number of motor vehicles and in the combustion of gasoline, installation and use of such partially effective emission control devices will, in the long run, only limit the rate of increase of pollution in our cities. More drastic measures are needed. Also, reduction of hydrocarbon emissions without a corresponding reduction of nitrogen oxides will free the latter for direct irritating effects and hence may not be as helpful as one would hope.

The number of automobiles operating in the city at any one time might be lowered by greatly enlarging the area covered by freeways and parking lots, which would speed up traffic and reduce the time spent in cruising the streets, looking for a place to park, but such structures would destroy much of the beauty of the city and many of its values. Development of publicly acceptable mass transportation is perhaps a more promising means of creating conditions under which automobile traffic within the city can be controlled.

Perhaps in the future our cities could be divided into two layers, one for automobiles and one for people. All vehicle traffic would be in tunnels and other enclosed spaces from which the air could be rapidly pumped and treated to remove noxious substances.

Alternatively, one might conceive of a system for penetrating the atmospheric inversion layers and replacing the polluted air with fresh air sucked from aloft. The construction of many very high stacks equipped with enormous pumps has sometimes been discussed by engineers for the Los Angeles area, but the costs and amount of energy required, not to mention the hazards to air traffic, seem prohibitive.

Perhaps ultimately the most satisfactory solution will be the development of means for energy conversion at low temperatures that would be inexpensive and light enough to be used in private automobiles. Low-temperature energy conversion probably is the only feasible means of eliminating the nitrogen oxides. These are inevitably formed when ordinary air is heated to the high temperatures prevailing in internal combustion engines. Both fuel cells and rechargeable electric batteries appear promising, but the development work required to make them economically competitive with internal combustion engines will take many years.

Although an increasing portion of the nation's new electric generating capacity is nuclear-powered, the capacity of fossil fuel generating plants may well double by 1980 and redouble by 2000. At present there are no effective and inexpensive processes for removing sulphur dioxide from flue gases, but several fairly promising methods are being investigated. If these were installed in all new plants, sulphur dioxide emission could be held at its present level up to 1980 and perhaps reduced by 20 percent or more between 1980 and 2000. Research and development are urgently needed to find more economic processes. The cost of the most promising of present devices, the alkali-alumina process, is estimated at a capital investment of about $11 per kilowatt of installed capacity and an additional operating cost of close to $4 per kilowatt per year.[19] Within the United States as a whole, the cost of installing these devices in new fossil fuel plants would be about $2 billion by 1980, and the annual operating costs would be around $750 million.

Air pollution raises some of the problems of government in the United States. Polluted air masses do not recognize political boundaries. In the eastern megalopolis, for example, the prevailing winds blow contaminants from New Jersey's oil refineries, smoke-belching factories, and smoldering trash dumps right over New York City. A charge on polluters for use of the public air supply as an atmospheric sewer has been widely advocated, but this must be national or at least regional in scope, otherwise polluting industries may simply move from one state or municipality to another one that uses its carelessness about pollution as a recruiting inducement for industry.

Water Pollution

The problem in general

Most of the rain and snow that falls on the United States evaporates or sinks into the ground. About a fourth of the total precipitation, averaging 1,100 billion gallons per day, runs off or seeps through the ground to rivers, where it is

[19] *Ibid.*, p. 241.

available for use. In 1954, 300 billion gallons per day were withdrawn from lakes and rivers and it is estimated that, by the year 2000, daily withdrawals will be close to 900 billion gallons, or 80 percent of the average river flows.[20] Only 150 billion gallons per day will be actually "consumed," that is, evaporated. The remainder will be returned to rivers, lakes, and estuaries, carrying a burden of pollutants from its contact with human beings and their farms and industries.

Though much of the river water will need to be reused several times, the principal water problem in the years ahead will not be quantity but quality. Without a radical change in sewage disposal methods or enormous expenditures for dams and other flow regulation devices it will be impossible to prevent serious deterioration of our bodies of water. Even to maintain enough water at acceptable standards for public health and industrial purposes will be difficult. The problem of water pollution in the heavily populated states could become overwhelming in the next few decades unless we adopt many technological and sociological innovations.

Under conditions of balance between men and their environment human wastes discharged into rivers are metabolized by bacteria and changed into nutrients for other organisms, plus carbon dioxide, water, and other harmless substances. The river cleanses itself, and the water may be used over and over again. But streams have only a limited capacity to handle waste materials, and they can be disastrously affected by overloading, particularly if the stream bed is affected. Organic sludges and other suspended solids settling to the bottom eliminate many higher forms of life from the bed of the river and stimulate the bacterial production of such stinking toxic substances as hydrogen sulphide and mercaptans. Oil accumulated in suspended particles and settling on the stream bed can destroy bottom-living aquatic life for several decades.

Highly toxic substances discharged into a river often cause spectacular fish kills and a public outcry. Low-grade toxins are more insidious. The continued addition of low-grade pollutants results in an increase in the population of certain

20 *Ibid.*, p. 137.

species, and others, which cannot tolerate contamination, disappear. Clear streams usually contain a large number of species, but the number is greatly reduced in a polluted stream. This reduction of diversity tends to lower the dynamic balance of the river system and to produce instabilities that result in further deterioration. Governor Rockefeller has thus described the Hudson River: "For ten miles south of Albany there are no fish but only sludge worms, leeches, rattail maggots, the larvae of flies—the handwriting on the wall that warns us to stop treating our waterways as if they were open sewers."[21]

Typically, American cities have turned their backs on their rivers. In Hartford a high wall hides the Connecticut River from the nearby streets and buildings. In other cities the banks are lined with factories and warehouses or they are used as a cheap source of land for freeways. Recently, some of our cities have recognized that a river in the city is a priceless asset. Boston was among the first; fifty years ago it laid out miles of parks and grassy slopes along the Charles, and in the last decade, Chicago has decided that the Chicago River can be used for recreation and beauty rather than as an open sewer.

With this new view of the river (which, of course, has long prevailed in many European cities) there has also arisen a strongly felt need to reduce or remove the pollution that has made our rivers unpleasant and useless for many human purposes.

Because of the large and specialized water requirements of different industries, the quality of water is also of direct economic importance. Most industrial uses of water are for cooling, washing, or transport of materials. Water is a raw material in some processes and as steam it is used for energy conversion. Avoiding scale formation from dissolved solids is necessary for the economic operation of a steam boiler, and rigorous control of water quality is essential in a brewery. Thus, though many industries are heavy contributors to water

[21] Robert and Leona Train Rienow, "Last Chance for the Nation's Waterways," *Saturday Review*, May 22, 1965, pp. 35–36 and 96–97.

pollution, others must have water of good to very high quality. It may be necessary in a metropolitan area to zone different sources of water for different uses and to establish control of polluting industries for the benefit of others that need water of good quality. Usually, however, industries requiring water of very high quality must treat their water supply, no matter what its source, and their incremental cost for handling polluted water is not high.[22]

A new set of economic demands is arising in many parts of the country, represented by the service industries associated with tourism and the recreational uses of water. Fishermen, swimmers, and scuba divers all demand clear and pure water.

There are special problems related to pollution of the seashore. Here we are dealing not with a two-dimensional area but with an essentially one-dimensional boundary zone between the land and the sea. Nearly half of all Americans live within a hundred miles of the ocean, and this proportion will probably increase in future decades. By the end of the century, some 150 to 200 million people may be struggling for places on the beaches and in the narrow coastal waters. With our present length of shoreline, this would mean about two people per foot, even if the entire coastal strip were a public beach.

Today, only a fraction of the shoreline is available for public recreation, which must compete with factories, power plants, shipping, and military uses. Much of the shoreline is privately held, and long stretches are already too polluted to be safe for swimming or water sports. Bays and estuaries, which are at the lower end of river basins and receive their undigested waste products, are the most seriously threatened parts of the coastal zone.

Varieties of water pollution

Eight kinds of water pollutants are recognized by the U.S. Public Health Service: organic sewage, infectious agents, plant nutrients, organic chemicals, inorganic and miscellane-

[22] *Delaware Estuary Comprehensive Study Preliminary Report and Findings,* Federal Water Pollution Control Administration, Washington, D.C., 1961.

ous chemicals, sediments from land erosion, radioactive substances, and waste heat.

1. Organic sewage. This is our most obvious water problem. Under favorable circumstances, organic matter in sewage is oxidized to carbon dioxide, water, phosphates, nitrates, and other plant nutrients by aquatic bacteria, which utilize the dissolved atmospheric oxygen in the water. For this reason, sewage is said to have a biological oxygen demand—that is, a certain amount of dissolved oxygen is required to transform its contained organic matter into innocuous substances. Most sewage is "treated" to a greater or lesser extent before being dumped into our rivers, lakes, and estuaries, and its organic matter content and biological oxygen demand are thereby lowered.

The volume of sewage waters produced in American cities usually ranges from 100 to 150 gallons per person per day. Typically, the suspended solid content of this sewage, and its biological oxygen demand, are 200 parts per million.[23] The amount of organic wastes entering municipal sewage treatment plants is only a few ounces per person per day. This is reduced by 80 to 90 percent in conventional primary and secondary treatment.

Rivers and other natural waters typically contain about ten parts per million of dissolved oxygen when this gas is close to saturation. For a stream of typical depth, say 15 to 30 feet, natural rates of re-aeration with oxygen are from one to two parts per million per day, depending on the turbulence of the stream and the degree of oxygen undersaturation. This is somewhat less than the rate of oxygen consumption by the sewage. Hence raw sewage with an oxygen demand of 200 parts per million must be diluted about fortyfold when it is dumped into a river if the oxygen supply in the receiving water body is not to be seriously depleted. Two thirds of the U.S. population, about 125 million people, are served by domestic sewers. Sewage from about a tenth of this number is discharged raw, and that from more than another quarter after only primary treatment. In total, sewage discharges correspond to the raw sewage from 50 million peo-

[23] *Restoring the Quality of Our Environment,* p. 160.

ple.[24] To avoid oxygen depletion, these discharges must be diluted with 200 to 300 billion gallons of river, lake, or ocean water per day.

About a third of the biological oxygen demand in municipal sewage comes from industrial wastes. In addition, industries discharge directly into our water bodies waste materials with an oxygen demand greater than that of all municipal sewage. The food processing industries, especially smaller operators, tend to be heavy polluters. Typical oxygen-demanding discharges include the offal from meat-packing plants, sugar-beet wastes, whey from dairies, pesticide-carrying cannery washings, and inedible parts of fruits and vegetables. Oil refineries discharge oils, waxes, and complex organic chemicals. The textile industry contributes fatty and oily residues from the bleaching of cotton, flax, and jute, and emulsions of dirt, bacteria, soap, and proteins from the washing of wool. Both the sulphite and kraft processes of the paper industry produce large residues of organic material—in the case of the sulphite process, about 500 pounds of oxygen demand per ton of pulp.[25] This industry alone probably puts more organic material into United States water bodies, in terms of biological oxygen demand, than is contained in all the municipal sewage in the United States.

In the Great Lakes and in harbors and estuaries on both coasts, the maritime transportation industry is an important source of pollutants. In spite of regulations to the contrary, cargo ships and other craft, including small pleasure boats, often dump raw sewage into harbors and bays. The federal government has also been lax. Its installations discharge over a hundred million gallons per day of untreated sewage into surface waters or onto the ground.[26] Pearl Harbor, the principal harbor in our youngest state, has long been filthy with ship sewage.

Industry can handle water pollution in several ways, four of which are especially important: (1) process changes

[24] *Ibid.*, p. 10.

[25] *Waste Management and Control*, p. 189.

[26] Donald E. Carr, "Death of the Sweet Waters; The Politics of Pollution," *The Atlantic*, May 1966, pp. 93–106.

(sometimes called "in-plant abatement"); (2) effluent treatment; (3) closed-cycle operations in which the water is not discharged, but treated and recycled through the plant; and (4) export of wastes to an environment that can receive them without deleterious effects.[27] The chemical companies have made the greatest contributions to in-plant abatement through process changes that have, in many cases, proven economical because they conserve valuable materials. Such changes often reduce the biological and chemical oxygen demand of effluents by more than 90 percent.

A wide variety of effluent treatment and disposal methods is used by industry, including screening, sedimentation, lagooning, centrifuging, filtration, flotation, flocculation, chemical oxidation, precipitation, polymerization, incineration, anaerobic digestion, deep-well disposal, barging to sea, piping to sea or to desert regions, and irrigation spreading. In spite of this diversity, treatment by industry of its waste effluents has apparently been pursued less vigorously than process changes. As Table 5 shows, the volume of industrial effluents discharged into our rivers, lakes, and estuaries is nearly twice as great as the volume of municipal sewage, yet the amount spent on operation of industrial treatment plants is only about a third that spent by municipalities. Municipal expenditures are more than 5 cents per 1,000 gallons of sewage, and industry spends only about 1 cent per 1,000 gallons.

Perhaps the best known example of a closed cycle for water used in manufacturing is that of the Kaiser Steel plant in Fontana, California. Here the motivation for closed-cycle operation is the shortage of water in a semi-arid region. More significant from the standpoint of pollution abatement is the action taken by the Wisconsin Steel Company, which was formerly a heavy polluter of the Calumet River in the Chicago area. The company has designed and installed a circulating water supply that discharges nothing to the river and takes in only moderate amounts of make-up water.[28]

In the so-called "Penjerdel Region" (the three metropolitan

---

[27] *Delaware Estuary Comprehensive Study Preliminary Report and Findings.*

[28] *Waste Management and Control,* p. 56.

Table 5. Municipal and some industrial expenditures for
treatment of waste waters, 1959.

Source	Return flows, in billions of gallons of effluent per day	Operating expenditures for waste treatment (millions of dollars)	Operating expenditures in cents per 1,000 gallons
Industry			
Steel	10.1	4.8	0.13
Chemical	6.5	40.3	1.7
Pulp and paper	4.3	14.0	0.9
Petroleum	3.3	30.6	2.5
Automobile	0.23	4.5	5.3
Bituminous coal	0.08	4.2	14.3
Total industry	24.5	98.4	1.1 (average)
Municipal sewage	14.6	300	5.7

Sources: For industrial effluents and expenditures: "Water in Industry," National Association of Manufacturers, January 1965. (Quoted in appendix 5 to *Waste Management and Control,* pp. 188 and 194.)

For municipal effluents and expenditures: various estimates in *Waste Management and Control;* and *Restoring the Quality of Our Environment.* It is assumed that the equivalent of two thirds of municipal effluents receive primary and secondary treatment at an average cost of 8.5 cents per thousand gallons.

areas of Trenton, Philadelphia, and Wilmington on the lower reaches of the Delaware River), the waste materials produced by industry have a biological oxygen demand equivalent to that of the sewage from 2.6 million people. One fourth of this material is removed by waste treatment, and three fourths, equivalent to a population of 1.9 million people, is discharged into the Delaware. However, the municipal sewage dumped into the river is even greater. It corresponds to the raw sewage from 2.3 million people, out of a total population of 5 million.[29]

[29] *Ibid.,* pp. 237–252.

An instructive contrast to the dismal record of Penjerdel is that of the Ruhr River Basin, which contains a large proportion of the entire industrial capacity of West Germany. The waters of the Ruhr River system are used, processed, and reused, eight times over, yet most of them remain clean enough for fishing and swimming, and, with only mild treatment, for drinking.[30] Their quality is maintained by the semigovernmental Ruhr Valley Administration, which levies an effluent charge, proportional to the amount of pollutant materials dumped into the river system, on every municipality and every industry that uses the waters. Each can choose the most economical trade-off between the level of treatment it will provide for its own wastes and the size of the effluent charge it will pay. The efficacy of the system hinges in part upon the use of the Emscher River as a recipient for the residual and hard-to-treat wastes.[31]

Construction of municipal plants for primary and secondary sewage treatment costs about $60 per capita population equivalent (the average amount of domestic or municipal sewage produced by one person). Annual operation costs decrease with plant size, and range from $3.50 to $2.25 per capita population equivalent.[32] Capital and operating costs of industrial waste treatment plants are apparently somewhat lower. New capacity to make up present deficiencies in municipal sewers and sewage treatment plants would require a capital investment of about $5 billion, and an annual operating cost of perhaps $200 million. These expenditures should be about tripled by 1980. Capital and operating expenditures for treatment of industrial wastes should be of the same order of magnitude.

The oxygen-demanding fraction of domestic and industrial wastes is growing more rapidly than the rate of installation and effectiveness of conventional waste treatment. Unless remedial measures are taken, the oxygen demand even of treated sewage effluents will be great enough in future decades

---

[30] Carr, "Death of the Sweet Waters."

[31] Kneese, *The Economics of Regional Water Quality Management.*

[32] *Waste Management and Control,* p. 244.

to consume the entire dissolved oxygen content of all the waters in all the U.S. rivers during the stage of dry weather flow.[33]

A quantitative light can be gained by considering the total municipal sewage flow in the 1950's of about 15 billion gallons per day and its projected increase to 37 billion gallons per day by 2000. If all the sewage in the 1950's had been dumped raw into the nation's streams it could use up the oxygen content of 600 billion gallons per day. Adding an equal biological oxygen demand from industrial wastes would raise the total amount of oxygen used to that contained in 1,200 billion gallons per day, whereas the average daily river flow in the United States is only 1,100 billion gallons. Fortunately, most of the sewage is treated so that the flow required at present for oxidation is only a few hundred billion gallons per day. But industrial wastes may increase seven-fold by 2000, and as we have seen, the municipal increase may be 250 percent.

2. *Infectious agents.* Typhoid and other disease-causing bacteria have been virtually eliminated from domestic water supplies in the United States, but a danger persists from infectious viruses—for example, hepatitis.

3. *Plant nutrients.* Conventional sewage treatment greatly reduces the content of dissolved and suspended organic matter, but the effluents contain dissolved nitrates, ammonia, phosphates, vitamin B complex, and other plant nutrients. The phosphate concentrations in treated effluents have actually increased in recent years, probably because of the wide use of phosphate-containing detergents. When discharged into a lake, or a sluggish river such as the Potomac, these nutrients cause a damaging overfertilization, or "eutrophication" of the water body. Livestock and poultry wastes and flows from heavily fertilized farm fields and suburban lawns also contribute to the process. As a result, many streams, lakes, and estuaries in the United States have become filled with objectionable growths of blue-green algae and other water plants. Particularly on cloudy days, the algal growth near the surface shuts off the supply of sunlight from deeper growing algae and other plants. The latter die and in their decay use up the oxy-

[33] *Ibid.,* pp. 12–13.

gen dissolved in the water, so that fish and other water animals suffocate. The process is contributed to by variations in nutrient supply, by sporadic release of toxins into the water, and by the excess supply of certain nutrients. The water is made unsatisfactory for domestic and industrial uses, and its recreational values are destroyed. Hundreds of water bodies scattered across the nation are affected; much public attention has been given to some of them, including Lake Erie, Lake Washington, and the Potomac. In Lake Mendota, near Madison, Wisconsin, about a quarter of the added nitrogen oxides comes from the air via rain and snow. Automobiles are probably the source of most of these atmospheric nitrogen oxides.[34]

Possible control measures include removing nutrients from municipal and industrial wastes by so-called tertiary or advance treatment. This is both difficult and expensive, costing 20 to 30 cents per thousand gallons.[35] Alternatively, waste waters can be diverted to streams below a lake, or to a well-flushed water body. Treatment of the lake itself by removal of weeds and debris and dredging of putrescent bottom material is also sometimes tried. Much research is needed on the nutrient requirements of different kinds of water plants. Perhaps addition of particular micronutrients or growth-promoting substances to the waters entering a lake would encourage the growth of desirable plants and diminish the obnoxious blue-green algae.

4. Organic chemicals such as insecticides, pesticides, and detergents. Technological advances have caused much of the problem of water pollution. Rachel Carson called ours the "age of poisons" and with good reason, for many of the 500 or so new chemical compounds produced each year are not only highly toxic to living creatures but dreadfully persistent. Until recently, detergents were among these persistent new chemicals. They contaminated lakes and streams because they were impossible to break down in ordinary sewage dis-

---

[34] *Report on the Nutrient Sources of Lake Mendota,* Nutrient Sources Subcommittee of the Technical Committee of the Lake Mendota Problems Committee, Madison, Wisconsin, January 3, 1966.

[35] *Waste Management and Control,* p. 193.

posal plants. Soap manufacturers are now producing new "biologically degradable" detergents that disappear by bacterial activity as other garbage does.

But the pesticides, herbicides, and related poisons we are spreading through the environment are more rugged. They are dispersed over the fields and washed into rivers by runoff from rain and irrigation, only to be gathered again in the bodies of wild animals, birds, and fishes, with consequent destruction of our fellow creatures and hazards to our own health.

5. *Inorganic and miscellaneous chemicals—chemical residues, salts, acids, sludges.* Chemicals such as alkyl disulphate do not usually kill fish, but they affect the gill structure and cause a slow loss of blood. Sulphates and ammonia may change the predominant species in a river's flora from diatoms, which are valuable links in the food chain, to blue-green algae, which are noxious and nearly worthless to other organisms. Some substances such as copper and lead accumulate over time and eventually become lethal to fish and other desirable animals.[36] Coal mine effluents flowing into rivers and harbors are often so acid they corrode ships' hulls and destroy aquatic life. Other chemicals, such as phenols, may cause unpleasant tastes or odors that must be specially handled in treating municipal water supplies.

6. *Sediments from land erosion.* Particles carried in suspension and as bedload, produced by the accelerated erosion of mistreated land, bring destruction to stream channels and reservoirs. They reduce a stream's ability to assimilate oxygen-demanding wastes and prevent sunlight required by aquatic plants from penetrating the water.

7. *Radioactive substances.* Present techniques for handling these substances largely prevent contamination of our water bodies at today's levels of production of radioactive substances. But a great increase in nuclear wastes can be anticipated within the next few decades as atomic electric power generation grows, and the problem of disposal will become more serious.

8. *Waste heat from electric power plants and from industry.*

[36] *Ibid.*, p. 45.

When river waters are overheated they can hold less oxygen, and the rate of oxidation is increased; thus, introducing heat into a stream has an effect similar to introducing oxygen-demanding wastes. Thirty years from now, the amount of water required for cooling could be larger than the entire present use of water for all purposes in the United States. Waste heat disposal may have serious consequences for fish and other aquatic organisms, because most of them are highly sensitive to temperature change.

About half the heat energy in the fuel used for electric power generators must be dissipated in the cooling system. For a 1,000-megawatt plant that disposes of this heat by dumping it in a river or other water body, about a billion gallons per day are required if the temperature of the water is to be increased no more than 15 degrees Fahrenheit. Heating of river waters can be entirely avoided by the use of large cooling towers, which are estimated to cost about $4 per kilowatt, with an operating cost of $2.50 per kilowatt per year.[37] For all new generating capacity in the United States, the capital cost of cooling towers would be about $800 million by 1980, and the annual operating cost around $500 million.

The special problem of storm drains

Even after adoption of sophisticated waste treatment methods, many cities continue to be major sources of water pollution, because of the nature of their drainage systems. The drains of a city carry two kinds of liquids: storm water from streets, roofs, lawns, and paved areas, and used or spent water from dwellings and industry. Storm water is sometimes collected, transported, and disposed of through a storm drainage system, and the spent water or sanitary sewage is carried by separate sanitary sewers. In most older cities, however, both types of waste water are collected in a single set of underground drains, called combined sewers. Such sewers have been in use ever since cities began. The problems they cause are still to be solved.

Before the development of sewage treatment plants, city sewers discharged directly into rivers or other water bodies

[37] *Ibid.*, p. 246.

through numerous outfalls. New York City has 218 of these old outlets, Chicago, 362, and Cleveland, 420.[38] When it was decided that sewage should be treated, interceptor sewers were built along the water fronts beneath the outlets to collect their drainage and carry it to a central treatment plant. These interceptors are large enough to collect all the drainage during dry weather. Regulating devices and weirs of several kinds are used to admit measured amounts of liquid to the interceptors. When it rains, the excess flow goes overboard through overflow or relief drains directly into a river, lake, or bay. The volume of storm runoff is 10 to 100 times as large as ordinary sewage flows, hence nearly all sewage during heavy rains enters the river raw and untreated with the storm water. Even if the interceptors were large enough to carry the storm water to the treatment plants, the capacity of these plants would be overwhelmed. Storms usually occur only four or five times a month, primarily in summer, and consequently a small percentage of the total sewage produced during the year is lost through overflows, but these may carry 20 to 30 percent of the organic solids, which tend to deposit in the drains during dry weather and to be scoured out during storms.

The Chicago Sanitary District collects and subjects to a high degree of treatment over 99 percent of the dry weather flow in the combined sewers of the city. During the summer season, however, raw sewage overflows four or five times a month, and as a result the dissolved oxygen becomes completely depleted in parts of the river and canal system. To abate the nuisance, the District must draw large amounts of water from Lake Michigan to flush out the canals, and the entire flow is subsequently discharged into the Illinois River, where it creates further pollution problems. The operation of the system results in an average diversion of about two billion gallons of water per day from the Great Lakes–Saint Lawrence River basin to the Illinois and Mississippi rivers.[39]

It is possible to separate, completely or partially, the two systems, provide holding reservoirs and large settling tanks

[38] *Restoring the Quality of Our Environment,* p. 159.
[39] *Waste Management and Control,* p. 169.

from which the excess runoff can be released gradually, reduce storm drainage, or install treatment devices in the larger combined sewers themselves. The technology is available for any of these approaches, but all are expensive. For complete separation, existing sewers can be used either for storm runoff or sanitary sewage and a new system built to carry the flows that are to be excluded. The direct costs are some $10 million per square mile, or $1,000 and above per household,[40] plus the economic loss and agony to the city caused by entrance into all the streets, properties, and buildings to break existing connections and install new drains.

Partial separation by construction of a new storm water system to drain streets, yards, parking lots, and new buildings would greatly reduce overflows without the necessity of tearing into existing buildings.

Newly developing suburban areas are nowadays almost universally provided with separate sewers even though the old city may be on the combined system. Separate drains can be installed also in redeveloped areas. Over the years as the city is rebuilt, the entire system will then gradually become separated. In the meantime, new "express sewers" can be built from the separated areas to carry sanitary sewage directly to the treatment plant.

The dust, oil, debris, and filth that settle in a city are usually swept or flushed into the drains, where they lie until the first good rain carries them to the outfall. Thus in many situations, partial treatment (as by sedimentation) of combined sewage might be more effective in reducing pollution than separation of the system.

Large shallow tanks can be built beside the combined sewers in such a way that the tanks must fill as the sewer fills. This damps out peak flow rates and allows a higher portion of the total surface runoff and contained solids to be handled by the interceptors. Columbus, Ohio, and communities in the Detroit area have such tanks; Halifax, Nova Scotia, is studying them.[41] Treatment by settling of solids from excess storm water flows has been practiced in England for many years.

[40] *Restoring the Quality of Our Environment*, p. 161.
[41] *Ibid.*, p. 164.

Storm standby tanks go into operation when the capacity of treatment facilities is exceeded. These stay empty in dry weather and serve both as storage tanks and settling basins during storms. The overflows from the tanks can be chlorinated.

The problems of combined sewers could be eliminated by reducing sufficiently either the rate or the amount of storm runoff. Urbanization usually greatly increases runoff rates, but it need not. At least one county is now requiring developers to provide designs that will not alter the natural runoff rate. The water should be stored, detained, and where possible allowed to soak into the ground to replenish ground water. In the humid regions of the United States, enough rain and snow fall on a city to supply all the water it needs. Unfortunately, the water is usually carried away as rapidly as possible. Roofs are steepened, yards graded, and streets sloped, to ensure rapid drainage. Planning for new or rebuilt cities should look toward conservation and use of the water that falls on them.

A possibly effective technological solution would be the use of large existing sewers as auxiliary treatment plants. This could be done, for example, by aerating them through perforated plastic tubing stretched along the bottom of the sewers.[42]

Pollution of the Land

Archaeologists, digging through the layers of old, long-inhabited cities, have found that these ancient settlements were rebuilt many times on their own debris. Evidently civilized man has always cohabited with trash. Today we try to get most of our trash out of sight. But our methods of ultimate disposal have advanced very little over those of ancient times, and the weight and volume of refuse have increased several fold.

Solid wastes produced each day in the households and offices of United States cities are probably equal to the weight

[42] Gordon M. Fair and John Geyer, *Water and Waste Water Treatment* (New York: John Wiley and Sons, 1958).

of air pollutants—around 4.5 pounds per person, or 125 million tons per year for the country as a whole. Refuse production is believed to be increasing at about the same rate as our gross national product, roughly 4 percent per year.[43] This is not surprising because a large fraction of consumer goods ends up as solid waste. Although estimates from different cities vary widely, the average household trash can will contain, by weight, 40 to 60 percent paper, 10 to 20 percent grass, brush, and garden cuttings, 5 to 15 percent garbage, 5 to 20 percent ashes and dirt, 8 percent metal cans and tubes, 3 to 9 percent glass bottles and jars, and 2 to 6 percent of various odd bits of plastic.[44] The proportions of ashes and garbage are diminishing, and other kinds of refuse are increasing.

In a less affluent society, much of this material would be separated and salvaged, but today in the United States it is mainly a source for pollution of city and suburban land, and to a lesser extent of our air and water.

In addition to household and office refuse, tens of millions of tons of solid wastes are produced by industry—12 to 15 million tons of metal scrap, around 20 million tons of scrap paper, perhaps a million tons of plastics and rubber. Although some of this industrial scrap ends up as an environmental pollutant, a large part of it, together with a small fraction of municipal wastes, is salvaged and recycled. Copper recovery equals 80 percent of newly mined domestic copper; reclaimed lead is almost twice domestic mine production; reused aluminum is 25 percent of the total aluminum supply.[45]

The junk and scrap industries are said to gross $5 to $7 billion a year. However, because of technological and other changes, the fraction of salvaged waste materials is diminishing. Replacement of natural fibers with synthetics in clothing has reduced the usefulness and value of rags. Market changes have almost ruled out the collection of waste paper by the Boy Scouts and the Salvation Army. Urban zoning and higher

[43] *Restoring the Quality of Our Environment,* pp. 134–156.
[44] *Ibid.,* p. 140.
[45] *Ibid.,* p. 146.

labor costs are eliminating junk collectors; Baltimore lost 50 percent of its junk yards in the last ten years.[46]

Demolition of old structures for freeway construction and urban redevelopment is yielding a growing mass of wastes. In some cities the weight of these materials produced each year is about equal to that of household and office trash. A fraction of demolition waste is burnable; part of it is salvageable (for example, bricks and steel girders), but much of it consists of large, awkwardly shaped pieces of concrete, masonry, plastic, glass, metal, and tile. These are useless for salvage and expensive to dispose of.

Solid wastes can be burned, buried, flushed, reused, or simply thrown away in more or less open country in the hope that they won't be noticed. The first three methods tend to produce problems of air, land, and water pollution, respectively. The fourth is becoming less and less widely used, for economic and other reasons. The fifth method, though condemned by all right thinking people, has always been and still remains very popular. It finds one of its latest expressions in the piles of junk automobiles that disfigure open spaces around our cities.

Data on the amounts of solid wastes disposed of in various ways in American cities are spotty, inaccurate, or nonexistent. Some of the best estimates come from Los Angeles County[47] and the city of New York. In New York, up to 7,000 tons of wastes are burned each day in eleven separate municipal incinerators.[48] About 800 tons of waterfront and harbor debris are hauled out to sea on giant barges and burned by private contractors. The residue from both the municipal incinerators and the barges is dumped by the city on 3,000 acres of tideland fill at Fresh Kills on Staten Island. The number of private incinerators in New York apartment houses is unknown, but it is probably of the order of 12,000,[49]

---

[46] Ibid., p. 144.

[47] Planned Refuse Disposal, Sanitation District of Los Angeles County, Calif., September 1955.

[48] Annual Report, 1963–64, Department of Sanitation, the City of New York, N.Y., 1964.

[49] Freedom to Breathe, Report of the Mayor's Task Force on Air Pollution in the City of New York, 1966.

serving two million people and burning perhaps 2,500 tons a day. Ashes from these incinerators are routinely collected by the city, and oversized and noncombustible items are collected on the request of householders. It is estimated that 40 percent of the municipal solid wastes produced in New York are transported directly to municipal dumps and land-fill sites without passing through any incinerators. At least until very recently, some of this material was subjected to open burning at the city dumps.

From these fragmentary figures, we arrive at an estimate of 16,000 tons per day of solid waste disposed of in apartment houses or by the city government.[50] This is 4 pounds for each of New York's 8 million inhabitants. Slightly more than half the total is deposited on municipal land-fill sites. The remainder is burned and disappears into the air, and in the process contributes to the serious air pollution problems of the city. This is particularly true of the emissions from private incinerators and open dumps. Besides the municipal wastes, a large but unknown mass of demolition materials, probably at least 5,000 tons per day, is hauled by private contractors across the Hudson River and dumped in the New Jersey marshlands.

Over-all, the city is using up lands available for "sanitary fill" at a rate of between one and two square miles per year. This large area is necessary because of the low density of the waste materials and the fact that the fill cannot be much more than ten feet thick without creating serious drainage problems.

In New York City, the Sunday *Times* often weighs eight pounds and costs 50 cents. To get rid of it through the municipal system costs 10 cents. Three quarters of the money goes for collection and transportation to the city incinerator, about a fifth for operation and amortization of the incinerator, and the remainder for transport and burial of the residual ash.

The total annual cost per person for municipal solid waste disposal is about $20. (The cost per ton is $19 to $29, including $15 to $20 for collection costs, $3 to $6 for incineration, and $1 to $3 for land fill.) These figures include about $1 per

[50] *Ibid.*, p. 49.

ton for amortization of the capital cost of the incinerators and for the purchase of vacant land for sanitary fill. Extrapolating to the country as a whole, annual expenditures on municipal solid waste disposal must be of the order of $2.5 billion, eight times the operating costs for municipal sewage treatment. This should increase to $4.5 billion by 1980. If we include in our comparison the amortization of capital costs for municipal sewer and sewage treatment systems, annual costs of solid waste disposal will still be twice the costs of handling municipal sewage by 1980.

Collected trash may be transported ten to fifty miles to a disposal site, but most of the cost is incurred in the first fifty feet from the household trash can. It is hard to see how the latter cost can be reduced without a radical change in the collection process—for example, development of home or apartment trash shredders that would allow paper and other dry solid wastes to be disposed of in the sewage system, much as garbage is now handled.[51] Experience with garbage grinders, which were at first viewed with great uneasiness by sanitary engineers, emphasizes both the potentialities of sewage waters as a medium for waste collection and transport, and the low loads of solid material they carry at present. Substitution of a mechanical method such as shredding and sewage disposal for present trash collection may become necessary in the future, because it may be impossible to find anyone willing to take a job as a trash collector at a wage anyone is willing to pay.

Air pollution from solid wastes can be reduced to negligible proportions by proper design and operation of municipal incinerators. But this kind of disposal is expensive compared to sanitary land fill. In any case, the residue from incineration is 10 to 20 percent by volume of the initial material, and this, plus the refuse that cannot be incinerated, must be got rid of somehow, either by burial on land or dumping at sea. For most cities, at least some land disposal is necessary. The problem is to find satisfactory sites, and here, just as with air pollution,

---

[51] *Proceedings, National Conference on Solid Waste Research,* American Public Works Association (Chicago, Ill.: University of Chicago, Center for Continuing Education, December 1966).

we come up against the difficulties posed by the many small municipal jurisdictions in the metropolis. The tradition has been for each city or town to find sanitary fill sites within its own boundaries. In the Boston area, with 79 separate jurisdictions, 61 dump wastes locally. Some municipalities will not even allow others to haul refuse through their streets on the way to a burial site. Organization of a metropolitan or regional waste disposal agency such as those in the Detroit and San Francisco Bay areas[52] would benefit all concerned. An agency of this kind could cooperate with metropolitan planners in selecting and laying out future recreational open spaces that could in the meantime be used for sanitary land fill. With the right kind of planning, solid wastes can serve to fill and improve areas for later use as parks, golf courses, and green belts.

The principal pollution problem of sanitary land fill comes from the dumping of garbage, sewage sludge, and other putrescible materials. Besides obnoxious odors and the formation of breeding grounds for flies and rats, there is a danger of ground water contamination, especially when the water table is close to the surface, as well as a hazard from toxic or explosive decay products if the filled area is later built upon. In general, putrescible matter forms only about 10 to 15 percent of the solid wastes produced in the city, and this proportion can be reduced to less than 5 percent by the use of household garbage grinders feeding into a sewage system and a treatment plant. In order to avoid pollution, putrescible wastes can be separated from other solids and incinerated, buried in especially selected areas, fed to pigs, or composted.

One of the unpleasant problems of solid wastes is the visual pollution produced by beer cans, glass bottles, plastic containers, and pieces of paper that litter the countryside. Because it is virtually indestructible, this trash accumulates from year to year. A most welcome innovation of modern technology would be a "biodegradable" beer can, a container with satisfactory storage properties and adequate shelf life that would be attacked and disintegrated by bacteria as soon as it was discarded. Steel cans have the virtue, in contrast to aluminum, that they disappear relatively quickly. This is an example of one of the key points of attack on the solid waste problem: product design needs to take into account, together with other factors, the possibilities of either reuse or easy disposal.

Another kind of visual pollution is the national eyesore constituted by scattered piles of junk automobiles and auto hulks that have been or are being processed for removal of spare parts. These unsightly objects have greatly increased in number and size during the last ten years.

About 5 million motor vehicles, each containing on the average a ton of salvageable scrap steel, are discarded each year. Although nominally a source of valuable metal, junk cars are now a surplus commodity. The cost of collecting, processing, and transporting auto hulks is more than the price of the #2 steel scrap into which they can be converted. Not only is this kind of scrap much less desirable than other grades, but changes in the steel-making process have resulted in a smaller demand for scrap of any kind.[53] At the same time, the rapid increase in motor car production has been followed by a steady rise in the number of automobiles junked each year.

To reduce the number of stored or abandoned automobile hulks, it has been suggested that the federal government support a price differential that would assure the recycling of hulks to the steel furnaces. In small or remote communities, this might include government financing of a "cleanup train"[54] that would collect and compress junked automobiles and other outsized steel objects.

Alternatively, a tax could be devised to provide an incentive for quicker salvage of spare parts and disposal of the hulks. An annual federal or state license might be imposed on all automobiles, except those currently licensed for road use, or a personal property tax might be placed on junk cars. Possibly a purchase excise tax could be imposed that would provide a sinking fund for ultimate disposal of the car

[53] *Restoring the Quality of Our Environment,* p. 154.
[54] *Ibid.,* p. 156.

at the end of its useful life. An excise tax equal to 1 percent of the purchase price of a new car would amount to about $20 per ton of metal, and this should be ample to ensure the reuse of automobiles as raw materials by the steel companies. Federally conducted or sponsored research is needed on means for producing more uniform scrap from auto hulks, on methods of storage of hulks in excess of current market demands, and on uses other than for scrap steel. For example, it has been suggested that auto hulks might be combined with taconite ore, in order to produce a magnetic material of improved characteristics.

Roles in Pollution Control

The problems of air, water, and land pollution have little regard for political boundaries, are a national concern, require large expenditures for their solution, and affect the quantity and quality of our natural resources. For all these reasons, the federal government must take a leading role in pollution abatement. Among the things it can and should do are:

1. Avoid being a polluter in all operations it conducts, supports, or controls.[55]

2. Provide tax incentives for pollution abatement by industry—for example, allowances for rapid amortization of waste treatment equipment, and credits for sums spent on research or development.[56]

3. Establish environmental quality criteria and standards for maximum allowable amounts of pollutant discharges. Among other benefits, such standards may effectively create markets for advanced abatement equipment and processes.[57]

4. Carry out and support those kinds of pollution research that are not likely to benefit individual firms, including the determination of the effects of pollutants on human beings, animals, and plants, the study of dispersion processes in the

[55] *Ibid.*, p. 16.
[56] *The Adequacy of Technology for Pollution Abatement.*
[57] *Ibid.*

environment, and the development of techniques for measurement and analysis.[58]

5. Underwrite industrial research and development on abatement devices that may later be widely sold. By establishing control regulations, the government creates a market for the successful developer, and it should be able to recoup its share of the costs.[59]

6. Test and demonstrate advanced control methods in its own operations. An army base could be used to test tertiary sewage treatment and complete recycling of water; the Tennessee Valley Authority might install a promising new device for sulphur dioxide removal in its coal-burning electric plants.[60]

7. Underwrite large-scale demonstrations of new control systems. Many developments in pollution control cannot be adequately tested or demonstrated on a small scale. It is not sufficient for a method to serve satisfactorily a single dwelling or neighborhood. New systems must be demonstrated in a complete community that has a complex mix of waste problems. The average city administrator feels that he cannot use the local taxpayers' money to take a chance, and consequently he is likely to recommend only economically proven systems. Hence demonstrations and full-scale trials of new systems need to be ensured or partly paid for with federal funds.[61]

8. Support the advanced training of technicians, engineers, economists, and scientists for many kinds of tasks in pollution control. Federal fellowships, training grants, and institutional support are needed to ensure that persons of ability and imagination are drawn into this broad field and trained in its intricacies.[62]

9. Provide meeting grounds for discussion and agreement on pollution problems and abatement measures among state,

[58] *Ibid.*

[59] *Ibid.*

[60] *Restoring the Quality of Our Environment*, p. 27.

[61] *Ibid.*, pp. 26–29.

[62] *Ibid.*, pp. 33–38.

county, and city officials, industrial managers, and public representatives.[63]

10. Stimulate formation of special governmental or quasi-governmental agencies designed to handle metropolitan or regional waste disposal and pollution control on an integrated basis.[64]

11. Provide information and educational materials that can be used by all governmental and private agencies to create better public understanding of pollution problems.[65]

In recent federal legislation, the Congress has expressed its conviction that programs for pollution control should be progressive and continuously developing and that they should be collaborative, engaging all levels of government and both public and private institutions. There is a strong reliance on both carrots and sticks: authorizations to establish federal standards and appropriations for programs of enforcement; subsidies to state and local governments for construction of abatement facilities and provisions for the conduct or support of research, technical assistance, and training. Formal lines of responsibility from the federal government down through state governments and local bodies of general jurisdiction are emphasized.[66]

At the moment, federal legislation may have outrun the development of administrative machinery for action and the knowledge on which action must be based. This legislation is directed almost entirely at the abatement of pollution after it has occurred. There has been little attention given to the prevention of pollution before it happens.

Control of water pollution was formerly considered to be solely a state and local responsibility. Legislation in the states developed as a public health program, and enforcement authority was vested in state health departments. In recent years, however, such legislation has recognized the need to protect all beneficial uses of water. The legislation of 35 states and Puerto Rico now gives a single state agency the

---

[63] *Waste Management and Control,* p. 26.

[64] *Restoring the Quality of Our Environment,* pp. 21–22.

[65] *Waste Management and Control,* pp. 6–7.

[66] *Ibid.,* pp. 203–221.

responsibility for developing comprehensive programs to deal
with all aspects of water pollution, including the establishment
of stream classification and water quality standards.

About two thirds of the states also have some type of legislation for air pollution control, but on widely varying bases.[67]
Only 12 states provide for any form of state financial aid to
help communities control air or water pollution. Federal legislation dealing with solid wastes (Public Law 89–272) came
into effect in 1965. Sixteen states have action programs.[68]

The new federal law authorized expenditures on solid waste
problems of $7 million in fiscal 1966 (rising to $20 million in
fiscal 1969) to finance surveys, technological development,
pilot plant and full-scale demonstration of improved disposal
methods, engineering feasibility studies of new methods, encouragement of interstate and local cooperation, graduate
teaching grants to universities, and research grants to universities, states, and research agencies.

Regional organizations for water-quality management have
a traditional standing in the United States—from the early,
single-purpose sewage, irrigation, or drainage districts to
such modern multi-purpose organizations as the Ohio River
Sanitary Commission (ORSANCO) and the Delaware River
Basin Commission (DRBC).[69] In Germany, the Ruhr Valley
Administration has shown that integrated regional management based on systems analysis and economic optimization
can be carried very far in practice, through cooperative organization, wise engineering, and ingenious use of workable
but theoretically sound rules of thumb. ORSANCO and
DRBC have shown that impressive progress toward basin-
wide planning and management can be attained in the United
States.

A regional agency needs a competent technical, planning,
administrative, and legal staff. In addition, it must have

[67] *A Study of Pollution—Air,* a Staff Report to the Committee on
Public Works, United States Senate (Washington, D.C., U.S. Government Printing Office, September 1963).

[68] *Waste Management and Control,* p. 149.

[69] *Ibid.,* p. 209.

adequate authority and resources to deal effectively with its responsibilities.[70] These include:

1. Investigation of actual or potential pollution problems and development of effective plans. To do this, the agency needs to obtain and interpret physical, biological, and economic data to forecast the occurrence and extent of pollution and to analyze the economic and other consequences of alternative courses of action.

2. Control and regulation of pollutant emitters—for example, industrial discharges into a river system or combustion exhausts into the atmosphere.

3. Taxation and assessment, both for control purposes, through charges on polluters, and for raising funds to carry out the purposes of the agency. The effluent charges levied in the Ruhr Valley are an example. Besides such revenues, the agency may also need to raise money by issuing bonds or by obtaining grants from other branches of government.

4. Establishment and operation of treatment or disposal facilities.

5. Cooperation with and advice to other governmental agencies, especially municipalities and counties, that have authority over land use.

Water, air, and land in part are a common resource, and in part are subject to individual possession or ownership. Traditionally in the United States, individual rights to water and air have been tied to the ownership and use of land. For pollution, as for other aspects of land-use control, planning, zoning, and standards have become the most commonly employed tools to attain a reasonable compromise between private property rights and the public interest.[71]

Under our system, the authority to implement these land-use controls is firmly lodged in local governments—counties and municipalities. This fragmentation of land-use controls is a hard fact of our political life, and it means that the federal government, the states, and regional authorities concerned with pollution must develop cooperative devices to deal with local governmental jurisdictions.

[70] *Ibid.*, p. 226.
[71] *Ibid.*, p. 213.

A pollution control unit, to be successful, needs the support of a constituency that can help it establish and enforce sanctions against pollution, particularly voluntary sanctions based on publicity and public opinion. An effective constituency must be "grown" through a continuing program of education. The public needs to be supplied, in readily understandable form, accurate and objective information on problems and opportunities. A nongovernmental organization can be especially effective within "problem sheds" that include a number of political units. An example is the Water Resources Association of the Delaware River Basin, which works with industry and community advisory groups to support the work of the Delaware River Basin Commission.[72]

Some Conclusions

As pollution problems become steadily more serious, we need to consider balances and choices within the environment as a whole and to take full advantage of its natural processes. For example, garbage disposal by incineration, land fill, or household grinding adds pollutants to the air, the soil, or the waters. Our choice of which method to use should depend on the character of the local environment and the total burden of pollutants we are adding to different parts of it. In windy areas that are steadily ventilated, a higher proportion of waste products can be disposed of to the air than in regions of light winds and frequent temperature inversions. Different streams may be devoted to different purposes. Some can be kept clean and sparkling, others used to oxidize relatively large quantities of organic matter.

We have seen that air and water pollutants do not recognize conventional demarcations. They move across city and county lines and ignore state boundaries. To limit or prevent pollution, therefore, control measures are needed over regions determined by meteorological and hydrologic realities, rather than by legal artifacts. We need to treat the entire urban-

[72] *Ibid.*, p. 210.

Table 6. Summary of estimated annual costs of pollution control in United States cities during the next fifteen years.

Kind of pollution	Annual costs (billions of dollars)		
	Capital	Operating	Total
Air pollution			
Automobile afterburners	1.5	1.0	2.5
Sulphur dioxide removal from stack gases[a]	0.3	1.0	1.3
Industrial control equipment[b]	0.3	NA	0.3
(Subtotal)	(2.1)	(2.0)	(4.1)
Water pollution			
Reservoirs for seasonal equalization of river flows for waste oxidation	0.4	–	0.4
Municipal sewage collection and treatment	0.9	0.6	1.5
Industrial effluent treatment	1.1	0.5	1.6
Separation of combined sewers and storage of storm waters[c]	0.5	–	0.5
Electric utility cooling towers[d]	0.1	0.6	0.7
(Subtotal)	(3.0)	(1.7)	(4.7)
Solid waste disposal			
Collection of municipal wastes[e]	–	2.6	2.6
Incineration of municipal wastes[e]	–	0.7	0.7
Land fill of municipal wastes[e]	–	0.3	0.3
Junk auto disposal[e]	–	0.2	0.2
Demolition waste disposal[f]	–	0.9	0.9
(Subtotal)	–	(4.7)	(4.7)
Total	5.1	8.4	13.5

Source: Except where noted, computed from estimates of unit costs and growth of pollutant emissions given in this paper. Operating costs are averages over the next fifteen years. Capital costs for water pollution control are annual investment costs for construction and equipment, assuming a discount rate of 4 percent and a twenty-five year useful life for the structures.

[a] Assuming that all present and future fossil fuel generating plants will install equipment for removal of sulphur dioxide.

[b] Los Angeles County expenditures from *Summary of Total Air Pollution,* projected to 1980 and multiplied by twenty.

[c] Based on an estimated population of 40 million people served by combined sewers, and an assumed cost of $200 per person for

suburban-rural complex that constitutes a modern metropolis as an entity. Existing levels of government need to cooperate in new ways, and it may be necessary to invent and test new types of governmental organizations.

The problem of pollution has many aspects—public-health, economic, sociological, political, and institutional. But in all aspects it is related to human beings. It would not exist except for man's activities. All living creatures are affected by pollution; only man has the ability to control or eliminate it. The sciences that deal with man, with his behavior and his institutions, are therefore central.[73]

Many kinds of social scientists and social engineers, as well as chemists, biologists, statisticians, and sanitary engineers, must be involved in handling the pollution problems of the future. Economists are needed to determine the real costs of pollution and its abatement, and the economically "efficient" allocation of these costs among different elements of society. Urban and regional planners should keep the goal of minimal pollution constantly in mind. Political scientists, public administrators, and lawyers will have the task of devising new forms of governmental organization, inter- and intra-governmental cooperation, and public-private interaction. They must find both incentives for right action and legal sanctions against wrong actions—carrots and sticks—and ways to apply them.

When stated in the aggregate, the sum of the costs estimated in previous sections of this paper for reduction of air, water, and land pollution is large. But even if all measures

---

sewer separation and/or storage of storm waters, from *A Study of Pollution—Water*. A Staff Report of the Committee on Public Works, United States Senate (Washington, D.C., U.S. Government Printing Office, June 1963).

d Assuming that all present and future electric utilities will construct cooling towers.

e Assuming that the amount of municipal wastes and junk autos will increase by 80 percent during the next 15 years.

f Assuming that amount of demolition wastes and unit costs of disposal are each half those of municipal wastes.

[73] *Restoring the Quality of Our Environment*, p. 42.

were taken to meet existing as well as future needs, the total per person per year on the average during the next fifteen years would represent only a small fraction of the national income—less than 3 percent (Table 6). As incomes continue to rise, it should be possible to increase the absolute amounts spent on waste disposal, even if the fraction of income for these purposes is not increased. With growing affluence, moreover, our people may be willing to allocate a larger fraction of their resources to maintain the quality of their environment, just as the fractions for education, health, and recreation are increasing.

RACE AND MIGRATION TO THE AMERICAN CITY

Charles Tilly

Not long ago, the movement of Negroes from rural to urban areas in the United States reached a crucial marker: a higher proportion of Negroes than of whites is now living in cities, especially big cities. For a long time, a majority of the nation's Negro population has lived outside the rural South. Most other "nonwhite" groups in the United States have spent most of their time in big cities; American Indians are the major exception. Anyone who keeps echoing the old idea of nonwhite migration to cities as simply an invasion of bewildered country folk is now, at best, behind the times.

Not that migration, or even migration from rural areas, has stopped. Americans are still very much on the move, and the countryside is still sending millions of people to the city each decade. But with increasing exchanges of inhabitants among cities and a shrinking share of the total population in

I am grateful to S. D. Clark, Roger Davidson, William Michelson, Morton Rubin, Louise Tilly, Ian Weinberg, and James Q. Wilson for advice and criticism, not all of which I had the wit or knowledge to act on.

rural areas, *the majority of migrants to most American cities, whatever their color, are now coming from other urban areas.*

One of the great American dramas—the mass movement of Negroes from the villages and open country of the South to the metropolises of both North and South—is ending a fifty-year run. It has left a mark; the very title of Claude Brown's *Manchild in the Promised Land* recalls the hopeful exodus to the North. A thousand theories about the peculiarities of Negro life in the United States rest on beliefs about the wrenching effects of that migration.

Migration could plausibly explain such serious matters as the pattern of racial segregation in large cities, the bad housing and inferior services in urban areas inhabited by racial minorities, the violent outbursts of the nation's ghettos during the last few summers, and the white flight from the central cities of major northern metropolitan areas. Plausibly, but not certainly. This analysis will review some of the plausible relationships between migration and the living conditions of Negroes in cities, consider which of those relationships are solidly established, and offer some thoughts on what might be done to change them.

How Many Migrants, Where, and When?

Although they have probably moved around locally more often, America's racial minorities have generally done less long-distance migrating than have whites. We know surprisingly little about the volume and direction of their migration before the last few censuses. As a rough-and-ready approximation, we might say that in an average recent year five million of the twenty-odd million nonwhite Americans moved from one dwelling to another. Of them, some four million stayed in the same county, and the remaining million divided more or less equally between people moving elsewhere in the same state and people moving from one state to another.[1]

[1] For an excellent review of national and regional data concerning American internal migration, see Henry S. Shryock, Jr., *Population Mobility within the United States* (Chicago: Community and Family Study Center, University of Chicago, 1964).

Even more so than in the case of whites, the long-distance migrants were only a small minority of all the nonwhite movers.

Where did the interstate migrants go? If you took a map of the United States and drew a broad straight line from Tallahassee to Boston, another heavy line from New Orleans to Chicago, and a spindly one from Houston to Los Angeles, then sketched branching lines leading to the cities along the way—thicker for the bigger cities and the ones farther south—the three trees on your map would represent quite well the main established paths of nonwhite migration. The 1960 Census showed the importance of those paths.[2] In most states outside the South, about half the nonwhite population consisted of persons born in other states. Migration, that is, has added enormously to the nonwhite populations of northern and western states.

The states of origin and destination are most commonly on the same tree. For example, the South Atlantic states (from Delaware down to Florida and Georgia) were by far the most frequent places of birth reported for nonwhite persons; such northern states as New York, New Jersey, and Pennsylvania drew very heavily on them for their nonwhite migrants. But the state contributing the most to Illinois' population was outside the South Atlantic area. It was Mississippi, with Tennessee, Alabama, and Arkansas next but far behind. The chief feeder to California was Texas, followed by Louisiana. The "migration trees" are still very much alive.

But their shapes are changing. A growing number of Negro migrants are moving from one northern or western metropolitan area to another, and the number going directly from the rural South to big cities of the North and West has shrunk. Although during the late 1950's most of the nonwhite migrants to big southern cities like Atlanta and Memphis were still coming from small towns and the country, the majority of nonwhite migrants to big northern metropolitan centers like Detroit and Philadelphia were coming from *other*

[2] See especially *U.S. Census of Population: 1960. Subject Reports: State of Birth,* Final Report PC(2)–2A, and *Lifetime and Recent Migration,* Final Report PC(2)–2D.

metropolitan areas. In the previous forty years so many Negroes had made the move from farm to village, village to town, and town to city that in 1960 the Negro population still contained much more than its share of people who at some time in their lives had made a major change in the *kind* of community they lived in. Nevertheless, only a fifth of the 1960 nonwhite population of American metropolitan areas (as compared with a tenth of the white population) consisted of persons born on farms. And the people then on the move were more urban than that.

Even in Wilmington, Delaware—a city of 100,000 located in a largely southern state with many Negroes in rural communities—well over half the nonwhite migrants by 1960 were coming to the city from other metropolitan centers.[3] In fact, by that time, once occupational differences were taken into account, there was little difference in urban experience between white and nonwhite migrants to Wilmington. Many Negroes were coming from Philadelphia, or Baltimore, or Detroit. The branches of the migration trees are crossing increasingly, and are growing to be more substantial than the trunks that used to support them.

The Impact of Big Cities

Most urban Americans have noticed at least one part of this complex process: the swelling of the nonwhite population of the central section of major metropolitan areas. They have noticed the changes in New York's Bedford-Stuyvesant, Chicago's West Side, Cleveland's Hough, Boston's Roxbury. In all these cities and many more, the white population has dwindled since 1940 or so, as the net effect of many moves into central cities and many more moves out of them. At the same time, Negroes in cities have more than reproduced themselves and migration has added mightily to their numbers. One result has been the familiar but still impressive

[3] Charles Tilly, *Migration to an American City* (Newark, Delaware: Division of Urban Affairs and School of Agriculture, University of Delaware, 1965).

rise in the proportion of Negroes in central cities. Over the decade 1950–1960 the percentage nonwhite in Washington went from 35 to 55, in New York from 10 to 15, in Cleveland from 16 to 29, in Boston from 5 to 10, in Chicago from 14 to 24; in all these cities the nonwhite population was over nine tenths Negro. If we play the risky game of projecting these increases in a straight line, for the year 1980 we arrive at the following percentages nonwhite:

Washington	95
Cleveland	55
Chicago	44
New York	25
Boston	20

As predictions, these numbers are worthless. As signs of what has been going on, they are very telling.

The less obvious part of this process was the bleaching of the suburbs through the addition of huge numbers of whites and almost no Negroes. Some of the bleaching occurred because of the flight of whites from the problems and people of the central city, some of it because jobs and housing attracted new white migrants directly to the suburbs rather than to central cities, more of it because, in the normal process of moving around and out toward the sites of new housing, low incomes and organized discrimination barred Negroes from taking part. A second result, then, has been the emergence of increasingly black central cities surrounded by increasingly white suburbs. This is the situation that gave one of the last decade's most intelligent essays on big cities the title *The Metropolitan Area as a Racial Problem.*[4]

At least the flight of the whites left some small benefits for Negroes. Though the piling up of families in the constricted central city housing market of the 1940's had actually increased crowding and decreased the average quality of dwellings available to Negroes in many cities, the loosening of the 1950's and 1960's gave them more choice, more room, and

---

[4] Morton Grodzins, *The Metropolitan Area as a Racial Problem* (Pittsburgh: University of Pittsburgh Press, 1959).

better quality. Many whites moved out of housing in good condition, public action like highway construction or urban renewal flattened many of the worst dwellings, a smaller number of new dwellings open to Negroes went up, and some landlords, faced with less of a seller's market than before, renovated their properties.[5]

Of course, these changes meant that Negroes ended up paying much higher rents; the regularity with which urban renewal programs subtract low-rent housing from the stock and replace it with fewer units of high-priced housing is only one example. These changes also look much less impressive when compared with the even greater gains in space, choice, and housing quality whites made throughout American metropolitan areas. The multiple shifts of population and housing stock, taken all together, left big-city Negroes with an absolute improvement and a relative loss.

These streams of migration, local moves, and housing changes depend on each other so intricately that it is hard to say what difference migration in itself makes. In a strict sense, migration—in the form of net movements of Negroes into big cities and net movements of whites away from central cities and from areas of expanding Negro population—accounts directly for the pattern of segregation. Furthermore, the tendency of those migrants who come to the city through contacts with friends or kinsmen to settle first with them or near them, as well as the tendency of other Negro families to seek protection and familiar surroundings near the ghetto, add a measure of self-segregation to the city. Yet these tendencies toward a voluntary clustering of the Negro population are surely far less important than the extraordinarily limited range of dwellings open to the newcomer; besides the deliberate discrimination of owners and agents, the range is limited by the insufficient information concerning the market which new

[5] Karl E. Taeuber and Alma F. Taeuber, *Negroes in Cities* (Chicago: Aldine, 1965); Bernard Frieden, *The Future of Old Neighborhoods* (Cambridge: M.I.T. Press, 1964); Charles Tilly, Wagner D. Jackson, and Barry Kay, *Race and Residence in Wilmington, Delaware* (New York: Bureau of Publications, Teachers College, 1965).

arrivals have at their disposal, their low incomes, and the problem of traveling to work in those central city enterprises which employ Negroes in any number.

These factors affect not only the location but the *quality* of housing available to racial minorities. A highly segregated market gives the minority group less room to compare or bargain, and in that sense any regional and local moves that raise the level of racial concentration also aggravate the housing situation. Still, it is not so simple. Despite the common-sense presumption that in a restricted market there would be more for everyone if fewer new people came to town, and despite the near certainty that the piling up of new arrivals during the 1940's worsened the housing of Negroes, it looks as though over the long run the vitality of new construction in a metropolitan area—which depends on the area's general prosperity and is therefore related to its attractiveness to new migrants—matters a great deal more than the number of Negro newcomers.[6] Where plenty of new suburban housing is going up, vacancies appear in the older sections of the central city, and Negroes are in a better competitive position. Under these conditions, to be sure, the whites are usually improving their housing at an even faster rate, so the gap between the races is remaining or increasing. The "trickling down" of used housing to Negro families does improve their lot; it falls far short of equalizing their opportunity.

Who Migrates? Why?

We often encounter the argument that if a town improves its living conditions and public services too energetically, it will simply see its resources consumed by a rush of new, poor, dependent migrants—drifters, welfare chiselers, and problem families. There are two things wrong with this idea. First, living conditions and public services play only a small part in determining the number of migrants to any particular city. Second, migrants to cities are drawn especially from favored and vigorous elements of the general population.

---

[6] See especially Taeuber and Taeuber, *Negroes in Cities,* chap. 7.

When interviewers ask American migrants why they have moved, the migrants give answers relating to jobs far more than any other answers; the largest number usually report a specific job brought them to the city, but another sizable number say they came looking for work.[7] This is about as true for Negroes as it is for whites. However, since workers in relatively unskilled occupations more often migrate without having a job already nailed down, and since Negroes include a higher proportion of workers in relatively unskilled occupations, Negroes who migrate are more often looking for work than migrating whites.

Our information on why migrants choose one destination rather than another is less abundant.[8] For people who have received specific offers of jobs, the climate, amenities, and services of a given city normally enter in a secondary way into their evaluation of the offer. For people retiring or in bad health they often determine the choice. But for people moving without a guarantee of a job the presence of friends and relatives matters a great deal more than such things as the housing supply or the availability of public assistance. If these conditions do make some marginal difference in the volume of a city's migration, most likely it is through the encouragement or discouragement friends and relatives already there give to potential migrants, rather than through a general spreading of the word among the would-be freeloaders.

If we move away from what people *say* about their own motives for moving and toward the *objective conditions* dif-

[7] Ralph H. Turner, "Migration to a Medium-Sized American City," *Journal of Social Psychology*, 80 (1949), 229–249; Shryock, *Population Mobility*, chap. 12.

[8] See Leonard Blumberg and Robert Bell, "Urban Migration and Kinship Ties," *Social Problems*, 6 (1959), 328–333; John S. MacDonald and Leatrice MacDonald, "Chain Migration, Ethnic Neighborhood Formation, and Social Networks," *Milbank Memorial Fund Quarterly*, 42 (1964), 82–97; Morton Rubin, "Migration Patterns of Negroes from a Rural Northeastern Mississippi Community," *Social Forces*, 39 (1960), 59–66; Harry Schwarzweller, *Family Ties, Migration, and Transitional Adjustment of Young Men from Eastern Kentucky* (Lexington: University of Kentucky Agricultural Experiment Station, 1964).

ferentiating cities receiving many migrants from cities receiving few, we find jobs looming even more important than before. In the United States, the net migration to an area corresponds very closely to its income level and its production of new jobs as compared with other potential destinations for migrants. An exhaustive analysis of net migration from 1870 to 1950 conducted by the demographers and economists of the University of Pennsylvania shows that during this period Negroes as a group, even though they had less to hope for, responded more sharply to changes and regional variations in economic opportunity than did whites.[9] We have no good reason to think the situation has changed. Though booming cities often have both good public services and numerous migrants, there is no sign that public services themselves affect the volume of migration, and there is every sign that new employment does.

Anyway, who comes?[10] The "Grapes of Wrath" picture of migrants as the dispossessed has such a grip on American imaginations that one of the most popular explanations of the big-city riots of 1964, 1965, and 1966 has been the arrival of unhappy wanderers from the South. In reality, cityward migrants tend to be *above* the average in education and oc-

[9] Hope T. Eldridge and Dorothy Swaine Thomas, *Demographic Analyses and Interrelations* (Philadelphia: American Philosophical Society, 1964), vol. III of *Population Redistribution and Economic Growth, United States, 1870–1950*. Memoirs of the American Philosophical Society, no. 61.

[10] In addition to Shryock, Taeuber and Taeuber, Rubin, Schwarzweller, and Eldridge and Thomas, cited above, see C. Harold Brown and Roy C. Buck, *Factors Associated with the Migrant Status of Young Adult Males from Rural Pennsylvania* (University Park: Pennsylvania State University Agricultural Experiment Station, 1961); Ronald Freedman, "Cityward Migration, Urban Ecology and Social Theory," in Ernest W. Burgess and Donald J. Bogue, eds., *Contribution to Urban Sociology* (Chicago: University of Chicago Press, 1964); C. Horace Hamilton, "Educational Selection of the Net Migration from the South," *Social Forces,* 38 (1959), 33–42; Arnold M. Rose, "Distance of Migration and Socioeconomic Status of Migrants," *American Sociological Review,* 23 (1958), 420–423.

cupational skill at their points of origin. They come heavily concentrated in the most energetic age groups—the late teens and early twenties. *And they even tend to rank higher in education and occupation than the population already in the city.* (Of course, those who leave any particular city also average high in occupation and education, so the net effect of migration in and out is often to depress the level of skill in a city's population.)

People moving off farms are a little different. They are not consistently better off than the people they leave behind: both the least and the most educated predominating in the younger ages, the least educated in the older ones. They tend to be even younger than other migrants, and they are on the whole below the standard levels of education and occupational skill for the city's population. But migrants from farms are only a small part of all people coming to any particular city, and so their arrival does not significantly depress the population's level of qualifications.

We already know that nonwhite migrants to cities have more often come from farms and from regions with generally low educational standards than have white migrants. We also know that nonwhite persons, whether migrants or not, generally get less education and hold poorer jobs than white persons. No one should be surprised to learn that the average nonwhite migrant comes to the city with less education and occupational skill than either the white migrant or the bulk of the urban population. *But compared to the nonwhite population already in the city,* the average nonwhite migrant has a distinct *advantage* in age, occupation, and education.

These complicated comparisons hold an ironic implication for those city fathers who wish they could speed the departure of Negroes from their towns and keep new Negro migrants from coming in. Such a strategy would be a very good way to depress the average level of qualification of the city's Negro population. It would probably increase the proportion, if not the absolute number, of the Negro population heavily dependent on public services. The way to insure a young and skilled Negro population would be to attract new migrants and make sure that the mobile people already in the city were too satisfied to depart. Of course, stimulating job opportunities and providing a decent education for Negroes already in the city would complement such a policy.

One part of this prescription is already in effect without much help from the city fathers. More and more of the recent Negro migrants to big cities are people with relatively good job skills and educational backgrounds moving in from other metropolitan areas. If these new migrants have not attracted as much attention as the displaced croppers from depressed farming areas of the South, maybe it is because they do not fit everyday prejudices so well.

Does Migration Disorganize?

If we come to realize that most Negro migrants are neither drifters nor dregs, we may have to abandon other common-place prejudices concerning the disorganizing effects of migration. No doubt it is true—as a long line of acute observers from W. E. B. DuBois to Gilbert Osofsky have noted—that migration from the South to an urban North in which Negro women had a niche (if not a very pleasant one), while Negro men often had no place at all, wrenched and reshaped the family lives of Negroes.[11] No doubt this wrenching even affected the later generations born in the city. Although the difference in family stability between whites and Negroes of the same income or occupations is less than many people think, Negro households do break up and regroup more often than do white ones. Rates of divorce and separation are generally higher for Negroes.[12] The greater frequency of divorce and separation in turn helps make families headed by women more common among Negroes. The figure below shows, for 1960, the proportion of female-headed families in various

---

[11] W. E. B. DuBois, *The Philadelphia Negro* (Philadelphia: University of Pennsylvania, 1899); Gilbert Osofsky, *Harlem: The Making of a Ghetto* (New York: Harper and Row, 1966).

[12] See, for example, *Divorce Statistics Analysis* (Washington: U.S. Department of Health, Education and Welfare, Public Health Service, 1965; National Center for Health Statistics, Series 21, No. 7).

income and color groups, within central cities.[13] This comparison suggests (but certainly does not prove) that income is the big factor and racial difference in family life a somewhat smaller one. A finer comparison by income, indeed, would show less difference between the racial categories, since within each of these broad income classes the nonwhites are concentrated toward the bottom. If so, Negroes still come out

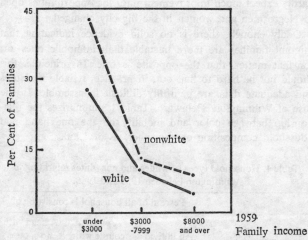

Percent of families headed by women, by income class: U.S. central cities, 1960

disadvantaged because their incomes are on the whole much lower and less reliable than those of whites. Though the majority of Negro families are unbroken, a substantially higher proportion of Negro children than of white children grow up without a father continuously at hand, and suffer both economically and psychologically from the absence of that father.

All this amounts to saying that the situation in the city, rather than the fact of moving, shook Negro family life in the

[13] Data from *The Negroes in the United States* (Washington: United States Department of Labor, Bureau of Labor Statistics, 1966; Bulletin No. 1511), table IVA-5.

time of the great northward migration. The distinction may seem academic: the impact of any move on the individual always includes the differences in living conditions between the origin and the destination. Yet it matters a great deal. For in the one case we might conclude that as migration slowed down and the immediate shock of moving faded, the troubles of Negro families would disappear. In the other case, we could hardly expect much improvement until the opportunities open to Negro men and women in the big city changed.

Oddly enough, there is no solid evidence indicating that migrant families are more unstable than immobile ones—or, for that matter, that the opposite is true. In principle, this should not be hard to find out; in practice, reliable measures and adequate data are painfully difficult to assemble. In the case of Wilmington, Delaware, Table 1 summarizes the relationship between color and mobility on the one hand and household composition on the other, as of 1960.

Table 1. Household types of whites and nonwhites migrating to Wilmington between 1955 and 1960.

	Percent of all households consisting of					
	An individual living alone		A married couple with or without dependents		A head with no spouse present, plus others	
Moves made from 1955 to 1960	White	Non-white	White	Non-white	White	Non-white
Stayed in same house	20	28	62	47	18	25
Moved within the city of Wilmington	24	20	61	52	15	28
Moved into the city from the suburbs	23	18	62	56	15	26
Moved in from another metropolitan area	30	14	64	61	6	25
Moved in from a non-metropolitan area	36	7	54	91	10	2
Total	22	22	61	51	17	27

Source: Unpublished tabulation of the 1960 Census of Population.

The white and nonwhite populations had about the same proportions of people living alone. But the relationship with mobility was quite different: among the whites, the bigger the move, the higher the proportion of solitary individuals; among the nonwhites, the bigger the move the smaller the proportion of solitary individuals. This does not mean there were more *unmarried* migrants among the whites, but that single nonwhite migrants were much more likely to lodge with friends or relatives instead of taking rented rooms. In fact, both single and married Negro migrants to Wilmington often come alone, and stay for at least a short time with friends or relatives. After finding jobs and getting used to the city, the married men ordinarily secure separate lodgings and then send for their families. The single men often continue to lodge with their friends or relatives for quite some time. The common picture of recent migrants as footloose, solitary individuals applies to the whites of Wilmington much more accurately than to the nonwhites.

The rest of the table contains an even more interesting message. Here we find the proportions of households headed by intact married couples contrasted with the proportions we might call "broken." The general comparison follows the national pattern: the whites have significantly more intact families. The comparisons in terms of mobility, however, look quite different for the two groups. The various categories of whites do not differ very much, except that the migrants from nonmetropolitan areas (which means essentially small towns and open country) include fewer married couples than the rest. Among the nonwhites, the bigger the move, the higher the proportion of married couples. The range goes from less than half for people staying in the same house between 1955 and 1960, up to more than nine tenths for people moving in from nonmetropolitan areas. The statistics directly contradict everyday ideas on the subject.

Among both whites and nonwhites, the long-distance migrants include *fewer* broken families (compare the last two columns of the table). There are two significant differences between the white and nonwhite patterns. The white migrants from other metropolitan areas do not look much different from the local population. The comparison between white and nonwhite migrants from nonmetropolitan areas goes the other way, with almost no broken families among the nonwhites coming from the countryside. If migration is disrupting family life in Wilmington, it must be doing so over a longer time span than the five years our table covers. Whatever the explanation of the greater instability of nonwhite households, it can hardly be the disruptive effects of migration.

While the great differences in size and in sources of migrants between the two cities produce some interesting variations in the pattern, both Wilmington and New York display the same general tendencies. Table 2 is a parallel tabulation

Table 2. Percentage of whites and nonwhites migrating to
New York City between 1955 and 1960
(according to household composition).

	Percent of all households consisting of					
	An individual living alone		A married couple, with or without dependents		A head with no spouse present, plus others	
Moves made from 1955 to 1960	White	Non-white	White	Non-white	White	Non-white
Stayed in same house	21	27	65	49	14	24
Moved within the central city	19	24	71	54	9	22
Moved into the city from the suburbs	28	23	63	64	9	12
Moved in from another metropolitan area	44	34	50	49	6	18
Moved in from a non-metropolitan area	38	23	50	63	12	14
Total	21	26	66	51	12	23

Source: U.S. Census of Population, 1960, Subject Report PC(2)–2C, Mobility for Metropolitan Areas, calculated from table 4.

for New York City. A higher proportion of New York's recent migrants are living alone, and a few more of the migrants from nonmetropolitan areas are in broken families. Yet the main conclusion holds: if anything, the recent migrants are less likely than the rest to have broken families, and this is especially true within the nonwhite population.

When it comes to the related matter of emotional adjustment, it now looks as though major mental disorders are more common among long-distance migrants than in the general population (although even that fact could not in itself establish that mobility *causes* mental disorder), but comparisons for other types of personal disorganization remain inconclusive.[14]

As for the crime and delinquency so regularly attributed to the newcomers, what evidence there is points the other way: it takes some time in the city for the migrant to catch up with the old residents. A long series of studies first stimulated by arguments offered for the restriction of immigration after World War I showed lower rates of criminal activity for immigrants than for the native population. In a careful recent study of about 900 Negro boys from a high-delinquency section of Philadelphia, Leonard Savitz found the boys born and brought up in the city to have delinquency rates about 50 percent *higher* than the migrants from elsewhere, even after making allowance for the greater number of years the natives had been around to be caught. As Savitz summed up: "There was no confirmation of internal migration as a disorganizing process in modern life. The migrants not only tended to be lower than the natives in the frequency and seriousness of delinquencies, but also were less likely to come from broken homes, have illegitimate siblings or engage in considerable intracity mobility."[15] Most of the studies seeming to show otherwise, it turns out, establish that crime, delinquency, illegitimacy, and family instability concentrate in *areas* of high mobility, but fail to show that the mobile *persons* in those areas create disorder.

---

[14] H. B. M. Murphy, "Migration and the Major Mental Disorders: A Reappraisal," in Mildred Kantor, ed., *Mobility and Mental Health* (Springfield, Ill.: Charles C. Thomas, 1965), plus other articles in the same volume.

[15] Leonard Savitz, *Delinquency and Migration* (Philadelphia: Commission on Human Relations, 1960), p. 16.

A detailed analysis of commitments to Pennsylvania prisons by Judith Kinman and Everett Lee brought out an even more interesting conclusion than that of Savitz.[16] As was already well established, they found the rates of imprisonment to be much higher for Negroes than for whites. Like Savitz, they also found that among Negroes the rates were higher for natives than for migrants. But among whites, it was the other way around: the migrants went to prison more often. Furthermore, the really big differences showed up among migrants from the South, with the whites, compared with the natives and the whites from other regions, having exceptionally *high* rates of commitment, and the Negroes (likewise compared to the natives and the Negroes from other regions) having exceptionally *low* rates. So the most convenient explanation for the greater frequency with which Negroes are convicted of crimes—the disorientation of the new arrivals from the South —appears to be wrong on every count. Perhaps one part of the correct explanation is that the white criminal has an easier time escaping detection, conviction, and imprisonment than the Negro criminal. Perhaps another is that the Negro migrant from the South is more often drawn temporarily into a protective web of kinsmen and fellow migrants, whereas the white Southerner is more often cast into miserable circumstances on his own. Whatever the ultimate explanation, it must have more to do with what happens to migrants *after* they are in the city than with the shock of moving itself.

The Assimilation of the Newcomer

Sociologists and politicians alike have often tried to analyze what has been happening to racial minorities as a process of assimilation "into the mainstream of American life." They have relied on analogies with the fairly regular ways in which Italians or Poles went from isolation, deprivation, and cultural distinctness toward the normal rewards and involvements of American life.

[16] Judith L. Kinman and Everett S. Lee, "Migration and Crime," *International Migration Digest*, 3 (1966), 7–14.

The basic argument stands out in both the title and the text of Irving Kristol's stimulating *New York Times Magazine* article: "The Negro Today Is Like the Immigrant Yesterday."[17] The article rightly reminds us how much of the ugly language and uglier fact of current accounts of Negro urban life applied to the Irish of our cities only a few generations ago and holds out assurances that this crisis, too, will pass away. A number of historians of American immigration and assimilation, like Oscar Handlin, have urged the same thesis.[18]

The idea is attractive because of its simplicity and its optimism. Even if they didn't come from overseas, many Negroes have recently made the big move from region to region and from country to city. Over the last century Negroes and Orientals have won access to significantly better jobs, incomes, and education. These changes make the assimilationist idea plausible. The argument also makes it easier for the descendants of nineteenth- or twentieth-century immigrants to reply to Negro demands with: "We made it on our own . . . Why can't you?"

The idea of an inevitable movement toward assimilation faces some difficult facts, however. The ancestors of most of America's Negro population were here well before most of the Europeans on whose assimilation the scheme is based. Some forms of racial discrimination and segregation (the World War II roundup of Japanese, the rising residential segregation of big cities in the 1940's, the earlier elaboration of Jim Crow legislation are examples) have worsened several times in the memory of living men. And Negroes (if not Orientals or American Indians) have publicly expressed a greater sense of alienation from the rewards and involvements of American life in recent years than before.

In some broad ways, to be sure, assimilation has been moving on. Over the last few decades Negroes have been gaining better jobs, more education, higher incomes, sounder housing,

---

[17] *New York Times Magazine,* Sept. 11, 1966.

[18] Oscar Handlin, *The Newcomers* (Cambridge: Harvard University Press, 1959). See also Marc Fried, "The Transitional Functions of Working-Class Communities," in Kantor, *Mobility and Mental Health.*

fuller medical care, even greater life expectancy. But so have whites. In all these respects, the gap between whites and Negroes has closed little (if at all) over the last twenty years. Negro unemployment rates remain consistently higher, especially in bad times. Broken families remain common, illegitimacy rates rise, the need of Negro households for public assistance persists. The essence of assimilation is not just material improvement in absolute terms, but a closing of the gap between a group of newcomers and the rest of the nation. For a process often billed as steady and irreversible, the assimilation of Negroes does not seem to be working right.

At the beginning of their discussion of the position of Negroes in New York City, Nathan Glazer and Daniel Patrick Moynihan seem to accept the standard argument: "The Negro population is still in large part new to the city. In 1960 half of the entire nonwhite population of the city above the age of 20 had come from the South. These Americans of two centuries are as much immigrant as any European immigrant group, for the shift from the South to New York is as radical a change for the Negro as that faced by earlier immigrants."[19] Then the qualifications begin. As their analysis unfolds, Glazer and Moynihan slowly come to the conclusion that the conditions for getting ahead have changed too much, that the Negro family has suffered too much damage, that the internal cohesion of the Negro population is too low, for anyone to expect an updated repetition of the classic American success story. Now, this is not exactly the argument of civil rights leaders or of radical critics of American society, but it differs greatly from the more optimistic assimilationist account of what is going on.

At first glance, these disagreements may look like tedious professorial wrangling over definitions and historical analogies. In fact, they set the terms of one of the great questions for research and action in urban life over the next decade. Has there been a standard process of assimilation into an American mainstream via the big city, one that is still working

---

[19] Nathan Glazer and Daniel Patrick Moynihan, *Beyond the Melting Pot* (Cambridge: M.I.T. Press, 1963), p. 26.

today for Negroes and other racial minorities? Or have the mechanisms broken down, has the economic situation changed too much, has the system of exclusion become too efficient, are the groups now seeking inclusion too different in character? Or is the notion of assimilation into the mainstream itself based on a misunderstanding of how American life works?

If the standard process of assimilation is still working, then designers of American public policy could reasonably seek ways to speed up an established pattern of change. If the process is not working, then they would have to envisage changes in the very structure of American society. For once, a problem with extensive theoretical implications and a question of great significance for public policy come together. Although I cannot guarantee that the social scientists, the policy makers, or the critics will come up with satisfactory answers, I am sure that they will all soon be pouring an extraordinary effort into the analysis of assimilation.

That prediction is all the safer because when forced to account for racial protests or ghetto riots, Americans so readily turn to migration and its aftermath as the explanations. The Governor's Commission on the Los Angeles Riots (the McCone Commission), after pointing out the hardships suffered by Negroes everywhere in the United States, had to ask, "Why Los Angeles?" Here is what they said:

> Yet the riot did happen here, and there are special circumstances here which explain in part why it did. Perhaps the people of Los Angeles should have seen trouble gathering under the surface calm. In the last quarter century, the Negro population here has exploded. While the County's population has trebled, the Negro population has increased almost tenfold, from 75,000 in 1940 to 650,000 in 1965. Much of the increase came through migration from Southern States and many arrived with the anticipation that this dynamic city would somehow spell the end of life's endless problems. To those who have come with high hopes and great expectations and see the success of others so close at hand, failure brings a special measure of frustration and disillusionment. Moreover, the fundamental problems, which are the same here as in the cities which were racked by the 1964 riots, are intensified by

what may well be the least adequate network of public transportation in any major city in America.[20]

Migration bears the blame

That migration is to blame seems at first glance to be confirmed by the special census of South Los Angeles conducted after the Watts riots. From 1960 to 1965, unemployment stayed almost constant (in the face of dramatic increases in employment elsewhere), incomes had dropped, housing had deteriorated, and broken families had become more common.[21] When unveiling the census report, Andrew Brimmer, Assistant Secretary of Commerce for Economic Affairs, interpreted it to mean that "the most successful families had moved to more desirable neighborhoods and had been replaced by lower income groups moving in from other parts of the state and nation."[22] The new findings seemed to corroborate the Commission's explanation of the riots.

But the facts are more complicated. If migration is such a powerful factor, we should find that cities receiving many underprivileged migrants are more violent than the rest, we should expect violence in those sections of cities where populations are swelling with new migrants, and we should discover that recent migrants are peculiarly prone to violence. What is the evidence?

The efforts of sociologists to get at the origins of collective violence have not revealed any reliable tendency for high-migration cities to produce more interracial mayhem or more frequent ghetto explosions than the rest. An analysis of 76 urban riots during the years 1913–1963 done by Stanley Lieberson and Arnold Silverman of the University of Wisconsin identified some revealing tendencies for riots to break out in cities where Negroes were underrepresented in the police force or in the city council, but detected no difference at-

[20] *Violence in the City—An End or a Beginning?* (Los Angeles: Governor's Commission on the Los Angeles Riots, 1965), pp. 3–4.

[21] U.S. Bureau of the Census, *Special Census Survey of the South and East Los Angeles Area, November, 1965* (Series P-23, no. 17, 1966).

[22] According to a report in the *New York Times,* March 9, 1966.

tributable to migration.[23] In any case, the Watts of just before the 1965 riots was actually a *declining* community in population as well as in standard of living, not a staging area for new arrivals. And the Los Angeles County Probation Department found:

1. Over half the juveniles picked up for participation in the riots were California born.
2. More than three quarters had lived in the country at least five years.
3. Only one in twenty had been there less than a year.
4. The proportions of natives and long-term residents were even higher among those juveniles whose cases the courts considered worth prosecuting.[24]

The findings sound something like the studies of crime and delinquency we reviewed earlier. It apparently takes time to learn to riot. Again we discover that the way assimilation to the city works is more important than how much stress and strain moving around creates.

Migration as a Problem for Public Policy

The most acute problems we have encountered in this survey of race and migration are not really problems created by migration at all. Some are difficulties faced by members of racial minorities wherever they are in America, difficulties

[23] Stanley Lieberson and Arnold R. Silverman, "The Precipitants and Underlying Conditions of Race Riots," *American Sociological Review*, 30 (1965), 887–898.

[24] *Riot Participant Study, Juvenile Offenders* (Los Angeles County Probation Department, 1965). According to a *New York Times* article of September 4, 1966, a similar study of adult offenders done by the state's Bureau of Criminal Identification and Investigation yielded the same conclusions. After I wrote this paper, in 1966, much more evidence pointing in the same direction came in. See especially Louis H. Masotti, ed., "Urban Violence and Disorder," *American Behavioral Scientist*, 2 (March–April 1968), entire issue.

that migration simply transplants and concentrates in cities. Job discrimination is one important example. In these cases, a change in the conditions of migration might affect which communities had to take the largest direct responsibility for meeting the problem, but it would not make much difference in the gravity of the problem as a whole.

Other problems are forms of discrimination more prominent in cities than elsewhere and therefore aggravated by the movement to the cities of more of the people they hurt. Big-city residential segregation is like that. In these cases, a slow-down of migration might ease the problem, but it certainly would not eliminate it.

As for problems directly produced by migration, my main message has been that they have been seriously misunderstood and exaggerated. Migrants as a group do not notably disturb public order, their arrival does not lower the quality of the city's population, they place no extraordinary demands on public services, and they do not arrive exceptionally burdened with personal problems. These things happen to them later. The difficulties faced by inhabitants of ghettos and by cities containing them are not to any large degree products merely of migration.

Yet in two ways the migrant *does* present a challenge to public policy. First, moving over long distances often imposes hardships and confusion on families at the same time as it cuts them off from the agencies that might be able to help them; instead of recognizing the special problems of people on the move, American public services tend to discriminate against them. Second, the newcomer—already by definition an innovator, having an advantage in age, education, and skill, bound to the old ways of his new city by fewer commitments and routines—is in an extraordinarily good position to take advantage of programs breaking down racial barriers, if only they are open to him. The challenge is to make maximum use of the migrant's talents, give him the greatest possible access to the rewards the city has to offer, make sure he can get past the personal crises almost all big moves involve without breaking down, and assure that he has attractive alternatives to the social and geographic isolation of the ghetto.

Open housing arrangements directed to the newcomers would make sense. Some of the recent migrants might be too dependent on friends and relatives already in the city to consider living far from them. But we have seen that the more detached and highly skilled migrants from other big cities are increasing in number. They might well be more interested in integrated housing than the long-time ghetto residents who are the prime concern of most current open-housing programs. Since the creation of new jobs so regularly stimulates migration, why not encourage or require expanding firms to assure the availability of unsegregated housing?

Because migrants normally face their grimmest moments shortly after arrival, the usual residence requirements for public services have an unpleasant illogic to them. So long as cities think of themselves as involved in a curious sort of market in which generous public services infallibly attract more of the dispossessed, it is not hard to understand the occasional temptation to erect high walls and long waiting periods. But in fact, as we have seen, the quality of public services does not seem to make much difference to the flow of migrants, and the migrants who do come place no exceptional demand on services. In any case, equalizing the assistance available to newcomers in one city or another (possibly through federal programs concentrated in the first year of residence) would eliminate the competition among cities to keep migrants away. It would also mean the responsibility of paying for such assistance would be equally shared. Facilities like public housing are mostly paid for with funds coming from outside the city anyway. They ought to be available to those new arrivals who need them.

There are other services that need to be specially designed for migrants. Since the Welcome Wagon rarely calls in the ghetto, and social agencies do not usually make contact with a family until its serious troubles have begun, something as simple as a reception service could be very effective. Many migrants do not know where they can get medical attention, job information, help in finding housing, or legal assistance; they can only get unreliable, fragmentary information from their friends and neighbors. They are at a point where established routines and obligations are less likely to keep them from taking opportunities—for jobs, for housing, for training —outside the cramped circle of minority group life.

A well-run urban reception service would produce an important extra benefit: a good pool of information about current migration and migrants. For a country that has done so famously in the collection and storage of other kinds of data, the United States has pitifully little reliable information on migration. The Census does provide sound, voluminous data on long-term trends and new movements of population. Some scholars have learned to squeeze sources like city directories long and ingeniously enough to produce finer detail on who migrates and fuller descriptions of short-run fluctuations. Their procedures are still no substitute for the rich, accurate, up-to-date quantitative picture of migration to be gained from an intelligent combination of data already in the records of utilities installations, real-estate transactions, truck movements, new employment, school enrollments, and voting registrations, or for the full qualitative picture to be gained from the household interviews a reception service might conduct. At present the feedback of information on migrants to and from American cities is far too slow and fragmentary to permit effective action in meeting the pains they face or the problems they pose.

Conclusion

Migration, as such, is not a major public problem. But it points up grave problems. In the long run, the assimilation of racial minorities into the social life and opportunities of the city is the fundamental problem of American civil rights. Negroes, Orientals, and members of other racial minorities are increasingly concentrating in the great metropolitan centers. That is where the new opportunities and the possibilities of massive change are opening up. How cities meet the needs and aspirations of their nonwhite citizens will determine how America as a whole meets those needs and aspirations. If Negro separatism of any kind works effectively, it will have to work in the city. That is why the simple question, "*Is* the Negro today like the immigrant yesterday?" matters so much, and is so likely to obsess scholars and policy makers over the next decade.

HOUSING AND NATIONAL URBAN GOALS: OLD POLICIES AND NEW REALITIES

Bernard J. Frieden

Federal housing programs in the past thirty years have helped millions of American families to improve their living conditions. Housing policy today, however, must be reconsidered in the broad context of contemporary urban problems, for it is becoming clear that the solutions of the past are no longer adequate. Housing standards remain important: several million families are still living in slum conditions that should no longer be tolerated in the United States. But new housing strategies are needed that will recognize more complex goals: freedom of residential choice, the elimination of racial barriers, and a chance for all families to have access to good schools, good public services, and job opportunities.

The housing problem, in its most basic and traditional form, can be defined as one of assuring an adequate living environment for people too poor to pay for decent housing at market prices. Other groups than the poor have also laid claim to a housing problem, however. Considerable government aid has in fact gone to middle-income families whose problem is not that of reaching minimum living standards but rather having a wide range of choice in the housing market or meeting the terms of home ownership. The most urgent conflicts over housing policy center on the still unmet needs of the poor and of Negroes and other minorities victimized by discrimination in the housing market. The issues at stake have important implications for the future of central cities, metropolitan development, racial equality, and the elimination of poverty. Serious conflicts over neighborhood change, the enforcement of fair housing laws, and the management of urban development programs arise directly from the shortage of decent low-cost housing in metropolitan areas.

This paper will focus on housing problems confronting the poor and minority groups—the nature and dimensions of these problems, the progress that has been made in dealing with them, and housing policies that may bring faster results. Although there has been substantial improvement in American housing since World War II, there are disturbing signs that progress so far has exposed a hard core of remaining issues that call for new approaches. In addition, housing policies that have worked in the past are now coming into conflict with other national objectives. Thus a review of past experience and a reconsideration of goals and strategies are in order.

Effects of Slum Housing

To earlier urban reformers, the elimination of slum housing was essential to cope with many social evils. Slums were thought to cause family breakdown, personal disorganization, crime, disease, and poverty. Contemporary social scientists are skeptical of such claims, and current research findings do not bear out simple causal relationships between physical housing conditions and social behavior. Experience with public housing also provides grounds for skepticism: families who move from run-down tenements into sanitary apartment projects do not necessarily resolve their other problems. In rejecting earlier simplistic views, however, there is a danger of falling into the equally questionable conclusion that housing conditions have no impact on social life. It is clear that housing interacts with other elements of the social and physical environment in influencing patterns of human behavior.

Current research suggests that crowding, inadequate plumbing and ventilation, and insufficient wiring and lighting clearly contribute to the spread of respiratory and digestive diseases and to home accidents.[1] Morbidity and mortality rates are sensitive to housing conditions; studies indicate that improved housing reduces the incidence of illness and death. Evidence on the psychological effects of crowding and the extent of stress resulting from dilapidated and poorly maintained housing is less clear-cut. Lack of space and of privacy appear to interfere with children's study and with parental control. There is evidence that housing is an important factor in self-perception. Houses that convey an obvious image of neglect and inferior status have been found to influence the self-evaluation and motivation of people who live there, leading to feelings of pessimism and passivity.

This quick sketch of the research evidence on effects of substandard housing is subject to two important qualifications. First, the amount of research focusing directly on housing conditions has been very limited. Much of what is known is deduced indirectly or as a by-product of studies focused on different subjects. It is possible that stronger connections do exist between housing and behavior, but that research to date has not been adequate to identify them. Second, such factors as morale, self-perception, and motivation appear to be related to a broader environment than the housing unit alone. Neighborhood surroundings, both social and physical, are extremely important—possibly more so than the living quarters. In recognition of the importance of the neighborhood, programs to improve slum conditions have given increasing attention to providing better local facilities and services—schools, parks, clinics—and to involving the residents more directly in planning their own communities. Although this paper is concerned primarily with housing, it should be

[1] For a review of evidence concerning the effects of substandard housing, see Alvin L. Schorr, *Slums and Social Insecurity* (Washington: U.S. Department of Health, Education, and Welfare, 1963). The following discussion is based on Schorr's findings.

understood that improvements in housing must be accompanied by related community development if they are to have significant impact on the lives of people who are now in inadequate housing.

One unmistakable aspect of the low-income housing problem is a simple matter of economics. Families living in poverty are often forced to spend a substantial share of their income—one third or more—for housing, thus cutting heavily into their budget for other necessities, such as food and health care. Other dissatisfactions resulting from inadequate heat and maintenance, rats and insects, and the many hazards and discomforts of slum housing have been compelling enough to lead to political action and direct pressure for improvement.

Rent strikes, demonstrations, protests, and local demands focused specifically on housing conditions have attracted national attention. A recent poll of Harlem residents put the need for better housing near the top of the list of "worst problems" (second only to drug addiction).[2] The Office of Economic Opportunity has found poor housing so frequent a concern in poverty areas that it has modified its antipoverty programs to give more attention to housing. Housing also ranked high among the problem areas identified by the first group of cities applying for aid under the model cities program. Communities entering this program were encouraged to survey the needs of their poverty areas broadly and to give attention to such subjects as education, employment, welfare, and health. Although many cities assigned first priority to a subject other than housing, housing was nevertheless ranked among the high priority items more often than any other problem.[3] Further, governmental activities that demolish housing—urban renewal, highway construction, other public works—have met with increasing resistance because they add to the housing problems of the poor. Thus the people

[2] "Negroes in Poll Ask More Police," the New York *Times,* Sept. 4, 1966, p. 1.

[3] U.S. Department of Housing and Urban Development, *Content Analysis of First Round Model Cities Applications* (Washington, April 18, 1968), pp. 2–4.

who live in slums have made it clear that they are not there by choice and that they want a chance to improve their living conditions.

Dimensions of the Problem

Defining and measuring the quality of housing raises many difficulties. A good definition would reflect our society's consensus as to what constitutes decent living conditions, and it would permit clear classification of housing units by field observers. We do not now have such a definition. Studies of housing since World War II have, however, made use of fairly consistent standards that allow reasonable approximations of housing quality to be made. Since these standards first came into use, society has upgraded its concept of adequate housing. By today's standards, the application of these measures thus yields a rock-bottom estimate of the extent of substandard housing, but it does make possible an estimate of change in the supply and distribution of housing from a single set of benchmarks.

Four aspects of housing enter into this set of standards: structural condition, presence or absence of plumbing facilities, crowding, and cost in relation to the income of the occupant. Surveys by the U.S. Census Bureau provide the basic data on all these subjects. National housing censuses were taken in 1950 and 1960 and national housing inventories, based on a more limited sample, were conducted in 1956 and 1959. Substandard structural condition is reported as "dilapidated" housing, which according to Census definition "does not provide safe and adequate shelter and in its present condition endangers the health, safety, or well-being of the occupants." To be classified as dilapidated, a house must have one or more "critical defects"—holes over large areas of the foundation, walls, roof, floors, or chimney; substantial sagging of floors, walls, or roof; external damage by storm, fire, or flood—or a combination of lesser defects sufficient to require considerable repair or rebuilding; or must be of inadequate original construction, such as shacks with makeshift walls or roofs or dirt floors. The absence of a private toilet, bath or shower, and hot running water is reported separately. In interpretations of the Census data, housing is generally classified as substandard if it is dilapidated or lacks one or more of these plumbing facilities.[4]

The other measures concern crowding and cost. The usual measure of overcrowding is an occupancy ratio of more than one person per room. The point at which the cost of housing becomes an unacceptable burden depends upon a judgment of the proportion of a family's income that can be allocated to housing without creating other deprivation. Welfare administrators and others concerned with low-income family budgets make widespread use of a norm of 20 percent of income as the maximum that can be spent for housing without cutting into expenditures on other necessities.

Condition, crowding, and cost are all related as measures of housing welfare and guides to public policy. Discussions of housing are often distorted when one or more of these factors are neglected. Thus slum clearance has been advocated as a way of eliminating the problem of substandard housing; instead, it may replace the slum problem with an overcrowding problem. Or strict enforcement of local housing codes may reduce the number of substandard and crowded housing units, while raising the price of housing so that high costs create fresh problems.

Taken together, information on substandard conditions, crowding, and cost provides a picture of current housing deficiencies in the United States. According to the 1960 Census of Housing, 8.5 million families (including one-person households) were living in substandard housing—in dilapidated conditions or lacking one or more plumbing facilities. This number constituted 16 percent of all families in the United States. At the same time, 6.1 million families—12 percent of the total—were overcrowded; we do not know how many were both overcrowded and in substandard housing.

[4] For a fuller discussion of Housing Census definitions and their interpretation, see Leonore R. Siegelman, "A Technical Note on Housing Census Comparability, 1950–1960," *Journal of the American Institute of Planners,* 29 (February 1963), pp. 48–54.

Substandard housing is clearly a problem of low-income families. Households with annual (1959) incomes of $4,000 or less constituted 38 percent of all households in 1960, but this low-income group accounted for three fourths of the total families in substandard units and for 42 percent of all families in overcrowded housing. Nor is this prevalence of inadequate housing among the poor a result of insufficient spending for housing. Among families who earned less than $4,000 and lived in rental dwellings, more than 80 percent were paying 20 percent of their income or more for rent. Nearly half (46 percent) paid 35 percent or more of their income for rent, clearly an excessive amount to spend. It is sometimes alleged that the majority of people who live in slums are there because they place a low value on housing and do not spend much for it, and that many slum dwellers can actually afford to live in better housing. The information at hand indicates, to the contrary, that low-income people strain their budgets to pay higher rents than they can afford, but that there is not enough decent cheap housing available to meet their needs.

Contrary to popular impression, there is more substandard housing in rural than urban areas. About 40 percent of the families in substandard housing in 1960 were living within metropolitan areas. Overcrowding is more an urban than a rural problem, however: almost 60 percent of the overcrowded families lived in metropolitan areas.

These figures add up to a very conservative estimate of inadequacies in American housing. They exclude a large amount of deficient housing reported in the Census as "deteriorating"; that is, having complete plumbing facilities but needing more structural repairs than would be provided in the course of normal maintenance. In 1960, 4.1 million families were living in housing of this type, 2.5 million of them inside metropolitan areas. Many other families live in housing that lacks central heating; still others live in housing that is sound but located in substandard surroundings, near heavy industry or truck terminals for example. Several million families live in quarters that are not dilapidated by Census standards but that are in violation of the higher standards set by local housing codes. In sections of Philadelphia, the number of units in violation of the building code has been found to exceed Census counts of deficient housing by as much as two to one.[5] Thus it has been estimated that at least one fourth of the American people are living in inadequate housing or an inadequate environment.[6]

Recent Trends

In the Housing Act of 1949, Congress declared as national policy "the realization as soon as feasible of the goal of a decent home and a suitable living environment for every American family." This goal is still far from achievement, and the situation today must be considered disappointing in view of the vast resources of the American economy. Yet the dynamics of the American housing market are more encouraging than a static overview would suggest.

Housing conditions in the United States improved substantially in the 1950's. The improvement was not only in percentage terms, but also involved a reduction in the actual number of families living in substandard and overcrowded housing. Thus the national housing problem is not a matter of an unyielding quantity of occupied slums, irreducible even by massive new homebuilding and unresponsive to public policies. Still less is it a matter of slums growing faster than efforts to improve them, though the rhetoric of slum reform is filled with such assertions. Instead, the problem confronting policy makers is one of maintaining or accelerating present rates of improvement—a difficult task in itself but more manageable than fighting a losing battle.

Since the extent of improvement in American housing is still debated and not yet widely acknowledged, it is useful to review the evidence gathered by the Census Bureau in 1950, 1959, and 1960. Because of certain changes in Census definitions, technical difficulties in making Census comparisons have opened the way for misinterpretations that tend to

[5] William Grigsby, *Housing Markets and Public Policy* (Philadelphia: University of Pennsylvania Press, 1963), p. 253, n. 2.

[6] *Ibid.*, p. 253.

obscure the substantial changes that have occurred. I shall
cite data from the Housing Census of 1950 and from two
separate surveys at the end of the 1950's: a 1959 Census survey on a sampling basis (covering approximately 180,000
units) which used exactly the same definitions as the 1950
Census; and the 1960 Housing Census, which counted for the
first time a number of single-room housing units and which
changed certain definitions of housing condition. Data for
1960 have been adjusted to approximate the same categories
of housing condition used in 1950 and 1959. The three surveys show declines in both substandard and overcrowded
(1.01 or more persons per room) housing:[7]

	1950	1959	1960
families in substandard housing (millions)	14.8	9.1	8.4
families in overcrowded units (millions)	6.6	6.0	6.1

(A further post-enumeration survey differed only slightly from
the 1960 Census results, estimating 8.5 million occupied substandard units. A later restudy of the 1960 data undertaken
by the Census Bureau found that the national trends in substandard housing from 1950 to 1960 were measured accurately, despite widespread errors in block statistics: measurement errors at the block level tended to cancel out at the
tract and city levels, and errors in structural condition classification were corrected by plumbing facilities data.[8]) The vari

[7] For the method used in making Census comparisons, see
Leonore R. Siegelman, "A Technical Note." The relevant sources
of data for 1950, 1959, and 1960 are: *U.S. Census of Housing
1950*, vol. I, *General Characteristics*, pt. 1, U.S. Summary, tables 7–
11; *U.S. Census of Housing: 1960*, vol. IV, *Components of Inventory Change*, Final Report HC (4), pt. 1A-1, 1950–1959 Components, U.S. and Regions, table 1; *U.S. Census of Housing: 1960*
vol. I, *States and Small Areas*, U.S. Summary, Final Report HC
(1)-1, table 9.

[8] U.S. Bureau of the Census, *Measuring the Quality of Housing
An Appraisal of Census Statistics and Methods*, Working Paper no
25 (Washington, 1967).

ous sources of data are not far out of line with one another. They all indicate that the number of families living in substandard housing was reduced by about 40 per cent in the 1950's, and the number of overcrowded families was reduced by 8 or 9 percent.

Comparable national surveys of housing conditions have not been undertaken since 1960, but FHA housing market analyses of some 65 cities in 1965–1966 indicated continuing reductions in substandard housing.[9] On the basis of preliminary data, the Census Bureau has estimated that the national total of families in substandard housing dropped from 8.5 million in 1960 to 5.7 million by 1966.[10]

Some observers who continue to question whether housing conditions improved in the 1950's have based their argument on that portion of substandard housing consisting of dilapidated units. Robert P. Groberg, formerly Assistant Director of the National Association of Housing and Redevelopment Officials, has contended that post-enumeration surveys conducted by the Census Bureau following the Censuses of 1950 and 1960 "revealed that there was no significant change in the number of dilapidated housing units over the decade. There were 4.1 million dilapidated units in 1950 and the same number in 1960!"[11] This statement conveys a misleading image of unchanging and seemingly incurable slum housing. It appears to refer to total dilapidated housing units, including those that are vacant. A more accurate measure of housing welfare is the number of occupied units; empty structures may be an eyesore but they should be distinguished from inadequate living conditions. Groberg's figures are derived from the post-enumeration surveys that supplied cor-

[9] U.S. Congress, Senate, Subcommittee on Executive Reorganization of the Committee on Government Operations, *Hearings, Federal Role in Urban Affairs,* 89th Cong., 2nd sess., 1966, pt. 1, pp. 148–149.

[10] U.S. Bureau of the Census, *Current Population Reports,* series P-23, no. 24, "Social and Economic Conditions of Negroes in the United States" (October 1967), p. 55.

[11] Robert P. Groberg, "Urban Renewal Realistically Reappraised," in *Urban Renewal: The Record and the Controversy,* ed. James Q. Wilson (Cambridge, Mass.: M.I.T. Press, 1966), p. 528.

rected estimates of the 1950 and 1960 Housing Censuses. These corrected estimates, for occupied dilapidated units, are 3,709,000 in 1950 and 3,485,000 in 1960.[12] The improvement indicated here is slight, to be sure, but dilapidated housing constituted only a fourth of all substandard units in 1950. The post-enumeration surveys provide no evidence for doubting the substantial reduction in other substandard housing. In fact, while the post-1950 survey indicated that the Census had overstated the number of occupied dilapidated units (thus exaggerating the apparent improvement registered in 1960), the same survey indicated that the 1950 Census had understated the number of units with plumbing deficiencies, which constitute the remainder of the substandard housing. On balance, the several Census surveys confirm the impressive decrease in inadequate housing during the 1950's

Further, it is important to note that the stock of dilapidated and other substandard housing does not consist of the same houses over time. Many units are improved every year, while others are neglected or altered so that they decline in quality. Between 1950 and 1959, 4,250,000 dwelling units were upgraded from substandard to standard condition, while 965,-000 went from standard to substandard.[13] In this respect as well as others, the housing policy problem is more complex than mounting an attack on enduring slums; it involves promoting the maintenance of sound housing as well as encouraging the renovation or replacement of inadequate dwellings.

[12] U.S. Bureau of the Census, *The Post-Enumeration Survey, 1950,* Bureau of the Census Technical Paper no. 4 (Washington, 1960), table 14; U.S. Bureau of the Census, *Evaluation and Research Program of the U.S. Censuses of Population and Housing, 1960: Accuracy of Data on Housing Characteristics,* series ER 60, no. 3 (Washington, 1964), table 2A.

[13] *U.S. Census of Housing: 1960,* vol. IV, *Components of Inventory Change,* Final Report HC (4), pt. 1A-1, table 5.

Extent of Improvement

How widespread were these improvements in housing in the 1950's? Several issues are important in evaluating recent housing trends: their impact on urban areas, the extent to which Negroes shared in housing gains, and the distribution of housing improvement among different income levels. One significant dimension of housing welfare—changes in cost—has so far been omitted from this account of the housing market, but will appear as a key issue in weighing the benefits received by different income groups.

Housing conditions improved more rapidly in metropolitan areas than in the rest of the country, despite the very large migration of low-income rural people into the cities in the 1950's. Because of the redefinition of many metropolitan areas between 1950 and 1960, aggregate information on metropolitan housing is not available on a consistent basis. Information on several key aspects of metropolitan area housing does tell a clear story, however. The major element in reducing substandard housing in the 1950's was renovation. Of the substandard units occupied in 1950, the number renovated to standard condition by 1959 exceeded the number removed by demolition or other means (fire, flood, etc.) by more than two to one, both in the country at large and in metropolitan areas. Inside metropolitan areas, more than half the housing that was substandard in 1950 had been put in sound condition by 1959 through structural repairs or plumbing additions. In the rest of the country, about a third of the substandard housing was similarly improved.[14]

Table 1 presents more complete information for the twelve largest metropolitan areas, with comparable data for 1950 and 1959. In all these areas, the proportion of substandard and overcrowded housing declined notably. In absolute numbers, the gains are substantial for housing condition but less im-

[14] *Ibid.*, tables 3, 5. For a fuller analysis of the improvement in urban housing, see Bernard J. Frieden, *The Future of Old Neighborhoods* (Cambridge, Mass.: M.I.T. Press, 1964), pp. 19–26.

pressive for overcrowding. The number of overcrowded families decreased in eight cities, but increased in four others. Statistics for both years make use of the 1950 definition of a dwelling unit, thus excluding a number of single-room units counted for the first time in the 1960 Census. As a result, figures for both years slightly understate both the total quantity of housing and the amount of substandard or overcrowded housing; but this qualification does not affect the basic trend toward improvement.

Further confirmation that the urban slums are yielding comes from New York City, where the image of constantly spreading slums has been nurtured for a long time. As recently as 1960, an official report to the mayor concluded that all the construction activity in New York in the 1950's added up to no progress in meeting the city's need for sound housing to replace slums and ease overcrowding.[15] In a subsequent study, Frank Kristof (formerly Assistant Chief of the U.S. Census Bureau Housing Division and then research director of the New York City Housing and Redevelopment Board) made the necessary adjustments in Census data and other sources to permit a definitive comparison of housing conditions in 1950 and 1960. Kristof's calculations indicate that substandard housing was reduced from 367,000 units in 1950 to 276,000 by 1960, and overcrowded standard housing from 87,000 to 73,000 units. Using a concept of housing need that takes into account substandard condition, overcrowding, and a desirable vacancy reserve, Kristof concluded that in the 1950's the city progressed about one quarter of the way toward achieving this goal.[16] (As of 1965, a special Census Bureau survey indicated a further reduction of some 40,000 units of substandard housing in New York City.[17])

[15] J. Anthony Panuch, *Building a Better New York: Final Report to Mayor Robert F. Wagner* (March 1, 1960), p. 35.

[16] Frank S. Kristof, "Housing Policy Goals and the Turnover of Housing," *Journal of the American Institute of Planners*, 31 (August 1965), pp. 232–245.

[17] U.S. Congress, Senate, Subcommittee on Executive Reorganization of the Committee on Government Operations, *Hearings, Federal Role in Urban Affairs*, 89th Cong., 2nd sess., 1966, pt. 1, pp. 147–148.

Table 1. Substandard and Overcrowded Housing in Twelve Largest Metropolitan Areas, 1950 and 1959

Metropolitan Area (Standard Consolidated Area or Standard Metropolitan Statistical Area)	Substandard dwelling units[a]				Overcrowded dwelling units[b]			
	1950		1959		1950		1959	
	Number	Percent of total	Number	Percent of total	Number	Percent of total	Number	Percent of total
New York SCA	482,737	12.2	356,035	7.4	528,766	14.0	477,981	10.2
Chicago SCA	371,002	22.0	202,220	9.4	224,639	13.8	198,677	9.7
Philadelphia SMSA	151,451	14.3	97,626	7.3	90,342	8.9	84,458	6.7
Los Angeles–Long Beach SMSA	136,799	9.1	61,981	2.6	149,125	10.3	202,016	9.2
Detroit SMSA	112,760	13.1	70,831	6.2	91,337	11.0	97,286	9.0
Baltimore SMSA	89,248	22.1	29,916	5.8	45,834	12.0	50,245	10.5
Cleveland SMSA	49,415	11.3	41,235	7.3	35,819	8.4	41,288	7.7
St. Louis SMSA	181,204	34.9	102,990	15.6	93,254	18.4	84,869	13.5
Washington, D.C. SMSA	54,069	13.0	29,820	5.0	52,063	12.8	49,680	8.6
Boston SMSA	83,590	12.1	57,346	7.4	63,781	9.6	52,410	7.1
San Francisco–Oakland SMSA	70,333	9.5	46,391	5.0	66,917	9.5	65,439	7.3
Pittsburgh SMSA	201,992	32.2	102,114	14.2	95,730	15.6	65,323	9.4

Source: U.S. Census of Housing: 1960, Vol. 4, *Components of Inventory Change,* Final Report HC (4), Part 1A, for respective metropolitan areas, Table 1.

[a] Substandard units are either dilapidated or lacking one or more plumbing facilities.

[b] Overcrowded units are defined as those with 1.01 or more occupants per room.

A fundamental question in appraising recent improvements in housing is the extent to which Negroes shared in the over-all gains. Negroes do not participate in the nation's housing market on the same terms as whites. They are victimized by widespread discrimination in the sale or rental of housing, their choices are limited, and their need for additional housing in urban areas is especially pressing. Particularly for Negroes, criteria other than condition, crowding, and cost are relevant, including freedom of locational choice, especially opportunities to leave segregated areas. These issues will be discussed later; for the moment it is useful to continue focusing directly on the housing unit and its characteristics.

In the country at large, the number of nonwhite families living in substandard housing was cut by about one fifth, from 2.8 million in 1950 to 2.3 million in 1960. Proportionally, the gain was greater. In 1950 Negroes were so poorly housed that 72 percent of all nonwhite families were living in substandard dwellings; by 1960 the proportion was down to 44 percent. Despite this improvement, the gap between Negroes and whites actually widened in the 1950's. Comparable figures for white families were 32 percent in 1950 and 13 percent in 1960.[18] Preliminary Census Bureau estimates for 1966 show further reductions in the proportion of both white and nonwhite families living in substandard housing, with whites down to 8 percent and nonwhites down to 29 percent nationally.[19] Information on changes in overcrowding is not available by race for the entire country, but Table 2 summarizes the urban situation for both crowding and condition.

The gains for nonwhites indicated in Table 2 are solely proportional; with the great increase of black population in the cities, the number of nonwhite families in inadequate housing increased even though their proportion dropped. In 1950, 1.4 million nonwhite families in urban areas lived in housing that

[18] U.S. Housing and Home Finance Agency, *Our Nonwhite Population and Its Housing* (Washington: Government Printing Office, 1963), table 24 (based on U.S. Census data).

[19] U.S. Bureau of the Census, *Current Population Reports,* series P-23, no. 24, "Social and Economic Conditions of Negroes in the United States" (October 1967), p. 53.

was unsound or lacked plumbing facilities; in 1960, 1.8 million. During the same period, the number of overcrowded nonwhite families increased from 700,000 to 1 million.[20] Further, even the proportional gains failed to narrow the differential between white and nonwhite housing conditions.

Table 2. Characteristics of Occupied Urban Housing Units

		1950	1960
Nonwhite:	Unsound condition or lacking plumbing facilities	60%	46%
	With 1.01 or more persons per room	30%	25%
White:	Unsound condition or lacking plumbing facilities	18%	14%
	With 1.01 or more persons per room	12%	8%

Source: U.S. Housing and Home Finance Agency, Our Nonwhite Population and Its Housing (Washington: Government Printing Office, 1963), table 32 (from U.S. Census data).

A look at the distribution of housing gains among different income groups is also in order. In evaluating current trends in housing, it is important to know whether the benefits of improved housing reach low-income groups as well as those who are in a better position to pay for improvements. Figure 1 depicts the proportion of families at different income levels who lived in substandard housing in 1950 and in 1960.[21] At every income level, including the lowest, smaller proportions lived in substandard housing in 1960 than in 1950. Of

[20] U.S. Housing and Home Finance Agency, Our Nonwhite Population and Its Housing (Washington: Government Printing Office, 1963), table 32.

[21] Figures 1 to 3 involve a minor inconsistency in the data reported for 1950 and 1960. Information for 1950 covers 34.0 million occupied nonfarm units but omits the 5.7 million farm dwellings that were occupied at that time. Information for 1960 covers all occupied housing, including 3.6 million farm units of a total 53.0 million. This compromise was necessary in order to obtain cross-classifications of housing characteristics by the income of residents; it does not appear to introduce errors of a magnitude that would change the findings significantly.

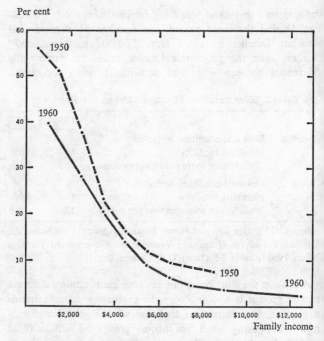

Per cent

Figure 1. Percent of Families in Substandard Housing, by Income Group, 1950 and 1960

Source: Calculated from *U.S. Census of Housing: 1950*, Vol. II, *Nonfarm Housing Characteristics*, Part 1, U.S. and Divisions, Table A-4; and *U.S. Census of Housing: 1960*, Vol. II, *Metropolitan Housing*, Part 1, U.S. and Divisions, Table A-4.

Information for 1950 covers only occupied nonfarm housing; information for 1960 covers all occupied housing, including 3.6 million farm units of a total 53.0 million. Income is that of primary families and individuals in 1949 and 1959.

Substandard housing is classified as dilapidated or lacking one or more plumbing facilities.

course, incomes rose substantially for most of the population between 1950 and 1960; thus the actual distribution of families along the income curve shifted to the right. To take account of changes in income, I have divided the Census income

categories into groupings representing roughly the bottom
third ($0–1,999 in 1950, $0–2,999 in 1960), middle third
($2,000–3,999 in 1950, $3,000–5,999 in 1960), and upper
third ($4,000 and above in 1950, $6,000 and above in 1960)
of the population in each year. The proportion of families in
each third who were living in substandard housing was:

	1950	1960
upper third	12%	4%
middle third	30%	14%
lower third	53%	36%

Thus the lowest-income groups did share substantially in the
improved housing conditions of the 1950's, but middle- and
upper-income groups made greater proportional gains.

Figure 2, dealing with changes in overcrowding by income
level, tells a somewhat different story. Here the improvements
are not distributed across the board but are most evident at
the low income levels. Between $4,000 and $8,000, the proportion of families living in overcrowded housing actually
increased between 1950 and 1960. Once again, the graph
itself does not take account of the changing distribution of
income, which alters the picture. Divided into thirds, the proportion in overcrowded housing becomes:

	1950	1960
upper third	10%	9%
middle third	17%	14%
lower third	17%	12%

At all income levels, the proportional reduction in overcrowding is less than the reduction in substandard occupancy.
When the changing distribution of income is considered, however, the proportional reductions in overcrowding are greatest for the low-income group, less for the middle-income
group, and still less for the top third.

The other key element in housing welfare—cost—is the subject of Figure 3. This graph reports the proportion of families
at different income levels who spend more than 20 percent
of their income for rent. It is therefore limited to renter-

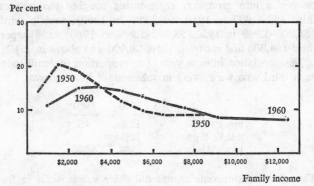

Figure 2. Percent of Families in Overcrowded Housing, by Income Group, 1950 and 1960

Source: Calculated from *U.S. Census of Housing: 1950,* Vol. II, Part 1, Table A-7; *U.S. Census of Housing: 1960,* Vol. II, Part 1, Table A-3.

Information for 1950 covers only occupied nonfarm housing; information for 1960 covers all occupied housing, including 3.6 million farm units of a total 53.0 million. Income is that of primary families and individuals in 1949 and 1959.

Overcrowded units are defined as those with 1.01 or more persons per room.

occupied housing in 1950 and 1960, and covers gross rent, including utilities where the tenant pays for them himself. The general upward shift in the curve from 1950 to 1960 answers the question of who is paying for the widespread renovation and general improvement in housing conditions. At every income level, a higher proportion of families paid more than one fifth of their income for rent in 1960 than in 1950. An analysis in terms of changing distribution of income indicates the extent of the upward shift for each of the three income divisions:

	1950	1960
upper third	9%	10%
middle third	37%	46%
lower third	81%	89%

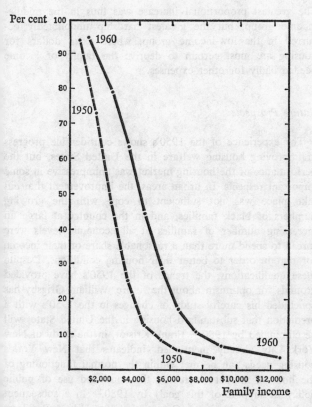

Figure 3. Percent of Families Paying More than One fifth of Income for Rent, by Income Group, 1950 and 1960

Source: See Figure 2.

Information for 1950 covers only occupied nonfarm housing; information for 1960 covers all occupied housing, including 3.6 million farm units of a total 53.0 million. Income is that of primary families and individuals in 1949 and 1959.

Gross rent is reported as a percentage of 1949 and 1959 income for primary families and individuals in renter-occupied housing. Gross rent includes utility costs where the tenant pays for these.

The greatest proportional increase was thus in the middle-income group, but the greatest hardship undoubtedly occurred in the low-income group, where extra dollars for housing are most certain to deprive the family of income needed badly for other expenses.

Future Prospects

The experience of the 1950's shows considerable progress in improving housing welfare in the United States, but the performance of the housing market was unimpressive in some important respects. In urban areas, the improvement that did take place was not sufficient to cope with the growing numbers of black families, and in the country at large an increasing number of families at all economic levels were forced to spend more than a reasonable share of their income for rent in order to better their housing conditions. Despite these qualifications, the trends of the 1950's have provided grounds for optimism about the future. William Grigsby has concluded his careful study of changes in the 1950's with a prediction that substandard housing in the United States will be eliminated by 1980.[22] Frank Kristof, in the study of New York City already mentioned, indicates that New York's housing needs can be met within the normal functioning of the housing market (including the continued use of public policy in support of this goal) by 1980.[23] In a subsequent study for the National Commission on Urban Problems (Douglas Commission), Kristof applied the same concept of housing needs to the country at large and concluded that the rate of progress of the 1950's has continued into the early 1960's and can reasonably be expected to continue in the decades ahead. Kristof's projections, which assume no significant increase in the federal role in housing, show a steady reduction from 20.5 million units needed in 1950 (to replace substandard housing, end overcrowding, and provide a 5

[22] William Grigsby, *Housing Markets,* p. 322.
[23] Frank S. Kristof, "Housing Policy Goals."

percent vacancy reserve of sound housing) to 5.7 million units needed by 1990.[24]

If these expectations are reasonable, they still pose the question of whether reaching the national housing goal by the 1980's is an acceptable rate of progress. There is widespread dissatisfaction with housing conditions now, particularly among Negroes and low-income groups. The prospect of waiting another twenty years to reach the goal of the Housing Act of 1949 will not evoke great enthusiasm in the slums. Further, the definition of substandard housing that enters into these projections is a minimal one, based on Census categories that do not include such factors as central heating, adequacy of light and air, blighted surroundings, or violations of local housing codes. In addition, our notion of what constitutes acceptable housing will continue to reflect constantly rising expectations. By the 1980's, much of the old housing that meets today's concept of minimum standards will be considered obsolete in size, layout, or appearance. In this sense, postponing the replacement of today's inadequate housing until then means that large numbers of people will continue indefinitely to live in conditions that they and the rest of society consider unacceptable.

Whether the rate of housing improvement can be accelerated depends upon many circumstances, including some that are independent of housing policies. The close connection between low incomes and inadequate housing has already been stressed. The elimination of poverty in the United States would go a long way toward eliminating substandard living conditions. Short of this goal, rising incomes for those who are now poor will be essential to maintain—if not increase—the rate of progress that was achieved in the 1950's. But aside from a general growth of income or the provision of a guaranteed annual income, the operation of the housing market will have much to do with future rates of improvement. The market mechanisms that contributed to improvement in the 1950's will not necessarily operate the same way in the future.

[24] Frank S. Kristof, *Urban Housing Needs Through the 1980's: An Analysis and Projection* (Washington: National Commission on Urban Problems, Research Report no. 10, 1968).

A closer look at the components of housing change is helpful in assessing future prospects.

A high volume of new housing construction has been one of the main forces for improvement. Total housing production between 1950 and 1959 (excluding farm units) averaged slightly more than 1.5 million units started per year.[25] This new construction more than kept pace with population growth, and triggered a series of changes in the rest of the housing supply. Two thirds of the new home building took place inside metropolitan areas, mostly in the suburbs. Millions of middle-income families moved from the central cities to new suburban developments, leaving behind a large stock of vacant housing. These vacancies freed the tight housing situation of the late 1940's and made it possible for other families to move out of crowded or unsatisfactory quarters. The turnover of existing housing was sufficient to provide living space for new migrants arriving in the cities as well as older city residents and newly formed families. In most large cities, the movement out to suburbia was greater than population growth resulting from migration plus natural increase. With this decline of central city population, crowding was eased considerably in the dense slum neighborhoods. Crowding was also reduced within the dwelling units: large households, in which grown children lived together with their parents and other relatives, split up to live in separate quarters. Since the population pressure was easing, many small units were merged to form larger apartments. Each wave of movement freed some housing that became available to others. Accompanying this turnover of housing was the impressive amount of renovation noted earlier. Housing that formerly lacked plumbing facilities or bathrooms or needed repair was put in sound condition.

The indirect effects set in motion by new construction emerged very clearly from a pilot study of housing turnover in New York City.[26] In the study sample, 64 new units gave rise to a chain of turnover involving 90 additional units. At each

[25] U.S. Department of Commerce, *Construction Statistics, 1915-1964* (Washington: Government Printing Office, 1966), pp. 17–18

[26] Frank S. Kristof, "Housing Policy Goals," pp. 241–242.

successive link in the chain, families with lower incomes moved into turnover units, improving the space or quality of their housing and in a few cases moving from a substandard to a standard unit. Most families increased their rent bill as a result of the move, though the new median rent generally remained about one fifth of family income. This turnover process is not necessarily the same as "filtering," a concept that implies a drop in the cost of old housing as a result of vacancies triggered by new construction. Nevertheless, the turnover of existing housing is a means of supplying additional sound housing for income groups unable to afford the price of new construction. Turnover can involve higher rent-income ratios for the movers, as indicated in the New York study and in the national data cited earlier. The widespread effectiveness of the turnover process in providing sound housing for lower-income groups can be seen in the fact that even at the lowest income levels in 1960 (Figure 1), a majority of families were living in standard housing.

Turnover is thus the basic process by which low-income groups improve their housing in the cities. It also has special significance as the way in which Negroes find places to live. Between 1950 and 1960, the nonwhite population grew from 9 million to 13.2 million in metropolitan areas, with more than 80 percent of this increase occurring in the central cities. Living space for this growing population came almost entirely from older housing formerly occupied by white people. Only a small proportion of Negroes who need housing manage to buy or rent new housing, or move into newly built public housing. Between 1950 and 1960, almost a million metropolitan housing units went from white to nonwhite occupancy; fewer than 100,000 went from nonwhite to white occupancy during the same period. Thus in 1959, as many as 30 percent of all nonwhite families in metropolitan areas were living in housing where white families had lived in 1950.[27]

Successful operation of the turnover process depends upon three major factors: a high volume of new construction, a

[27] *U.S. Census of Housing: 1960*, vol. IV, *Components of Inventory Change*, Final Report HC (4), pt. 1A-1, table 2.

low volume of demolition of existing units, and adequate maintenance and upgrading of older housing. During the 1950's all these factors interacted to produce a substantial improvement in housing in urban areas and in the country at large. Within metropolitan areas, 9.8 million new units were built and only 1.0 million were lost through demolition and another 700,000 through such means as fire and flood; 1.8 million dwellings were upgraded from substandard to standard condition and 600,000 downgraded from standard to substandard.[28]

These same components of housing change do not look as promising for the late 1960's and beyond. An increased volume of new construction is needed to keep pace with population growth and mobility, to offset demolitions and losses at the 1950's rate, to continue progress in eliminating substandard and overcrowded conditions, and to allow for a reasonable vacancy reserve. Current estimates, prepared by both governmental and private studies, are that at least 2 million new units per year are needed now and 2.5 million within a few years.[29] Actual production continued to average about 1.5 million units a year through 1965, but dropped starting in 1966 and is unlikely to recover during the high interest rate period at the end of this decade. Further, housing demolition in urban areas will increase substantially in the late 1960's and 1970's. The acceleration of urban renewal and of highway construction alone is expected to result in 100,000 demolitions a year, mostly in urban areas.[30] The total effect

28 *Ibid.*, pp. 21–24.

29 U.S. Congress, House, Committee on Banking and Currency, Subcommittee on Housing, *Hearings, Demonstration Cities, Housing and Urban Development, and Urban Mass Transit,* 89th Cong. 2nd sess., 1966, pp. 66, 246; U.S. National Commission on Technology, Automation, and Economic Progress, *Technology and the American Economy,* vol. 1 (Washington: Government Printing Office, 1966), p. 87; Charles Abrams, *The City Is the Frontier* (New York: Harper and Row, 1965), p. 277.

30 U.S. Congress, House, *Study of Compensation and Assistance for Persons Affected by Real Property Acquisition in Federal and Federally Assisted Programs,* printed for use of the Committee on

may be to double the yearly demolition of 100,000 units in metropolitan areas in the 1950's, when urban renewal and federally aided highway construction were just getting under way. Nor is demolition limited to substandard housing: in the 1950's, more than 40 percent of the units demolished in metropolitan areas were in sound condition with all plumbing facilities.

The third major component—renovation of substandard housing—is more difficult to anticipate. Home repairs and improvements constitute a major industry in the United States. By 1967, outlays for maintenance, repairs, and improvements to nonfarm housing reached $11 billion per year.[31] We do not know, however, what proportion of the total is spent on improving substandard housing. Almost two thirds of the expenditures were for owner-occupied single-family houses,[32] and a large part of the remainder was undoubtedly for maintaining and improving rental housing already in sound condition. There is some evidence to suggest that the high rate of renovation in the 1950's has already taken care of many of the easy jobs, and that property owners will be slower to renovate the remaining substandard housing that is in poorer condition.[33] One careful analysis of the hard-core slums of Newark, New Jersey, has found disturbing signs that most slum-owners have little interest in property improvements, regardless of market conditions, tax policies, or the availability of financing. When the demand for tenement apartments is very strong, the landlord sees no need to improve his property; when the demand is weak, he does not improve because he fears for his investment.[34]

Thus the current outlook is for a slowing of the rate of housing improvement that occurred in the 1950's. In the

---

Public Works, 88th Cong., 2nd sess., 1964, p. 258; Alvin L. Schorr, *Slums and Social Insecurity,* p. 61.

[31] U.S. Department of Housing and Urban Development, *Housing and Urban Development Trends,* 22 (May 1969), p. 29.

[32] *Ibid.,* p. 30.

[33] William Grigsby, *Housing Markets,* p. 269.

[34] George Sternlieb, *The Tenement Landlord* (New Brunswick, N.J.: Rutgers—The State University, Urban Studies Center, 1966).

1950's, we built more than enough new housing to keep pace with new household formation, we demolished relatively little old housing, and we renovated a large number of substandard units. In the 1960's, new construction appears to be falling behind the needs created by urban population growth and housing losses, the volume of demolition is increasing, and the prospects for maintaining a high level of renovation are uncertain.

Problems with the Turnover Process

Among possible strategies for meeting the national housing goal, one approach would be to accelerate the forces that operated successfully in the 1950's. Policies could aim at stimulating a higher volume of new construction, faster turnover of existing units, and greater investment in maintenance and renovation of low-cost housing. But exclusive reliance on this turnover process creates other problems and leads to some bewildering dilemmas for public policy.

Urban growth in the United States has been pushing outward from the core of the central city, with new housing added in a series of rings wrapping around the central city and covering more and more suburban territory. Each ring of development tends to contain housing built at about the same time. Thus the old housing that middle-income families abandon when they move to new quarters is generally concentrated in the inner part of the metropolitan area. Some years ago, these areas of declining middle-class occupancy constituted only a small part of the central city just beyond the downtown business district. By the 1950's, with more housing considered obsolescent, and with a larger number of middle-income people able to move to newer housing, the area of declining middle-class occupancy blanketed very large parts of the central cities and even a number of the oldest suburbs just beyond the city boundary. With low-income people relying almost entirely on older housing abandoned by more affluent groups, it was inevitable that the economic and racial composition of the central cities and some adjoining suburbs would undergo drastic changes.

As a result, the same process that brought about a striking improvement in national housing conditions yielded a plentiful harvest of acute social and economic problems in the central cities. The combination of new suburban development and housing turnover in the older cities led to a massive dispersal of the population along racial and economic lines. By the late 1950's, the suburbs had succeeded in attracting a concentration of white, young, middle- and upper-income families with children; while the central cities were left with higher proportions of the elderly, broken families, Negroes, low-income workers, and the unemployed. These social and economic disparities between central cities and suburbs do not hold true throughout the country, but they do apply to virtually all the large metropolitan areas and to urban areas of all sizes in the Northeast.[35]

The consequences have been severe, both for the people involved and for city governments. One result has been a growing social and cultural isolation of the poor from the rest of society. In neighborhoods where the poor are concentrated, models of success are few and unemployment among youth is sometimes so prevalent that it becomes the normal pattern. It is difficult to judge just how significant this type of isolation is for the poor, and social science evidence is by no means definitive. Other effects of the same social separation are more direct. Workers in the central cities are increasingly cut off from blue-collar jobs in expanding suburban industrial centers, while manufacturing and related lines of employment continue to decline in the central cities. Transportation is difficult to the new industrial parks, and central-city workers are not sufficiently in touch with suburban firms to learn about job opportunities.

For Negroes, these problems are intensified. Even many of those who can afford to move to new housing in suburbia are blocked by discrimination or hostility, and are forced to

---

[35] For documentation and analysis of central city-suburban differences, see U.S. Advisory Commission on Intergovernmental Relations, *Metropolitan Social and Economic Disparities: Implications for Intergovernmental Relations in Central Cities and Suburbs* (Washington: ACIR, 1965).

stay in central-city ghettos. One recent analysis of 1960 data makes it clear that white families with low and moderate incomes are finding their way to the suburbs, but black families in the same income brackets are not. Richard Langendorf carried out calculations for eleven large metropolitan areas to test where Negro families would be living if, at every income level, an identical proportion of Negroes and whites were homeowners and an identical proportion of Negroes and whites in both homeowner and tenant categories lived in the suburbs. Under these assumptions, which imply that household income is the key determinant of where people live, the proportion of Negroes in the suburbs would increase substantially. For all eleven areas combined, 16 percent of nonwhites actually lived in the suburbs in 1960; under the new assumptions this figure would rise to 40 percent. The number of suburban nonwhites in New York, Los Angeles, Pittsburgh, and St. Louis would double; in Washington and Baltimore it would more than triple; in Detroit it would increase four times; in Chicago five times; and in Cleveland it would increase about twenty times.[36]

Where people live has much to do with the quality of public services available to them, and this connection leads to one of the most fundamental problems posed by current urban development: the gap between local needs and local resources. Disadvantaged groups in the central cities are highly dependent upon public services. They need high-quality educational programs for both children and adults, they have special needs for health and welfare assistance, recreation facilities, and police and fire protection. Central cities face high service demands, but many of their prosperous taxpayers have left and their commerce and industry are also moving to the suburbs. The cities have been struggling to cope with this gap between service needs and local tax resources. One result has been steady pressure for state and federal help; the recent proliferation of federal aid programs for the cities is a direct consequence. Another typical city strategy has been to

[36] Richard Langendorf, "Residential Desegregation Potential," *Journal of the American Institute of Planners,* 35 (March 1969), pp. 90–95.

develop urban renewal programs intended to win back (or hold onto) middle-income families, retail stores, and industrial firms. Despite the increase in federal aid and the more questionable effects of renewal programs, public services in the cities have had to be held far below the levels that are needed to enable disadvantaged groups to compete with others on equal terms.

In this sense, it is fair to say that our solution to the national housing problem has been creating a national urban problem. Federal housing policies seem to be at odds with other federal objectives. Some programs—chiefly FHA mortgage insurance, federal aid for highways that stimulate suburban growth, and aid for suburban water and sewer systems—accelerate the pace of new housing construction in the suburbs and the turnover of central-city housing. Others—principally urban renewal and aid for mass transit—aim at reviving the central cities and stemming the flight to the suburbs. Urban renewal in turn depletes the supply of low-cost housing and thus slows the turnover effects stimulated by national housing policy. The programs that favor suburban growth promote population dispersal along racial and economic lines, setting the stage for race segregation between central cities and suburbs, which runs counter to civil rights goals. This same dispersal handicaps the central cities in their efforts to supply adequate services for low-income groups, countering other national goals of eliminating poverty and providing equality of educational opportunity.

Continued dependence upon the turnover process to accommodate low-income groups is also producing open social and racial conflict in many central-city neighborhoods. In the 1950's, the growing black population of the central cities was able to take over a great deal of housing left behind by mobile white families who chose to move to suburbs. Even in the 1950's, however, this turnover process failed to reduce the number of urban Negro families living in substandard and overcrowded housing. The continued growth of black population in the cities means that many Negro families have nowhere to go but into whatever vacancies turn up in white areas. But as the more mobile white families have departed, a core of deeply rooted people have remained in old neighborhoods—people who cannot afford to move to the suburbs or who want to stay where they are. Many established ethnic neighborhoods remain in the central cities, where people are tied to friends, family, churches, clubs, and the other loyalties that develop in a close-knit community. Often they are fearful of invasions by Negroes or other newcomers. Some neighborhoods have tried to stabilize the situation by supporting urban renewal programs designed to remove pockets of low-cost housing and price out potential invaders. Others express their fears in backlash voting or open hostility to black newcomers.

The time has come to diversify our mechanisms for meeting the housing needs of low-income groups. The turnover system is working, but it is producing too many objectionable by-products. These by-products in turn have generated new policies that will interfere with the future turnover of old housing. In particular, many central cities have found their changing population composition unacceptable and have developed urban renewal programs to stabilize existing neighborhoods or to attract back middle-income families—both of which will sacrifice low-income housing needs in order to diversify the city's population.[37]

Still another reason for supplementing the turnover process with other approaches lies in the nature of national housing goals. The goal of a decent home and a suitable environment for every family is too limited for the needs of urban life today. In our spreading metropolitan areas, mobility is a prerequisite for equal opportunity. Families need to be able to move to keep up with changing work locations, to have access to specialized services or institutions, and to have some measure of freedom in choosing a type of housing or type of community. Most middle-income families now enjoy this freedom of movement through the operation of the housing market, though many middle-income Negroes still do not. Most low-income families have very limited freedom of movement: the turnover process restricts their choice to

[37] See Bernard J. Frieden, "Toward Equality of Urban Opportunity," *Journal of the American Institute of Planners*, 31 (November 1965), pp. 320–330.

areas where old housing is concentrated. A more adequate statement of national housing goals would go beyond decent shelter and surroundings, and would include diversity of choice in housing and freedom of movement throughout metropolitan areas.[38] New strategies are needed to achieve this more complex goal.

Diversifying Housing Strategies

Widening the choices available in the urban housing market does not necessarily mean rejecting the turnover process. The continued use of old housing that is in sound condition is surely desirable in itself; further, it does provide for one significant choice by enabling many people with low and moderate incomes to live in the central cities and older suburbs. Although some families now in the cities are living there reluctantly, the majority are probably there by choice. Middle- and upper-income groups can generally afford to move elsewhere if they want to. (At all income levels, however, Negroes have little freedom of movement.) Poorer families are more constrained by the shortage of suburban housing at prices they can afford, but many would be reluctant to leave in any case. Recent research and relocation experience in low-income neighborhoods demonstrate clearly that a high proportion of the people living there want to stay nearby in order to keep up their ties with friends, relatives, organizations, churches, and with a style of life that can hardly be found in the newer suburbs.[39] The growth of urban renewal and highway construction is forcing many of them to leave their old neighborhoods and to look for other housing in the city. Others, however, are potentially mobile

---

[38] See *ibid.*

[39] See Marc Fried, "Grieving for a Lost Home," in *The Urban Condition*, ed. Leonard J. Duhl (New York: Basic Books, 1963), pp. 151–171; Herbert J. Gans, *The Urban Villagers* (New York: Free Press of Glencoe, 1962); Chester Hartman, "The Housing of Relocated Families," *Journal of the American Institute of Planners*, 30 (November 1964), pp. 266–286.

and want to leave the city. If they have to stay where they are, they may be unable to take advantage of suburban job possibilities or to achieve their aspirations for a more middle-class life style.

Widening the housing choices available, therefore, means maintaining the turnover process and the options it offers, but developing additional strategies that will open other opportunities. Three general approaches are worth exploring: (1) reducing the cost of new construction so that more people can afford new housing; (2) making the turnover process work more effectively to offer wider choices of location, cost, and ownership as well as rental; (3) providing direct subsidies for new housing, managed so as to counter imbalances resulting from the turnover system.

1. Reducing the cost of new housing

Past efforts to reduce costs and widen the market for new homes have relied mainly on financial mechanisms to attract investment funds into home mortgages and make mortgages readily available to home buyers, plus some special programs to finance housing at below-market interest rates. More attention should be given to promoting cost reductions in construction, through the introduction of new technology, simplification of building controls, and the removal of obstacles to large-scale production and land development. The cost of new housing today prices most American families out of the market. By 1968, the median sales price of new single-family houses had risen to $24,600. Seventy percent of all new homes sold for $20,000 or more, and only 8 percent for under $15,000.[40] Ownership of new homes is effectively limited to the top half of white families and the top quarter of black families, who earn $8,000 a year or more.

The homebuilding industry, despite its significant role in the national economy, has lagged far behind other industries in sponsoring research and development, in applying technology, and in benefiting from mass production and large-scale operations. Several factors contribute to this lag: the structure of the

[40] U.S. Department of Housing and Urban Development, *Housing and Urban Development Trends,* 22 (May 1969), p. 28.

industry, with a predominance of small firms; consumer reluctance to accept innovation; resistance to change from manufacturers of building components who fear new materials; and resistance from labor unions that fear a loss of jobs. Other obstacles result more directly from government policies. Builders and parts manufacturers have little incentive to develop a technology suited to mass production as long as the housing market is fragmented by separate building codes and land development controls in every local community. Some 5,000 separate jurisdictions in the United States have building codes. Many of these communities have adopted one of several national model codes or a state or county code, but typically with enough local variation so that there is little over-all uniformity. The manufacturer of a new building component or system has to design his product to meet the most stringent local requirements in whatever market he intends to enter, or he will have to produce costly variations to meet each local regulation. Code variations thus add to manufacturing cost and inhibit mass production.

Aside from lack of uniformity, many codes reflect very conservative building practice and contain requirements that are far in excess of what is needed for safety and durability. Further, most codes specify particular materials or methods rather than stating performance standards that could be met as well by newly developed building components. New materials, such as plastic piping, may not be permitted in the specifications. Widespread adoption of performance standards would encourage manufacturers to introduce new, cost-saving materials and methods.

A useful approach to these problems was tested recently in the California School Construction Systems Development program. Thirteen school districts in California agreed to merge their building programs in order to create a market large enough to stimulate the development of new school components and building systems. With foundation support, a staff was organized to devise performance standards that would meet the needs of all thirteen districts, and manufacturers were invited to bid for a contract to build twenty-two new schools. Twenty-six firms submitted bids, and five collaborating manufacturers were chosen from among them.

Industry spent over $12 million to develop the new components, many of which are now being marketed elsewhere in the country. The California school districts together offered a market of $35 million worth of construction to be awarded in a single bid. Cost estimates indicated savings of about 18 percent, as well as shorter construction time.[41]

Similar approaches can be applied to stimulate technological change in the housing industry. A series of federal advisory groups have all recommended governmental action for this purpose. The Panel on Civilian Technology, established jointly by the President's Special Assistant for Science and Technology, the Chairman of the Council of Economic Advisers, and the Secretary of Commerce, designated a sub-panel on housing which reported in 1963. This group noted the obstacles created by fragmentation in the housing industry, the proliferation of local building codes and development controls, and the lack of sufficient research and information on which to base public policies. It recommended federal support of needed research which private companies cannot be expected to finance in the near future, federal assistance for university activities in this field, and use of federal housing construction (such as military housing) as a laboratory for experiments in technological innovation. The final report pointed to precedents for this federal role:

> The Government has traditionally undertaken expensive and marginal experiments which were deemed in the national interest and which were too risky, or too central to the Nation's security, to be left to private ventures. We believe that the same technique and logic should apply in civilian technologies such as housing.[42]

[41] "Architecture by the Carload," *Architectural Forum,* 122 (April 1965), pp. 81–85; U.S. Congress, House, Hearings before a Subcommittee of the Committee on Government Operations, *The Federal Research and Development Programs: The Decision-making Process,* 89th Cong., 2nd sess., p. 114 (statement of Ezra D. Ehrenkrantz, Project Architect, School Construction Systems Development Project).

[42] U.S. Executive Office of the President, *Better Housing for the Future,* a report to the Panel on Civilian Technology, Office of

Later the Assistant Secretary of Commerce for Science and Technology, J. Herbert Holloman, established a Panel on Engineering and Commodity Standards of the Commerce Technical Advisory Board to review the broad requirements for industrial and commodity standards in the United States. This panel, chaired by Francis L. LaQue, Vice President of International Nickel Company, took up the question of building codes in reporting its findings in 1965. It concluded that a uniform national building code capable of accommodating the special needs of different regions is technically feasible at this time; and that such a code would help eliminate arbitrary restrictions that add unnecessarily to construction costs and would stimulate innovation on the part of material suppliers and builders. This panel recommended that the Department of Commerce set up a panel on building codes, in co-operation with private code development groups, to extend their own investigation and propose action toward establishing a uniform national building code.[43]

In 1966, two more advisory groups recommended public action in this field. The Advisory Commission on Intergovernmental Relations completed a detailed study of building codes and reached several familiar conclusions as well as a number that extend earlier findings. The commission found that obsolete code requirements, unnecessary diversity of codes among local jurisdictions, and inadequate administration together place unjustified burdens on the technology and economics of building; that too many building codes contain unnecessarily high standards beyond the establishment of minimum requirements for public health, safety, and welfare. The cost of adhering to excessive requirements, in the view of the commission, limits the economic range of housing that can be made available within a community. Further, the problems of code uniformity were found to be greatest in

Science and Technology, Executive Office of the President, from its Sub-panel on Housing (April 1963), p. 11.

[43] U.S. Department of Commerce, "Report to the Panel on Engineering and Commodity Standards of the Commerce Technical Advisory Board to the Assistant Secretary for Science and Technology" (Feb. 2, 1965), pp. 13–14.

metropolitan areas. The commission pointed to extensive federal involvement in building code preparation and administration—through direct construction, specifications for housing (such as FHA minimum property standards), housing guarantees, support of research and testing, and grants to local governments for preparing and enforcing building codes—but concluded that the federal government has followed no consistent path or objective toward modernization and uniformity of codes. The commission also concluded that the present state of knowledge is insufficient for preparing complete "performance codes" (codes based upon performance standards rather than specification of types of materials), and that this is a high-priority area for research.[44]

The Advisory Commission's proposals constitute a program for modernizing building codes and working toward greater uniformity. They include federal support for a co-operative public-private program to develop national performance criteria and testing procedures, establishment of a federal commission to develop a model uniform national building code (for voluntary adoption), preparation of uniform standards for all direct federal construction, and development of state model building codes.

The National Commission on Technology, Automation, and Economic Progress went further in advocating more vigorous use of federal assistance and incentives in the housing field. This commission's appraisal of the current situation recognizes the technological advances that have already been made but calls attention to their limitations:

Recent years have seen many improvements in building materials, but few in building techniques. The typical construction firm is too small to conduct its own research. While the structure of the industry provides pressure to reduce the costs of doing things the traditional way, there is little pressure for new methods. The use of power equipment in site preparation, the hoisting of materials, and improved hand tools have increased efficiency but have made no basic change in methods. Complex

[44] U.S. Advisory Commission on Intergovernmental Relations, *Building Codes: A Program for Intergovernmental Reform* (Washington: ACIR, 1966), pp. 81–82.

patterns of special interests, fragmented local governments, and lethargy perpetuate outmoded building codes which stand in the way of whatever incentives to innovation exist.[45]

The National Commission, like other advisory groups, calls for federal support for research in housing and community development, for research to establish performance criteria, for co-operative action to develop a model national code, and for experimentation in federal building activities. It goes beyond other recommendations in urging the federal government to apply the California school district approach to federally aided public housing. Where large initial markets are required to stimulate advanced production methods, the commission urges the federal government to provide them within public housing programs. Further, the commission proposes that after a model national code has been developed, the federal government should limit its housing aid, mortgage insurance, and direct construction of facilities to those localities which modernize their building regulations in line with the model code. The commission expects technological progress in housing to create a new industry and many new jobs; but in the event that new techniques cause certain crafts to suffer, the commission proposes federal subsidies for retraining, severance pay, and retirement costs for technologically displaced workers.

In 1967, President Johnson appointed two more commissions to conduct detailed studies of urban development and housing problems: the National Commission on Urban Problems, authorized in the Housing and Urban Development Act of 1965 and chaired by former Senator Paul H. Douglas; and the President's Committee on Urban Housing, chaired by Edgar F. Kaiser. Both these groups conducted fresh research and published excellent reports by the end of 1968. (The high quality of these reports, following upon that of the Kerner Commission, prompted the observation that government reports were getting better as the problems got worse.) Both these commissions took a guarded view of the pros-

[45] U.S. National Commission on Technology, Automation, and Economic Progress, p. 87.

pects for cost reduction through new technology and warned that dramatic savings are not likely in the near future. Thus they both recommend greatly increased housing subsidies for low-income families. But they both note that even limited reductions in construction cost will have significant cumulative effects amounting potentially to billions of dollars each year in the national economy. Further, dollars saved in construction also reduce other cost items based on construction, such as profits and overhead, interest on loans, and property taxes.

The Douglas Commission proposes the establishment of a National Institute of Building Sciences to formulate construction standards, test technological innovations, and provide for research, evaluation, and dissemination of information on building technology. The commission also urges the federal government to withhold water and sewer and other facility grants from communities that maintain building codes more restrictive than nationally recognized model code standards; to develop building code standards for rehabilitation housing; and to eliminate unnecessary variations in federal construction standards. It urges the states to adopt building codes and to require metropolitan areas either to conform to national model code standards or to adhere to the state code; and to strengthen state supervision over building code administration.[46]

The Kaiser Committee gave more of its attention to the problems of housing production and drew up a series of detailed proposals for reducing costs. The major elements of their strategy are to eliminate existing institutional impediments to innovation and cost reduction, promote research and development, stabilize patterns of construction, and create new institutions which a high-technology housing industry would need. They estimate that a combination of these policies might reduce monthly housing costs by at least 10 percent in the next few years.

The Kaiser Committee's specific recommendations include proposals to increase federal appropriations for housing re-

---

[46] U.S. National Commission on Urban Problems, *Building the American City* (Washington: Government Printing Office, 1968), pp. 254–272, 417–450.

search and development to $100 million a year (a tenfold increase over recent levels); to authorize the Secretary of Housing and Urban Development to exempt federally subsidized housing from restrictive state and local building codes; and to establish a semi-public Building Standards and Testing Institute which would develop national performance standards for building materials and systems, draft more uniform federal construction standards, and coordinate the testing of building products and subsystems.[47]

The various proposals for federal action range from modest research programs in support of private industry to active use of federal resources to create new markets and stimulate changes in local building controls. Virtually all the proposals presuppose the establishment of a clear and consistent federal policy to promote technological advances in the housing industry as a means of widening the market for new housing. As a first step, current federal activities in housing and construction should be aligned in support of such a policy. Federal agencies responsible for direct construction of housing, for example, should develop a uniform set of performance standards for their own projects.

To make a significant impact on the housing industry, the federal government will clearly have to go far beyond putting its own house in order. Studies, code development, and experimentation will have to be supplemented by the use of federal incentives that can offset some of the deep-seated resistance to change within the housing industry and within local government. New markets created with federal assistance may be able to stimulate private investments in new housing systems and components. Creating markets beyond government-built housing, however, does mean achieving greater uniformity in building and land development regulations, and here the obstacles are considerable. Many local building codes contain provisions that are not designed to help consumers of housing, but rather to protect manufacturers of particular

[47] U.S. President's Committee on Urban Housing, *A Decent Home* (Washington: Government Printing Office, 1968), pp. 187–205.

components or craftsmen with particular skills.[48] Further, local building codes and land development controls often reflect deliberate policies to limit the volume of new housing by raising its cost. This situation is particularly true in the suburbs of metropolitan areas, and it seems to be more widespread in zoning and subdivision controls than in building codes. For the creation of a mass market, greater consistency is needed in all these development controls.

Local resistance to new housing is a growing threat to national goals that stress support of urban development and a high volume of residential construction. Much of this resistance is a result of local tax considerations. New low- and moderate-cost housing brings with it demands for new local services—particularly schools—that typically cost more than the amount of local property tax produced by the new housing. For suburban governments coping with tax increases to pay for new schools and other service increases resulting from sudden population growth, preferred development strategies usually favor some mixture of luxury housing, "clean" industry, and shopping centers—all of which tend to yield more in local taxes than they cost the local community to service. "Fiscal zoning"—requiring large minimum lot sizes for new housing in order to discourage low-cost subdivisions—is one means to this end. Excessive subdivision requirements and building code provisions also add to the cost of whatever housing may be built, thus slowing the rate of new development and improving the prospects for high assessed valuations. In addition to the tax motives, local policies to discourage development often reflect determination to exclude unwanted people—principally those with low status, low income, or black skin.[49]

To overcome these complex sources of resistance, several measures are needed that have little to do with building code

[48] U.S. Advisory Commission on Intergovernmental Relations, *Building Codes*, p. 7; Martin Meyerson, Barbara Terrett, and William L. C. Wheaton, *Housing, People, and Cities* (New York: McGraw-Hill, 1962), pp. 130–131.

[49] See Bernard J. Frieden, "Toward Equality of Urban Opportunity," pp. 323–324.

reform directly, but represent other facets of federal urban policy. One important strategy consists of reducing local reliance on the property tax to pay for service costs. The growth of federal and state aid to local communities has worked in this direction and will undoubtedly continue, whether through a plan for federal revenue-sharing with states and local governments or through further growth of grant-in-aid programs. Another approach involves metropolitan-wide consideration of development controls, such as review of local regulations by metropolitan planning councils. A combination of local interest and state and federal policy has been instrumental in establishing metropolitan planning agencies in most metropolitan areas of the country. Federal policy in this area can be extended to strengthen the role of metropolitan planning agencies and of state government in working toward more uniform development controls and high levels of new housing construction.[50]

Two new programs illustrate the more direct use of federal incentives to encourage code reform. The model cities program makes available a wide variety of federal aids for city development projects that meet a number of special criteria. A project is eligible for assistance only if local laws and regulations are consistent with the objectives of the program, and the Secretary of Housing and Urban Development is directed to encourage "maximum possible use of new and improved technology and design, including cost reduction techniques." Among the objectives of the program, with which local regulations are to be consistent, is the provision of "a substantial increase in the supply of standard housing of low and moderate cost."

Similarly, federal grants to assist planned metropolitan development (authorized in the Demonstration Cities and Metropolitan Development Act of 1966 but not yet funded)

[50] See Joint Center for Urban Studies of the Massachusetts Institute of Technology and Harvard University, *The Effectiveness of Metropolitan Planning*, prepared in cooperation with the Subcommittee on Intergovernmental Relations, Committee on Government Operations, U.S. Senate (Washington: Government Printing Office, 1964), especially pp. 99–123.

are limited to projects that meet specific objectives related to metropolitan planning. The Secretary of HUD is to give special consideration to whether the local government applying for aid is conforming to metropolitan planning through "the establishment and consistent administration of zoning codes, subdivision regulations, and similar land-use and density controls."

Other federal initiatives have begun in the past few years, although none has yet been carried very far. In 1968, the Department of Housing and Urban Development began an "in-city experimental housing program," a series of experiments planned to make use of new construction methods for low-income housing in twenty cities. Whether the Nixon administration will carry this program forward appears problematical at present. An amendment to the Housing and Urban Development Act of 1968 introduced by Senator Proxmire directs the Secretary of Housing and Urban Development to conduct a series of tests of new housing technologies in projects to be built on federal land or on local sites where building regulations permit experimental construction methods. Federal mortgage insurance is made available for these projects, and each one is to aim at production of at least a thousand units a year for five years. Finally, Secretary Romney has given considerable emphasis in his public statements to the need for improving construction technology. He has begun to organize "operation breakthrough," which will attempt to create a unified market for new low-income housing units in a number of cities where experimental building systems may be tested.

Despite these examples, however, measures to promote technological innovation in housing have generally been neglected as an area of federal action, and increased attention is clearly warranted. It is possible, however, that the payoff may come in terms of better housing rather than cheaper housing. Conceivably the building industry will focus on innovations to provide more space, equipment, or flexibility at present prices rather than cost-saving techniques that will enable more low- and moderate-income families to enter the market. If this is the case, middle- and upper-income families may enter the new housing market on a larger scale, giving up the houses where they are now living in favor of a superior product. The results would benefit national housing goals by providing for additional turnover of existing housing, but might fail to supplement the turnover approach and to offset its shortcomings. Careful monitoring of public policy will be necessary to assure that some effort, at least, goes into cost reduction. The difficulties standing in the way of technological change in housing, and the possibility that such change may not reduce costs significantly, both argue for continued development of other strategies for meeting national housing needs.

2. Improving the turnover process

The turnover process itself would produce fewer objectionable by-products if it enabled more poor people to move into a wider variety of existing housing, including older housing in the suburbs. With about a fifth of American families moving every year, a large supply of existing housing becomes available for occupancy. The problem is to get a larger share of this housing for people whose choices are now very limited, principally Negroes and low-income families.

Eliminating racial discrimination in the sale and rental of housing would contribute measurably toward improving living conditions for Negroes as well as countering the patterns of segregation that now result from the turnover process. Because black people are not free to move throughout urban areas, they are unable to take full advantage of vacancies that would meet their pressing housing needs. Racial segregation between suburbs and central cities has attracted a great deal of attention, but Negroes are also segregated *within* central cities. The sound housing that becomes available in white neighborhoods often makes no contribution to solving the housing problems of black families who live in the ghettos. Further, many Negroes who can afford used suburban housing are kept out of the suburbs by discriminatory practices.[51]

[51] For an analysis of potential Negro housing demand at middle-income levels, see U.S. Housing and Home Finance Agency, *Potential Housing Demands of Non-White Population in Selected Metropolitan Areas* (Washington: HHFA, Office of the Administrator, 1962).

Both public and private activities have developed to combat housing discrimination. Government approaches have involved federal action to prohibit discrimination in the sale or rental of federally aided housing, a number of state and local laws to prohibit discrimination in private housing, and the federal Civil Rights Act of 1968, which will apply to most private housing by 1970. The coverage of these laws and federal policies together still leaves certain gaps, but the major problem is implementation. Enforcement of the open housing provisions of the 1968 civil rights law, assigned to the Department of Housing and Urban Development, has been crippled by scanty appropriations for staff and other costs. Even in the case of federally aided housing covered since 1962 by President Kennedy's executive order "Equal Opportunity in Housing," federal agencies responsible for enforcement have failed to adopt effective procedures.[52]

The most important missing ingredient needed to allow equal access to housing is governmental will to enforce laws, hire sufficient staff, and mount affirmative programs that do more than respond to complaints. More serious government action is long overdue in this field, but in addition there is much to be said for joining together public and private efforts.

Private groups have played a major role in stimulating government action, and they have also worked directly at the local level. Citizen organizations and private developers have sponsored housing planned for racially mixed occupancy from the outset. Neighborhood associations have worked to prevent panic selling and to stabilize areas of racial transition. More than a thousand local fair-housing organizations have been established to find homes for black families in white neighborhoods on an individual basis. Though these groups have focused mainly on helping middle-income Negroes, there is growing evidence that a broadening of their strategy to include families with somewhat lower incomes might yield

---

[52] See Richard and Diane Margolis, *How the Federal Government Builds Ghettos* (New York: National Committee Against Discrimination in Housing, 1967), p. 27.

more impressive results.[53] In addition, governmental support for these private efforts—such as staff assistance—should be considered. Greater co-operation between public and private agencies can be particularly important in making fair housing laws more effective. Private organizations have been able to test whether real estate brokers comply with state laws against discrimination and to furnish public agencies with the evidence they need to enforce the laws. Government measures can strengthen the work of private groups by providing a needed context of public policy and leadership, while private groups can often operate more effectively in sensitive local situations.

The importance of ending racially restrictive practices in housing has become clouded by conflicting views of how to achieve racial equality. Militant black separatism has shaken the civil rights consensus of the early 1960's, which stressed racial integration. Separatists as well as others committed to racial equality have given first priority to the development of racial pride and solidarity, the improvement of existing ghettos, and the building of large black voting blocs in the core cities—all of which seem threatened by attempts to help Negroes break out of segregated neighborhoods.

There is less in this conflict than meets the eye. First, the rapid growth of Negro population in northern urban areas will continue for some time and will create constant demands for more living space. If existing ghettos had to contain all Negro population growth, their physical plant and services— already inadequate—would deteriorate still further under the pressure. Present plans to rebuild black communities with improved housing, new schools, industrial centers, and recreation areas would fail in the face of new and divisive conflict over limited space. Thus programs to help some Negroes move out of the ghettos ought to be seen as complementary

---

[53] See George B. Nesbitt and Elfriede Hoeber, "The Fair Housing Committee: Its Need for a New Perspective," *Land Economics,* 41 (May 1965), pp. 97–110; and George and Eunice Grier, *Equality and Beyond: Housing Segregation and the Goals of the Great Society* (Chicago: Quadrangle Books, 1966), pp. 68–82.

to plans for improving living conditions there, and not as a contradictory alternative.

Further, many Negroes want to move out of segregated neighborhoods, as indicated both by attitudes and by actual moves in the recent past. An indication of attitudes emerged from the extensive opinion survey in fifteen cities sponsored by the Kerner Commission in early 1968. Negroes in the sample were asked: "Would you personally prefer to live in a neighborhood with all Negroes, mostly Negroes, mostly whites, or a neighborhood that is mixed half and half?" Nearly half—48 percent—said they preferred a neighborhood mixed half and half; 37 percent said it makes no difference; only 8 percent said they preferred an all-Negro neighborhood and another 5 percent said "mostly Negro."[54]

Negroes have also been expressing their preferences by "voting with their feet." Several of the older black communities—Harlem, Hough, and Watts—have been losing population. Many others are continuing to grow, but at a slower rate than would be the case without substantial outmigration. In northern urban areas, most of this movement is to other neighborhoods in the central city. Even in the suburbs, however, the numerical increase of Negro population has been substantial although it is very small in comparison with growth in the central cities. Between 1950 and 1960, Negro population in the suburbs of metropolitan areas grew by an average of 60,000 people per year. On the basis of 1950–1960 population trends, projections prepared for the Douglas Commission indicate that this figure may rise to an average of 160,000 people per year in the period 1960–1985.[55] (Current estimates made since 1960 have fluctuated widely, but they suggest that the Negro suburban growth average from

[54] U.S. National Advisory Commission on Civil Disorders, *Supplemental Studies* (Washington: Government Printing Office, 1968), p. 15.

[55] Patricia Leavey Hodge and Philip M. Hauser, *The Challenge of America's Metropolitan Population Outlook—1960 to 1985* (Washington: U.S. National Commission on Urban Problems, Research Report no. 3, 1968), p. 26.

960–1968 may be as high as 100,000 people per year.[56])

Projections do not necessarily come true, and these in particular may depend upon deliberate action to open the suburbs to more Negro families. The most important message of these projections and of recent movement patterns is that there will be continuing pressure for access to housing in predominantly white neighborhoods, both in the central cities and in the suburbs. This pressure will result from the growth of black population and from the choices of people who want to move out of presently segregated areas. The freedom to make this choice is an important right which should be upheld by government. Commitment to freedom of residential choice in no way minimizes the need for improving the ghettos, however; they, too, should become communities of choice, not areas of forced segregation.

So far this discussion has focused on making the turnover process more effective for people who can afford to pay their own way in the housing market but are blocked by discrimination. For low-income families, the major obstacle to more effective use of the turnover process is the price of older housing in good condition. Existing houses could be a valuable resource for poor families if moderate subsidies were available and if these subsidies allowed them freedom to choose where they live. Federal subsidy programs, however, have generally been directed to newly built housing and they have been difficult to use in the suburbs. Recent policy changes have begun to make federal housing subsidies more flexible, but there is still a long way to go.

Federal aid for low-income public housing, which used to mean large housing projects, has been broadened to include units in existing buildings as well as new developments. Local housing authorities are authorized to buy (and rehabilitate) older housing or to lease individual units for low-income families. Rent supplements, a more flexible form of subsidy,

[56] U.S. Bureau of the Census, *Current Population Reports,* series P-20, no. 181, "Population Characteristics," (1969), p. 1; and U.S. Bureau of the Census, *Current Population Reports,* series P-23, no. 27, "Trends in Social and Economic Conditions in Metropolitan Areas," (1969), p. 2.

make it possible for low-income families to live in privat developments, either newly constructed or renovated, unde nonprofit, limited dividend, or co-operative sponsorship. Al though these programs have made a start at using existin housing, they are still concerned mainly with new construc tion. Further, they both rely on local government action—t establish a housing authority and approve its plans, or to mee certain federal requirements placed on local government t establish community eligibility for rent supplements. As a re sult, suburban governments that want to keep out low-incom people can easily block the use of these programs.

Subjecting housing subsidies to what amounts to a loca government veto has in fact established another formidabl obstacle keeping low-income families out of the more affluer suburbs. Critics of housing policy have suggested several way of removing or minimizing this obstacle. The Douglas Com mission has proposed eliminating requirements for local gov ernment action in connection with the rent supplement prc gram and has also recommended that the states authorize loca housing authorities to lease housing anywhere in the metro politan area, subject to certain limitations. The U.S. Cor ference of Mayors has urged a more forceful use of federa influence to open the suburbs to low-income housing. A res olution adopted at the mayors' 1966 annual conference cal on Congress to make all federal grants for water and sewe systems, open space, and other community facilities contir gent upon a local agreement to provide a "reasonable share of the low- and middle-income housing in the area.[57]

Two major new subsidy programs authorized in the Hous ing and Urban Development Act of 1968 are designed to re move this obstacle by operating without requiring any explic involvement of local government. The new programs for low income home ownership (section 235) and low-incom rental housing (section 236) follow the pattern of other mort gage assistance programs rather than that of earlier low income subsidy programs. A private developer—not a loca government agency—is the agent for producing housing. Th

[57] "U.S. Told Suburbs Must Help Cities," the New York Time. June 16, 1966, p. 1.

developer (normally a non-profit or limited-dividend sponsor) makes his financial arrangements with a lending institution and with the FHA, and builds or renovates housing for low-income buyers or tenants. The federal government then makes subsidy payments on behalf of the low-income residents to the mortgage lender, within certain statutory limits. No local government approval is needed, other than the same review given to any new development for compliance with zoning and building regulations. Although there are still possibilities for local government harassment by means of extra-stringent building inspections, these new programs promise to go a long way toward taking subsidized housing out of local politics and treating it instead as part of normal housing market operations.

The new program for home ownership also offers another significant option to low-income families. Most federal subsidy programs in the past offered tenancy but not ownership to the poor. Yet it is clear that many families at all income levels want to own their homes, and it is also clear that owner-occupancy generally means better maintenance. In the 1950's, rates of renovation were greater in owner-occupied properties than in rental units. In 1960, a substantially higher proportion of low-income *owners* lived in sound housing than low-income *tenants*. Further, it has commonly been found that rental property, as well, is kept in better condition if the owner lives in the same building than if he is an absentee landlord.[58] Subsidy programs that promote home ownership thus hold the prospect of increased satisfaction for new owners and their tenants, as well.

Even the new programs, however, have built-in rigidities that will prevent them from making full use of turnover housing. Both the ownership and rental programs are designed mainly for the production of new housing. In the case of ownership subsidies, the 1968 legislation sets specific limits on how much aid can go for existing housing: not more than 25 percent of appropriations in the first year, declining to not more than 10 percent by the third year. This restriction will have the effect of pricing most housing in the program

[58] See George Sternlieb, *The Tenement Landlord*.

beyond the reach of families with very low incomes, even after maximum-assistance payments authorized by the law are supplied. In many cities, the supply of older vacant housing is increasing, and much of this housing can be put in sound condition at a far lower cost than that of new construction. A number of private non-profit organizations have been operating small-scale programs to help low-income families renovate and buy this housing, most notably the Bicentennial Civic Improvement Corporation in St. Louis.[59] These pilot programs have demonstrated the feasibility and desirability of home ownership as an option for low-income families. Their success helped build the case for a federal home ownership program; but the federal law now rules out more widespread use of the same housing supply that has made it possible for the poor to afford the costs of ownership.

This feature of the new federal program has been prompted by the same rationale that ties subsidies to new housing production in almost all federal programs. As long as there is little good housing vacant and available at moderate cost, subsidies to low-income families for existing housing may do little more than inflate its cost. This is a reasonable fear, borne out by experience with families on welfare whose housing allowances often prop up the cost of the slums where they live. While the shortage of vacant housing in low or moderate price ranges does persist nationally, it is not uniform from city to city or over time. Substantial numbers of vacancies and even abandonments have been occurring in the old neighborhoods of several cities.[60] This housing could be a valuable resource for poor families who want to become homeowners or want to live in areas where it is located. What is needed is a federal policy that will recognize local variations in housing supply and individual choices, and will allow subsidies for existing housing where it is appropriate.

[59] See Bernard J. Frieden and JoAnn Newman, "Home-ownership for the Poor," *Trans-action*, forthcoming.

[60] See Charles Abrams, "Housing Policy—1937–1967," in Bernard J. Frieden and William W. Nash, Jr., eds., *Shaping an Urban Future: Essays in Memory of Catherine Bauer Wurster* (Cambridge, Mass.: M.I.T. Press, 1969), pp. 35–45.

3. Subsidizing new housing

In principle, the fastest and surest way of providing decent housing for every family would be to subsidize a large volume of new housing directly for the poor. This strategy would eliminate the delays and uncertainties of waiting for the turn-over process to produce vacancies. It could also forestall many of the urban problems resulting from the turnover process, provided that new housing for the poor were distributed broadly throughout urban areas as is new housing for other people.

Federal aid for new low-income housing began in the 1930's, but actual production has always been small. The largest and oldest federal program, low-rent public housing, was authorized in 1937, and by 1967 had produced some 635,000 units. This number must be compared with the 8.5 million families still living in substandard housing (by conservative definition) in 1960. It is a disappointing performance even in comparison with past congressional authorizations: the Housing Act of 1949 authorized construction of 810,000 public housing units in the next six years alone. In the mid-1960's, all the major federal subsidy programs together—public housing, moderate-income housing, rent supplements, and housing for the elderly—were providing some 50,000 new units a year. In 1968, the last year of the Johnson administration, a special effort to increase production succeeded in starting about 120,000 new units under these programs.

Not only has the volume of this housing been too small to accelerate national housing progress significantly, but subsidized housing has been concentrated disproportionately in the central cities. As of 1967, nearly half of all low-rent public housing in the country (47 percent) was located in 51 major cities with populations over 250,000. (These same cities contained 34 percent of the country's urban population in 1960.) The reasons have already been noted: public housing and other subsidy programs until 1968 were subject to a local government veto which was exercised freely in the suburbs.

The new federal programs enacted in 1968 can help open the suburbs to more low-income families. The landmark 1968 act also authorizes a dramatic increase in the production of subsidized housing. President Johnson's 1968 message on housing and cities proposed a new goal of six million subsidized units in the next ten years, an output sufficient to rehouse all the families then estimated to be living in substandard housing. The act itself includes authorizations to fund 1.5 million units in the first three years (950,000 in the new ownership and rental programs, plus 375,000 public housing units and 209,000 units covered by rent supplements).

When the time comes to make actual appropriations, Congress has shown a great reluctance to put its money where its authorizations are. For the first year under the 1968 act, Congress appropriated only a third of what it had authorized for the new ownership and rental programs, and less than half of what it had authorized for rent supplements. In early 1969, deep cuts in housing budget requests once again seemed all too likely. In the years ahead, the promising machinery established in 1968 will do very little to solve the country's housing problems unless much greater appropriations are forthcoming.

Another way of accelerating new housing production for low-income families could be through a program to encourage the development of entire new communities on open land at the edge of built-up urban areas. A limited federal program to insure mortgages for the development of new communities was enacted in 1966 and a more important form of aid —debenture guarantees—was authorized in the 1968 law. New communities could offer opportunities to build low-income housing on vacant land, in desirable surroundings, and with a high level of services.

The federal program, however, gives relatively little emphasis to housing for the poor as a component of new communities. The 1968 law states only that the Secretary of Housing and Urban Development shall determine that the new community's development plan "will include a proper balance of housing for families of low and moderate income." The major federal purposes seem to be to counter the trend toward scattered suburban growth, rationalize the use of land for urban development, and assure provision of adequate public services. Former Secretary of HUD Robert Weaver, speaking outside his official role, minimized the possibility of using

ederally aided new communities to provide new housing
or the poor and for Negroes:

> Although I am a firm and long-time advocate of open oc-
> cupancy and economic diversification in housing and have
> repeatedly emphasized the importance of such patterns in
> suburbia, I cannot delude myself into the belief that new com-
> munities will be a principal or the exclusive means of achiev-
> ing these objectives . . . For one thing, the new communities
> will not be numerous enough. For another, many private
> sponsors of new communities are sufficiently affluent to ob-
> tain financing from conventional sources which are not sub-
> ject to federal standards.[61]

The most significant study of privately built new communities
in the United States more than confirms Dr. Weaver's views,
and concludes that these communities are not likely to differ
much from typical new suburbs in their social composition.[62]

That the federal program is intended mainly to build better
communities for middle-income families has been clear
enough to its critics. Big-city mayors have opposed it precisely because it promises to strengthen and extend the patterns of racial and economic segregation that result from current housing policies. Though the mayors have a vested
interest in wanting to slow the movement of middle-income
groups to the suburbs, their views make sense from the standpoint of national housing goals as well. The U.S. Conference
of Mayors and the National League of Cities have urged
Congress to oppose new communities legislation until it is
established that "the program would not discriminate against
older central cities and would not promote further economic
and social disparities between central cities and new growth
areas."[63]

[61] Robert C. Weaver, *Dilemmas of Urban America* (Cambridge,
Mass.: Harvard University Press, 1965), pp. 29–30.

[62] Edward P. Eichler and Marshall Kaplan, *The Community
Builders* (Berkeley and Los Angeles: University of California
Press, 1967).

[63] U.S. Congress, House, Committee on Banking and Currency,
Subcommittee on Housing, *Hearings, Demonstration Cities,* p. 200.

A revised program to promote new community develop
ment could conceivably serve as a useful supplement t
present housing policies. Clear social purposes will have t
be defined for these communities, with high priority for low
income housing. If the developers of new communities ar
unwilling to include housing for low-income groups, as D
Weaver implied, the program will have to be reshaped t
provide either stronger incentives for private sponsors or som
means of increased public involvement.

Future Policy Issues

All the strategies discussed here will involve greater nationa
commitment to meeting housing needs. Accelerating techno
logical change in the housing industry, equalizing access t
housing markets, or mounting new and bigger programs wil
be impossible without increased political support. Building thi
support will require a great deal of work to clarify the natur
and consequences of present policies and to propose and de
bate alternatives. The distribution of housing subsidies, fo
example, is not well understood. Many middle-income voter
oppose aid for low-income housing because they consider it
unique and unwarranted subsidy for the poor. Few peopl
take special note of the enormous federal housing subsidie
given to middle-income groups by means of income-ta:
deductions on mortgage interest payments. In reality, th
situation has been well described as "socialism for the rich
free enterprise for the poor." Middle- and upper-incom
groups receive much greater housing subsidies than the poo
but in forms that seldom attract public attention.[64]

Evaluating present policies is important, but the majo
challenge to housing analysts and political leaders is to revis
these policies to deal with changing problems. Several issue
need special attention to lay the groundwork for new policies
First, the overly simple and outmoded housing standards no
in use need to be replaced. Housing progress in the futur

[64] Alvin L. Schorr, "National Community and Housing Policy,"
Social Service Review, 39 (December 1965), 433–443.

hould be judged by more than criteria of physical shelter. Freedom of residential choice, opportunities for ownership, and access to good neighborhood facilities, jobs, schools, and services are equally important. Further, housing problems are becoming less a matter of meeting standards that remain stable over long periods of time. We are dealing with a gap between living conditions of the poor and those of the rest of society, and we need to know whether this gap is closing or becoming wider.

Housing policies should also be related more closely to economic and community development goals. Housing programs ought to be considered not only from the point of view of their end-products, but also of their conduct and operation. In particular, more attention should be given to opening economic opportunities in housing to the poor (jobs in construction, real estate, property management, and maintenance) and to involving residents in decision making and control. If these goals turn out to conflict with the need for increased production, policies will have to be adjusted to make reasonable compromises.

Finally, the nature of housing subsidies needs close review. The continued improvement of American housing is likely to mean continuing cost pressure on low-income families. Even if technological developments hold down construction costs, subsidies will continue to be needed if the poor are to have decent housing. Many of the problems with present housing programs, however, can be traced to the way in which subsidies are handled—through the supplier of housing, not the consumer, and sometimes with local government participation required. An important object of future housing policy should be to minimize the extent to which low-income families are restricted by the subsidies they receive. As housing market conditions change, it may be possible to relate subsidy programs more closely to income policies instead of tying them to the production of new housing. Improved income policies may make it possible eventually to solve the housing problems of the poor by a combination of adequate incomes, an adequate and diversified housing supply, and equal access for all families to the housing market.

DESIGN AND URBAN BEAUTY IN THE CENTRAL CITY

John Burchard

"Urban design, architecture, and landscape architecture are
inescapable; they are the only arts that cannot be avoided.
People can insulate themselves from painting, sculpture, lit-
erature, music, the dance. But they cannot avoid exposure
to the design of buildings and open spaces or to the occasional
but growing number of examples of urban design; the design
of combinations of buildings and spaces."[1]

"Since urban design, architecture, and landscape architecture are the only arts that cannot be avoided, they have a
uniquely *public* character. They ought, in consequence, to be
the special concern of all public-spirited people whether they
guide the decisions of business, institutions, or government.

[1] Martin Meyerson, *et al.*, *Face of the Metropolis* (New York:
Random House, 1963), p. 7. This book should be used as a *vade
mecum* for this essay. It has the most comprehensive collection of
photographs and intelligent comment about them of any work
available today on the subject of urban design. And although the
urban world changes rapidly, it is still not out of date.

It is upon an alliance between good taste and public-spirited leadership that the future of urban design depends."[2]

Urban design can aim at other things but as discussed in this essay its aim is beauty.

What Is Urban Beauty?

"Beauty" is, unhappily, a slippery word. The philosophers will tell you almost anything you want to hear—you have only to choose the right one. But if beauty is to be found in efficient conduct of practical operations, that is not what this essay is about. If beauty is to be found in the good and moral life, that is not what this essay is about. If beauty needs to be put in a straightjacket of definition, that is not what this essay is about. It will not help us much, either, to fall back on Keats's poetic restatement of Socratic aspirations, "beauty is truth, truth beauty." That is not all we need to know.

If the tests of pragmatism, of operationalism, of ethics and morality are not to be applied, what possible tests remain?

There is the test of "essence." In some ways it is the only one that can be applied to the totality of an urban esthetic. Great cities *do* have great flavor, and the flavor of each is unmistakable. It is quite impossible to confuse Istanbul with Rome or Paris or London or New York or San Francisco. The only difficulty with the standard of essence as a guide to design is that these totalities have not been designed. They are rather the consequence of the accumulation of components, usually over a long history. Some of the details have been designed; others have just been happy accidents. Having met with general approval the latter were not allowed to wither. And so each city took its tone.

A city with essence naturally has some stake in preserving it. There are risks in this. What are the essential and delightful elements of the essence? Which people have found what essential or delightful and on what authority? When does nostalgia become absurd? We are plunged at once into the conflict between the preservationists and the modernists, the antiquarians and the destroyers. Happy the city, no doubt, where the past offers much that is really worthy of the solicitude of its guardians. But if the preservationists were to win every issue they would end by making their city into a morgue, or at best a museum. The real life of Venice *for Venetians* is no longer in the Piazza San Marco but in bustling Mestre; the tourists may like gondolas but citizens find motor boats more convenient.

Moreover, few cities and especially few American cities have as much worth preserving as Venice has. San Franciscans would do better not to flutter and preen themselves every time an undistinguished house that belonged to an unknown sea captain is temporarily spared the wrecker's ball. Boston did well, in the end, to stop worrying about a building in which *The Liberator* may once have been printed, but it was not hard, for Boston has genuine antiques to preserve. A city that tries to keep too green the memory of too many Kilroys will also fail to be a city with a live and contemporary beauty.

Thus the problem of what to save and why is a thorny one. The great cities of the world are those in which constant and tempered change is going on. There are things worth saving from the past for three quite different reasons. (1) Their beauty may be absolute and beyond challenge even if they have no present utility; the Taj Mahal is an example.[3] (2) Beautiful or not, they may have been the home of a truly historic event of which it is wise to keep reminders; Independence Hall is a good example, bedrooms in which people may or may not have slept are not.[4] (3) Though

[3] The white marble mausoleum built by the Shah Jahan in Agra for the interment of his beloved consort Mumtaz Mahal (1592–1631). Jahan planned a facing one of black marble for his own remains but it was never completed. In the end, thanks to the frugality and puritanism of his son Aurangzeb, who was more interested in mosques than in mausolea, Jahan was stuffed in with Mumtaz when he died 27 years later. A warning to those who postpone achievement!

[4] Independence Hall, Philadelphia, 1732. The events were major in American history, the building a handsome and moving one of

having grace and historical merit of a slighter degree, they may yet be convertible into some presently useful purpose of a different sort; Castello Sforzesca in Milan is a fine specimen.[5] These tests can be applied with reasonable objectivity. If any one of them is satisfied then the preservationists should not be run over by "progress." Use of such tests would never threaten the destruction of the genuine landmarks of any historically important or historically beautiful city. They would, for example, have saved the Larkin Building in Buffalo[6] and at least the cage of the Pennsylvania Railroad Station in New York,[7] but not the Metropolitan Opera House in the same city or the Palace of the Fine Arts in San Francisco.[8] Cities with little history should be worrying about their role in future history and not busily engaged in inventing an important past. A hole in a wall that *may* have been made by one of Wild Bill Hickok's bullets is little more than a hole in a wall.

A long debate can obviously be opened on the matter of when to preserve and when not to. It is an important issue but not the most important issue and must be left here with

---

its time, though rather small. It is hurt today by the scale of the urban buildings around it and especially by an overly gigantic mall recently created by over-zealous designers.

[5] The conversion effected in 1956 by Peressutti, Belgiojoso and Rogers is a brilliant one, preserving the appearance and meaning of the militant old fortified castle and yet serving the new galleries and their distinguished collections very well.

[6] The Larkin Building, 1904, was one of the great and prophetic buildings of Frank Lloyd Wright and deserved to be an historical monument.

[7] Built in 1906–1910 by McKim, Mead and White.

[8] Completed as part of the Panama Pacific Exposition of 1915. This quite conventional piece of exposition architecture of another day and in the manner of Piranesi became important only because its architect, Bernard Maybeck, a beloved and often usefully influential man (Berkeley campus), was a leading symbol of the claims the people of the Bay Area were making for a place on architectural Olympus. Maybeck himself had more sense and thought it ought to be torn down. The restorers still have a building in search of a user, at a cost that could have provided San Francisco with the great plan it lacks.

the notation that cities with any history should probably have a skilled Historical Monuments Commission, should finance approved restorations, and should not be swayed by the enthusiasm of amateurs, who generally want to save everything.

But not many cities anywhere, and certainly very few large American cities (not over a dozen at most), have a positive essence that can somehow be preserved. Essence, on the other hand, is very hard to design from scratch. They are finding this out in Chandigarh and Brasilia, where unplanned areas have a perverse way of being more interesting if not more beautiful than the planned. But exclusively governmental cities can sometimes achieve an instant character, sprung full-panoplied where almost no other kind can.[9]

If essence cannot be the test of design for urban beauty, we are left only with hedonism. There is nothing disgraceful or sinful about hedonism save for those who believe that man was created to mourn. The only difficulty is that we have to ask, whose hedonism? It cannot be the hedonism of the experts alone because they cannot always agree even about individual buildings. Elite consensus will be a little less capricious than one might imagine but nonetheless it is not authoritative enough in a democracy to permit us to dismiss everything it rejects. General consensus is almost certainly even less reliable. There must be a vast number of Americans who feel no active reaction of discomfort or displeasure as they use one of our strips of filling stations; fourth-rate supermarkets; used-car lots; hot dog, shrimp, and doughnut stands; inferior motels; and other ugly examples of the degree to which frail and inexpert but quite uninhibited retail business can degrade the vision of the city. If there were any active

[9] Whether the character is desirable is moot. The great capital cities have been places like London, Paris, Rome, Vienna, where other kinds of life were as important as the political. Canberra, Ottawa, Washington, and no doubt the new ones are a consequence of monumental building, the housing of hordes of civil servants, and a sterile cultural life where the political gossip transcends everything else in interest and where the governors are more or less shielded from the pulse of the people.

dislike amounting to a consensus, obviously these things could not endure.

Moments of great urban beauty have often, indeed usually, been achieved by dictatorial decisions. These produced the square of St. Peter's in Rome;[10] the Place de la Concorde and the Rue de Rivoli in Paris;[11] the Place Stanislas in Nancy.[12] These were situations in which an autocrat with taste found an architect of genius to match his desires and a great collaboration of client and artist ensued. The democratic substitute for this is not easy to find.

It would be dangerous to trust the decisions of even thoroughly respectable groups whose primary missions and skills lie elsewhere, whether they be the PTA or NAACP, the DAR or the American Legion, the NAM or the CIO; the justices of the United States Supreme Court might be no wiser. Even the consensus of the most relevant professional societies would almost by their nature be too conservative. Least of all can esthetic decisions be trusted to the United States Congress.[13] It is a puzzlement.

In the meantime a philosophy of hedonism drives us inexorably to the conclusion that a beautiful city, in a democracy at any rate, must have a variety of beauties appealing to a variety of tastes. It should not eschew monumentality because some liberals fear its symbolism. It should not tear down

[10] Particularly under Pope Alexander VII and the baroque genius, Giovanni Lorenzo Bernini (1598–1680).

[11] Commissioned by Louis XV and executed by Jacques Ange Gabriel in 1755.

[12] Commissioned by Stanislaw Leszczynski, Duc de Lorraine, and laid out by Here de Corny in 1753.

[13] This statement hardly needs documentation, especially in so far as the Congress is concerned. Witness, for example, the absurd hearings concerning the Air Force Academy and especially its chapel. Reflect on how the winners of the Smithsonian and the Franklin D. Roosevelt Memorial competitions were swept under the rug. Observe how the Congress, under the lash of such connoisseurs as the late Sam Rayburn and his successors, has supported nonarchitect George Steuart (who none the less is called Architect of the Capitol) in his expensive desecrations of a dignified and important piece of American architectural history.

its Broadways or North Wells Street in Chicago because some thin-nosed people find them vulgar. It needs beauties of large size and beauties of small size, noisy beauties and quiet beauties, refined beauties and vulgar beauties. Jane Jacobs likes Madison Avenue because she finds action and "life" in the shop windows there and she thinks Park Avenue is "dead." That does not mean that Park Avenue should be at once converted into Madison Avenue. There are other equally able people in New York, even in Greenwich Village, with quite different views.[14] Great cities have in fact offered great contrasts of beauty from the monumental to the intimate, from the classic to the romantic, from the urban to the bucolic, although the essence of any given city may be slanted one way or another. Paris, probably still the most beautiful of all, has great variety. It is fortunate that this diversity of components is an advantage; without it, it might be hard to accomplish anything. For components can be designed and can be preserved or changed and so improvement is possible. Also fine components can and need to be beautifully articulated with one another. This is a second element of urban design for beauty that is within the bounds of feasibility. To go beyond this, to seek a master plan for the total urban esthetic is to soar too near the sun.

The "Value" and the Price of Urban Beauty

The plain fact is that beauty and economy are not synonymous and that no urban beauty comes free.

It costs money to refrain from desecrating a coast or a river bank or a hillside, and a developer's private interests may too often appear to be consonant with the public interest in increasing tax revenues. It costs less, in the beginning anyway, to dump garbage in a harbor or on a piece of idle land than

---

[14] Jane Jacobs, *Death and Life of Great American Cities* (New York: Random House, 1961). This entertaining expression of a point of view had a transitory acclaim. But it is so personal and so erroneous as not to be included in the brief bibliography of this essay.

to dispose of it efficiently and cleanly. A town may lose some immediate advantage if it does not make some land out of an adjacent lake or harbor. A sand dunes park may seem an ideal location for a new and needed steel mill and other locations may be more costly; but the dunes may be irreplaceable. More people, measured in numbers, will benefit from electricity supplied by new Grand Canyon dams than will be deprived of the erstwhile beauties of the undrowned or undried-up river bottom. It is going to cost someone, probably all of us through the federal government, something of the order of an additional $50 million to take a freeway through a tunnel under a picturesque and modestly historical piece of Monterey, California. It costs more to plant a tree than not to plant it, to tend it than not to tend it, to cause flowers to grow in a bank or post office. At the other extreme, magnificent buildings cost a great deal more than merely workable ones. Each and every one of these additional costs can be calculated and demonstrated by any half-way competent accountant. The liability column is easily verified. Unhappily, the same thing cannot be said of the asset column. What is the monetary value of an urban tree; of the wading pool in the Tuileries Gardens of Paris; of the Mall in London; of an unspoiled Golden Gate? Disneyland may perhaps be measured in strictly box-office terms, but even when a charge is made can this be said of the delightful San Diego Zoo, or the Children's Fairyland and Madison Square Playground in Oakland?[15] Various assertions can be made. It can be said that beautiful cities will pay for themselves because they will attract tourists. This was a common rallying cry in New York in the late nineteenth century. Beautiful cities *have* attracted tourists and that can be verified. But so have enough convention halls, large-capacity hotels, and bars. The gross income the outsiders bring to a city can also be calculated. But where does the fiscal profit finally come to rest? Is the city better for its in-

---

[15] The zoo is well supported, as it should be, by entrance fees for adults and by annual popular subscriptions. The free playgrounds in Oakland were both developed by the Park Department but with large contributions and impetus from private organizations such as the Lake Merritt Breakfast Club or The Lions' Club.

habitants when it is always full of conventioneers and tourists? The suspicion is that it is not. Even the economic case is not well established.

There are more elaborate defenses for building the beautiful city. For example, it is sometimes argued that intellectuals, and especially "productive" intellectuals like scientists and engineers, definitely add to the wealth of the community where they live. If it is also true that they will elect to congregate only in communities where cultural advantages and urban amenities abound, then should the city not invest in the production of these magnets? But is it true? And, if true, what are the economic details?

The fact is, of course, that convincing ones do not exist. Perhaps they could be arrived at, perhaps not. It is hard to believe that a lot would not have still to be left to faith. But it would be desirable nonetheless to have studies of this subject. Until they exist it would be as well for the believers in urban beauty who feel impelled to defend it to seek other currencies. A common one is the soft currency of social benefit.

But even this soft currency may be hard to trust. It seems superficially reasonable to guess that, if one had to be poor, it might be more tolerable to be poor in Paris than in Lille, in London than in Sheffield, in Charleston than in Birmingham. But is this really so? We do not know. *We* can perhaps say that if *we* were poor we think we might have such preferences. But we are not poor. Moreover, we can judge only our own city from the point of view of a resident. What the city looks like to the tourist is quite a different matter. There may be compensations of other sorts in Glasgow or Birmingham that do not spring up to pleasure the eye of the tourist, who is always more avid in his quest for urban beauty when abroad than when at home. This is not to say that modern social scientists might not be able to find out some things about this question—to determine what kinds of measurable social benefits arise from urban beauty, and how much, if at all, they compensate for the failure to enjoy other social benefits.

But we do not have such studies today. We do not know how much edge would be taken off Watts if Copenhagen's

Tivoli Gardens[16] or London's Green Park were near at hand. The suspicion is, not much. Indeed, beautiful cities of the past have been among the more turbulent, not among the more somnolent. Perhaps that is one of the reasons they became beautiful.

All one can say on present evidence is that urban beauty is probably worth something in a financial way and something in a social way. Whether it is worth what it costs is not possible to prove. In the end, and waiting much more study, cities will be beautiful if citizens, logically or illogically, want them beautiful and are willing to pay for it themselves. Handing the bill over to the federal government is no long-range answer. It is popular now because the remote federal government can collect taxes locally that local politicians would not

[16] Tivoli Gardens were started more than a century ago under a five year concession from the King of Denmark to George Cartensen to build and operate a forty acre pleasure garden just outside the city gates. Today these famous gardens, enveloped by the city, offer pleasure for young and old, cultural and popular amusements, food at the level of sausage and a dill pickle or a soufflé and a caneton rouennaise, trees, paths, flowers, marching bands, fireworks in an array unequalled anywhere else in the world and perhaps not transferable. Admission is charged, ground rent is paid to the city, and the stockholders have for years received a dividend of 10 percent. Tivoli seems to be admired equally by Danes and foreigners. Efforts at something comparable but more firmly based in folk art in Stockholm and Oslo have fallen far short. The nearest approximation in the United States is perhaps the complex of buildings and activities in Balboa Park, San Diego, although, despite the zoo, these are weighted heavily on the cultural and international side; or the more specialized Disneyland and the various Marinelands. One essence of Tivoli is that it is "downtown" and does not demand an expedition, so the visitor can go with or without children and for a "little" day as well as a "big" one. Not many American cities could offer comparable sites, although the Boston Common, part of Central Park, or lower Grant Park in Chicago might do. But Americans cannot be made into Danes quite so easily and the very Americans who patronize Tivoli every day they are in Copenhagen might never patronize a local Tivoli if they had one. Still it might be worth trying in some newly developing city if the design and management could be held to the standards of Tivoli.

dare to try to collect and because its credit is or seems more secure. But in the long run the federal government cannot collect more for urban development than cities can themselves provide. At most it can redistribute it. One of the weaknesses of this is that cities with no aspiration or taste for beauty will, willy nilly, indulge in minor beautification at the expense of the great cities. Who in Monterey would not vote for a freeway tunnel at someone else's expense? Would a majority in Monterey vote for it if the money could be used for something else in Monterey? This is not an argument against the tunnel but merely a statement that the citizens of Monterey have been deprived of a free choice in the use of what was probably, at bottom, their own money. There will be no more national gain for urban beauty in such procedures than in any other kind of egalitarianism. Until a substantial amount of the revenues are fed back to the cities without strings that determine how much goes to relief, and how much to education, and how much to housing, and how much to roads, and how little for beauty, with rules for each of these, the particular aspirations of a city to be beautiful or distinguished in some quite different way will inevitably be subdued and the whole result cast in the image of what seems decent and desirable in Washington. There seems no real doubt that a large part of the federal budget earmarked for urban improvement of all sorts should go back to the cities to be foolish about in their own way. Then there may be some beautiful cities. Otherwise there may be none.[17] In the view of the General Accounting Office all the great and beautiful cities of history have been "foolish." Let then some of our cities be beautiful if they choose and let those who will, be wise.

[17] How to distribute the funds fairly would not be easy to work out—but the notion is so logical and has been so often advanced that it needs careful attention by the bureaus in Washington, where its popularity is predictably doubtful, and by the Congress, who might understand the reasoning better.

The Contest of Priorities

Even so, the city would of course have very difficult decisions to make as to what to spend for beauty, out of a finite pot, when so many other things need to be done.

"The major problem facing the big cities of the world for the rest of this century is the improvement of the quality and meaning of life for the general population and especially for previously deprived sectors at the bottom of the social ladder, or off the ladder altogether."[18] These are recent words of the San Francisco poet journalist, Kenneth Rexroth. He was aiming his shafts first at the culture of the "establishment," which he says, rightly, does not touch enough people to matter much, and then at the bureaucratic, cautious, even censorious actions of most of those who run urban recreational facilities such as parks. The latter, says Rexroth, again with some truth, fear to let the parks be used for spontaneous neighborhood affairs. "We need, as a first step, to open up to the widest, most varied, most intensive use the public facilities we now have which can enable us to stimulate and foster cultural activities at the grass roots, or rather, pavement and street corner level . . . Both as to membership, personnel and function, all our city commissions dealing with cultural questions are obsolete. The committee members are all living in a bygone age and the only power they have is to make mischief, to halt and hamper creative action."[19]

The target of this statement might have been a much larger one. It might have included urban beauty in the physical sense as well as the beauty of urban life in the quite different sense of pavement play. Both are presumably parts of urban joy.

To discuss them implies the assumption that a joyless city may be meaningless to its ordinary citizens, however well it serves as a fort, a warehouse, a production center, a place of pilgrimage, or a seat of government. Joy, of course, is not

---

[18] "Arts for the Street Corner," by Kenneth Rexroth, *San Francisco Sunday Examiner and Chronicle*, July 3, 1966, sec. 1, p. 16.
[19] *Ibid.*

always a sufficient antidote to pain. There are surely some other urban problems that can establish some sort of priority over the problem of urban joy. A throbbing tooth may make it impossible to listen to a great performance of great music. If pain is incessant—the pain of poverty, of rejection, of starvation, of hopelessness, of fear, even the pain of hate—there may be no energy left to seek or relish urban joy. It may even come about that the only positive joy is that of defying the city, of desecrating its most cherished monuments, of destroying its most delectable beauties. This paper has then to take it for granted that the urban problems of health, welfare, education, opportunity, public safety, and so on have to be at least partially solved before it can be reasonable to think about urban joy at all in any terms, much less the terms of urban beauty.

But there is a risk here. What do we mean by partially? Despite campaign oratory by benevolent white fathers, the deep social problems will never really be solved for *everybody*. They do need to be solved for many more people than they now are; and they can be. But the solution will cost much more money and much more imaginative and experimental efforts than are being spent now and will take a much longer time than Americans like to allow for the solution of any problem. It will be tempting, therefore, to try to put all the money and all the imagination and all the effort into working on situations where the disease is self-evident and attracts more personal human sympathy than can be attracted to urban beauty. This in turn can lead to postponing any effort toward urban beauty to some later, better time. One might even feel quite moral about "putting first things first." This is a dangerous temptation.

The lesser danger is that we may be satisfied with trying for urban beauty on the cheap, in planting a few forlorn trees or indulging in praiseworthy but not very far-reaching neighborhood litter collection, to the obbligato of an occasional speech from on high. The greater danger is that the whole idea of urban beauty will be postponed to another day when the intervening corrosion and decay will be too much even for people as affluent as we to remedy.

The idea of postponing beauty has long had an appeal for

Americans. John Adams in his frequent letters from France bewailed the fact that culture would have to wait a few generations while other things were done. Shortly before he died a few years ago, a leading American board chairman asserted in full confidence that if Americans had wasted their money on fountains the way the foolish Romans had, there would not have been enough resource and power left in America to permit us to "save the world." More recently a presidential adviser has noted, after the usual perfunctory curtsey to urban beauty, that we might have to postpone any efforts in that direction for a long time in view of the necessities in Asia.

Thus in the name of public health, of education, of welfare, of safety, of civil liberties and all the way up to national security it is easy for the practically minded to find excuses for deferring "extravagant" expenditures on urban beauty. Take no more land for parks, do not refurbish the opera house, build the cheapest possible freeway become watchwords so long as a single citizen lacked a hot meal or a hospital bed yesterday. This of course means forever. In such a view no urban beauty is as valuable as a rendezvous in space. Whom the gods would destroy they first make mad.

Even if reform were to attain all its objectives—if everyone were well fed, decently housed, healthy, gainfully employed, gorgeously dressed, sufficiently educated to use abundant leisure, and even if in the city there were no dark corner in which it was unsafe to be alone, and even if a few of the citizens were daily commuting to Mars or for that matter Pluto—the city might still be an unhappy city. For happiness is positive; it is something more than the state of not being unhappy. That is why one is tempted to paraphrase Virgil "quidquid id est, timeo censores et dona ferentes." "However it may be, I fear the reformers when they come bearing gifts." The gifts are likely not to be generous enough and almost certain not to be amusing enough; they will not be designed for urban joy but only for the alleviation of urban pain.

This essay, then, firmly beds itself in the premise that the pursuit of urban beauty cannot wisely be postponed; that it has pragmatic if unmeasurable value and that major efforts should be made to foster it, enhance it, and achieve it at the same time that other, more humanely attractive and demonstrably useful, projects are being vigorously executed.

The essay also stretches its boundaries a little beyond the central city. The periphery enhances the central city and vice versa, or at least it should be so. The problem is not the crass one of making the central city beautiful so that it can survive the hegira or turn the tide a different way. That may or may not transpire. The problem is for the whole metropolitan area to be beautiful. In this the central city can hardly fail to play a principal role—in communities where there really is one—because such centers have now so much of the greatest urban beauties. And if a modern city does not have a center it will still have more or less to create one (or perhaps several). All this implies the assumption that the interdependence of the core and periphery must be more firmly established politically and economically than it now is.

It is something more than a metaphor to say that the professors in Berkeley ought to pay something to the city of San Francisco to help preserve the view they hold in such esteem at the cocktail hour; or that the people of Marin County should pay the same city to support the privilege of working in skyscrapers they decline to permit to rise on their own terrain, thus getting the best of both possible worlds practically for nothing—or so it seems. On the assumption that the necessity for some metropolitan governmental entities and some greater coordination will be emphasized in many other essays in this volume, where the relevance is even more obvious, this study will take it for granted so far as urban beauties are concerned.[20]

---

[20] The idea of super-metropolitan governments with large overriding powers is by no means universally accepted by scholars, let alone by politicians and suburbanites. See, for example, Martin Meyerson and Edward C. Banfield's position on this for Metropolitan Boston. "There is much to be said for letting people decide locally how much of each service they wish to pay for and consume . . . Politics would not go out the window just because metropolitan government came in." *Boston: The Job Ahead* (Cambridge: Harvard University Press, 1966), p. 21. But they concede certain metropolitan functions that do call for central management, such as real

The Elements of Urban Beauty

The elements of urban beauty include the total city-scape, the approaches from which the resident may see it, a variety of middle-sized urban details such as great avenues, squares, and other open spaces, water and water fronts, gardens and parks, smaller backwaters, and finally an abundance of little details sometimes called street furniture. Evidently these are subject to an increasing amount of design as they become smaller, but that is no reason to despair of the big ones or to leave them to chance.

It is possible in architecture for a great over-all design to be ruined by unhappy details,[21] but it is impossible for even magnificent details to save a fundamentally bad design. This is also true for a city.

Architecture is only one of the details of a city; an important one but not the only one. There have been beautiful cities with little or even no distinguished architecture (San Francisco, Lisbon) and there have been ugly cities which possessed some fine buildings (Helsinki, Tokyo). The most totally beautiful cities undoubtedly will contain some great architecture. But it is theoretically possible to have too much. Restraint is as helpful to the beauty of a city as it is to that of a Christmas tree. That is why Architecture with a big *A* is stressed here mainly in the discussion of landmarks and the design of major spaces. Good architecture with a small *a* should pervade a beautiful city; and the small *a* will often, though not always, imply modesty, even neutrality.

1. The city-scape. Not every pleasant city has a visible city-scape. The city-scape is certainly the most difficult thing to design and control. It depends on how men have accommodated themselves to the natural terrain or accommodated

---

estate taxes, water supply and waste disposal, air pollution control, major outdoor recreational areas, and transportation. All these functions bear on urban beauty.

[21] Unhappily, this situation arose in Penn Center, Philadelphia. See Meyerson, *et al., Face of the Metropolis,* pp. 61–65.

it to themselves and after that the sensitivity they have shown toward the works of their predecessors. The city-scape is as much a combination of urban space as of buildings enclosing it or enclosed by it. The relations between space and buildings are subtle; not all designers are sensitive to them; among those who are sensitive are those who allow their personal arrogance to override their presumed good taste.

The classic city-scapes can be seen almost all at once and even from several different directions. Almost inevitably they belong to small cities. Examples are Toledo in Spain, a number of the Italian hill towns, and a few other places that are dramatically visible from every approach. Occasionally this has been possible on the flat; for example the minarets of Esfahan beckon over the desert; the spires of Chartres across the wheat fields.

City-scapes that can be seen from only a few advantageous positions are naturally more common. This is the case for the appearance of New York City from the sea, whence the supra-Gothic grandeur of lower Manhattan island is breathtakingly apparent to passengers on ocean liners, to commuters on Staten Island ferries, and to every Tug Boat Annie who steams by. The old and great panorama of San Francisco across the bay from Oakland, sweeping far south from Mt. Tamalpais and the Golden Gate, is reserved for East Bay sundowners and not seen daily by many San Franciscans or even tourists who are not indulging their curiosity about Berkeley. The contours of Rio de Janeiro are such that there are many places where emergent drama occurs fleetingly for the traveler but the great views are from the hilltops or from airplanes and thus in this case are reserved for the poor and the tourist.

Chicago has one of the most spectacular waterfronts in the world, its new lake edge enhanced by intelligent land filling, provided with a spectacular facade, respected even by the sewage disposal plants. But the great view from the east is reserved for the few who come in from or over Lake Michigan. Even the air traveler sees it less often than he once did, since the new air patterns for O'Hare airport do not often come over the city. In any event, we ought to ignore the air view; it is brief and special and its irrelevance to our general problem is evident from the fact that practically every city in the world looks beautiful from high enough up or when it displays only its electric lights.

Partial availability of the great panorama is open to citizens of Istanbul who quite commonly arrive by water, to those who course the Grand Canal in Venice, to Bostonians who enter their city along Memorial Drive on the Cambridge side of the Charles River Basin.

But for every example of a brilliant urban scape that is seen by at least some of the citizens daily it is possible to cite an equally beautiful city that has no one dominant city-scape or that cannot be seen over-all by any approach the citizen may make. Paris and London are outstanding examples. In Paris one may, of course, ascend Montmartre or take an elevator to the top of the Eiffel Tower, thus obtaining something approximating a static airplane view. This sort of privilege is open to an increasing number of people in an increasing number of cities but it cannot be regarded as a central contributor to urban beauty, though some of the towers may be.[22] What, if anything useful, can then be said of the city-scape? Two lines of thought may be worth noting; one deals with how a city-scape may be protected from damage; the other with how it may be seen.

The existence of a great city-scape does not have to be only a matter of nature's bounty. Cities have generally been established for other reasons than the force of their dramatic terrain. Such great terrains are therefore to be found in but a few cities that were originally attractive as sites for forts or monasteries or seaports. Many of the most exciting city-scapes are, like those of Chicago, almost entirely man-made. The terrain has been skillfully altered as in Venice or Boston; rivers have been controlled as in Pittsburgh or assiduously

[22] The examples multiply yearly: the Top of the Mark, the Empire State Building, the Prudential roof gardens in Boston and Chicago, the television towers in Tokyo and Stuttgart. Almost every city has its Top of Something. But this is hardly a way of life for a citizen unless he has too many visitors to entertain. Some of these platforms even rotate as in Seattle. Many serve meals whose quality generally is in inverse ratio to the altitude of the restaurant.

tended as in Paris. Then on these altered sites exciting congeries of constructions have been erected: the mountain of lower Manhattan, the wall of Chicago, the romantic spires of Zurich, the variety of intimate and palatial buildings on the Seine in Paris (which is adorned almost as much by the variety of its bridges as by the variety of its riparian life). The improvement of sites has been self-conscious, even designed. The congeries may have been more the consequence of laissez-faire or of history. But as an urban style developed it became a treasured thing and tended to be protected by law, sometimes mostly by economic law as in lower New York, more often by an array of statutory laws and ordinances as in most European cities, which seem to have taken more pride in their inheritances than American cities.

The more brilliant the natural landscape, the greater its scale, the harder it is for men to ruin it. But it is never quite impossible. San Francisco's munificent site has not been damaged, perhaps it has even been enhanced, by an ill-conceived, speculation-oriented gridiron street plan, by a nondescript set of buildings none of which, at least until recently, has had any genuine distinction. The Bay Bridge and especially the Richmond Bridge, ugly as they are, have been unable to ruin it. Probably the scale is such that even the most bombastic new cathedral tower or ill-sited skyscraper can do little harm. San Francisco has benefited by a few constructions, such as the Golden Gate Bridge,[23] and by the constant zeal of conservationists who are as ardent and as ruthless as any to be found in the nation. Nonetheless even this site can be eroded. The bulldozers and the split levels have desecrated the Twin Peaks; there is a constant threat to the Marin hills, less that they be developed with high rise buildings than that they be whittled away by trivial developments of single family houses on stilts, earnestly pursuing the "Marin County Way of Life." There is a constant struggle to prevent the shrinkage of the Bay by individual communities, seeking to increase their taxable acreage by fill and to reduce the amount of contamination of the waters by municipal effluent and

[23] Golden Gate Bridge, opened 1937, Oakland-Bay Bridge, opened 1936, and Richmond-San Rafael Bridge, opened 1956.

industrial waste. The new bridges that will be needed to the north may enhance or deface the landscape and the cheapest possible bridges are certain to deface it, while over the hills there hangs on too many days the leaden smog that has none of the visual or emotional beauty of the fogs that boil out of the Pacific in memory of Jack London.

But San Francisco has thus far been fortunate. Other cities have not fared so well. The bulldozers have scarred the hills of Los Angeles and San Diego beyond visual repair and offer a constant enticement to landslide. Seattle long ago sold her great front for a freeway. The cities of the Middle West, especially those of the Mississippi Valley, turned their backs on the great rivers long ago. No Great Lakes city save Chicago has begun to realize the possibilities for lakeside beauty and recreation. Most of the time Robert Moses has given Manhattan's river banks over to expressways and not to the people of the island, many of whom rarely ride on them.[24]

Some of these ill consequences have been the result of deliberate choice, more no doubt the result of lack of foresight or overzeal for the satisfaction of a different need. They are to be found in greater or less degree in every city. There is a general need first to stop the erosion and then to reclaim at least some of what has been despoiled, expensive as it has now become to do it. We have several good examples to follow: there is first of all the brilliant, almost heroic, recovery of the banks of the Chicago River; there is the renewal of the Golden Triangle at the confluence of the Allegheny and Monongahela rivers in Pittsburgh although the architecture may be institutional and banal; Philadelphia's achievements

[24] This generalization is not universally valid. There are a few good green spaces on the northern stretches of the West Side Highway. On one short span of East River Drive there are grassed terraces carried over the traffic lanes right out to the edge of the East River, a special boon for nearby apartment dwellers. The solution was perhaps triggered by the fact that space between the established building lines and the river was so narrow as to force the superposition of the north and south lanes. But this did not do more than suggest the opportunity. Applause goes to those who grasped it but none to those who with the good example in view so consistently ignored it thereafter.

on the Schuylkill and Delaware rivers should not go unnoticed. All these demonstrate that a great deal of recovery is possible if a city wants it enough. There can even be said to be a trend toward such recoveries. But they will not occur by themselves. It is only a figure of speech to say that a city wants anything. What happened in Chicago, Pittsburgh, and Philadelphia is owed not to the "city" but to a handful of dedicated men who in one way or another joined tenacity and imagination and generosity to power.

But even with a trend toward reclamation, negative measures against decay are also necessary to keep things as good as they are. Even if London ever succeeds in cleaning up her filthy Thames, on which the scum rides up and down the tides and which seldom reaches the sea, there will be need to guard against later polluters. There are plenty of statutory ways in which major desecrations of urban landscape can be forbidden. But like zoning they will never be effective unless they are steadily and unflinchingly enforced; and this in turn will never happen unless the public cares more than it now seems to. Not very many urban newspapers even bother to keep their public on the alert.

But prevention, though necessary, is not a very imaginative thing at best. It is more interesting to indulge a flight of fancy as to what the Twin Cities and the University of Minnesota might have done, and still might do, to exploit the great gorge of the river. Will St. Louis manage to make its levees into a place of public delight? A wishbone memorial to Jefferson is not much of a start. Boston made a fine urban asset by damming a minor river, the Charles, to provide the Charles River Basin and a tidal stream, the Mystic, to make two substantial lakes. What other cities might do more with their inconsequential streams? It is technologically practical today to make big lakes right in the heart of town if one wants to enough and to provide Dallas, for example, with its own Lac Leman (without Mt. Blanc). Much more can be done in cultivating the advantages of little rivers as San Antonio has done most brilliantly; but even more modest efforts will pay, such as the fifty foot Strawberry Canyon that meanders down the campus of the University of California at Berkeley.

There is another way to affect the city-scape besides that

of abusing, conserving, or even creating nature. There is a city-scape of buildings. When a new building is being considered it would be possible to see whether its proposed masses and heights will embellish the existing city-scape or damage it severely or simply be neutral. Architects and clients have not often been willing to look beyond their selfish noses on this point and one or two architects with the highest reputations for sensitivity have been among the most ruthless desecrators. So also (and more frequently) have been the mediocre designers.

The enormous change of scale imposed on the Boston skyline by the new Prudential Tower[25] would have been provided by any building of that vertical scale no matter how refined its details.

However, this subject must be approached with caution, since prediction sometimes turns out to have been wrong. For example, people who liked the old Park Avenue with its uniform building heights and its modest frenchified facades were full of foreboding when Lever House[26] broke the peace of that street both in scale and texture. But havoc was not wrought. In the end a number of other distinguished buildings, such as Seagrams, Pepsi-Cola, and Union Carbide[27]

[25] Proposed originally in 1953 by students at Harvard; followed up by a team of famous architects including The Architects Collaborative, Walter F. Bogner, Hugh Stubbins, Jr., Pietro Belluschi, and Carl Koch and Associates, with Stevens Development Corporation as the promoter. In the end the Prudential Insurance Company became the developer; the architectural wand, now devoid of magic, fell to Charles Luckmann and Associates, whose design, though low in land coverage, bears no relation to the older scheme. The story of how this imaginative use of obsolete railroad lands right in the heart of the city came to fall short of the potentials for urban beauty, whatever it may have provided in the way of economic advantage, is well told in Meyerson's *Face of the Metropolis*, pp. 69–73.

[26] Skidmore, Owings and Merrill, 1951–52.

[27] The House of Seagram, 1957, by Ludwig Mies van der Rohe and Philip Johnson, associated with Kahn and Jacobs. Pepsi-Cola, 1958–59, by Skidmore, Owings and Merrill. Union Carbide, 1957–1960, by Skidmore, Owings and Merrill.

joined Lever on the same street. There was a new Park Avenue
—different but not less beautiful and no doubt better suited to
the needs of modern Manhattan. Then came the proposal to
build the gargantuan Pan-Am Building[28] over the Grand
Central Building and another great outcry, which has not yet
abated. This building, to be sure, lacks the architectural distinction of some of the other Park Avenue buildings previously cited but, even if its quality were greater, its mere size
and bulk and the way it stops the street would be its important
effect. Whether it will in turn stimulate a new and benign
scale on Park Avenue cannot be predicted today. I think not.

Sometimes new buildings can be injected into the city-scape
with very little difficulty, aside from the consideration of
difficulties of traffic patterns, deeper-canyoned streets, and the
like. Lower Manhattan has been remarkably resistant in this
sense. New tall buildings such as the Chase-Manhattan Bank[29]
have slipped into the rubric of towers comfortably because
they have not fought the scale or even the spirit of the en-
semble. Of course each new and higher one does change the
profile; the older lower buildings recede in importance and
even disappear so that memory sees something that can no
longer be seen in fact, but the new remains impressive and not
less beautiful than the previous version in which the Wool-
worth Building was a central feature.[30] But even such a complex may not be absolutely immune. If enough equally high
buildings were to rise on the edges of the present constella-
tion so that it was widened and therefore visually flattened,
something quite unpleasant might result. Or some newcomer
might be simply just too high, for example if plans go ahead
for the proposed New York World Trade Center.[31] If so, it
could do the same sort of harm as Prudential's tower has un-

---

[28] Pan-Am Building, c. 1959, by Emory Roth and Sons with
Walter Gropius and Pietro Belluschi as design consultants. It is
hard to know who was the responsible designer, which may be one
of the troubles.

[29] Skidmore, Owings and Merrill, 1961.

[30] Cass Gilbert, Architect, 1909–1913.

[31] Minoru Yamasaki, Architect. The work is just in the project
stage.

doubtedly done to the Boston skyline at least for a long time
to come. This is the kind of thing that San Franciscans fear
as their towers climb out of Montgomery Street and up onto
Nob and other hills.

What kind of checks could a city possibly provide to defend
and enhance its city-scape? One that has worked well in Europe, the limitation of heights, is probably no longer possible here. Even industrious Germany has needed no building
higher than 26 stories though there are rumors that one a mile
high has been proposed. Why is great height needed in Dallas
or in many other of our newer cities? Though our new cities
need not copy New York and Chicago, they are doing so with
gusto. It is not much of a compliment to the sophistication of
San Franciscans that someone there thinks it important
whether the city now boasts the highest building west of
Chicago.

The idea of limiting heights has served Paris and London
beautifully in the past as it once served Boston. The Boston
dike was breached years ago and once broken it could never
be stuffed again. The London dike is crumbling west of West-
minster. Paris is more adamant in the center city but the
old beautiful central Paris is rapidly being encased by an un-
beautiful high rise periphery. Paris, unlike London, may keep
a Hilton out of its front yard but it talks of a new parallel and
higher Paris nearby.

Though absolute height controls may be archaic and simply prevent urban growth, it would still be possible to think of
a city of zoned heights related to a desired ultimate skyline
that can be designed without designing the details of the buildings, just as the towers of San Gimignano can be looked at
as a whole and not merely as a collection of individual vertical elements. Personal ambitions to have the highest building
somewhere if only for a minute, delusions that the mere height
will pay off in prestige are likely still to encourage entrepreneurs to break the rules; obsequious politics, even when
not venal, is likely to encourage the amendment of such restrictions at the behest of what seems to be an urban tax advantage. Still it might be tried.

In trying it, it could be reasonable for cities that have some
pretension to a city-scape to demand that the proposals upon

which a building permit is to be issued must not only conform to a profile but must also include studies of the city-scape both before and after the intrusion of the new building; that these shall be published; that public discussion should be encouraged and perhaps that the proposal should have to be approved by an appropriate body with requisite powers—not the building department, needless to say. After all, if the Florentines dueled about a new cornice profile, Americans might duel about the whole envelope of their city. Without yet defining the details of how such a body might work (this will appear later), the notion of the power of such qualified judgment is taken as acceptable. The difficulties of enforcement and the probabilities of evasion are admitted. Even if in the end refusal of permits proved spongy, the very act of having to air the proposed studies, and the subsequent public brouhaha, might deter at least some entrepreneurs and their architects from their rashest deeds. There is, after all, an increasing corporate concern about the corporate image and the effect of the corporate buildings on that image. There is also a desire to contribute to the amenity of the city in which the corporation is domiciled.

The direct involvement of corporations in the good taste of their buildings, whether in the whole city-scape or viewed as separate entities, tends to be less effective in the United States than it might be because of the fact that so many corporations are not directly involved in making urban buildings with their own capital and under their own direction. This has been the general pattern for corporate buildings in Germany. It has produced such excellent examples of corporate and municipal buildings as the Mannesmann and Thyssen buildings in Dusseldorf, the BAT building in Hamburg, and the Telefunken and IBM buildings in Berlin. Too often in our cities the big urban buildings are built entirely as speculative rental space by none too esthetically minded entrepreneur-builders with very little public image to risk, and then rented with the name being granted to the largest and longest tenant. With the exception of perhaps two or at most three American entrepreneurs not a single distinguished building has been produced this way. Almost every distinguished office building in our country is in fact the product of a corporation building primarily for its own long-range needs and having a good deal of public image to lay on the line. Though it might be a good thing, the bad entrepreneur-builders cannot be suppressed by law. The only antidote is that still more corporations shall take their personal urban responsibilities seriously.

2. *Approaches.* A city-scape is in any case not very meaningful if it cannot be seen. A few city-scapes are generally noticeable as one runs around the city, say, of Istanbul, Paris, or Zurich. But urban viewing on the grand scale will occur for citizens mainly as they approach the city. Some of the attractive but dwindling approaches over water have been mentioned. They might be revived in a few places where other approaches are slow and unpleasant, by using new, faster water vehicles and by being ingenious about the termini —easy parking at the outer terminus, very pleasant transport at the center with a quick and perhaps free trip to a nearby concentration using moving sidewalks, Disney-type trailers, and even canals, or cable cars. But such opportunities if they exist at all are obviously the privilege only of a few cities.

Railroad approaches have from the outset been unpleasant. They have so corrupted the adjacent land that it is hardly retrievable now, at least in an esthetic sense. New rapid transit systems that do not use buses are almost certain to have to go underground in central cities and so the city-scape does not concern them much.

This does not mean that a great deal cannot and should not be done to make the new transit rides a delightful experience and not like that of the New York subways. Noble proposals have been made in San Francisco, but those who have high aspirations for final elegance must always fight a generally losing battle against citizens who are trying to meet schedules of time and cost and who find aspirations expensive and time consuming and probably not very important anyway. Subway systems could be remarkable. They are unlikely to be, though they will no doubt be more pleasant for a time than the old ones were. Station plaza design does have a positive role to play in the beautiful city, however, and cities should be well aware of the opportunities they throw away when they do not view them in that light. But the principal approach to cities, barring the jet propulsion of individuals, is likely for a long time to be by highways, at least for the local residents. This may not be desirable but it is the fact. Transportation facilities as a whole occupy at least a quarter of urban space and of this the streets and highways claim more land than any other use. They obviously represent a great opportunity or a great liability. In recent years as the automobiles have multiplied they have become an increasing menace in almost every way. This accounts no doubt for what is not a trivial or ephemeral citizens' revolt against the federal freeways and their management, noisiest in San Franciso but real in San Diego, in Monterey, in New Orleans, in Boston, even in Los Angeles. There is ample justification for this, but it is already very late.

However, it will be self-defeating to carry the revolt too far. Cars could be given less freedom in American cities without a counter revolt, but it is doubtful that any American city could succeed in imposing an absolute and small number of urban parking spaces as Stockholm has done. Some courage should be shown in making it more expensive and awkward to bring cars into town; on-street parking really could be stopped, with an enormous freeing of the traffic pattern. But there will still have to be freeways and downtown parking and there are examples here and there in the country that show they can be esthetic assets and not esthetic liabilities. A few freeways have rights of way wide enough to permit gracious planting both as a visual and auditory buffer, creating no diseconomies along their rights of way. Here and there they have not cut neighborhoods in two; instead, by the device of handsome bridges and even extensive overhead plazas, they have connected one side with the other, though the exploitation of air rights as in Hartford has not been sufficiently done. Here and there they have opened new vistas of urban scape to the drivers who course them and some of these are remarkable; here and there, principally at complex intersections, they have brought new and handsome forms to the city. All these they have done here and there but never often enough and especially never often enough in any one place. The solution to this problem of urban beauty is not to abolish freeways through cities but to insist that they be as good as isolated examples have shown them capable of being. This would be far more creative than the unimaginative and more costly scheme of putting them all in tunnels.

The reason we get what we get is partly because the federal managers are unimaginative and stubborn, partly because city engineers are not artists, partly because politicians never dare to take the land of people who vote when they can take the land of a park whose trees and grass cannot vote, and partly because of an effort to build the most possible freeway for the least possible money. The cost of highways is so majestic already that to change our attitudes in the direction of even more expensive networks can be the action only of daring city or state officials somewhere, prepared (and likely) to lose their jobs. This is not a task which private enterprise can help on, save by supporting the official if he comes along. Wise federal policy might, however, engage in large grants to a few schemes as a way of establishing bellwethers and inducing emulation; this would surely be more productive than frittering the money away on tunnels for all the Montereys that can make a loud enough noise. The risks of such a program in the sequel are obvious and a very long line might form on the right. Even then it would perhaps be better to have fewer freeways and nicer ones.

3. Parking. In the end the car must come off the freeway, preferably in the central city, or at least in an important ganglion. We know by now that parking lots are not good looking and that on-street parking is little more attractive. Underground garages such as those at Mellon Square in Pittsburgh or Union Square in San Francisco are pleasant and useful, although the overhead parks have somehow failed and more design could have been lavished on that aspect of the problem. There are excellent examples of above-ground ramp garages that are also an esthetic asset and they can be seen from Cologne to New Haven to San Francisco. Certainly a city that wants to be beautiful had better be committed to full control over the entry and stabling of cars in its midst. In this process it will become abundantly clear that there should be substantial areas in a city, some even up to a half mile square, into which no automobile should ever intrude unless beneath the ground. People should be able to walk safely, shielded from noise and smell in the very center of their city;

they, not the automobile, should breathe the air and feel the sun. That this can be designed into a city can be seen by even the most casual inspection of Edmund Bacon's proposals for Philadelphia and especially for Market Street. Nor does such a proposal require that all those Americans who have forgotten how to walk shall now have to relearn the art. There are ingenious devices to take one from his car door to wherever else he wants to go. It was a sad day in American experience when Fort Worth decided not to put Victor Gruen's imaginative and contemporary scheme to test.[32] This called essentially for a downtown pedestrian core of commodious size from which private motor vehicles were to be excluded.

4. *The modern plaza and other landmarks*. We rightly admire the great old European squares, although they are less attractive when they are used for parking, as in Nancy or Paris, than when they have been kept inviolate for pedestrians, as in Venice. But in literal terms they are obsolete. The large public assemblies they once served are possible now only over television. To make them large enough for modern uses would destroy them. They enjoy a nice proportion of wall height to horizontal distances that cannot lightly be altered. Yet their buildings are too low for a modern central city. If you raise the buildings you must enlarge the horizontal dimensions or else all is lost. When you make the horizontal dimensions that great, the space is simply too big for people on foot and if you put them into vehicles you have destroyed the square in another way. The problem of the new urban scale both in space and in time is esthetically thorny. It has been understood by only a handful of urban designers, though they all talk about it. Yet that does not mean that the square is obsolete. It just needs to be a different kind. The city could

[32] The Downtown Plan for Fort Worth, designed by Victor Gruen Associates, was commissioned by J. B. Thomas of the Fort Worth Edison Company. A committee of twenty citizens undertook to execute it after the plan was first published in 1956. But the opposition was violent and, though the plan has influenced many subsequent ones, ten years after it was proposed it still has not obtained the legislation or the bond issues it needs. See Meyerson, *et al.*, *Face of the Metropolis*, pp. 74–76.

profit from a considerable number of squares or plazas with well-designed linkages from one to the other, perhaps even through quite narrow pedestrian channels going through buildings and almost certainly on multilevels by which pedestrians could make the journey from one square to another without being aware of an automobile. All this is fairly easy to effect but we are not doing it. Yet we do have the prototypes. There are by now enough examples of successful urban plazas around office buildings[33] or of equally relevant first-class shopping centers[34] to show what is possible. The designs can be improved, one can be better related to another one and so on, but the pilot work has been done and demonstrated.

On the other hand we may not be prone to make new boulevards in the image of Commonwealth Avenue, Boston,[35] especially of a residential tree-lined sort. If they carry cars

[33] For example, Mile High Center, 1955, and Courthouse Square, 1959, Denver, I. M. Pei, Architect; Rockefeller Center, New York, begun in 1931 by a host of architects headed by Reinhard and Hofmeister; the new Chase-Manhattan Plaza, New York, completed 1961 by Skidmore, Owings and Merrill; Penn Center, Philadelphia, Vincent Kling, Architect, 1952–1962; the Charles Center Plan for Baltimore, revealed in 1958. The details are worth studying and are sufficiently presented in Meyerson, *et al., Face of the Metropolis.*

[34] For example, Midtown Plaza, Rochester, New York, by Victor Gruen, opened 1962; the earlier and pioneer Kalamazoo shopping mall, 1959; Southdale Shopping Center, Minneapolis, 1956, also by Victor Gruen; the shopping plaza in Vallingby, Sweden, completed 1957, architects Sven Backstrom and Leif Reines; or the shops and department store of the Lijnbaan in Rotterdam, completed 1953, the shops by Broek and Bakema, the store by Marcel Breuer. Of interest also is Schulstrasse in the heart of Stuttgart. There are other noteworthy American examples and the much greater number of cheap, crude, and disagreeable ones, often unfortunately connected with national corporations that have the resources to do better.

[35] Other examples are the magnificent Outer Drive in Chicago, a 1930 offshoot of the earlier proposals of Daniel Burnham; Drexel Boulevard, Chicago; Summit Avenue, St. Paul; Euclid Avenue, Cleveland; and the even more majestic ones of Europe such as London's Mall or the Champs Elysées in Paris. A new one is proposed for Market Street, San Francisco.

their boulevard aspects are destroyed, and it is hard to con ceive of them without cars. Cities that have such streets shoul of course try to make civilized use of them. But the moder counterpart will be the beautiful freeway, the magnificen new square, the articulation of the pedestrian paths of th city. Sidewalk cafes are more pleasant on the autoless street

This cavalier abolition of the boulevard does not imply th abolition of shade trees and grass or that only straight lines ar suitable for a city. There are some doctrinaire modernist who make such assertions and regret having the city in th country or the country in the city but they are mostly Euro peans telling us what to do; they are Europeans, moreover who are forgetting the clear testimony of all their most beau tiful cities, at least of the West.

The modern plazas were perhaps started in America by th Rockefeller Center project of 1931 and given a nudge b Lever House in 1952. Now they have multiplied and new ones are in various stages of planning. None is perfect but eac has contributed enormously to the good character of its city Here we will not engage in criticism of the defects but onl point out briefly how they came about.[36]

Almost without exception they represent an initiative pro vided by private citizens or private corporations, the Rocke fellers in New York, the Mellons in Pittsburgh, operatin almost as great Greek citizens might once have done; some times the initiative was that of a corporation with a messag to convey, such as Lever Brothers or the House of Seagram or the more recent Chase-Manhattan. Occasionally, if no often, they have been the product of the ambitions of ex traordinary builders such as Webb and Knapp under th leadership of William Zeckendorf when he developed Mil High Center in Denver and, later, Place Ville Marie in Mon treal. Some of the projects have had city help, some little o none. The owners of Chase-Manhattan, for example, trade some of their land to permit the widening of four streets an agreed to guarantee a permanent plaza. In return the cit closed Cedar Street and increased the permissible groun coverage from 25 to 30 percent. Penn Center in Philadelphi

---

[36] See note 33 above.

was more directly the product of municipal impetus and the support of two strong mayors, Joseph (now Senator) Clark and Richardson Dilworth, but the achievement would have been impossible without some cooperation from the Pennsylvania Railroad.

The Charles River Center in Baltimore was planned by a private, nonprofit group under contract to the Committee for Downtown Inc., a group of Baltimore businessmen who financed the study through contributions. The city's Urban Renewal and Housing Agency made only minor revisions before accepting the plan. The city voters approved an urban renewal bond issue to cover part of the city's share in the financing. Execution was placed in the hands of the Urban Renewal and Housing Agency.

From the examples it seems clear that a great deal can be done. But what is surprising and disappointing is that so little is done and that so little seems to be learned from excellent and bad previous examples. The Avenue of the Americas in New York right behind and even embracing a part of Rockefeller Center has developed in its own chaotic way with a group of ill-assorted, unconnected, blatantly and vulgarly selfish buildings as though Rockefeller Center had never existed. Many of the newer buildings on Park Avenue have made no effort to relate themselves or even their plazas, when they have them, to those of the House of Seagram or Lever House. The one period of the year when cooperation seems possible on Park Avenue is in the Christmas season when the street and the window displays, and the churches, the hotels, and the office buildings become fantastically beautiful in a secular way.

The development of large communal complexes for commerce and management is the area in which private enterprise has made and probably can continue to make the greatest contribution to urban beauty. What is needed is a much more considerable collaboration in the planning stages between the holders of adjacent properties. Chicago could, for example, have had a far more brilliant development of the new Loop around the Civic Center and the Federal Center and the First National Bank had one other large owner felt disposed to cooperate. Investments will need to be as generous as they have been and perhaps even more lavish. There must be a careful selection of architects for such projects. There are none too many who are up to it, but there are perhaps enough if they are used wisely.[37]

When such combinations have been effected they need more help from city governments than they have usually been getting; more sensible interpretation of building codes and especially revision of the frequently obsolete ones; more sympathy with a quid pro quo on the closing of streets; perhaps even some tax benefits. Certainly they should never be punished for having improved the city. Yet this has been done. "New York City recently raised taxes on the Seagram Building by one third of a million dollars a year on the ground that by building so beautiful a building the company had enhanced its prestige and value. If this decision stands (the company is appealing it) other companies will probably take steps to avoid any suspicion of architectural excellence for fear of having their taxes raised."[38] (The decision was upheld on

---

[37] Architects really equipped for this sort of design thinking and the necessary previous analytical study are not legion and they are all very busy, but nonetheless appropriate ones can be commissioned. It is not always the largest firms that can do the best work, although one of the largest firms is among the very best as some of the other largest ones are among the most ordinary. It may take a little courage even for a private corporation, in a chauvinistic city, to choose a man from out of town, but it may be necessary, since the best architects tend to cluster where the action is. Fortunately regional pride need not be flaunted! Considering only men who are fully arrived, there are eight to ten who could be called great by world standards, eighteen to twenty who are very good, and another dozen who are probably good enough. These forty-odd are distributed over three different East Coast cities; three Middle Western cities; three Pacific Coast cities; and there is one in the Southwest. The concentration is largest, naturally, in the northeast quadrant, but only the South is a little shy of this high level of demonstrated talent.

[38] See Meyerson and Banfield, *Boston: The Job Ahead,* p. 112. Also Joseph E. Seagram and Sons, Inc., *vs.* Tax Commission of the City of New York, 14 NY 2nd 314, 251 NYD 2nd 460 (1965). The company was obviously in an awkward bind. Presumably it had had to justify its $45 per square foot costs to its stockholders

ppeal.) The city should not engage in such practices. It might ccasionally cede some land on a long ground rent or other roper protection to guarantee a park-like plaza or contract) maintain an existing park so that a mutually beneficial ollaboration could result, such as that between the Phoenix-hein-Ruhr Company (Thyssen Haus) and the park de-artment in Dusseldorf. The city might undertake to main-ain the plazas or even to embellish them with art approved y the owners. The measures usually proposed by municipal overnments are, on the contrary, parsimonious, suspicious, mid, restrictive.

There are obviously other combinations for the center city han those of office buildings or shopping areas. There is high ise housing, both public and private; hotels, of which the uality is consistently downwards; there are new amusement enters such as Lincoln Center, the success of which is not et tested. But even Lincoln Center suggests that as yet most reat civic improvements in America's most affluent cities ill have to be financed by private subscriptions if they are ultural, although new cities, at least, can get their citizens) pay for covered stadia for various spectator sports. All that ays, perhaps, is that more people care to see football and base-all than care to go to opera and ballet and symphony and vant-garde theater. After all the Colosseum in Rome was uch larger than the Theater of Marcellus.

5. American public architecture. The present standards of merican public architecture, with a few notable exceptions uch as the Marin County Civic Center, and more common xceptions among school buildings, are not high. In the days f the early republic a civilized set of officials built well in ccordance with accepted classic principles.[39] In the middle

---

n precisely the same grounds it later had to deny were relevant to tax appraisal. Nonetheless, the tax policy was obviously short-ghted.

[39] Thomas Jefferson may have been the last president with a ell-developed and sure-footed taste and interest in architecture; ut President Madison at least knew enough to consult Charles Bul-nch. From Madison on the presidential interest has been mostly issing, which may have been just as well. Hope flared briefly in e administration of President Kennedy.

years under various Supervising Architects of the Treasury
the styles varied with the fashions but the results were no
always bad.[40] In the early part of the twentieth century
the Beaux Arts eclecticists actually built notable examples o
their fashion[41] and even made a few innovations, but thei
product has generally been scorned by the prophets of th
modern revolution. After the revolution began, the skill of th
eclectics diminished. The new revolutionary architects wer
seldom commissioned for public buildings; when they wo
competitions, ways were usually found not to build their win
ning designs. The first serious chink in the federal armor wa
made by a sensible committee of architectural advisers wh
persuaded the State Department to take some large chance
in embassies and chancelleries that were being built almos
everywhere.[42] But this barely spread to other public buildings
advances like the Air Force Academy in Colorado Springs
and especially its Chapel, were the source of heated discussio
in which even President Eisenhower appeared as an adversary
though not a very determined one.[43] Under President Ken
nedy there seemed hope for wider gains and these may stil

[40] For example the Louvre types under Alfred B. Mullett; an
the Victorian Gothic types under William Appleton Potter.

[41] There were a number of excellent architects of the quality c
Paul Philippe Cret (Pan-American Union), Bertram Grosveno
Goodhue (Nebraska State Capitol), Charles Follen McKim (Bos
ton Public Library), and Cass Gilbert (Brooklyn Army Ware
house). Their successors tried to speak the same language, but th
results were tired and dull. Gilbert himself would have preferre
to be remembered by the U.S. Supreme Court or the Minnesot
State Capitol.

[42] For example, in Athens by The Architects Collaborative; Nev
Delhi by Edward Stone; in Ghana by Harry Weese; in Bangkok b
John Warnecke. Some other distinguished American designers suc
as Eero Saarinen and Ralph Rapson did not achieve their best wor
in this program.

[43] Architects for the Air Force Academy (Chapel 1960) wer
Skidmore, Owings and Merrill. The hearings were salty if not in
formative; they revealed one of Frank Lloyd Wright's worst side
and the tastes of a number of individual senators.

take place under the present advice of Karel Yasko.[44] Similar trends can be seen at state and municipal levels but change remains slow. Industrial corporations and more recently universities have tended to commission more imaginative architecture than public bodies. An important exception is Boston's City Hall.

It is not hard to advance a number of reasons as to why. Our nation has long ago built most of the buildings for which a symbolic architecture seemed demanded. This would have been the kind of architecture for which it is easiest to defend "extravagance" and even imagination, although the image of classic democracy would have died hard. On the other hand, the administrative space needed by governments has increased enormously. These buildings, especially office buildings, might have taken a cue from good commercial buildings had there not been a natural political reluctance to housing civil servants in quarters as luxurious as those provided, say, for the typists of Deere, Lever, Seagram, or Union Carbide. Another important sector of governmental building was devoted to housing. So much of this was subsidized that there was a corresponding reluctance to "pamper" the subsidized. This often reached the point of seeming to forget what the housing was for.

Then there was and is the question of the significance of public taste in a democracy. Nothing has happened until recently to raise the general taste and most of what has happened is owed to a few national magazines. Only one or two newspapers in the United States maintain professional architectural critics; the others rely on amateurish personal comments by a strange assortment of entirely unqualified columnists who assert that "they like what they like."[45] Television comments are spasmodic and scarce. No one has

---

[44] Karel Yasko is Assistant Commissioner for Design, Public Buildings Service of the General Services Administration.

[45] Solid criticism appears regularly in *The New York Times* (Ada Louise Huxtable), the *Louisville Courier Journal* (Grady Clay), and occasionally in *The Washington Post* (Wolf Von Eckhardt). I know of no other newspaper critics of architecture in our country who deserve to be taken seriously.

known quite how to have a public interest. "While a democracy of taste permits delegation of certain responsibilities to design experts (just as political democracy permits delegation of responsibilities to elected and appointed officials) the general public must possess sufficient acumen to choose among experts; to temper them and to inspire them to higher standards of performance."[46] However, some architects who have been on many commissions and are much in demand as consultants seem to despair of ever raising public taste to a decent pitch and regard the danger of missing the goal as making it unwise to try. Very little has, in any event, been done to provide the public with this acumen; the very subjects which might have helped in school curricula have often been decried by educational leaders as "soft," especially since Sputnik.

When the elected representatives have not been timid in esthetic matters they have been even less helpful. They have not often been able to rise above their personal tastes, generally untutored and often instinctively bad. This is not surprising. They were not elected because of their presumed competence in such matters.

Again the doctrine of frugality in public works is still a popular one although it is applied more to individual building than to the number of buildings to be proliferated.

Finally, good design can never be achieved without the employment of first-class designers. Such men simply do not reside in every city. Indeed, there may not be over a dozen cities in the country[47] that could honestly claim today to be the domiciles of first-class and tested architects and designers. But every city has architects who, in lesser practical matters, are fully competent and who aspire to more. The political pressures on local politicians to employ local "talent" are real and incessant.

For some of these difficulties there can be no remedy save the slow one of time. It would be advantageous if more cities were to have five-year capital budgets like Philadelphia's, so that better and less capricious forward planning was possible. Some cities might even dare to impose a statutory percentage

[46] Meyerson, et al., Face of the Metropolis, p. 37.
[47] See note 37 above.

of cost on public buildings to provide for art, landscaping, fountains, and other embellishments and that would be kept inviolable by law from incursions for other elements of the budget. This is quite common abroad. More difficult politically would be drastic changes in the requirements of competitive bidding. This is costly and inefficient and does not protect the public more than constant public scrutiny.

The savings might be spent for better architecture. Conscious effort to change secondary school patterns for the cultivation of public taste would have a real if delayed effect. Television stations could do much more than they now do; some imaginative sponsor might find it interesting to do a great cities series on prime time with as high a budget as a few others spend for high-grade music and drama programs.[48]

The political decision makers might in such circumstances be led to stop exercising incompetent personal judgments about the arts and brought to rely as much on unquestioned local experts[49] as they now do, say, about controls to be put on a local nuclear reactor where they are conscious of their ignorance. One way to achieve this would be to appoint official and manifestly qualified nonpartisan, unpaid, citizens commissions but not more than one at any one time in any one city. These commissions should be made up of experts and not of people chosen to represent all the presumably appropriate economic, social, religious, and other irrelevant blocs. They could act as a standing body or, perhaps preferably, on an ad hoc basis for each important project. They should not have power, because the final responsibility must rest with the mayor and other elected officials, but they should

[48] For example, the Esso drama series, the Bell Telephone Hour, and the musical programs of Firestone. A brilliant series on cities might be productive for the right national sponsor.

[49] These experts are in every city of size; some are attached to museums; some to universities; some architects might be willing to sit above the melee; and then there are in every city some talented patrons, men like Stanley Marcus in Dallas, Edgar Kauffmann, Jr., in Pittsburgh, August Heckscher, Jr., in New York, William Hewitt in Moline, Illinois, and so on. Such a group can be backed by outside people when it is necessary—as it surely will not always or even often be.

have funds to publicize their recommendations and their reasons; and the public should be made fully aware of the occasions when the responsible officers elected to disregard the commission's advice—and what is more important, why.

But all these measures will not produce good enough results unless men of exceptionally high talent are commissioned at least for the major public works. This may very often mean men from out of town, although their services may be supplemented by the services of local architects. Great cities have never hesitated to import great talent wherever it may have resided; a man may often be more convincing out of town than he is at home, and not through any defect on his part.

Once a decision has been made to brave local chauvinism there are, fortunately, several ways by which the selection of an architect can be made so that the final decision-making power is that of refusing or accepting a single recommendation. Either method makes it possible to take the pressures for local employment out of the offices of decision. One is the method of the public competition, which produced such interesting results in Boston and Toronto for their city halls and in Sydney, Australia, for its Opera House. There must be one warning here. It is positively immoral to hold a competition and then to decline to commission the winner. Competitions ought to be played for keeps. This is not, unfortunately, the way the world wags. It is a commentary on how common it is to walk out on the winner that former mayor John Collins of Boston was much and properly praised for his courage in sticking by the winning design and designers of the Boston city hall. Another alternative is to leave the recommendation of a single architect in the hands of a specially appointed panel of distinguished and obviously qualified citizens, with or without outside consultants. This was done successfully in determining the architect for the new city hall in Dallas. There are advantages and disadvantages to each of these procedures that need not be rehearsed here.

Beyond this there would seem to be no reason why cities should not be encouraged in such boldness by a very large national prize, given by the federal government to the city that brought in the most distinguished civic architecture each year or each four years. Such a prize should be big enough to attract real notice to client, architect, and mayor; it should be conferred by the President and could properly be in the amount of several million dollars so that the winning city could do something else it had expected to have to postpone.

6. *"Street furniture" and other details.* American cities need more shade and trees downtown than they generally have. They need more fountains. They need more small and intimate backwater squares in which neighborhood children may play safely and in peace and in which the old can sleep in the sun. Probably not many center cities will ever be able again to put together a great midtown area like Central Park unless some enormous disaster forces a fresh start; and it is not even certain that more smaller ones, as well kept, would not do as much for a modern city. Smaller squares (and they can often be very small) that are restful and humane, now found in such different places as Cordova, London, Stockholm, and Kyoto, could be made. Land can and should be taken for these purposes now and then, with or without the help of a single private patron. But the location and the details and the protection and the maintenance of these all need to be part of a plan.

A great deal could be done if a color expert like Alexander Girard were called on to define the colors of at least the leading taxicab companies and of public vehicles. The beautiful effect of this is more than one might expect until he sees a row of yellow cabs in the rain. The light fixtures of most of our cities could be redesigned to their benefit both for form and utility; and so could the trash containers, the alarm boxes, the street signs, the benches on which people should be encouraged to sit (not all city sitters are bums or pigeon feeders). None of these things needs to be standardized from neighborhood to neighborhood; so personalities and healthful competitiveness can be fostered. Public sanitary stations can be clean and safe as they are in San Francisco and not dirty and dangerous as they are in Boston and New York. Sidewalk pavements can be made more cheerful by the use of simple mosaics as one can see in cities from ancient Ostia to modern Lisbon, and these can be used for advertising too.

All fountains are not wasteful. Some of the most interesting contemporary ones are wedded to practical uses, as the cool-

ing ponds in front of Deere and Company in Moline, Illinois
or the spectacular Jet d'Eau in Geneva, which, spurting 452
feet high in Lac Leman, was originally created to help equalize
pressure changes in the civic water supply. A hilly city can
connect pools all of which at different levels enjoy the same
run-off of water, which can be collected and recirculated at
the bottom, thus resembling some of the nicest Persian gar
dens. The sculpture of Carl Milles is an important asset to
the public spaces of Stockholm and Göteborg. American
cities would do well to get more of their sculpture out of the
museums and into the streets, but like the Florentines of old
they would need to be more interested in sculpture than in
memorial statues of anybody. The advertising kiosks of Vienna
and Paris, the billboards of Rome, the neon lights of the Ginza
show other pleasures. Each of these details can be seen in
some city, many in the best. They are not common enough
in America. They can be experimented with in selected neigh
borhoods and even competitively at relatively low cost (we
are not talking about hand-made amateur designs) and with a
consequent neighborhood pride and sense of place. Merchants
could make great contributions in this area and to their profit
It is said, perhaps apocryphally, that an influential Fort Worth
banker, opposing the Gruen scheme, snorted that he did not
want to do business in a palm garden. Even a Fort Worth
banker can be wrong. The much publicized and highly suc
cessful Ghirardelli Square in San Francisco has surely demon
strated this.[50] Other cities can have Ghirardelli squares with
out waiting for a local candy factory to become obsolete.

Many of these littler things can certainly be designed pro
fessionally at local levels. To some extent they might even
be designed in the design offices of public bodies although it
might be well to go slow here. Not many cities, if any, will be

[50] This prize-winning square by Wurster, Bernardi and Emmon
was opened in 1965. Plans for enlargement have already been an
nounced. The successful shops are admittedly specialized and high
priced and the restaurants very crowded. It is not exactly a people's
plaisance though the coffee bar comes near to being so. But the
example is, nonetheless, provocative, and a good many things have
to start at the top.

able to put together a very good design office. No modern city can afford to be without a powerful and able city planning commission and a first-rate full-time staff to support it. Such staffs can be assembled although the competition is increasingly keen. But design for beauty is something else again.

No city can afford to pay for the full-time talents of even one first-class designer who, anyway, would not be content to work in splendid isolation. Almost any man of real repute in this field earns today much more than the top city officials. Moreover, he works better as a free man. It would be an unusual designer of the first rank who could stand continually the conditions and limitations that are almost inevitable in American public work and civic service regulations. For design the city would do better to have one sharp-nosed and sensitive talent picker who was reluctant to undertake work himself but who was happy in finding the right men for the right jobs. The United States government has partially learned this lesson. Industrial corporations found out long ago that they got better design from outside architects than they did from their own staffs or even from a single outside architect who did all their work.

Summary

In Martin Meyerson's book frequently cited above there is an interesting, final section called "Constraints and Possibilities."[51] It will not be recapitulated here. It should be consulted; many of the ideas have appeared somewhere in this text. A short summary would merely say that we certainly have both the financial means and the esthetic know-how to have beautiful cities if we want them enough. But we may want other things more. If we do want beautiful cities they will be the result of large collaborations with much give and take between governmental agencies and private management. For years to come the private sector may have to continue to supply more than its share of leadership, imagination, daring, and civic-mindedness.

[51] Meyerson, *et al.*, *Face of the Metropolis*, pp. 233–238.

There is a major hazard as well as the minor ones that this essay has been describing. "What is everybody's business is nobody's business. The greatest need in our cities is not so much for a giant rebuilding program as for a giant upsurge of popular concern for and pride in the urban environment."[52]

But popular concern is not self-generating. The grass roots are nurtured by examples, not by theory. The examples can be provided only by courageous and "foolish" men of public and private affairs who dare to stick their necks out—and are not embarrassed to be known as promoters of urban joy. Their cities in the end might laud their memories. It has happened before.

BIBLIOGRAPHY

Out of the myriad books and articles on the city and its beauties, old and new, the following, all relatively new, are suggested as having the most relevance to the topic of this essay.

Bacon, Edmund N. *Design of Cities.* New York: Viking, 1967.

Burchard, John E. "Megalopolitan Inurbanity," *Technology Review,* vol. 68, no. 3 (Jan. 1966), pp. 15 et ff.

Cullen, Gordon. *Townscape.* London: Architectural Press, 1961.

Gibberd, Frederick. *Town Design.* London: Architectural Press, 1959.

Kouwenhoven, John A. *Made in America.* Garden City: Doubleday Anchor, 1962.

Logie, Gordon. *The Urban Scene.* London: Faber & Faber, 1954.

Lynch, Kevin. *The Image of the City.* Cambridge: M.I.T. Press, 1960.

Meyerson, Martin, *et al. Face of the Metropolis.* New York: Random House, 1963.

Meyerson, Martin, *et al. Metropolis in Ferment,* Philadelphia, *The Annals,* 1957. In this edited symposium see John E. Burchard, "The Urban Aesthetic."

Nairn, Ian. *Counter Attack.* London: Architectural Press, 1957.

Sitte, Camillo. *The Art of Building Cities* (Chas. T. Stewart, tr.). New York: Reinhold, 1945.

[52] *Ibid.,* p. 23.

Tunnard, Christopher. *Gardens in the Modern Landscape*. London: Architectural Press, 1948.

Tunnard, Christopher, with Henry H. Reed. *American Skyline*. Boston: Houghton Mifflin, 1955.

Zucker, Paul. *Town and Square*. New York: Columbia University Press, 1959.

Of interest on larger theoretical, philosophical, or historical grounds would be many of the published works of Steen Eiler Rasmussen, Sigfried Giedion, José Luis Sert, Walter Gropius, Sir Herbert Read, Eliel Saarinen, Clarence Stein, J. M. Richards, Vincent Scully, and particularly Sir John Summerson and Le Corbusier. There are also books about a good many individual architects and individual projects.

URBAN CRIME

Marvin E. Wolfgang

The Volume and Character of Urban Crime

Official police statistics consistently indicate that in general urban areas have higher crime rates than rural areas. Moreover, the rate of serious crimes per 100,000 population appears to increase with the size of the community.

Table 1, derived from the *Uniform Crime Reports* of 1965, shows the number of "index" offenses—the seven crimes the FBI considers most serious—and rates per 100,000 popula-

---

Source: Uniform Crime Reports, 1965, p. 51.

[a] Population by area for each state is 1965 estimate; total population for each state is Bureau of the Census provisional estimate as of July 1, 1965, and subject to change. All rates were calculated on the estimated population before rounding.

[b] The percentage representing area actually reporting will not coincide with the ratio between reported and estimated crime totals because these data represent the sum of the calculations for individual states, which have varying populations, portions reporting, and crime rates.

Table 1. Index of crime, United States, 1965.

Area	Population[a]	Total offenses	Murder and non-negligent manslaughter	Forcible rape	Robbery	Aggravated assault	Burglary, breaking or entering	Larceny, theft, $50 and over	Auto theft
United States total	193,818,000	2,780,015	9,850	22,467	118,916	206,661	1,173,201	762,352	486,568
Rate per 100,000 inhabitants		1,434.3	5.1	11.6	61.4	106.6	605.3	393.3	251.0
Standard metropolitan statistical area	129,796,000								
Area actually reporting[b]	97.4%	2,268,555	6,801	17,408	108,682	155,479	937,583	615,931	426,671
Estimated total	100.0%	2,312,351	6,978	17,844	110,623	158,843	956,038	627,054	434,971
Rate per 100,000 inhabitants		1,781.5	5.4	13.7	85.2	122.4	736.6	483.1	335.1
Other cities	24,338,000								
Area actually reporting	88.5%	215,748	716	1,170	3,951	17,412	97,106	65,950	29,443
Estimated total	100.0%	242,345	851	1,317	4,433	20,435	109,121	73,408	32,780
Rate per 100,000 inhabitants		995.7	3.5	5.4	18.2	84.0	448.4	301.6	134.7
Rural	39,684,000								
Area actually reporting	75.0%	173,735	1,296	2,412	2,786	17,684	86,019	48,816	14,722
Estimated total	100.0%	225,319	2,021	3,306	3,860	27,383	108,042	61,890	18,817
Rate per 100,000 inhabitants		567.8	5.1	8.3	9.7	69.0	272.3	156.0	47.4

tion by different types of areas in the United States. The total crime index rate in large metropolitan areas (1,782 per 100,000) is nearly two times higher than the rate in other cities (996) and about three times higher than in rural areas (568). In each of the seven offenses used in the crime index (murder and nonnegligent manslaughter, forcible rape, robbery, aggravated assault, burglary, larceny of $50 and over, auto theft) this direction of decreasing rates from standard metropolitan areas to other cities to rural areas is evident except for murder and nonnegligent manslaughter, which has a rate of 3.5 for smaller cities, compared to 5.4 for SMSA's and 5.1 for rural areas, and for forcible rape, which is 5.4 for smaller cities, 13.7 for SMSA's and 8.3 for rural areas. (It should be noted, however, that these slight variations are not to be found with consistency over the 35 years of national crime reporting, and no great significance should be attached to them. The mark of consistency over long stretches of time is found, however, in the high crime rates reported for communities with large populations.)

When crime rates are examined by groups of cities of decreasing size, the consistency of decreasing rates is especially striking. In general, the larger the city category, the higher the crime rate for all "serious" crimes combined, as well as for most offenses. Table 2 shows that the differences between the most populated and the least populated communities are extremely large. For example, the 56 cities with over 250,000 inhabitants have rates that exceed the 2,119 cities under 10,000 inhabitants in the following respects: over twice as high in murder and nonnegligent manslaughter, four times higher in forcible rape, sixteen times higher in robbery, over three times higher in aggravated assault, over twice as high in burglary and larceny, and five times higher in automobile theft.

In 1965 the 56 largest cities with a total population of 42,573,000 reported nearly three times the total number of robberies (76,115) that occurred in all the other 4,017 cities with a population of 74,401,000 (27,561 robberies). A dramatic example of the fact that the highest probability of robbery—which is mostly a street offense—occurs in the largest cities may be found in a comparison of Chicago with groups of smaller cities. The Chicago metropolitan area alone, with only 6,641,000 estimated population in 1965, reported about twice as many robberies (16,224) as the combined number (8,293) reported by all "other cities" of less than metropolitan size and rural areas, together representing 64,022,000 inhabitants. In general, the rate of robberies recorded by the police ranged from 11.8 in cities of less than 10,000 population to 178.8 in cities of over 250,000.

Not only do big cities have more crime, within those cities crime is concentrated at the center. The percentage of stores that were burglarized, or in which persons were robbed, decreased regularly from the center of the city (Chicago) toward the city limits, and the decrease continued steadily for 125 miles except in one area where the rate increased slightly because of the presence of a medium-sized city.[1] Similar findings were noted for the metropolitan area of Detroit relative to the offenses of homicide, assault, rape, and robbery.[2]

Recent data from Norway and Denmark are also suggestive of the "criminogenic" (producing crime or criminality) character of cities. Christie[3] reported that, of all males born in Norway in 1933, 5 percent were registered as offenders by 1958. Nine percent of males from the big city of Oslo became offenders, compared with 8 percent from other cities and 4 percent from rural areas. Wolf[4] examined a sample of over 3,000 males in Denmark who were 21 years of age or older in 1953–54, and found that 9.6 percent were offenders: 13 percent lived in Copenhagen, 9 percent lived in towns of between 2,000 and 19,000 inhabitants, and only 6 percent lived in small towns under 2,000 population.

[1] Edwin Sutherland and Donald R. Cressey, *Principles of Criminology*, 7th ed. (Philadelphia: Lippincott Co., 1966), pp. 188–189.

[2] Stuart Lottier, "Distribution of Criminal Offenses in Metropolitan Regions," *Journal of Criminal Law and Criminology*, 29 (May–June 1938), 37–50.

[3] Nils Christie, *Unge norske lovovertredere* (Oslo, Norway: Universitets for laget, 1960).

[4] Preben Wolf, "Crime and Social Class in Denmark," *British Journal of Criminology*, 13 (July 1962), 15–17.

Table 2. Crime rates, offenses known to the police, 1965, by population groups (1965 estimated population).[a]

Population group	Crime index total	Murder and non-negligent man-slaughter	Forcible rape	Robbery	Aggravated assault	Burglary, breaking or entering	Larceny, theft, $50 and over	Auto theft
Total cities, 4,073; total pop. 116,974,000								
Number of offenses known	2,115,860	6,474	14,512	103,676	149,433	857,088	575,498	409,179
Rate per 100,000 inhabitants	1,808.8	5.5	12.4	88.6	127.7	732.7	492.0	349.8
Group I								
56 cities over 250,000; pop. 42,573,000								
Number of offenses known	1,106,313	3,936	9,112	76,115	85,236	418,341	269,622	243,951
Rate per 100,000	2,598.6	9.2	21.4	178.8	200.2	982.6	633.3	573.0
Group II								
96 cities, 100,000 to 250,000; pop. 13,704,000								
Number of offenses known	277,040	873	1,536	10,017	20,691	119,380	76,156	48,387
Rate per 100,000	2,021.7	6.4	11.2	73.1	151.0	871.2	555.7	353.1

Group III 230 cities, 50,000 to 100,000; pop. 15,788,000							
Number of offenses known	254,002	545	1,312	7,652	13,442	106,516	77,621	46,914
Rate per 100,000	1,608.8	3.5	8.3	48.5	85.1	674.6	491.6	297.1
Group IV 468 cities, 25,000 to 50,000; pop. 16,280,000							
Number of offenses known	216,457	499	1,018	5,353	11,515	91,450	72,036	34,586
Rate per 100,000	1,329.6	3.1	6.3	32.9	70.7	561.7	442.5	212.4
Group V 1,104 cities, 10,000 to 25,000; pop. 17,003,000							
Number of offenses known	170,821	387	949	3,170	11,343	78,514	52,575	23,883
Rate per 100,000	1,004.7	2.3	5.6	18.6	66.7	461.8	309.2	140.5
Group VI 2,119 cities under 10,000; pop. 11,626,000							
Number of offenses known	91,227	234	585	1,369	7,206	42,887	27,488	11,458
Rate per 100,000	784.7	2.0	5.0	11.8	62.0	368.9	236.4	98.6

Source: Uniform Crime Reports, 1965, p. 95.

a Population figures rounded to the nearest thousand. All rates were calculated on the population before rounding.

Arrest data from the FBI's *Uniform Crime Reports* (*UCR*) must be interpreted with considerable caution because police practices vary widely from one city to another.[5] Nevertheless, the 1965 *UCR* produces some dramatic examples of crimes that are concentrated in big cities. Perhaps the most striking arrest statistics are those that indicate the magnitude of narcotic drug law violations, gambling, prostitution, and commercialized vice in cities over 250,000 population. For cities in this category (Group I in Table 2) the narcotic arrest rate is 85 per 100,000. A sharp drop to a rate of 21 occurs among cities between 100,000 and 250,000 and continues in descending order to a rate of 6 for cities under 10,000 (Group VI). This same pattern is found for gambling arrest rates, which are 223 in the largest cities and show a sharp decrease to a rate of 70 in Group II cities and a continued regular decrease to a low of 10 in Group VI cities. Finally, prostitution and commercialized vice also follow this pattern: an arrest rate of 72 in the largest cities, 17 in Group II cities, and a steady decline to a rate of 2 per 100,000 in the smallest cities.

Within cities, delinquency and crime vary widely among different neighborhoods. The classic study of Shaw and McKay[6] in Chicago still remains as one of the most revealing. Among its major conclusions were the following: (1) Rates of delinquency and adult crime went down as one moved out from the center of the city. Thus, those areas nearest the center had the highest rates and those farthest from the center had the lowest rates. (2) Zones with high rates of truancy from school also had high rates for delinquency and adult crime. (3) The areas with the highest rates of crime and delinquency were characterized by physical deterioration,

---

[5] See Appendix below describing and evaluating criminal statistics used in America, especially the FBI *Uniform Crime Reports*.

[6] Clifford R. Shaw and Henry D. McKay, *Juvenile Delinquency and Urban Areas* (Chicago: University of Chicago Press, 1942); also, C. R. Shaw, *et al., Delinquency Areas* (Chicago: University of Chicago Press, 1929). For a summary and critique of ecological studies of delinquency, see Terrence Morris, *The Criminal Area* (London: Kegan Paul, 1958).

declining population, high density, economic insecurity, poor housing, family disintegration, transiency, conflicting social norms, and an absence of constructive, positive agencies. (4) The areas with the highest rates in 1930 also had the highest rates in 1900 despite the fact that the ethnic composition of the population had changed greatly. *Whether occupied by Swedes and Germans at one time, or then replaced by Poles, Italians, Syrians, Negroes, and other ethnic groups later, the delinquency rates for the areas near the center of the city remained high.*

These conclusions have been confirmed by similar investigations in at least fifteen cities. Moreover, the findings reported by Pauline Young[7] on an immigrant settlement in Los Angeles add weight to the argument expressed by Sutherland and Cressey that "the delinquency rate is more likely to be a function of social pressures in an area than of the biological or psychological traits of people who reside there."[8] Young found that the original delinquency rate of 5 percent rose to 46 percent within five years after the immigrant group moved to Los Angeles; that within another ten years no less than 83 percent of the immigrant children had accumulated records in the juvenile courts.

Bernard Lander[9] in Baltimore, David Bordua[10] in Detroit, and Roland Chilton[11] in Indianapolis have presented

[7] Pauline V. Young, "Urbanization as a Factor in Juvenile Delinquency," *Publications of the American Sociological Society*, 24 (1930), 162–166; also, her book, *The Pilgrims of Russia-Town* (Chicago: University of Chicago Press, 1932).

[8] Sutherland and Cressey, *Principles of Criminology*, p. 196.

[9] Bernard Lander, *Towards an Understanding of Juvenile Delinquency* (New York: Columbia University Press, 1954).

[10] David J. Bordua, "Juvenile Delinquency and 'Anomie': An Attempt at Replication," *Social Problems*, 6 (Winter 1958–59), 230–238.

[11] Roland J. Chilton, "Continuity in Delinquency Area Research: A Comparison of Studies for Baltimore, Detroit and Indianapolis," *American Sociological Review*, 29 (February 1964), 71–83.

For other factor analytic studies of urban crime, see Karl Schuessler, "Components of Variation in City Crime Rates," *Social Problems*, 9 (1962), 314–323; Karl Schuessler and Gerald Slatin, detailed and sophisticated studies of delinquency, seeking by statistical analysis to relate the characteristics of the population with differences in the rates of delinquency in various areas of a city. Although there are some differences among the findings of these authors, and interesting methodological questions are raised, Chilton concluded: "[Statistical analysis] for Detroit and Indianapolis indicated that *overcrowded* housing, [low] *income, unrelated individuals* and [low] *education* may . . . be importantly related to delinquency. Regardless of the label applied to these variables, it seems reasonably clear that the factors associated with delinquency in Baltimore and Detroit in 1940 and 1950, respectively, were also associated with delinquency in Indianapolis in 1950."[12]

Especially in cities, crime occurs close to the places where criminals live. This generalization holds best for crimes against the person (such as homicide, rape, and assaults) because the offender and the victim in these offenses are usually of the same race and from the same neighborhood and economic class. Henry Bullock[13] noted in a homicide study in Houston, Texas, that 40 percent of victims and their assailants lived at the same place where the homicide occurred or within the same city block. About 75 percent of the offenders and 87 percent of the victims lived less than two miles from the homicidal confrontation. R. Clyde White's earlier study in Indianapolis[14] revealed that petty crimes against property are likely to occur near the places of residence of the offenders, and more serious property crimes are committed farther from their residence. Recently, Calvin Schmid[15] reported that in Seattle even serious property crimes like robbery and

---

"Sources of Variation in U.S. City Crime, 1950 and 1960," *Journal of Research in Crime and Delinquency,* 1 (July 1964), 127–148.

[12] Chilton, "Continuity in Delinquency Area Research," pp. 81–82.

[13] Henry A. Bullock, "Urban Homicide in Theory and Fact," *Journal of Criminal Law, Criminology and Police Science,* 45 (January–February 1955), 565–575.

[14] R. Clyde White, "A Study of Residence and Place of Origin of Felons in Indianapolis," *Social Forces,* 10 (May 1932), 498–509.

[15] Calvin F. Schmid, "Urban Crime Areas: Part II," *American Sociological Review,* 25 (October 1960), 655–678.

burglary both occur to and are committed by residents in the central areas of the city. About 40 percent of burglaries and over 60 percent of robberies were committed in the central area, and over 30 percent of persons arrested for burglary and 40 percent arrested for robbery resided in this same area.

Urban crime trends are extremely difficult to determine from the data presently available. In general it appears that crime rates for some offenses, especially property crimes, have decreased since the end of World War II and that the rural rate has increased more rapidly than the urban rate. But there are inconsistencies and qualifications that are described in more detail in a later section of this analysis.

Limitations and Interpretations of Urban Crime Statistics

Although the *UCR* is diligently compiled by the FBI, there are many reasons for questioning the usefulness, reliability, and validity of these statistics. Some of these reasons stem from the difficulties inherent in any effort to collect crime statistics; other reasons are associated with faulty or poor methods of classifying and counting the phenomena of crime. These problems have recently been reviewed elsewhere in detail.[16] We shall only outline them here.

Variations in the definitions of crime in the 52 jurisdictions of the United States are broad, making extremely difficult the task of fitting separate state penal code violations into a uniform definition to be applied nationally. Moreover, the collection of statistics is localized, and the 8,000 law enforcement agencies participating in the *UCR* collection vary widely in their practices, administrative policies, and the ratio of police to population.

---

[16] See, for example, Marvin E. Wolfgang, "Uniform Crime Reports: A Critical Appraisal," *University of Pennsylvania Law Review*, 111 (April 1963), 708–738; Sophia M. Robison, "A Critical View of the Uniform Crime Reports," *Michigan Law Review*, 64 (April 1966), 1031–1054; and the defensive article by Peter Lejins, "Uniform Crime Reports," *Michigan Law Review*, 64 (April 1966), 1011–1030.

Research on "hidden delinquency" reveals that much crime is never reported to the police, either because they are never discovered or because they are concealed by the offender or the victim. Among these are fornication, adultery, sodomy, seduction, rape, desertion, nonsupport, gambling, weapons law violations, tax evasion, embezzlement, shoplifting, and so on.[17] Federal crimes are generally not included in the *UCR*, and rules governing commerce and industry, laws concerned with unemployment and social security benefits, although carrying legal sanctions when violated, are usually handled by administrative agencies (such as the National Labor Relations Board or the Securities Exchange Commission) rather than by federal district courts.

Not all crimes reported to the police are properly recorded by the police. The reorganization of the New York City Police Department in 1950 resulted in an "increase" of 400 percent in robberies, 200 percent in assaults with weapons, 700 percent in larceny over rates for 1948 and 1949. The changed reporting and recording procedures that accompanied a central control system enabled police headquarters to follow the process closely. This same experience has been noted in several major cities during the past fifteen years, most recently in New York City when the new Police Commissioner, Howard Leary, announced on April 4, 1966, that an audit of the crime reports revealed an apparent under-reporting by the police in six of the seven index crimes. Auto theft and rape had been under-reported by 22 percent, aggravated assault by 45 percent, larceny by 54 percent, robbery 90 percent, and burglary 96 percent. If corrected, New York State figures would have shown an over-all 1965 crime rate of 2,203 per 100,000 population instead of 1,608, and the rate

[17] For a full discussion of these offenses, see Thorsten Sellin and Marvin E. Wolfgang, *The Measurement of Delinquency* (New York: John Wiley & Sons, Inc., 1964), pp. 31–32, 121–127, 165, 173, 302. See also, Harry Shulman, "The Measurement of Crime in the United States," paper presented at the Fifth International Congress of Criminology, Montreal, Canada, September 3, 1965.

or crimes of violence would have been 279 rather than
193.[18]

In the crime classification system used by the FBI, the seven
crime index offenses are set apart from the nonindex offenses,
as if the former are much more serious. Yet it is known that
arson, kidnapping, and assault and battery (all nonindex
offenses) may in fact involve acts with some physical injury
more often than many index offenses like forcible rape and
even aggravated assault. Forgery, embezzlement, malicious
mischief, and disorderly conduct, which do not appear in the
crime index, can on many occasions result in more property
damage than some property offenses listed in the crime index.

In multiple events, the FBI follows the rule of counting only
that criminal act that is highest in the list of index offenses.
The amount of physical harm or the loss or damage to property is not counted as such and many criminal acts are therefore not recorded statistically. Thus, if an offender commits
forcible rape, burglarizes the house, physically injures the
victim to the point requiring hospitalization, and steals the
victim's automobile, only the rape is counted. Besides this loss
in the statistics, it is obvious that the seven offenses in the
important Crime Index cover a wide range of criminal
behavior. However, under the present *UCR* system, an equal
weight is given the seriousness of each offense. A robbery of
five dollars has the same weight statistically as murder, for
each act contributes equally to the computation of the crime
rate. If the number of criminal homicides in a city increases
and the number of burglaries decreases, there is no way of
determining from the crude crime rate for the city whether
the over-all crime situation has become more serious. Moreover, except for homicide, attempted acts are counted in the
same way as completed acts, despite the patent differences in
injury, loss, or damage.

Statistical deficiencies, especially with respect to urban crime
trends, are too numerous to describe in detail, but until
revisions were introduced in 1958, the most glaring error had

---

[18] Ronald H. Beattie, "Crime in the United States—1965," paper
presented at the Bureau of Criminal Statistics, July 27, 1966
(mimeo), p. 2.

been the computation of crime rates each year on the basis of the last decennial census. Thus, the late 1930's, 1940's, and 1950's (until 1958) regularly contained increasing rates partly (and perhaps primarily) due to the use of the 1930, 1940, and 1950 population figures. Even if the true rate of crime had actually remained the same, this traditional manner of attributing, for example, 1949 crimes to the 1940 population resulted in a recorded high increase in crime.

In addition, absolute percentage changes are commonly reported without reference to population changes. The 1956 *Report* showed that in 353 cities with over 25,000 inhabitants, 1950 had an increase of 11.3 percent over 1940, with increases ranging from 2.5 percent for robbery to 59.3 percent for aggravated assault. Each crime index offense showed a percentage increase. Yet, when these same city data are computed in relation to population they show a 5 percent *decrease* in the rate for 1950 (1,724 per 100,000) compared to 1940 (1,814 per 100,000) instead of the 11.3 percent increase. The actual range is from a decrease of 16.4 percent for robbery to an increase of 36 percent for aggravated assault.[19]

The 1960 *UCR* refers to the fact that "from 1950 to 1960, crime increased 84 percent."[20] There is no indication that this figure refers to absolute numbers and is therefore misleading. Based on rates adjusted for 1950 to include only crimes used in the index for 1960, the increase was actually around 22 percent. Moreover, murder and nonnegligent manslaughter did not change, aggravated assault and robbery dropped slightly, and forcible rape increased slightly. The 22 percent increase was almost entirely in property crimes. The 1965 *UCR* reports a rate increase of 25 percent in violent crime (murder, forcible rape, robbery, and aggravated assault) and an increase of 36 percent in property crime (burglary, larceny of $50 and over, and auto theft) between 1960 and 1965. It is interesting that although the U.S. population increased 8 percent between 1960 and 1965, the total number of arrests of persons

[19] See *Uniform Crime Reports*, 1956, pp. 80–81, table 27. I have made new computations.

[20] *Uniform Crime Reports*, 1960, p. 12.

of all ages and for all reported offenses increased only 9.5 percent.[21]

Efforts to calculate city crime trends over long periods of time are currently being made, as are attempts to provide a more valid measure of crime statistics in general. There is a general belief that crimes are increasing, not only in the central city but also and perhaps more rapidly in the suburban and rural areas. There is also a belief that juveniles are mostly responsible for these increases and that youthful offenders are committing more violent crimes than previously. These assumptions require much closer examination, however, before they can be accepted.

Youth and Violent Crime in the City[22]

If our crime statistics are hard to interpret, our delinquency statistics are in even worse shape. Recording techniques have changed over time, more juvenile police officers are engaged in handling young offenders, and certain minor juvenile offenses such as running away, being incorrigible, or truant, are now being counted as "delinquencies." For over a decade most city police departments have used such categories as "nonofficial arrest" or "remedial-arrest" or "warned-arrest" for apprehending juveniles, but not for arresting adults. Yet these special forms of juvenile disposition are recorded and rates of delinquency are computed on the total. Whole books have been written on these matters,[23] which we cannot pursue here in detail.

The public image of a vicious, violent juvenile population

[21] *Uniform Crime Reports,* 1965, pp. 5, 110.

[22] This section is abstracted in part from my recent White Paper, *The Culture of Youth,* prepared for the National Council on Crime and Delinquency, May 1966.

[23] See, for example, Sellin and Wolfgang, *The Measurement of Delinquency.* A new summary of these problems from around the world may be found in T. C. N. Gibbens and R. A. Ahrenfeldt, *Cultural Factors in Delinquency* (London: Tavistock Publications, 1966).

having a seemingly steady increase in violent crime is not substantiated by the evidence available. There may be more juvenile delinquency recorded today, but even that is predominantly property offenses. Rather consistently we are informed by the *UCR* that two thirds of automobile thefts and about one half of all burglaries and robberies are committed by persons under 18 years of age. Among crimes of personal violence, arrested offenders under age 18 are generally low; for criminal homicide they are about 8 percent; for forcible rape and aggravated assault, about 18 percent.

What this actually means is not that these proportions of these crimes are *committed* by juveniles but that among persons who are taken into custody for these offenses these proportions hold. Most police officers agree that it is easier to effect an arrest in cases involving juveniles than in cases involving adults. Most crimes known to the police are not "cleared by arrest" of the offender and the general clearance rate is roughly 30 percent. Thus, the adult-juvenile distribution among 70 percent of so-called major crimes is not known and cannot safely be projected from the age distribution of offenders arrested.

In addition, the crude legal labels attached to many acts committed by juveniles give a false impression of the seriousness of their acts. For example, a "highway robbery" may be a $100-theft at the point of a gun and may result in the victim's being hospitalized from severe wounds. But commonly, juvenile acts that carry this label and are used for statistical compilation are much more minor. Typical in the files of a recent study were cases involving two nine year old boys, one of whom twisted the arm of the other in the school yard in order to obtain twenty-five cents of the latter's lunch money. This act was recorded and counted as "highway robbery." In another case, one nine year old boy engaged in normal exploratory sexual curiosity with an eight year old girl on a playlot. The girl's mother later complained to the police, who recorded the offense as "assault with intent to ravish."

Nothing now exists in the official published collection of crime statistics to yield better information about these variations in seriousness. Weighted scores of seriousness are possible and available for producing a weighted rate of crime and delinquency, but they are almost never used.[24] Without a weighted system it is only the incautious observer who is willing to assert that youth crime is worse today than a generation or even a decade ago.

Moreover, computing rates of crime or delinquency per 100,000 is an extremely unsatisfactory and crude technique. Even a rate for all persons under 18 years of age fails to account for the bulges in specific ages like 14, 15, 16, 17, 18 that have occurred because of high birth rates shortly after World War II. Without age-specific rates, most criminologists are reluctant to make assertions about trends or even the current amount of juvenile crime and violence. Research is now in progress under the auspices of the President's Crime Commission and at the Center of Criminological Research at the University of Pennsylvania with these issues in mind. It is hoped that, if proper data can be gathered, new and more meaningful age-specific rates will be available. It would not be unexpected if, when these rates are computed, much of the recorded increase in violent juvenile crime for the past eight years or so will be such that it could be attributed to statistical error.

Though the results are not in, we can make some educated guesses now. By making certain gross assumptions about the proportion of the juvenile population between the delinquency-prone ages of 10 and 17 for cities of 2,500 and over[25] it has been possible to provide juvenile rates for violent or assaultive crimes against the person. The number of juveniles under 18 years of age arrested for specific offenses, divided by the population of persons aged 10 to 17, multiplied

[24] For details of one such weighting system, see Sellin and Wolfgang, *The Measurement of Delinquency,* chaps. 15–20.

[25] *Uniform Crime Reports,* 1958 to 1964. See also the report of the New York Division of Youth on this period, "Youth Crime—A Leveling Off?" *Youth Service News,* 17 (Spring 1966), 3–5; and the succinct analysis of *UCR* and California data by Ronald H. Beattie and John P. Kenney, "Aggressive Crimes," in Marvin E. Wolfgang, ed., *Patterns of Violence, The Annals of the American Academy of Political and Social Science,* 364 (March 1966), 73–85.

by 100,000, yielded a rate for each of the years. Table 3 shows these rates.[26]

Caution must be applied to these figures because of the two major assumptions that had to be made: (1) that the *UCR*

[26] Computations were made in the following way: The population of all cities of 2,500 inhabitants and more, included in the Uniform Crime Reporting area, was summed for each of the seven years from 1958 through 1964 (1958 was a year of important revisions in the *UCR* classification system; hence, a safe year with which to begin the analysis). The total populations of the United States and of children from ages 10 through 17 were obtained for each of the seven years from reports of the Bureau of the Census. The respective proportions of the 10 to 17 year old population for each year were readily obtained from these census reports and then applied to the *UCR* survey population.

The following data were used for computing the rates:

The *UCR* survey populations of cities of 2,500 and more inhabitants for the years 1958–1964 were as follows: for 1958— 52,329,497; 1959—56,187,181; 1960—81,660,735; 1961—85,158,360; 1962—94,014,000; 1963—94,085,000; 1964—99,326,000 (from *UCR*, tables 18, 17, 18, 21, 21, 28, 27 for the respective years).

The United States population for the years 1958–1964: 174,882,000; 177,830,000; 180,684,000; 183,756,000; 186,591,000; 189,417,000; 192,119,000 (from Estimates of the Bureau of Census, United States Department of Commerce, *Current Population Reports,* series P-25, no. 314, August 1965).

The percentages that the *UCR* survey population represented of the total U.S. population were: 29, 31, 45, 46, 50, 50, and 52 (computed).

The U.S. population aged 10 to 17 for the years 1958–1964 was: 23,443,000; 24,607,000; 25,364,000; 26,023,000; 27,983,000; 29,119,000 (from Estimates of the Bureau of Census, Department of Commerce, *Current Population Reports,* series P-25.).

The *UCR* child population aged 10 to 17 for the years 1958– 1964 was: 6,798,470; 7,628,170; 11,413,800; 13,468,000; 13,999,150; 15,141,880 (assumed and computed).

The number of persons under 18 years of age arrested for each of the five offenses over each of the seven years may be found on the specific table in the *UCR* annual reports.

The author had the assistance of Bernard Cohen, Research Assistant, Center of Criminological Research, University of Pennsylvania, in gathering and computing these data, and is grateful to

Table 3. Urban arrest rates for crimes of violence, 1958–1964: persons arrested aged 10–17, for cities with population 2,500 or more.

Crime	1958	1959	1960	1961	1962	1963	1964
Murder and non-negligent man-slaughter	1.9	2.3	3.0	3.2	2.9	2.9	3.1
Negligent man-slaughter	1.15	0.98	1.10	0.96	0.79	1.00	0.87
Forcible rape	10.0	9.8	10.9	11.4	11.2	10.3	10.0
Aggravated assault	34.4	35.5	53.2	60.1	61.6	63.0	74.5
Other assaults	95.9	118.0	118.7	126.0	139.2	153.7	163.6

survey population contained roughly the same proportion of persons aged 10 to 17 as the general population of the United States; and (2) that the overwhelming bulk of arrests of juveniles under 18 years of age, for offenses against the person, involved offenders no younger than age 10. It is assumed that little error is involved in this latter assumption because most juvenile court statutes with a lower age limit do not go below ages six or seven, and very few of these offenses are ever recorded for ages below ten. Moreover, computing a rate based on the entire population under 18 years would continue the unsatisfactory practice of including in the denominator preschool and infant children.

With this caution and these assumptions, Table 3 can nevertheless be said to show substantially the same rates in 1964 as in 1960 for murder and nonnegligent manslaughter and for rape. Murder and nonnegligent manslaughter reached a peak in 1961 (3.2), was under a rate of 3.0 per 100,000 in 1962 and 1963, and was 3.1 in 1964. These slight variations are of no statistical consequence, considering the operation of chance errors. Negligent manslaughter was highest in 1958

Philip Sagi, Professor of Sociology, for suggestions for statistical applications.

(1.15), had no statistically significant increase in the years since then, and in 1964 was down to 0.87. This offense mostly refers to automobile deaths, and despite the fact that more teenagers are driving today, the rate has not increased. Forcible rape has not significantly changed over the seven years: the high was 11.4 in 1961 and has dropped to 10.3 in 1963 and 10.0 in 1964. Aggravated assault jumped from 34.4 in 1958 to 53.2 in 1960, had a relatively stable rate of 60.1 to 63.0 between 1961 and 1963, and then rose to 74.5 in 1964. Other assaults (not part of the *UCR* index offenses) climbed steadily from 95.9 in 1958 to 163.6 in 1964.

There is little in these figures of criminal homicide or rape that should promote alarm. Assaults appear to be the main area of violence that should cause concern. But not until better data are available from some of the studies previously mentioned can we draw the proper conclusions. The President's Commission on Law Enforcement and the Administration of Justice is presumably preparing to make appropriate recommendations about the display of adult and juvenile crime statistics that should improve our knowledge of the extent and character of violent and other types of crime.

Among city gangs selected for their reputation for "toughness" and studied in detail by detached workers, the amount of violent crime, reports Walter B. Miller, is surprisingly low. Twenty-one groups numbering about 700 members yielded cumulative figures of 228 known offenses committed by 155 boys during a two-year period and 138 court charges for 293 boys during a twelve-year span. Miller remarks: "Violence appears neither as a dominant preoccupation of city gangs nor as a dominant form of criminal activity,"[27] for even among these toughest of gang members, the yearly rate of assault charges per 100 individuals per year of age was only 4.8 at age 15, 7.2 at 16, 7.2 at 17, and 7.8 at 18, after which the rates dropped through the early twenties. Violent crimes were committed by only a small minority of these gang

[27] Walter B. Miller, "Violent Crimes in City Gangs," Marvin E. Wolfgang, ed., *Patterns of Violence, The Annals of the American Academy of Political and Social Science*, 364 (March 1966), 96–112.

members, represented a transient phenomenon, were mostly unarmed physical encounters between combating males, did not victimize adult females, and were not ideological forms of behavior.[28]

Crimes of violence appear to be considerably more common among boys from lower social classes.[29] In their recent study of delinquents, Leon Fannin and Marshall Clinard reported: "One of the more important of the tests was a comparison of the frequency with which reported and unreported robberies and assaults were committed by members of the two class levels [middle and lower]. The vast majority of all lower class delinquents, 84%, had committed at least one such offense compared to 28% of the middle class (p = .01); 28% of the lower and 8% of the middle class had committed 10 or more violent offenses. Class level was also related to the frequency of fighting with other boys. Lower class delinquents fought singly and in groups significantly more often (p = .05) than middle class delinquents, with 20% of them averaging five or more fights per month compared to 4.0%."[30]

It should be kept in mind that the proportion of the entire juvenile population under 18 years of age who, in any year, are processed by the police and juvenile court is generally no higher than 3 to 5 percent. There are, however, several fac-

[28] Ibid. For a new, detailed listing of research and theory in this area, see Dorothy Campbell Tompkins, Juvenile Gangs and Street Gangs—A Bibliography (Berkeley: Institute of Governmental Studies at the University of California, 1966).

[29] See Robert Hardt and George E. Bodine, Development of Self-Report Instruments in Delinquency Research (Syracuse: Youth Development Center, Syracuse University, 1965). This is a conference report on methods of doing research on hidden delinquency and includes a good bibliography of major items in that area. See, also, Nils Christie, Johs. Andenaes, and Sigurd Skirbekk, "A Study of Self-Reporting Crime," and Kerstin Elmhorn, "Study in Self-Reported Delinquency among School-Children in Stockholm," in Karl O. Christiansen, ed., Scandinavian Studies in Criminology, vol I (London: Tavistock Publications, 1965).

[30] Leon F. Fannin and Marshall B. Clinard, "Differences in the Conception of Self as a Male Among Lower and Middle Class Delinquents," Social Problems, 13 (1965), 205–214; p. 211 cited.

tors concealed by this commonly reported statistic: (1) Arrest or juvenile-court-appearance statistics include double counting of the same juveniles who have run away, been truant, or committed malicious mischief, and so forth, more than once during the year, and for some types of offenses this amount of duplication can be sizable. (2) The figure ignores the fact that children have been delinquent during preceding years. In many areas in large cities 70 percent or more of all juveniles under 18 years of age, at one time or another, may have been delinquent. Solomon Kobrin[31] and others have drawn attention to this perspective. Nils Christie[32] in Norway has done the most elaborate study on the topic by analyzing a birth cohort. Thorsten Sellin and Marvin Wolfgang[33] are presently engaged in large-scale research on approximately 10,000 males in Philadelphia in order to compute a cohort rate of delinquency, examine their cumulative seriousness by age and over time, and provide a prediction model that might aid in decisions about the most propitious time in a juvenile's life for effective social intervention.

In sum, the data needed to describe the volume of youth crime are inadequate at present, but an alarmist attitude does not appear justified. Age-specific and weighted rates are required before trends can be analyzed. Because of the known rise in the adolescent population due to high fertility rates of the late 1940's, there is reason to suspect that any over-all increase in juvenile delinquency can be largely attributed to the population increase in the ages from 14 to 18. The absolute amount of delinquency can be expected to increase for some time for this same reason, but there is no basis for assuming that rates of juvenile violence will increase.

[31] Solomon Kobrin, "The Conflict of Values in Delinquency Areas," *American Sociological Review*, 16 (October 1951), 653–661.

[32] Nils Christie, *Unge norske lovovertredere* (Oslo, Norway: Institute of Criminology, Oslo University, 1960).

[33] Thorsten Sellin and Marvin E. Wolfgang, "The Extent and Character of Delinquency in an Age Cohort," research project of the Center of Criminological Research, University of Pennsylvania, sponsored by the National Institute of Mental Health.

As more families move to suburbs and more suburban families have teenage children, the amount of juvenile delinquency can be expected to rise in these areas even without a rate increase. In addition, as lower-middle class families move to suburbia, the higher rates of delinquency of this group will probably travel with them. As Robert Bohlke[34] has suggested, what is often viewed as "middle-class delinquency" is not middle class in the sense of the traditional middle-class value system or life style but only in terms of membership in a middle-income group, not all of whose members can be expected to accept the dominant values.

Finally, a certain amount of delinquency has always existed, will continue to exist, and perhaps should exist. In the sense discussed by Emile Durkheim,[35] crime is "normal," and perhaps even in some quantity desirable. Not only does the existence of delinquency provide the collective conscience an opportunity to reinforce its norms by applying sanctions, but the presence of deviancy reflects the existence of something less than a total system of control over individuals. Moreover, there appear to be personality traits among many delinquents that would be viewed as virtues if behavior were rechanneled. For instance, Sheldon and Eleanor Glueck noted in *Unraveling Juvenile Delinquency*[36] that delinquent boys could be characterized as hedonistic, distrustful, aggressive, hostile, socially assertive, and defiant of authority. The nondelinquents were more banal, conformist, neurotic, insecure, and anxiety-ridden. The attributes associated with the delinquents sound similar to descriptions of the "Renaissance Man" who defied the authority and static orthodoxy of the

[34] Robert H. Bohlke, "Social Mobility, Stratification Inconsistency in Middle Class Delinquency," *Social Problems*, 8 (Spring 1961), 351–363. See also, Ralph W. England, Jr., "A Theory of Middle-Class Delinquency," *Journal of Criminal Law, Criminology and Police Science*, 50 (April 1960), 535–540.

[35] Emile Durkheim, *Rules of Sociological Method*, 8th ed., trans. Sarah A. Solvay and John H. Mueller and ed. George E. G. Catlin (Glencoe, Ill.: The Free Press, 1950), pp. 66–73.

[36] Sheldon and Eleanor Glueck, *Unraveling Juvenile Delinquency* (Cambridge, Mass.: Harvard University Press for the Commonwealth Fund, 1950).

Middle Ages, who was also aggressive, richly assertive, "this-world" rather than "other-world" centered, and was less banal and more innovative than his medieval predecessors. The Glueck delinquents also sound much like our nineteenth-century captains of industry and our twentieth-century political leaders and corporation executives. The freedom to be assertive, to defy authority and orthodoxy, may sometimes have untoward consequences like crime and delinquency. But it is well to remember that many aspects of American ethos—like this freedom, or our benevolent attitude toward rapid social change, our heritage of revolution, our encouragement of massive migrations that uproot families and shift friends, our desire to be in or near large urban centers, our wish to travel fast and in our own vehicles—and many other values that we cherish may produce the delinquency we deplore as well as the many things we desire.

The Fear of Being Victimized

There appears to be a widespread fear throughout the United States, especially in central cities, of being assaulted, robbed, and raped on the streets. As gleaned from a presidential campaign that emphasized this theme, the establishment of a President's Commission on Law Enforcement and the Administration of Justice, private conversations, professional conferences, and mass media, most social analysts agree that the fear is present and real, although there is dispute about whether the fear is justified.

As the mass media present more news about crime more rapidly to more consumers over wider areas and about wider areas, there is a propensity for these consumers to assume that the incidence or frequency of crime is increasing, whether or not it is in reality. This kind of "instant" news, with a cultural tradition of interest in crime, may be partially responsible for the production of the fear of being victimized.

Official rates of some crimes of violence are moderately increasing. Improved methods of recording, greater use of civilian employees to tabulate and correctly calculate crime statistics in city police departments,[37] increased citizen willingness to report crimes, and other such factors probably increase apparent crime rates, but by how much is not known.

Despite the tendency of some criminologists to de-emphasize the crude rates of increase of crime in the city and to draw attention to age-specific rates by reference to the increase in the teenage population because of the high postwar births, there is nonetheless a probability of being victimized that may have increased considerably over the past fifteen years.

For example, let us for the sake of argument assume that violent crime *rates* have changed little over this time but that, as the *UCR* figures indicate, the *volume* of these offenses has greatly increased. The perspective of the potential victim is not concerned about the crime rate of *offenders*, or even the rate at which persons become victims of crime. He is concerned, rather, with the probability of becoming a victim in a given urban space, like on a certain street corner, on a given block, or near a certain place of business. The population of a neighborhood may have increased over fifteen years, the number of youths in crime-prone ages may have increased even though the crude rate of violent crime or even the rate of juvenile crime may have remained fairly steady. Since the size of the neighborhood has not increased (a street intersection retains the same square footage), the result is that the chances of a given citizen's being assaulted at that intersection have increased. It is not "moral decay" of the city that provides the answer to the question of why it is now less safe to walk past that intersection. Even without an increase in the crime rate, the higher proportion of persons in the ages of highest crime rates converging in greater numbers on that street corner will increase the chances that a person living near that corner will become a victim.

We have omitted reference to the greater vehicular mobility of youth and other ages and the greater freedom of movement around the city, and an increase in the space they oc-

---

[37] For this suggestion the author is grateful to Philip Sagi and Charles Wellford, who are preparing a paper on the periodicity of certain crime rate increases that are correlated with recorded increases of civilian employees in urban police departments.

cupy. These and other factors could readily be added to the central notion already expressed. Unfortunately, there have been few data on crime collected from the viewpoint of what Stanton Wheeler[38] has called the "consumer" or victim. Rates of burglaries by number of places to burglarize, rates of street robberies by the estimated number of persons on public streets at given times of the day,[39] rates of auto theft by the number of registered automobiles—all are typical forms in which victimization data might be collected and thereby illuminate the more orthodox offender-oriented crime statistics.

It should be kept in mind that certain types of fear of being victimized appear to have little or no support from available data. For two particular types of assaultive crimes—homicide and rape—there are some useful and consistent data on victim-offender relationships. It is unfortunate that we do not have more information about offenses like robbery, which would be of larger numerical concern. But from the viewpoint of gravity, death and rape are more disastrous and of more social consequence.

There is an oft-expressed fear among white females of being killed or raped by nonwhite offenders. National crime statistics provide no ready information on the race of victims and offenders in the same crime episode. However, in a five year study of nearly 600 criminal homicides in Philadelphia between 1948 and 1952, the author[40] noted that in 516, or 94 percent, of the 550 identified relationships, the victim and offender were members of the same race. In only 34, or 6 percent, of these homicides did an offender cross the race line:

[38] Stanton Wheeler, "Critical Statistics: A Reformulation of the Problem," paper read at the annual meeting of the American Statistical Association, Philadelphia, September 1965.

[39] For an interesting effort in this direction, see W. F. Greenhalgh, *A Town's Rate of Serious Crime Against Property and Its Association with Some Broad Social Factors* (London: Home Office Scientific Adviser's Branch Police Report, SA/Pol. 2, 1964); W. F. Greenhalgh, *Police Correlation Analysis: An Interim Report* (London: Home Office Scientific Adviser's Branch Police Report, SA/Pol. 5, 1964).

[40] Marvin E. Wolfgang, *Patterns in Criminal Homicide* (Philadelphia: University of Pennsylvania Press, 1958).

14 were Negro victims slain by whites, and 20 were whites slain by Negroes. In terms of rates per 100,000 population, Negroes were victims of white offenders approximately three times more frequently than were whites of Negro offenders. In this study, the number of Negro women slain by white men equals that of white women slain by Negro men, but of the three white victims, two were prostitutes with long criminal records, but of the three Negro victims, none had a criminal record. Only three cases of each interracial and inter-sex offense occurred in a community of two million inhabitants over a five year period.

In a similar study of rape in Philadelphia covering the years 1958 and 1960, Menachem Amir[41] recorded the race of victim and offender in each situation. Of the 646 cases of identified relationships, 497, or 77 percent, were Negro-Negro; 105, or 16 percent, were white-white (the rest were mixed). Thus, among the 44 cases in which the offender was of one race and the victim of another, 23, or 3.6 percent, contained a white male offender and a Negro victim; and 21, or 3.3 percent, had a Negro male offender and a white victim. Once again, the amount of race crossing is small, and the danger to white women is as minimal as to Negro women— probably much less if reference is made to the nearly institutionalized access white males have had to Negro women, from slavery to recent times, without much fear of reprisal or retribution.

As mentioned earlier, most homicides and lesser assaults occur within the same racial and social group, and victims and offenders reside not far apart. Perhaps the greatest danger to strangers in the city (or elsewhere) is from psychotic personalities like the recent cases of Speck in Chicago and Whitman in Austin, Texas. These are rare, albeit horrendous and dramatic, cases that are difficult to control or even predict. In homicide, the relationship of stranger between victims and offenders generally exists in less than 10 percent of the cases, and these include police officers killed on duty.

---

[41] Menachem Amir, "Patterns of Rape and the Female Victim," unpub. diss., University of Pennsylvania, 1965.

Assaults are most likely to come from the victim's universe
of friends, relatives, and acquaintances.

Criminogenic Forces of the City

There are forces within an urban community that generate
conditions conducive to criminality. Urban living is more
anonymous—it releases the individual from community re
straints and gives him more freedom to deviate. Living in the
more impersonalized, formally controlled urban society
means that conduct is often regulated by distant bureau
crats. The police are strangers executing these prescriptions on
at worst, an alien subcommunity and, at best, an anonymous
set of subjects. Minor offenses in a small town or village
are often handled without resort to official police action, and
as desirable as such action may seem to be, it nonetheless
results in fewer recorded violations of the law, compared to
the city. The villagers are unwilling to tolerate formal, ob
jective law enforcement.

Urban areas, with mass populations, greater wealth, more
commercial establishments, and more products of our technol
ogy, also provide more frequent opportunities for theft. Vic
tims are impersonalized, property is insured, and consumer
goods in more abundance are vividly displayed and are more
portable.

Urban life is commonly characterized by high population
density, spatial mobility, ethnic and class heterogeneity
reduced family functions, and, as we have said, greater ano
nymity. When these traits are found in high degree, and when
they are combined with poverty, physical deterioration, low
education, residence in industrial and commercial centers
unemployment or unskilled labor, economic dependency
marital instability or breaks, poor or absent male models for
young boys, overcrowding, lack of legitimate opportunities
to make a better life, the absence of positive, anti-criminal
behavior patterns, higher frequency of organic diseases
and a cultural minority status of inferiority, social and psy
chological mechanisms leading to deviance are more likely
to operate. These factors include frustration, lack of motiva

tion to obey external demands, conflicting norms, anomie, and so forth. The link between these two conditions—the physical features of parts of a city and its social psychological aspects—has not been fully studied to the point where the latter can safely be said to be the highly probable consequences of the former. To speak of a tradition of lawlessness as a further consequence of the conditions of urban life is an even more tenuous scientific position. Nonetheless, these are the assumptions under which the community of scholars and public administrators operate today. The assumptions are the most justified and logically adequate we can make unless or until successfully refuted.

It has often been suggested that high crime areas of a city (meaning both residence of offenders and places of crime occurrence) contain high numbers of new migrants, the residue of earlier residential groups that have mostly moved out, and competitive failures from better districts who were forced to move back to the cheaper rent areas. This "selective migration" thesis may have some validity, as Donald Taft[42] discovered in a study of Danville, Illinois, many years ago. But he also noted that most of the criminals in the high crime areas had been reared in delinquency areas of other cities.

It is abundantly clear even to the most casual observer that Negroes in American society are the current carriers of a ghetto tradition, that they, more than any other socially defined group, are the recipients of urban deterioration and the social-psychological forces leading to legal deviance. And for this reason, concern for crime in the urban community is commonly a concern for Negro crime. Although there are good reasons for raising serious questions about criminal statistics that report race of the offender and the fact that Negro crime rates are in general three or four times higher than white rates,[43] and although Negroes probably suffer more injustices than whites in the law enforcement process from arrest

[42] Donald R. Taft, "Testing the Selective Influence of Areas of Delinquency," *American Journal of Sociology*, 38 (1933), 699–712.

[43] For a more expansive treatment of this topic, see Marvin E. Wolfgang, *Crime and Race: Conceptions and Misconceptions* (New York: Institute of Human Relations Press, 1964).

to imprisonment, it is no surprise that the most painstaking efforts to measure crime correctly still find Negro crime rates high. When the untoward aspects of urban life are found among Italians, Germans, Poles, or almost any other group, their crime rates are similarly high. Relative deprivation and social disqualification are thus dramatically chained to despair and delinquency.

All of this is not meant to obscure the fact that poverty also exists in small towns and rural areas. But when multiplied by thousands, congested, and transmitted over generations, poverty becomes a culture. Expectations change; irritable, frustrated parents become neglectful and aggressive. Their children inherit a subculture of violence[44] where physically aggressive responses are either expected or required by all members sharing not only the tenement's plumbing but also its system of values. Ready access to weapons in this milieu may be essential to protection against others who respond in similarly violent ways in certain situations. The carrying of knives or other protective devices becomes a common symbol of willingness to participate in violence, to expect violence, and to be ready for it.

The use of violence is not generally viewed by the subculture as illicit conduct, and the users therefore do not have to deal with feelings of guilt about their aggression.[45] Violence often becomes part of the life style, the theme for solving difficult problems or monetary conflicts. Members of the dominant nonviolent culture are not usually the direct targets

[44] The theory of a subculture of violence was first used by me in *Patterns in Criminal Homicide*, 1958. Since then, various articles on the topic have appeared. The most detailed statement appears in Marvin E. Wolfgang and Franco Ferracuti, *Subculture of Violence: Towards an Integrated Theory in Criminology* (London: Tavistock Publishers, forthcoming); also in the Italian edition already published under the title, *Il comportamento violento* (Milan: Giuffre, 1966).

[45] On this point, in addition to *ibid.*, see the succinct and cogent analysis by Daniel Glaser, Donald Kenefick, and Vincent O'Leary, *The Violent Offender* (Washington, D.C.: U.S. Department of Health, Education and Welfare, Office of Juvenile Delinquency and Youth Development, 1966).

of criminal aggression from the subculture of violence, but the support of members willing to display their protest against powerlessness can promote riots that attack outsiders. When there are few alternatives for action to meet the demands of competitive social life, violence may become a typical response.

A subculture of violence is not the product of cities alone. The Thugs of India, the *vendetta barbaricina* in Sardinia, and the *mafioso* in Sicily have existed for a long time. From this subculture, it is suggested, come most violent crimes like homicide, rape, robbery, and aggravated assaults.

Crime Control—Prevention and Treatment

One of the major questions about programs to control crime is where the major effort (that is, time, manpower, money) should be made. Given that resources are limited and that it is desirable to allocate them in the most efficient and effective manner, insufficient attention has been given to the problem. Instead, city and other government agencies often distribute resources in a shotgun fashion under the assumption that every crime control area must be covered. It is not clear whether the major thrust of crime control efforts should be (1) to prevent people from ever committing crime, (2) to prevent first offenders from becoming second offenders, or (3) to concentrate on the recidivist (the very repetitive offender).

These three goals provide a focus for viewing almost all crime control processes. Anti-poverty programs, Project Head Start, better education, urban redevelopment and housing, equal job opportunities, the domestic peace corps, community legal counseling centers, community health centers, publicly supported day school nurseries, Mobilization for Youth, recreational facilities, the Police Athletic League, Big Brothers—all are primarily designed to improve the social system in order to prevent deviance in social interaction and personality. Striking at the forces that appear to yield delinquent products, at the criminal social system that recruits new representatives each generation, is assumed now by man to be in the long run the most effective means to reduce th volume of crime. This social engineering approach make the whole milieu the object for mounting an attack on crime These programs are costly, affect the economic and politica structure of society, and are meant not only to reduce crim and delinquency but to eliminate reasons for riots, improv the condition of men generally, and provide opportunitie for participation in power and the dominant culture's decision making features.

A more direct attack on delinquency, once manifested, i found in social action programs like the Chicago Are Project and other similar plans for what has become know as "detached workers"—that is, social workers and others wh work in the poorer neighborhoods and are attached to stree gangs. These workers gain the respect and confidence of gan leaders and try to rechannel their energies away from crim inal to more constructive or at least neutral activities. Gan control units in juvenile aid divisions of city police depart ments or in public and private agencies have reported suc cessful years of preventing gang wars, rescuing young live from careers of crime, and halting many acts of violenc Financial support for private foundations and the federal gov ernment has expanded these programs to the point wher they have become the institutional mode of prevention i many large cities.

With recent passage of the Law Enforcement Assistanc Act, many police departments are engaging in research an technological innovations connected with crime control an investigation. Improved record keeping, communicatio systems, crime laboratories, computerized operations researc techniques for patrol assignments, upgrading education i police-community relations, and new recruiting practices ar part of these activities to aid in prevention, detection, an deterrence.

The field of correction is concerned with treatment of th offender and ranges from court disposition through priso and release procedures. The principles of probation an parole suggest that offenders sent back to the communit as an alternative to incarceration require supervision both as a further protection to society and as a counseling help to the offender. The philosophy appears appropriate; the practice is often poor. Underpaid and understaffed probation offices and parole boards cannot provide the attention and assistance needed to carry out the principles of these programs. But despite great population increases and rising crime rates, fewer persons are in prison today than thirty years ago, primarily because these alternatives to imprisonment are widely used.

In work camps, correctional schools and cottages, and state farms new approaches to manipulate the attitudes, values, and behavior of prisoners are being tried with more funds and administrative support than these facilities have ever experienced before. Most bureaus of correction still maintain mediocre correctional systems that are concerned with securely housing offenders but that allow little innovative work and no sustained therapy program. But some states are regularly experimenting and improving their correctional systems. Group and individual therapy are only part of these relatively newer approaches.

The correctional task is generally not that of city governments, but one of the chief contributions cities can make is to permit, even encourage, state and county correctional institutions to be located physically within the city borders. The principal reason is that the large urban center provides a cluster of professional talent sorely needed in research and clinical practice within these institutions. In the past, many mental hospitals and prisons were placed in isolated rural settings, but facilities found in bucolic beauty have not successfully attracted bright young men, research teams, or experienced psychiatrists and psychologists. The city, with its medical and educational centers, should be the site of new correctional institutions of the future.

Predicting delinquency, or the success and failure of treated offenders, is a special area of interest to research criminologists and should be to public administrators. The work of Sheldon and Eleanor Glueck, Harvard's husband-wife team throughout a whole generation, has dealt extensively with a "social prediction table"[46] designed to predict delinquen propensity before it occurs. Concentrating on discipline supervision, parent-child affection, and the degree of cohe siveness of family life, these researchers attracted the interes of the New York City Youth Board and led it to experimen over ten years with the prediction model.[47] The results gratif some and disturb others. In general, the Glueck Socia Prediction Table has been claimed by the authors and th New York City Youth Board to be about 85 percent accura in predicting that delinquency will occur sometime prior t age 16 when the boys being predicted are studied at age six, a the time they enter first grade. There has been, in these studie a higher proportion of false positives (that is, predicting that boy will be delinquent when in fact he was not) than of fals negatives (predicting non-delinquency when in fact delin quency occurred.) Methodological issues raised by statist cians question the validity of the predictions, and a fear exis that children at six years of age who are "labeled" potenti delinquents will fulfill these prophecies.

Because over half of known delinquents who have com mitted a first offense do not commit a subsequent offense, it sometimes argued that trying to predict all delinquency economically and in other ways inefficient. Moreover, th one-time juvenile offender does not generally commit a seriou act. Therefore, it is suggested, the major effort at prever tion should be made with the vastly reduced population those juveniles who have first come into contact with th law. From this sub-universe, prediction models could b constructed to determine the probabilities of continued de linquency. Once the probability profile is produced, inter vention to prevent the expected delinquency could be unde taken. Major research of this kind is in progress now.

Statistical prediction of success or failure on probatio

[46] For original details of this effort, see Sheldon and Eleano Glueck, *Unraveling Juvenile Delinquency* (Cambridge, Mass Harvard University Press, 1950).

[47] Maude M. Craig and Selma J. Glick, *A Manual of Procedur for Application of the Glueck Prediction Table* (New York: Ne York City Youth Board, 1964).

and parole has at least a thirty year history.[48] By analyzing
various factors in the backgrounds of men who succeed (no
recidivism) or fail (recidivism) when released on parole,
studies in this country and abroad have reached as high as
80 percent accuracy in predicting parole violation of any
kind. Efforts to predict *violent* offenses committed by men
released on parole are much more difficult because only about
5 percent of men currently released on parole commit new
crimes of violence. A parole board trying to predict violent
crimes would have to identify, out of 1,000 releases, 50 men
(or 5 percent) who would commit new crimes of violence and
950 who would not. Such a board, given 80 percent accuracy
in their techniques, would predict violence for 20 percent
of 950, or 190 cases, and for 80 percent of the 50, or 40
cases. Errors would amount to 200 cases, or 190 nonviolent
designated as violent and 10 violent who were not designated
as violent. These are errors apart from others that might be
made in predicting more common types of parole violations,
such as burglary, other theft, and so forth.[49]

Sophisticated techniques requiring computer services have
been introduced for some time and with sufficient accuracy,
reliability, and validity to make their application highly
profitable as aids in determining whom the courts and prisons
can most safely release into the community, and when. But
administrators of public agencies have been reluctant to use
these statistical aids to their intuitive decision making. The
reluctance has come in part from skepticism, a lack of understanding of how statistical analyses have been done, and an
unwillingness to yield intuitive judgments to more objective
criteria for assessing probabilities. The developers of prediction instruments have regularly contended, however, that
their findings should not be used mechanically but only as

[48] For a discussion of this history, see Sheldon and Eleanor
Glueck, *Predicting Crime and Delinquency* (Cambridge, Mass.:
Harvard University Press, 1959); and the most recent review by
W. H. Nagel, *Het voorspellen van kriminell gedrag* (Staatsuit-
geverij s'Gravenhage, 1965).

[49] The author is indebted to the analysis of this problem found
in Glaser, Kenefick, and O'Leary, *The Violent Offender*, p. 36.

additional aids to the decision-making process. Judges and parole boards are only now becoming aware of prediction studies as a means to supplement their disposition decisions.

The urban forces that generated crime and focused official attention on the offender reassert themselves once he is returned to the community after serving a sentence. This social feedback mechanism requires that attention be given to insuring that the released offender is not returned to the same milieu that produced him. If, for example, there is validity to the notion of a criminal or violent subculture, it is necessary not merely to treat the offenders who rise to the surface of law enforcement involvement. It is also important for cities to consider the most appropriate means to disperse the group that shares a subculture of violence in order to weaken the impact of that value system. Wider economic opportunities, freedom of residential mobility, urban redevelopment that distributes the subculture population rather than merely housing it intact in new buildings, and other techniques should help to integrate these group members into the larger society and thereby destroy or at least reduce the size and impact of a delinquent subculture.

When rational decisions are made on the basis of research analyses using the best available information at the disposal of decision makers (the police, judges, probation and parole officers), there should be an improvement in the methods of crime control and effectiveness in the treatment of offenders. Traditionally, untested assumptions and unplanned procedures have operated in most police, court, and correctional systems of law enforcement and the administration of justice. Urban crime might be reduced by significant proportions if more talent, time, and funds were put into public use to produce the kind of research findings necessary to make more rational informed decisions.

APPENDIX

The Source of Criminal Statistics in the United States

The major source of criminal statistics in the United States is the *Uniform Crime Reports* (*UCR*) published since 1930 by the Federal Bureau of Investigation from data submitted voluntarily by police departments throughout the country. The number of cooperating police agencies has increased regularly through the years, from 400 in 1930 to over 8,000 in 1965, representing 92 percent of the national population. Offenses reported are violations of the criminal law of the separate states; no violations of federal law per se are tabulated or included in the *UCR*.

Since 1958, when important revisions were made in the presentation of data, crimes have been reported by geographical areas, following as closely as is practical definitions used by the Bureaus of the Budget and the Census. Standard metropolitan statistical areas (SMSA)—generally made up of an entire county or counties having certain metropolitan characteristics and at least one core city of 50,000 or more inhabitants—have the largest absolute population and coverage as reported in the last *UCR* (1965). The SMSA's represented 129,796,000 people, with 97.4 percent of the areas actually reporting to the FBI. "Other cities" are urban places outside the standard metropolitan statistical areas, most of which are incorporated communities of 2,500 or more inhabitants. In the 1965 *UCR* of "other cities" containing a population of 24,338,000, 88.5 percent of these areas actually reported to Washington. Finally, "rural areas," which are made up of unincorporated portions of counties outside of urban places and standard metropolitan areas, had a population of 39,684,000 in 1965, of which 75 percent reported to the FBI. Sheriffs, county police, and many state police report crimes committed within the limits of a county but outside cities, but the police departments within urban places report crimes committed within the city limits.[1]

The crime classification system used by the FBI is based on legal categories of offenses and is derived from an analysis performed originally by the Committee on Uniform Crime Records of the International Association of Chiefs of Police in 1929.[2] The original survey of the committee clearly showed the wide range of variation in statutory definitions of crime in the states. Therefore, offenses such as robbery, burglary, and larceny were broadly defined so that crimes committed under each of the varying state statutes could, for statistical purposes be embraced by the uniform classification system. Crimes were divided into two categories. The first, originally known as Part I, included criminal homicide, rape, robbery, aggravated assault, burglary, larceny, and automobile theft. All other crimes were subsumed in Part II which came to include in 1965 twenty-two subcategories, ranging from minor assaults to parking violations and juveniles who run away from home. Only Part I offenses were recorded under the term "crimes known to the police"; Part II offenses were reported according to the number of "persons charged" by the police. Part I offenses were traditionally referred to as the "major" or "more serious" offenses. These were assumed most likely to be reported to the police in some consistent fashion and to maintain, more than the other offenses, most of which do not come to the attention of the police. The Part I offenses came to be used as a crime index, much like a price or cost-of-living index. The wisdom of using police statistics for such a purpose has best been expressed in modern times by Thorsten Sellin, who suggested that "the value of criminal statistics as a basis for the measurement of criminality in geographi-

[1] *Uniform Crime Reports* (Washington, D.C.: United States Department of Justice, Federal Bureau of Investigation, 1965), pp 43–44, 51.
[2] *Uniform Crime Reporting: A Complete Manual for Police* (New York, N.Y.: Committee on Uniform Records, International Association of Chiefs of Police, 1929).

areas decreases as the procedure takes us farther away from the offence itself."[3]

All the arguments concerning the establishment of a crime index cannot be reviewed here. The use of the term "crime index" in the *UCR* did not appear until 1958, although Part I offenses were traditionally used in that sense. The initial rationale for using these seven offenses as an index appeared in the original work of the Committee on Uniform Crime Records, and is still currently offered: "The total number of criminal acts that occur is unknown, but those that are reported to the police provide the first means of a count. Not all crimes come readily to the attention of the police; not all crimes are of sufficient importance to be significant in an index and not all important crimes occur with enough regularity to be meaningful in an index. With these considerations in mind, the above crimes were selected as a group to furnish an abbreviated and convenient measure of the crime problem."[4]

All law enforcement agencies in the United States receive from the FBI a series of blanks, requesting information for the *UCR*. From completed forms returned by cooperating agencies, the Bureau tabulates crime rates and trends for presentation in the current quarterly preliminary reports and in the annual *UCR*. The kinds of data requested may be found in the *Uniform Crime Reporting Handbook*. For index crimes—formerly Part I offenses—the FBI requests the number of offenses reported to the police, the number of complaints that were found to be false, the number of actual or founded offenses, and the number of offenses cleared by arrest. "Cleared by arrest" means that one or more suspects have been taken into custody by the police and been made available for prosecution. Only the number of founded offenses and the number of offenses cleared by arrest are reported in the *UCR*. The index crimes are the ones most completely tabulated by rates according to population groups: for instance, the age, sex, and race of persons charged; monthly variations; the type and value of property stolen and

[3] Thorsten Sellin, "The Basis of a Crime Index," *Journal of Criminal Law and Criminology*, 22 (1931), 335.

[4] *Uniform Crime Reports*, 1965, p. 50.

recovered; murder victims according to weapons used; and murder victims by age, sex, and race. The rural-urban distribution of index crimes is determined from the police department's location. For crimes other than those that appear in the index, the cooperating agencies report on the number of persons charged (held for prosecution) but not the number of offenses known to the police, as occurs with index crime.

We have said that police records, published in *Uniform Crime Reports,* are our best source for measuring the amount of crime. But we must emphasize that if there is a universe of committed but unrecorded crime, and that if this universe differs from the first level of public knowledge, "offenses known to the police," there is an almost equally huge gap to the next level of knowledge, "offenses cleared by arrest," and any characteristic about the persons arrested. As is well known, the mere fact that someone complains to the police that an offense has occurred does not guarantee discovery of the offender. Only when offenders are taken into custody, however, are we able to say anything in a statistically analytic way about the attributes of offenders in general. This means that in order to analyze juvenile delinquency we must use that group of offenses that result in the arrest of juveniles, and we can only speculate about offenses committed by juveniles not arrested. The same must be said about our analyses of the sex and race of offenders.

In the *UCR,* "cleared by arrest" means that a reported offense is "cleared" (from the police record) by taking into custody one or more suspects and making them available for prosecution. This definition does not mean that the offender is cleared, or exonerated, but that the police are satisfied that the person they have taken into custody is a good suspect and that they can therefore clear their record of concern for that offense. The proportion of offenses cleared by arrest has been fairly constant over many years, and the percentage cleared by type of offense does not appear to vary significantly over time.

In the United States in 1960, a census and typical year for our purposes, we are told that 26 percent of all offenses known to the police were cleared by arrest.[5] Variations (rounded) among the index offenses are striking, for murder and non-negligent manslaughter had a clearance rate of 92, forcible rape 73, robbery 39, aggravated assault 75, burglary 29, larceny 20, and auto theft 26. Figures for other offenses are not given, but for these important crimes used for measuring the volume of crime in general, it is clear that we have only about a 25 to 30 percent sample of all known offenses from which we are required to make judgments about persons arrested. That is, about 70 to 75 percent of offenses are not cleared and leave us with no knowledge of the offenders. Whether we can safely project from the one fourth sample to the total group is only conjecture.

But the problem of projection is further complicated by the uneven rate of clearance among the seven offenses from which the 30 percent sample comes. Notice that acts commonly designated as "offenses against the person"—murder, rape, aggravated assault—have relatively high rates of clearance, while "offenses against property"—burglary, larceny, auto theft—have relatively low rates of clearance. In those offenses involving a face-to-face relationship between victim and offender, there is a greater likelihood of personal identification. When property is stolen without the victim's presence, obviously there are greater difficulties of investigation. Moreover, the ratio of police investigatory teams in offenses against the person, particularly criminal homicide, is much greater than the ratio of staff to complaints regarding property. Finally, many if not most offenses involving bodily injury are intragroup offenses and the victim and offender were known to one another prior to the offense. Homicide, for example, is one of the most personalized of offenses, usually involving a relative, mate, close friend, or at least acquaintance. The domain of probable suspects is therefore much more limited than the more common stranger relationship which the offender and victim have in purely property crimes. Robbery, we may note, has a clearance rate about halfway between the two major groups of offenses and statistically reflects the anomalous character of the crime, which is mainly an acquisitive one

[5] *Uniform Crime Reports*, 1960.

but does involve at least a personal confrontation and intimidation if not always a personal injury. In general, then, we see that about three fourths of the offenses against the person known to the police result in some suspects' being taken into custody, but arrests occur in only about one fourth for offenses against property.

Quite the contrary percentages occur when we examine the proportion found guilty among persons who have been charged with committing these offenses. The shift from a base using offenses to a base using offenders is significant. An offense may be "cleared by arrest" when one or more suspects are taken into custody; and one suspect may clear up one or more offenses. More specifically, one burglary may result in the arrest of three offenders; contrariwise, one arrested suspect may be responsible for three burglaries. The relationship between number of persons and number of offenses, therefore, is never entirely clear. We do know that in 1960, of every 100 index offenses known to the police, 26 were cleared by arrest and 20 persons were charged with having committed these offenses; and of every 190 persons charged, or held for prosecution, 76 were found guilty.

In short, the probability of being arrested for a property offense is low, but if arrested, the probability of being convicted is relatively high; the probability of being arrested for an offense against the person is high, but if arrested, the probability of being convicted is relatively low. Now it is of special interest to point out that offenses against the person comprise a very small percentage of all seven offenses in the crime index. If robbery is included among offenses against property, 92 percent of these index offenses are against property and only 8 percent are offenses against the person.

It should, perhaps, be mentioned that since 1946 there have not been available general national judicial statistics that are concerned with the number and kinds of criminal complaints filed and the method of their disposition. The Children's Bureau of the United States Department of Health, Education and Welfare does collect data on a sample basis from juvenile courts, and a few states have annual judicial statistical reports. But, as one author has indicated in a survey of such reports, there are confusing variations among the states in the agency making the report, the frequency of the report, the presentation of data, and the choice of reporting unit (offense, case, or defendant).[6]

Prison statistics are published by the Federal Bureau of Prisons in *National Prisoner Statistics*. There are occasional reports on state and federal institutions derived from data submitted voluntarily by the state agencies. Although detailed and accurate for their purposes, correctional statistics are of little or no use for measuring the extent and volume of crime that occurs in a community. The "mortality" of information about crime as one moves from one statistical level to another—from offenses recorded by the police to persons arrested, defendants found guilty, criminals imprisoned—is of such large dimension and variance over time and jurisdiction that most criminologists are convinced that only crimes known to the police can be used for valid measurement of the amount of crime and delinquency.

[6] Edward B. McConnell, "Judicial Criminal Statistics," *National Probation and Parole Association Journal,* 3 (July 1957), 250–262.

RIOTING MAINLY FOR FUN AND PROFIT

Edward C. Banfield

"Picketing and marching ain't getting us anywhere, man,"
said Byron Washington, a 16-year-old 11th-grader who was
arrested during this week's riots for having a rock in his hand.

"The whites got to face it, man, this is a new generation.
We aren't going to stand for the stuff our mamas and fathers
stood for.

"Look at me, I've got a B average, but I can't get a summer job. And if you don't work, you can't afford to go to
college."

New York Times report from
Waterloo, Iowa, July 14, 1967

In the law of most states a riot is a lawless act engaged in
by three or more persons and accompanied by violence or
breach of the public peace. If the rioters are Negroes it is
usually taken for granted that the riot is in some sense racial.
Probably the most widespread view is that Negroes riot because they can no longer contain their pent-up fury at the
mistreatment they receive from whites. The Watts riot, we
are told "was a manifestation of a general sense of deep

"Rioting Mainly for Fun and Profit" will be incorporated in
Edward C. Banfield's book The Unheavenly City, *to be published
in 1970 by Little, Brown and Company. The essay is included in
this volume by permission of the author and Little, Brown and
Company. Copyright © 1968, 1970 by Edward C. Banfield.*

outrage, outrage at every aspect of the lives Negroes are forced to live, outrage at every element of the white community for forcing (or permitting) Negroes to live such lives."[1]

On this view it follows that the way to end rioting—the *only* way to end it—is to stop mistreating the Negro and, so far as possible, to repair the damage already done him. "Doing such things as punishing police misconduct, providing decent housing and schooling, ending job discrimination and so forth are essential, but the problem goes deeper than that. The ghetto itself, with all the shameful economic, social, political, and psychological deprivation it causes, must be done away with once and for all. The riots have 'let America know' that this is what must be done. Now America must do it."[2]

This is not the view that will be taken here. The assumption that if Negroes riot it must be *because* they are Negroes is naive. If one rejects this as a starting place and looks at the facts instead, one sees that race (and, incidentally, poverty as well) was not *the* cause of any of the Negro riots and that it had very little to do with many of them. Indeed, it is probably not too much to say that many of the riots would have occurred even if (other things being the same) the people in the riot areas had all been white and even if they had all had incomes above the poverty line. The implication of this view is, of course, that punishing police misconduct, providing decent housing, and so on will not significantly affect the amount of Negro rioting. The causes of rioting, it will be argued, will continue to operate for another twenty years or so no matter what is done. But although more and possibly worse riots are to be expected, rioting will not destroy the cities. Dr. Kenneth B. Clark's warning that "The dark ghettos now represent a nuclear stock pile which can annihilate the very foundations of America,"[3] need not be taken very seriously

---

[1] Report of the Task Force on Assessment of the President's Committee on Law Enforcement and Administration of Justice, *Crime and Its Impact—An Assessment,* U.S. Government Printing Office, Washington, D.C., 1967, p. 121.

[2] *Ibid.,* p. 122.

[3] Kenneth B. Clark, "The Wonder Is There Have Been So Few Riots," *The New York Times Magazine,* September 5, 1965, p. 10.

if his metaphors refer to rioting of the sort that has occurred
in recent years.

    a. Two thousand juveniles break windows after an amuse-
ment park closes early leaving them without transportation.

    b. A gang of hoodlums robs a clothing store and smashes
the display windows of three other stores, stealing watches,
cameras, and rings.

    c. A young man has been shot and killed by the police dur-
ing a burglary and a crowd, shouting "This is for Willie," pelts
the police with rocks, bottles, and fire bombs.

    d. Following an inflammatory speech by a racist politician,
a mob overturns automobiles and assaults motorists.

To that strict behaviorist, the man on the moon, all four of
these events probably look alike: all are "riots" and, if the
rioters are Negro, presumably "racial." But to an observer
able and willing to take motives into account (that is, to
take note of the meaning of an act to the actor) the events are
very different and some are not in any sense racial. The first
(a) is a rampage by frustrated teenagers who happen to be
black. The second (b) is a foray for pillage by young toughs
who find "taking" things the easiest way of getting them. In
this case, too, race is not a motive and is in fact irrelevant to
behavior: the toughs are Negro, but they could as well be
white. The third event (c) is an outburst of righteous indignation on the part of people who have witnessed what they
think is an act of gross injustice. The young man who was
killed was black and the policeman who killed him was white,
but it is possible that the indignation the crowd feels is mainly
or even entirely against the police rather than against whites
as such. (In September, 1962, Negroes in the all-Negro village of Kinlock, Missouri, rioted when a Negro policeman shot
a Negro youth.) Indeed, some members of the crowd may be
indignant at whites, others at the police, and still others at
both whites and the police, and so it might be impossible to
say whether or not the riot was "mainly racial," even if one
had full knowledge of the subjective state of all rioters. In
the final case (d) the event is a demonstration carried on for
the express purpose of calling attention to a political position;

since the position is a racist one, the riot can easily be called racial.

Each of these four motivations implies a corresponding type of riot. (This is not to say that a certain type of riot is *caused* by a certain type of motive; as will be explained later, it is more useful to look elsewhere for causes). The four types are:

1. *The rampage.* This is an outbreak of animal—usually young, male animal—spirits. Young men are naturally restless, in search of excitement, thrills, "action." Also, as David Matza has explained, they are apt to feel "pushed around"; one who is caught in this mood of fatalism (as Matza calls it) wants dramatic reassurance that he can "make things happen," and breaking the law is one of the few actions open to him which immediately and demonstrably makes things happen.[4] Rioting (which Matza does not mention) is a way of making them happen on a wholesale scale. "These young people, to whom a voter registration campaign, a picket line, or an economic boycott mean very little, have found that they can stun an entire community by engaging in rioting. They can mobilize entire police forces and National Guard companies, keep mayors at their desks through the nights, and bring representatives of the news media from all over the country."[5]

A rampage may start either with an incident, for example an argument or an arrest, or "out of the blue." If it starts with an incident, the incident is more in the nature of a pretext than (as in a riot of the outburst of indignation type) a provocation—that is, the rampage begins not because the incident made the rampagers angry (although they may pretend that) but because they were looking for an excuse (signal?) to rampage. There is no pattern to the violence once it starts: it involves destruction for the sake of destruction and fighting for the sake of fighting. The police are frequently attacked by rampagers; this is not because they are hated (although they may be) but because they are at hand and will put up a good fight. Rampaging by teenagers has always been a problem in

---

[4] David Matza, *Delinquency and Drift,* Wiley, 1964, pp. 189–190.

[5] Fred Powledge in *The New York Times,* August 6, 1964.

the cities. From the very earliest times harassing the watch, vandalism, and arson have been favorite pastimes of the young.[6] In Pittsburgh in 1809 an editor proposed satirically that the city establish a "conflagration fund" from which to buy twelve houses, one to be burned each month in a civic celebration.[7] Until the middle of the last century fire companies in the large cities were manned by volunteers, mostly boys and young men, and were in many cases what today would be called conflict gangs. Whether they put out more fires than they started is a question. In Philadelphia, for example, firemen used to riot almost every Sunday using bricks, stones, and firearms, apparently with intent to kill.[8] In the slums of the large cities there were also street gangs, some claiming more than a thousand members, which fought each other and the police almost constantly.[9] Usually the authorities did not try very hard to interfere with these activities, which were regarded as in the nature of sporting events.[10]

Youth rampages occur today not only in the slums but elsewhere. Thousands of college boys rioted at Hampton Beach, New Hampshire, and at Seaside, Oregon, in 1964, the year the inner-city riots began, and there have been large rampages of white boys on the Sunset Strip of Los Angeles, in

[6] See Richard C. Wade, *The Urban Frontier*, University of Chicago Press (Phoenix Books), 1964, p. 90, and Howard O. Sprogle, *The Philadelphia Police, Past and Present*, Philadelphia, 1887, p. 50.

[7] Wade, *op. cit.*, p. 92. In Boston one house a month would not have been nearly enough; more than fifty buildings were fired by incendiaries in 1844. (Arthur Wellington Brayley, *A Complete History of the Boston Fire Department*, Boston, 1889, p. 207.) In Philadelphia thirty-four boys aged five to fifteen were arrested in three summer months of 1862 for starting fires. (Sprogle, *op. cit.*, p. 318.)

[8] Sprogle, *op. cit.*, pp. 90 and 106. See also E. K. Price, *The History of the Consolidation of the City of Philadelphia*, J. B. Lippincott Co., 1873, pp. 118–119.

[9] Cf. Richard O'Connor, *Hell's Kitchen*, J. B. Lippincott Co., 1958. See also Herbert Asbury, *The Gangs of New York*, Alfred A. Knopf, 1927.

[10] Roger Lane, *Policing the City, Boston 1822–1885*, Harvard University Press, 1967, p. 29.

Atlantic City, and elsewhere since. It is not only American boys who behave this way, but boys almost everywhere. In Stockholm, for example, hordes of teenagers hang around the subway stations committing acts of vandalism and harassing the police. "The police say that if a constable has to arrest a drunk who is disturbing the peace, the youngsters will often set upon the policeman, and a major riot looms before reinforcements can be called."[11] Probably many of the student "political demonstrations" reported in this and other countries are actually rampages.

In the upper classes the norms of culture tend to restrain the restlessness of youth and to encourage its sublimation. In the lower classes, on the other hand, cultural norms reinforce feelings of restlessness and the "mood of fatalism." Accordingly, lower-class youths are more apt than others to be caught up in frenzies of mob activity, and even adults of the lower class are, by comparison with those of the other classes, highly susceptible to the same influences.

2. *The foray for pillage.* Here the motive is theft, and here also boys and young adults of the lower class are the principal offenders. Stealing is ordinarily most conveniently done in private, of course, but when disasters—earthquakes, fires, floods, power failures, blizzards, enemy invasions—interrupt law enforcement it may be done as well or better in public. On these occasions, when "Everyone is doing it" and "If I don't take the stuff it will just go to waste," upper working- and middle-class adults who, under normal circumstances, would not steal, are likely to join the looters. (In 1711 the selectmen of Boston passed an act to punish persons "taking advantage of such confusion and calamities [as fire] to rob, plunder, embezzle, convey away and conceal the goods and effects of their distressed neighbors.")[12] From the standpoint of the youth or of the lower-class adult who makes a practice of stealing, it would be convenient to have a riot every day. Riots are seldom started by thieves merely to facilitate stealing, however. One reason for this is that the culture of the lower class renders it incapable of the planning and organization

11 *The New York Times,* September 16, 1965.
12 Brayley, *op. cit.,* pp. 15 and 31.

that would ordinarily be necessary to start a riot by design. Another and perhaps more important one is that although all thieves would benefit from a riot, no one thief would benefit enough from it to justify his taking the trouble and running the risks of starting it. (As an economist would put it, the riot is from the standpoint of the thieves a "collective good.")[13] But if thieves rarely start riots, they are always quick to join ones that are under way, and their presence in sufficient number may transform one from, say, a rampage to a foray for pillage. "I really know of no instance of a riot occurring in New York, or in any other large city, during which robbery did not play a prominent part," New York's Police Chief Walling wrote toward the end of the last century.[14]

3. *The outburst of righteous indignation.* Here the rioters are moved by indignation at what they regard, rightly or wrongly, as injustice or violation of the mores that is likely to go unpunished. Their indignation is partly at the wrong act and partly at the wrongness of its going unpunished. A riot of this type is always spontaneous—people do not become indignant according to plan. Indignation is aroused by an incident of some sort (which may, of course, have been contrived by someone for the purpose) and in the nature of the case, the indignant people are without leaders. The incident itself may help to make up for this lack by serving a coordinating function; as Thomas C. Schelling has pointed out, "Without something like an incident, it may be difficult to get action at all, since immunity requires that all know when to act together."[15]

A righteously indignant mob usually consists mainly of working-class people. The lower-class individual is too alienated to be capable of much indignation, especially in a matter that he thinks does not affect him personally and directly;

[13] See Mancur Olson, Jr., *The Logic of Collective Action,* Harvard University Press, 1965. The theory as applied to small groups is particularly relevant here; it is summarized on pp. 33–36.

[14] George W. Walling, *Recollections of a New York Chief of Police,* Caxton Book Concern, Ltd., 1887, p. 85.

[15] Thomas C. Schelling, *The Strategy of Conflict,* Harvard University Press, 1960, p. 90.

middle- and upper-class people are usually confident of their ability to get wrongs righted by making appeals through proper channels and, besides, they abhor violence. The working class is not under any of these limitations: it has a capacity for righteous indignation, distrusts lawyers, public relations people, and "channels" generally, and does not greatly mind—indeed, sometimes very much enjoys—a good brawl and the spilling of some blood.

Under favorable circumstances, that is, where the working class is large and consists of people who have enough in common so that they will respond with indignation to provocations of the same sort, an outburst of righteous indignation may involve a great many people—far more, certainly, than a rampage or a foray, both of which by their nature ordinarily draw upon relatively small "constituencies." All of the large riots of the nineteenth century were mainly outbursts of righteous indignation. Some of them were very large indeed. For example, the Boston riot of 1837 (a native-American working-class attack on Irish immigrants) is supposed to have involved more than 15,000 persons, roughly one sixth of the city's population.

In an outburst of righteous indignation the pattern of violence and destruction reflects the mob's wish to end, and also to redress or avenge, the wrong which aroused its indignation. As Rudé says in his account of popular disturbances in pre-industrial France and England, it imposes a conception of "natural justice": "Strikers tended to destroy machinery or 'pull down' their employers' houses; food rioters to invade markets and bakers' shops and enforce a popular price control or *taxation populaire;* rural rioters to destroy fences and turnpikes or threshing machines and workhouses, or to set fire to the farmer's or landlord's stacks; and city rioters to 'pull down' dissenters' meeting houses and chapels, to destroy their victims' houses and property, and to burn their political enemies in effigy."[16]

4. *The demonstration.* Here the motive is to advance a political principle or ideology or to contribute to the mainte-

---

[16] George Rudé, *The Crowd in History,* Wiley, 1964, p. 238.

nance of an organization. The riot is not a spontaneous, angry response to an incident. Rather it is the result of pre-arrangement by persons who are organized, have leaders, and who see the riot as a means to some end. The word "demonstration" is descriptive, for the event is a kind of show staged to influence opinion. Those who put it on are usually middle or upper class, these being the classes from which the people who run organizations and espouse political causes are mostly drawn. Demonstrations characteristically involve breach of the public peace rather than violence (if they involve neither they are by definition not riots); the middle- and upper-class cultural style favors the use of mock-violence (for example, the spraying of slogans with paint and the throwing of steer's blood), "happenings" (for example, halting traffic with police whistles), and behavior calculated to make the demonstrator the object, or the apparent object, of violence inflicted either by himself (as when he chains himself to something) or by the authorities (as when he "goes limp"). The middle and upper classes' abhorrence of violence is so great that techniques like these, which trade upon it without requiring the demonstrator to hurt anyone but himself (and usually not himself either) are often effective as a means of putting "the other side" at a moral disadvantage in the eyes of the middle- and upper-class television viewers for whose benefit the demonstration is staged.

These four types of riots are presented as analytical models. Some concrete riots very closely approximate a "pure" type, but most riots—and probably all large ones—are compounds of two or more of the types. The New York Draft Riot of 1863, for example, was a compound of at least three. It was a rampage of young toughs from the slums (three fourths of those actively engaged in violence were boys and men under 20 years of age who were not subject to the draft, a *Times* writer estimated); it was a foray for pillage (houses and places of business were ransacked all along Eleventh Avenue); and it was also—and perhaps mainly—an outburst of righteous indignation on the part of the Irish working class at the prospect of having to compete with freed Negroes for jobs and against the alleged injustices of the draft law.[17] Large riots tend to be compound, if for no other reason, simply because they attract looters. But it is likely that the fact of their being compound also tends to make them larger: that is, that inter-action among types of rioters tends to reinforce the motives and heighten the activity of each type. For example, the looters and rampagers in the Draft Riot no doubt got some moral support from having all about them rioters motivated by righteous indignation; at the same time, the presence of the looters and rampagers, most of whom were not clearly identifiable as such, must have added to the general sense of confusion and frenzy and by so doing must have helped sus-tain the fury of the righteously indignant. That these latter had *two* objects of indignation—Negroes and the draft law—must also have increased the interaction. One may conjecture that the greater the variety of motivational elements appealed to, the larger the number of rioters who will be recruited and —what is more important—the more interaction tending to sustain and escalate the riot there will be among the rioters.

Looking from this perspective at the recent series of inner-city riots, one is struck by the fact that for twenty years prior to July 18, 1964, there had been very few riots by Negroes and these few, with only one exception, had been protests against racial injustice. In 1961, for example, white mobs in six cities attacked Negroes, but there were no riots by Ne-groes. In 1962 there were four Negro riots—one was a demon-stration by Black Muslims, two seem to have been outbursts of righteous indignation provoked by incidents of alleged police brutality, and the fourth—the exception—was a ram-page by high school students after a football game in the District of Columbia stadium. In 1963 and the first half of 1964 there were eleven Negro riots, all apparently outbursts of righteous indignation and all but three occurring in the South. In none of these years was there a major Negro riot

[17] See E. C. Banfield, "Roots of the Draft Riots," *New York Magazine,* July 29, 1968.

—involving several hundred rioters and lasting more than a day.[18]

On July 18, 1964, a riot began in Harlem that proved to be a turning point. Two days before an off-duty white police lieutenant had shot and killed a 15 year old Negro youth he said had attacked him with a knife. The incident created widespread anger, and there was a protest march on the precinct police station the next day. The following evening (July 18) a second group of marchers refused to disperse; instead it began throwing bottles and stones at the police station and was soon joined in this by a band of Black nationalists who had been meeting nearby. The riot, which lasted in Harlem for three days, spread to the Bedford-Stuyvesant district of Brooklyn and six days later, for no apparent reason, to Rochester.[19] (The incident—an attempt by a policeman to arrest a drunk and disorderly adolescent at a street dance—seems to have been a pretext rather than a provocation.) A few days later the rioting spread, also for no apparent reason to three New Jersey cities, an industrial suburb of Chicago, and Philadelphia.

In Harlem when it first broke out, the rioting was mainly an outburst of righteous indignation at the police. There was little looting; the mob was chiefly occupied in bitter fighting with the police. As the rioting continued and moved to other cities, however, its nature changed. Looting and rock throwing became the mob's principal activities, with attacks on the police sporadic and incidental. In Rochester, the city manager said later, the riot had "racial overtones" but was not actually a race riot.[20] In Philadelphia, the first policeman attacked was a Negro. Nowhere did a Negro mob invade a white neighborhood or assault whites as such. Opinion leaders

[18] This section depends heavily upon a chronology compiled by the Legislative Reference Service of the Library of Congress. It appears in the *Congressional Quarterly* special report on Urban Problems and Civil Disorder, no. 36, September 8, 1967, pp. 1708–1712.

[19] The Harlem and Bedford-Stuyvesant riots are described in Fred. C. Shapiro and James W. Sullivan, *Race Riots, New York 1964*, Thomas Y. Crowell Co., 1964.

[20] *The New York Times*, November 7, 1964.

and publicists did not at this time see the riots as manifestations of deep unrest or anger on the part of Negroes. At the
end of the summer, J. Edgar Hoover, whose views were probably close to one end of the spectrum, reported to the President that although racial tensions had been a factor, none of
the disorders—not even the Harlem one—was a race riot in
the accepted meaning of the term (that is, race against race);
they were, he said, purposeless attacks in which youths were
responsible for most of the violence, and he classed them with
the college boy riots that occurred at about the same time.[21]
Others made similar assessments. Most civil rights leaders
dismissed the idea that the riots were conscious protests; that
was not merely an after-the-fact rationalization, Kenneth B.
Clark said, it was an "independent of the fact" one.[22] Bayard
Rustin was applauded by an audience of New York planners
when he explained that the violence was caused by "merely
a few confused Negro boys throwing stones in windows or a
Molotov cocktail at a cop who was perfectly capable of duck-
ing."[23] The police commissioner of New York said in effect
that they were rampages and forays. "They riot either out of
sheer cussedness or for criminal reasons, and in some instances because mob action seems to be taking on the aspects
of a fad . . . Bedevil the police, strip stores, shout and yell,
crush anyone who opposes you . . . and if the police try to
stop it, just yell 'brutality.' This is the pattern . . ."[24]

The view that riots did not manifest feelings of outrage
widespread among Negroes was consistent with the findings
of an elaborate survey of Negro opinion made late in 1964
by Gary T. Marx. It showed that most Negroes were neither
sunk in hopelessness nor consumed with anger. Only about a
third were in any sense militant, and the proportion of Negroes
who were strongly anti-white was much smaller. Most
thought that things were getting better for the Negro (81
percent of a sample in non-Southern metropolitan areas

[21] *The New York Times,* September 27, 1964.
[22] *The New York Times,* September 11, 1964.
[23] New York City Planning Commission, "The Future by Design," October 14–16, 1964, Transcript, p. 55.
[24] *The New York Times,* October 7, 1964.

thought this), that America was worth fighting for (87 percent), that a day would come when whites would fully accept Negroes (70 percent), and that the police treated Negroes either fairly well or very well (59 percent). "The overwhelming majority of those questioned," Marx concluded, "felt that progress is being made and that integration is being pushed by the government at the right speed and were optimistic about the future."[25] That most Negroes held these opinions does not necessarily mean that the rioters held them, of course; in fact, however, there is some reason to suppose that most of them did.[26]

The 1964 riot pattern was repeated the following August in the Watts district of Los Angeles. This area was not a slum in the usual sense (it was an area of single-family, detached houses, most of which were in good condition) and Los Angeles was a city in which the Negro fared better than in most places (the Urban League rated it first among 68 cities on the basis of a "statistical portrait" drawn in 1964). In this case, too, the incident that supposedly set off the riot could hardly have aroused a great deal of righteous indignation (a drunken Negro motorist had been arrested in what seems to have been a proper manner). Apparently the incident was mainly important as a pretext for a rampage by teenage Negro boys and young men who began throwing whiskey and beer bottles and pieces of asphalt and cement at motorists on Avalon Boulevard.[27] Two hours after the incident the mob,

[25] Gary T. Marx, *Protest and Prejudice,* Harper and Row, 1967, p. 39. See also the survey reported in the special issue of *Fortune,* December 1967.

[26] Comparing a sample of Negro males arrested during the Detroit riot of 1967 with a control group chosen from the area most affected by the riot, Luby found that the arrestees had no more grievances than the controls, that both arrestees and controls felt that they had made substantial progress in the past five years, and that both were remarkably optimistic about the future. (Eliot D. Luby, M.D., "A Comparison Between Negro Riot Arrestees and a Riot Area Control Sample," Paper presented at the annual meeting of the American Political Science Association, 1968.)

[27] Jerry Cohen and William S. Murphy, *Burn, Baby, Burn!* Avon Books, 1966, pp. 62–63.

which then numbered about 1,500, consisted mostly of these boys and young men. There was nothing "racial" about what they were doing. "One thing that impressed me was that these Negroes who were hurling stones were throwing them right into their own people. That's why I believe this didn't start out to be a race riot. These were just young hoodlums working off their frustrations. They were out to do destruction. They just wanted to hurt anybody, black or white."[28]

The statistics on arrests at Watts provide some slight basis for inferences about the motives of the rioters. About 15 percent of those arrested were juveniles. (The percentage would have been much higher, it has been suggested, were it not for the fact that the police, being short-handed, arrested the people who were easiest to catch.) Of the 3,438 adults arrested, nearly one third had been convicted of major crimes (that is, crimes for which they had received sentences of more than 90 days) and fully one third had minor records (that is, arrest only or conviction with a sentence of 90 days or less).[29] Since the police may be quicker to arrest Negroes than whites, it is hard to say what significance should be attached to the proportion having minor records. It is more noteworthy that one third had never been arrested.

Although the Watts riot followed the pattern that had been set the year before, Negro spokesmen at once proclaimed that it was politically motivated—it was, they insisted, a revolt, not a riot. Bayard Rustin wrote that it was carried on for an "express purpose" and was "the first major rebellion."[30] No one gave a very clear or convincing account of what the rioters were revolting against, however. The facts did not support the view that they were expressing hatred for the white man; even Rustin said that the rebellion was against the Negro's "own masochism." Nor did the facts support very well the view that the rioters were asserting that (in Rustin's words) they "would

[28] Newspaperman Don Cormier, quoted in *ibid.*, p. 71.

[29] Governor's Commission on the Los Angeles Riots, *Violence in the City—An End or a Beginning?*, Los Angeles, December 2, 1965, p. 24.

[30] Bayard Rustin, "The Watts 'Manifesto' and the McCone Report," *Commentary*, March 1966, p. 30.

no longer quietly submit to the deprivation of slum life"; after all, most Watts people lived comfortably in fairly good housing. It was somewhat more plausible to claim that they were angry about mistreatment by the police, but even this view did not fit the facts entirely, for the rioters had shown themselves more interested in burning and looting than in fighting the police.

However unjustifiably, Watts was regarded by many Negroes as something to be proud of—a kind of black Bunker Hill. This definition tended to make the rioting of the year before appear in retrospect as a kind of black Concord and Lexington and to establish a moral basis for any battles that might yet be fought in a black revolution. As one would expect, the frequency of rioting increased after Watts. In 1966, there were 11 major (that is, two day or more) and 32 minor riots, and in 1967 there were 25 major and 30 minor riots. In most instances, the rioting began either without any precipitating incident, boys and young men simply smashing windows, starting fires, and assaulting passers-by for no apparent reason, or with an incident that was a pretext rather than a provocation. Only two of the major riots in 1966 (those in Jacksonville, Florida, and San Francisco) seem to have started from a provocation and only eight (six of which were in Southern cities) of those in 1967 seem to have started from provocations.

The Detroit riot of 1967, although vastly more destructive, was in many ways typical. Like Los Angeles, Detroit was a city of relative prosperity and opportunity for the Negro; it had no real "ghetto" and its police had for several years been under very enlightened and determined leadership. The incident with which the riot started seems to have been a pretext rather than a provocation: when the police raided a speakeasy early one Sunday morning a crowd began pelting the policemen with stones. This might not have led to a riot were it not for the fact that at that particular time very few policemen could be mustered. (Early Sunday morning was a "low crime" period and the stronger day-time shift was not scheduled to report for duty at precinct stations until 8 a.m.) For several critical hours the police were conspicuous by their absence. It was well known, too, that the police would not use their guns except in the most extreme circumstances. For five or six hours after the speakeasy raid Negroes and whites mingled on the streets and looted amicably side by side. On the second day of the riot Governor Romney said that it was "not primarily a civil rights disturbance but rather lawlessness and hoodlumism by Negroes and whites," an opinion with which Mayor Cavanagh agreed.[31] Almost all the arrests made were for looting, and of those arrested nearly half were aged 19 through 24. The pattern of destruction was what one would expect in a foray for pillage. Stores having things that could be consumed directly—liquor, cigarettes, drugs, clothing, television sets, appliances, furniture—were looted no matter who owned them. Stores having things that would have to be "fenced"—jewelry—were usually left untouched, as were all buildings symbolic of the "white power structure"—banks, public offices, and schools. As one of the rioters, a child, explained, "There was nothing to steal in the school. Who wants a book or a desk?"[32]

It would appear, then, that what requires explanation is not so much rebellion by Negroes (whether against the white, the slum, their "own masochism," the police, or something else) as it is outbreaks of animal spirits and of stealing by slum dwellers, mostly boys and young men and mostly Negro. (A few non-Negroes participated, mostly as looters, in the Detroit riot and possibly in some of the others, and one major riot, a rampage-foray for which there seems to have been no pre-

[31] *The New York Times,* July 24, 1967. John Howard, a sociologist who observed the Detroit riot later wrote that poor whites played a major role in it. He found the Detroit (and also the Newark) riot to be a "lower-class, rather than racial, revolt." (William McCord *et al., Life Styles in the Black Ghetto,* W. W. Norton and Co., 1969, p. 273.)

[32] Quoted in *Education News,* October 16, 1967, p. 16. Luby's study (*op. cit.*) of a sample of Detroit arrestees and a control group also found the arrestees to be younger than the controls, less often married, more often raised in the urban North, more often raised in a family in which the father was not present during the first eleven years, less affiliated with organizations, less conscious of political leadership, and no more unemployed.

cipitating incident, was carried on entirely by Puerto Rican youths in Perth Amboy, New Jersey, at the end of July 1966.) In framing an explanation, it will be useful to begin by listing certain events ("accelerating causes"), each of which independently increased the probability of such riots occurring. This listing will be followed by a description of a set of states ("background causes"), the concurrent existence of which established *some* probability of their occurring.[33]

Accelerating Causes. Without attempting to pass on their relative importance, several such causes may be listed.

1. Sensational television coverage of the riots recruited rampagers and pillagers. As the mayor of Plainfield, New Jersey, explained, "The sensational coverage of the Newark riot showed persons looting stores while the police took no action to halt them. This view of looting appealed directly to the criminal and susceptible element."[34] Prior to the advent of television, it would have been very difficult for the authorities to have brought the possibilities for fun and profit in rioting to the attention of the lower class even if they had wanted to do so. Lower-class people do not read newspapers but practically all of them have at least one television set.

2. By carrying vivid accounts of rioting to cities all over the country television not only eliminated the necessity that would otherwise have existed for the independent discovery of certain techniques of rioting (for example, the use of fire bombs) but also, and especially, it established the *possibility* of it. That by throwing rocks, smashing windows, and setting fires one can throw a great city into turmoil is something that the ordinary person does not recognize until it happens. Once the possibility of an action has been established, the probability of someone's taking it is very much increased. "Some cats come in the bar and talk about how they are going to start burning again next month—down about Broadway. Mostly, it is just talk, but they know that they could do it."[35] The main

---

[33] For the distinction between "accelerating" and "background" causes, the writer is grateful to Mr. Bruce Jacobs.

[34] *The New York Times*, December 7, 1967.

[35] *The New York Times*, November 7, 1965.

point here is that, thanks to television, knowledge that "they could do it" was widely disseminated to people who otherwise would have been slow to discover it for themselves. In 1935 and 1943 Harlem had riots, but for lack of television coverage these did not provide a model that was known and imitated in cities all over the United States.

3. The rioters knew that they had little or nothing to fear from the police and the courts. Under the pressure of the civil rights movement and of court decisions and as a result of the growing "professionalism" of police administrators (these developments in turn being consequences of "middle-classification" of the population), the patrolman's discretion in the use of force declined rapidly after the war. At the same time courts were lenient with juvenile offenders. "Tough kids" had always attacked policemen when they got the chance, but by the 1960's the amount of toughness required was not very great, for in most cities it became more and more apparent that a policeman who shot a boy would be in serious trouble. Not being able to use force, the police could not effectively use the *threat* of it. It was not uncommon for a gang of boys to disarm and beat a policeman who, following orders, would not use his gun against them. During a riot, the police were especially ineffective: because their offenses were not very serious most rioters could not be successfully threatened; the only thing that could be done with them was to take them into custody, and this was something the police were seldom numerous enough to do. Sometimes the police had to stand by and allow looting to go on before their eyes. This circumstance, of course, increased the tempo of the rioting.

"Those first hours, when the cops pulled out, were just like a holiday," recalls one young man who joined in the looting of shops on 12th Street that morning. "All the kids wandered around sayin', real amazed like, 'The fuzz is scared; they ain't goin' to do nothin'.' I remember one day me and another kid, we was locked in the school and there wasn't any teachers around and we had a ball, we did all the things we'd been wantin' to do for a long time. We set some fires in the baskets and we emptied the teachers' desks and we stuck a whole mess of toiletpaper in the principal's mailbox. Well, that's what it was like out on the Street."[36]

4. The probability of rioting was increased by several factors that tended to give it legitimacy in the eyes of potential rioters. One was an outpouring of vivid television and newspaper portrayals of outrages against Negroes and civil rights workers in the South; perhaps Sheriff "Bull" Connor of Alabama created much of the indignation that was discharged in Harlem against the officer who shot the boy in July, 1964. Another was a barrage of statements by leaders of both races that represented the Negro's problems as entirely, or almost entirely, the result of racial injustice, implying that only white racism stood between the Negro and affluence. Another was the discovery that rioting was possible; as David Matza points out with reference to juveniles, learning through experience that an infraction *can* be done leads, by an illogic characteristic of childish thought, to the conclusion that it *may* be done.[37] Another factor was the spread of the rioting to several cities; the knowledge that "Everybody is doing it" tended, by more childish illogic, to the conclusion that doing it could not be very wrong. "If they can do it in Detroit, we can do it here," Milwaukee teenagers cried as they began smashing store windows. But what probably did most to make rioting seem legitimate was acceptance of the claim that the Watts riot was a "revolt" and that the rioting everywhere had some political purpose. Byron Washington, the Waterloo, Iowa, youth whose words appear at the head of this chapter, doubtless threw his stone with the strength of ten because he knew (having heard it over television perhaps) that he was not a boy out raising hell but a victim of injustice fighting for a college education. Whether correct or not, explanations that find the cause of rioting in the rioters' environment are bound to be taken as justifications, or at any rate extenuations, of their behavior and therefore tend to reinforce the irresponsibility that is characteristic of the age and class culture from

[36] J. Anthony Lukas, "Postscript on Detroit: 'Whitey Hasn't Got the Message,'" *The New York Times Magazine*, August 27, 1967, p. 44.

[37] *Op. cit.*, p. 184.

which they are largely drawn.[38] Rustin may have been right in saying that the looters were "members of a deprived group who seized a chance to possess things that all the dinning affluence of Los Angeles has never given them."[39] But, right or wrong, the effect of such statements is to make it easier for the potential rioter to justify his behavior, and therefore the statements are themselves a contributing cause of rioting. One can see this process clearly enough in something a twenty-year-old Watts rioter said to a reporter: "The white power structure looks on us as hoodlums when actually we are deprived people."[40]

If explaining the riots tended to justify them, so did predicting them. One who said that if drastic measures were not taken to end injustice riots could be expected might be correct, but correct or not his words would help form an impression in the public mind that rioting is a natural and perhaps even laudable response to the continuance of an injustice. From the very beginning of the civil rights movement its leaders have been wont to predict that violence will occur if reforms are not accepted at a faster pace; the riots, of course, made these predictions much more credible and therefore

[38] "Modern guides written for those who work with juveniles stress the importance of supporting the child. Whenever supporting the child leads to statements excusing or understanding his behavior, as they occasionally must, the precepts of subcultural delinquency are also supported.

Statements reinforcing the delinquent's conception of irresponsibility are an integral part of an ideology of child welfare shared by social work, psychoanalysis, and criminology. This ideology presents a causal theory of delinquency which, when it attributes fault, directs it to parent, community, society, or even to the victims of crime." (*Ibid.*, p. 95.)

[39] *Op. cit.*, p. 30. Vice President Humphrey helped to extenuate the rioting when he said in New Orleans that if he lived in a slum tenement with rats and with no place to go swimming "You'd have more trouble than you have already, because I've got enough spark left in me to lead a mighty good revolt [sic] under those conditions." (*The New York Times*, July 19, 1966.)

[40] *The New York Times*, November 7, 1965.

gave the civil rights leaders more incentive than ever to make them.[41] At the end of 1966, Dr. Martin Luther King, Jr., after acknowledging that "a prediction of violence can sometimes be an invitation to it," went on to predict that "failure to pursue justice" would result in more riots.[42] Rustin at about the same time told a Senate subcommittee that if the President asked for only a small increase in funds for the poverty program the Negro leadership "can no longer be responsible for what happens," and Senator Robert Kennedy said that unless "major steps" were taken "we will reap a whirlwind that will be completely uncontrollable."[43] Even if these predictions had been based on actual knowledge and even if by making them—and *only* by making them—it had been possible to secure the needed reforms, one would have to say that making the predictions increased the probability of there being riots; obviously it was impossible for the reforms to achieve their effect in time to prevent them. Realistically, however, those who made the predictions could not be at all sure that the measures they were proposing, some of which—for example, "pursue justice"—were so vague as to be almost meaningless, would have any tendency to prevent rioting; moreover, they had little or no reason to believe that their making the prediction would bring about the adoption of the measures they advocated. Rustin, for example, could not have supposed that his words to the Senate subcommittee would cause the President to ask for a larger increase in the poverty program. The one thing the predictions *were* likely to do was to make rioting appear more natural, normal, and hence justifiable.[44]

[41] There is a striking parallel between the rhetorical strategy of the civil rights leaders in the early 1960's and that of James Mill prior to the passage of the Reform Bill of 1832. See Joseph Hamburger, *James Mill and the Art of Revolution*, Yale University Press, 1963.

[42] *The New York Times*, December 16, 1966.

[43] *The New York Times*, December 7, 1966.

[44] In March 1968, the process of explanation and, by implication, justification, reached its apogee with the publication of the report of the National Advisory Commission on Civil Disorders (the Kerner Commission) which found that "white racism," poverty,

Background Causes. For there to be *any* probability of rioting of the kind here under discussion several conditions had to exist concurrently.

1. Without a large supply of boys and young men of the lower classes to draw on, major rampages and forays would be impossible. In the 1920's and 1930's the number of such people in the inner cities was very much reduced from what it had been in the previous century because of the aging of the immigrant population and the movement of the relatively well-off to outlying neighborhoods and suburbs. During the depression it looked for a while as if the inner-city slums and semi-slums might be permanently depopulated. During and after the war, however, these districts were filled or nearly filled once again by a new migration, this one from the rural South (and, in New York, from Puerto Rico). Being a young population with a very high birthrate, the newcomers quickly put more boys and young men on the streets than had been there before. The new (black) generation of inner-city youth may be somewhat more prone to violence than the earlier (white) ones. (Southerners, both white and black, tend to be violent as compared to other Americans.) But if so the difference is not great. Lower-class youth in every generation and in every ethnic and racial group is extremely violent as compared to middle- and especially upper middle-class adults.

2. The lower- and lower working-class people who now comprise most of the inner-city residential population are largely cut off from participation in institutions that in times past regulated and restrained the behavior of people whose class culture and situation were similar to theirs. Racial discrimination, although obviously a factor, is not the main thing that cuts them off from these institutions; rather what cuts

---

and powerlessness were mainly responsible for the riots. The next month there were riots in several cities following the assassination of the Reverend Martin Luther King, Jr. These riots followed the familiar pattern of looting, burning, and vandalism, and it was apparent that despite all that had been done to give a political character to these events most rioters were not there in order to protest. "It wasn't vengeance," a Chicago poverty worker said, "just material gain." (*The Wall Street Journal,* April 10, 1968. See also *The New York Times,* April 12, 1968.)

them off is the changes that have occurred in the nature of the institutions because of the "middle-class-ification" of the population of this country. In the last century, for example, the volunteer fire company gave boys and young men of the lower classes opportunities to express animal spirits under conditions that were to some degree controlled: the firemen fought *each other,* usually for the "honor" of their companies. Today, of course, fire departments are run on a professional basis and are open only to mature men who have placed well in an examination. More or less the same thing has happened in politics. Not so long ago party machines labored to establish claims on even the lowest of the low; the trading of jobs and favors in return for loyalty tended to create some sort of bond between the individual and the government. Now that the machine, precinct captain, and corner saloon have been replaced by the welfare bureaucracy, the nonpartisan election, and the candidate who makes his appeal on educational television, the lower classes no longer participate in politics at all and are therefore no longer held by any of the old ties. Even in criminal activities there has been the same trend. Like firefighting and politics, the money-making kinds of crime (as opposed to "kid stuff") are organized in such a way as to exclude—and therefore to exert no discipline upon—the unskilled and incapable.

This exclusion from institutions of those who are not able or willing to participate on the terms set by the now predominant middle class has the effect of reducing the influence within the lower classes of those persons who, although not able to perform according to the standard set by the middle class, could nevertheless lead and set an example for—and thus place some restraint upon—less able members of their class. The situation is strikingly like that which, when it occurs in prisons, is said to cause riots. "It is the cohesively-oriented prisoner committed to the values of inmate loyalty, generosity, endurance, and the curbing of frictions who does much to maintain the prison's equilibrium. When the custodians strip him of his power—when the custodians destroy the system of illicit privileges, of preferential treatment and laxity which has functioned to increase the influence of the cohesively-oriented prisoner who stands for the value of keeping things quiet—the unstable elements in the inmate population have an opportunity to capitalize on the tensions of prison life and to rise into dominance. The stage has been set for insurrection."[45]

3. A considerable number of upper working-, middle-, and upper-class people who have made large income and status gains in recent years and are impatient to make even larger gains live in the inner city in close physical proximity to the lower classes. Upwardly mobile members of earlier slum populations very quickly left not only the slum but the inner city as well, and usually the neighborhoods they vacated were occupied by some different newly arrived ethnic group. In the case of the Negro the outward movement has been rather slow, partly because of job and housing discrimination and partly because of a preference Negroes have for living near other Negroes; moreover, in the case of the Negro the places of those who *have* moved away have usually been taken by newly arriving Negroes. Upwardly mobile Negroes who for one reason or another live in or near the slum tend, of course, to be very sensitive to the dangers and unpleasantnesses of slum life and to blame them not on conditions common to the white and the Negro (for example, lower class culture, low income, and so on) but on racial injustice past and present, real and imaginary. If, like the upwardly mobile members of earlier groups, these Negroes lived in suburbs far from the inner-city slums they would not be available physically (and perhaps psychologically) for participation in riots. As it is they do not participate in them actively in large numbers. They do provide enough politically motivated rioters, however, to make possible the interaction effect that, it was argued above, tends to escalate a rampage-foray into a major riot. Even those who do not participate in the rioting tend to help legitimate it in the eyes of potential rioters by putting forward or concurring in the claim that it has a political purpose.

Several conclusions bearing on policy may be drawn from this analysis. One is that there is likely to be more rioting for many years to come, and this no matter what is done to prevent it. So long as there are large concentrations of boys and young men of the lower classes on the streets rampages and forays are to be expected. Without some support from righteously indignant members of the working class and from politically minded members of the middle and upper classes such outbreaks probably will not reach the scale that was reached in Los Angeles, Newark, and Detroit, but even so some of them will probably be well beyond the ability of local police forces to deal with. Eventually much of the inner-city population will move to the suburbs; this change, which is already under way, will reduce the potential for very large riots by physically separating the lower class from the working class and the working class from the middle and upper classes and thus (a) curtailing the number of persons available in any one place as recruits for a riot and (b) making interaction between rioters of different motivational types (for example, rampagers and demonstrators) less likely. For at least another twenty years, however, there will be enough potential rioters of all types in the inner cities to produce frequent rampage-forays and some major riots.

It is naive to think that efforts to end racial injustice and to eliminate poverty, slums, and unemployment will have an appreciable effect upon the amount of rioting that will be done in the next decade or two. These efforts are not likely to be very serious or, if they are, very successful. But even if they are both serious and successful they will not significantly affect the factors that produce riots. Boys and young men of the lower classes will not cease to "raise hell" once they have adequate job opportunities, housing, schools, and so on. Indeed, by the standards of any former time, they have these things now. It may be that in the very long run good opportunities and a high standard of living will bring about the assimilation of the lower classes into the middle and by so doing will make them less violent. But this will happen over the long run—say from one generation to the next—if it happens at all, and, besides, even middle- and upper-class boys riot sometimes. As for the upwardly mobile and politically minded Negro who has a potential for outbursts of righteous indignation and for demonstrations, even serious and successful efforts at reform are likely to leave him more rather than ess angry. The faster and farther the Negro rises the more impatient he is likely to be with whatever he thinks prevents his rising still faster and still farther. As the HARYOU manual, *Youth in the Ghetto,* remarks, "The closer the Negro community gets to the attainment of its goals—the closer it gets to the removal of the determinants and manifestations of racial exploitation and powerlessness—the more impatient individual Negroes will become for total equality.[46]

It is not only the Negro who will become more disaffected as his situation improves. The process of "middle-" and "upper-class-ification" is making the whole society more sensitive to departures, both real and imaginary, from the ideal, inherently unrealizable, of how things ought to be. As the economy becomes more productive and social arrangements more decent, the well-off—and among them youth especially—become more restless and more intolerant of the continual failure to achieve social perfection. Demonstrations, confrontations, protests, dialogues, and so forth, are bound to be more frequent as the middle and upper classes grow and more and more people have the leisure to act upon what the Judaeo-Puritan tradition tells them is a positive obligation to make society over. Paul Goodman, who, it seems likely, is a portent of things to come, says that he looks forward to a "conflictual community" that will "combat the emptiness of technological life."[47] No doubt most of the blood spilled by the middle and upper classes will be steer's blood carried for the purpose in plastic containers. The effect on the lower classes of this sort of behavior by the upper classes may be much more serious, however.

Although the underlying factors making for riots will not change for quite some time, there may be changes in accelerating factors. Television coverage of riots may be less provocative; if it is, one force making for the growth and spread of riots will be reduced (It will not, however, undo the main damage already done; the discovery that burning

[46] Harlem Youth Opportunities Unlimited, Inc., *Youth in the Ghetto,* New York, 1964, p. 20.

[47] Paul Goodman, "Utopian Thinking," *Commentary,* July 1961, 26.

and looting on a wholesale scale is possible will not be for gotten.) The ability of the police to bring incipient riot under control may be improved by the introduction of bette methods and equipment; of importance, perhaps, is the chem cal Mace, which if it proves to be both effective and acceptabl to public opinion may change the situation significantly b giving police the upper hand in dealing with juveniles an other offenders whom it would be wrong to shoot. On th other hand, one accelerating factor will doubtless gain i strength. This is the opinion that rioting is a way of protestin injustice and is therefore in large degree justified. As wa remarked above, the spread of this opinion has made eac successive wave of rioting somewhat more ideological tha the last. Now that the rationale of rioting has been well worke out, future riots may be mainly for protest rather than fc fun and profit.

Insofar as the motives of the past few years predominat in the future, however, it is safe to say that none of the fo lowing will make riots less likely: the election of Negro ma ors, a mayor's courageous strolling in the slums, the elimin: tion of police brutality and the improvement of polic manners, efforts to placate, coopt, or restrain Negro extremi leaders, the measurement of the "grievance level" of the Negr community, and the provision of jobs for the "hard core unemployed. Politically motivated persons may perhaps be i fluenced by such things, but looters and youthful rampage will not be.

There is no intention here to extenuate the crime of riotin It is easy, however, to exaggerate the harm that riots of th kind that have occurred since 1964 have done and are like to do. In the first place, not many people were killed seriously injured by the rioters; in all of the more than 1C riots from 1964 through 1967, apparently no more than abo twenty persons were killed by rioters.[48] It is angry

---

[48] Some deaths were undoubtedly accidental. That the riote deliberately killed so few may be regarded as additional eviden that they were not motivated by hatred for whites. On the oth hand, there have been many riots which unquestionably were ou

panicky policemen who do most of the killing and maiming, and when the police are equipped with nonlethal weapons there will probably be much less of this. Because "routine" crime sometimes ceases or is much reduced during a major riot, there may even be some net saving of life and limb by virtue of riots.

The property losses are not as staggering as may be supposed either. In the majority of the recent riots the damage consisted mainly of smashed windows, the theft of liquor, and the burning of some not very valuable buildings. It would not take a very heavy snowfall to cost a city and its people more than an average-sized riot costs them. Major riots are another story, of course, but even they do not cause destruction very different in kind or amount from what would be caused by a sizable urban renewal program. Wasteful as it is to destroy useful structures in either way, the costs of doing so are well within the ability of a very affluent society to bear. In the course of time, too, property losses will be cut as people adapt to the likelihood of rioting by changing the location of structures or the design of them. In Europe, heavy metal shutters are used to protect store windows; doubtless the same thing will be done here (in the worst slums it long has been, of course) when the danger to windows becomes great enough. (On the other hand, if, as seems likely, the government compels insurance companies to insure properties in high-risk areas at normal premium rates, incentives to make such adaptations will be removed.)

The danger that a riot will so disrupt essential services—sewage disposal and water supply, for example—as to create a major public health hazard is very small. To inflict serious damage of this kind would require a considerable degree of expertise and organization. If anything of this sort is to be feared, it is to be feared from a highly disciplined band of political zealots, not from a mob—least of all from a mob of rampagers and looters.

There are those who think that up to now at least the riots have been a good thing on the whole because (the Negro

bursts of righteous indignation and in which the rioters, although furious, did not kill. (See Rudé, *op. cit.*, p. 225.)

view) they have impressed white society with the necessit
of drastic action to improve the Negro's conditions of life o
(the white view) because they have helped to instill in th
Negro a sense of pride. According to the executive secretar
of the Milwaukee Teachers Education Association, "There i
a certain amount of Negro pride which resulted from th
riot. The pride factor is evident when you walk or drive dow
the street. Caucasians are sensitized to Negroes; they ar
aware that they exist. Before, they could psychologically dis
miss them as inferior . . . The Negroes feel this focus o
them. And when they are in school, they are going to expec
something to happen. Frankly, I think it's great."[49]

Such claims are impossible to evaluate and yet they cannc
be ignored.[50] Very probably the immediate effects of th
burning, looting, and killing are of little importance as com
pared to the enduring changes in attitudes, feelings, an
opinions that have been brought about by the rioting. No on
now can have the least idea of the nature of these change:
however, and even in retrospect the cause and effect relation
will remain unclear. The rioting may have given Negroes
new pride (that the facts do not justify it is of course besid
the point), and this may do more for the lower-class Negr
than all of the compensatory education, public housing, jo
training, and community organization that could be provide
with a dozen Freedom Budgets. It may also have impresse
whites as nothing else would with the need for immediate an
far-reaching reforms, and this may—although there is littl
reason for confidence—lead to much good and little or n
harm. If one could be certain that these effects were indee
produced by the rioting, one would be tempted to conclud

[49] *Education News, op. cit.,* p. 16.

[50] A claim that might be expected but does not seem to hav
been made is that the rioting has produced some natural leader
of the slum neighborhoods. That such leaders have not been pr
duced (and there is no reason to believe that they have) is perhap
further evidence of the essentially non-political character of th
rioting. In any case, it is interesting that, according to Rudé (*op
cit.,* p. 251) very few of the leaders who were produced by the pr
industrial riots were ever heard from again once the riots were ove

that it was a good thing in spite of its cost in life and property. But one cannot be certain. Moreover, even if these effects were produced, others that are disastrous may also have been. A racial myth may be very helpful to the Negro lower class and very harmful to the society as a whole. It may be that the principal effect of the rioting has been on white opinion, that it has checked a growing disposition on the part of the working and lower-middle classes to accept reforms, and that it has established as something beyond question for everyone the mistaken notion that the "problem" is mainly one of race rather than, as has been maintained here, of class. Explaining as "racial" behavior what can as well or better be explained in other terms would seem to be a dangerous game even when played with the best of motives.

THE SCHOOLS IN THE CITY

Theodore R. Sizer

It is said that the schools of our largest cities are in trouble inadequate and wanting in comparison with schools in the suburbs. Good schools, the argument goes, give children the chance to succeed in life and to be happy, law-abiding citizens. City schools, or at least slum schools, are successful if they provide people with the skills to leave the slum and its cultural misery. By this criterion, however, our big city school systems have over time been enormously successful institutions, one of the most staggeringly successful in American history. Millions have left the slums, and schools have played a central part in making this possible.

But the slum remains and within it the people and their children who for one reason or another cannot leave. For these it appears that the schools have been failures; but here one confronts the chicken and the egg. Are these children hostile to school and unsuccessful in its terms, so conditioned by their surroundings against entering middle-class culture that no institution could alter them? Is the fact of the frequent racial barriers to leaving the slum one that schools cannot overcome? Are today's city schools trying to educate only

he children of those who failed to pass or who cannot pass
-and have they accordingly become barren institutions,
ruelly symbolizing the inevitable despair of the situation? Put
nother way, can schools "succeed" for those whom society
olds down irrespective of merit?

It is in this context that one must see the "trouble" in our
urban schools—and, in an appreciation of their past roles,
heir opportunity. Lumping together all schools found in big
ities distorts the picture—there is as much variety of quality
nd kind within "big city" school systems as within the country
s a whole. Nonetheless, the schools in our central cities in-
lude among them those that serve a majority of our most
esperately disadvantaged population.

It is toward these schools that this essay is directed. Some
imple facts show the extent of the present trouble of fifteen
f our largest cities.[1]

Thirty-one percent of the children who completed the
inth grade in the big cities failed to receive their high
chool diplomas, as against 24 percent nationally.

At least 6 percent of the children who start fifth grade in
he big cities never start tenth grade.

---

[1] New York, Chicago, Boston, Los Angeles, Philadelphia, De-
roit, Baltimore, Houston, Cleveland, Washington, D.C., St. Louis,
Milwaukee, San Francisco, Pittsburgh, Buffalo. These communities
ave banded together, with the help of the Ford Foundation, in the
Great Cities Program for School Improvement." (San Diego has
oined the program since the writing of this article, and others may
oin in the near future.) Sources for these figures, which are sur-
risingly sparse, include R. A. Dentler and M. E. Warshauer, *Big
City Drop-outs and Illiterates* (New York, 1965); M. Harrington,
The Other America (New York, 1964); "Facts on American Edu-
ation," *NEA Research Bulletin,* May 1966; U.S. Office of Educa-
on, *Digest of Educational Statistics* (Washington, 1965); D.
chreiber, *Holding Power* (Washington, 1962); J. B. Conant, *Slums
nd Suburbs* (New York, 1961); and D. J. Brooks, *A Study to De-
ermine the Literary Level of Able-Bodied Persons Receiving Pub-
c Assistance* (Chicago, 1962). For the searching out of these and
ther data and for excellent editorial advice, I am indebted to
awrence Robertson, now with the International Business Machines
Corporation.

In one city, the rate of unemployment for male school leavers between the ages of sixteen and twenty-one is 15 per cent higher than the rate for high-school graduates.

In the same city, 48 percent of the boys sixteen to twenty-one *with* high-school diplomas were unemployed; this pattern is found in other cities.

Eighty-eight and four tenths percent of the applicants for General Assistance in Cook County (Chicago) for a six-week period had not completed high school; again, this situation is found elsewhere as well.

Though difficult to demonstrate statistically, it is clear that a great majority of school-leavers and a large percentage of high-school graduates are unemployable save for unskilled work.

Again difficult to document, there is considerable evidence that mental illness is higher among many of the groups that these schools serve.

These figures cannot be taken to prove the failure of schools alone or in part; they may reflect conditions that other agencies as well as the schools must seek to correct. But they do suggest that the urban schools face a task far harder than the suburban schools, a task requiring imagination, considerable resources, and the concern of all Americans, not just those who live in cities. These fifteen great cities enroll over five million children, over 10 percent of the country's pre-college student body. Further, these children's families are highly mobile, some leaving the city for the suburbs. Over two thirds move within the city, some moving again and again. The former, if ill-educated, become other communities' wards. The latter, often drawn from groups that the suburbs absorb inadequately—the racial minorities—are only more frustrated and caught.

A typical inner-city school is on a slight rise in a previously "respectable" part of the city. Many of the houses nearby have a kind of late nineteenth-century grandeur left, with high windows, bay turrets, and flights of imposing stone steps. Pressing in upon them are frame "triple deckers" thirty to fifty years old, with porches out back covered with drying

aundry. The school's yard is very small and backs onto the
ouses. Trash is in abundance.

The door of the school is locked, not to keep the children
n, as some critics would think, but to keep undesirables out.
'o get in, one pushes a button that rings in the classroom
earest the front door. An assigned student comes out, peers
t those who wish admittance, and either lets them in or in-
orms the office.

The building dates from Grover Cleveland's second admin-
stration. It is solid, high ceilinged; the floors are well polished,
ut the sickly green walls need paint badly; the rooms are
urprisingly cool on a warm June or September day, but the
ntique steam heating system is raucous on winter mornings.
'he windows in each classroom are decorated pane by pane
ith colorful paper cutouts made by the teacher after school.
ome rooms have new, tan-colored wood and steel movable
able-desks; others have older, lift-top models. In each case,
he desks are arranged in rows, though only the older ones
re screwed to the floor. The hall outside has a line painted
own the middle; during class breaks, "no talking" and "keep
o the right." Teachers are on duty at each point where the
all turns.

The teachers are proud and defensive; devoted and cynical;
n many ways the most interesting, important, and neglected
art of the school. They are stereotyped as rigid and out-of-
ate, and they deeply resent this. They are local people, by
nd large, and locally trained, but they protest, quite rightly,
hat this does not necessarily mean that they are parochial
nd ill informed. They look on most visitors much as they
ook on the battalion of behavioral scientists that has rushed
orward to explain the "pathology" of the urban school—with
he contempt for (and fear of) the witch doctor who never
eems to get at the root of the illness. They are at once
ritical of and loyal to the "central office," their own school
dministration, and they doubt the sincerity of a federal gov-
rnment that largely ignores them while it makes political
ay out of a national "teachers' corps" scheme to send eager
ut wholly inexperienced youngsters for brief tours into their
chools. There are superb professionals among them, more
an most critics suspect, but buried in the impersonality of

the system and under a staggering load of work. Compare
with but five years ago, they are an outspoken lot, drawir
together as never before in the face of difficult teaching co
ditions, hostile children and parents, low salaries, and a flou
dering and impoverished city government. Many now belor
to a labor union and speak more of "teacher power" than
"professionalism." As a group, the teachers display a new ar
in many ways refreshing truculence.

The children are quiet, well-disciplined: no "blackboar
jungle" here. The rein is tight and one can feel the pressur
but order and quiet are maintained. Few of the children a
ragged, though some are clearly undernourished. Several
the teachers, at their own expense, keep packets of dry cere
and a bottle of milk to serve as breakfast for those youngste
who come hungry to school. Attendance at school is, hov
ever, poor. Many of the students' families are constantly c
the move, from one rented space in the city to anothe
from one school district, inevitably, to another. Statisticall
50 percent of the children in this school in September wi
not be there in June.

The children's studies are a mixture of the old and the nev
all in basic subjects such as reading, writing, arithmetic, soci
studies, civics. The older authorities, "Dick and Jane," Muzze
and the rest are there along with the new Science Researc
Associates reading kits, Elementary Science Study material
and more. All are used, however, in almost identical way
the teacher teaching and the child listening, recording, reviev
ing in a workbook, and taking tests. One is struck by tl
paradox that the key "teachers" are the materials—the bool
—and yet they "teach" only as the human teacher allows ther
Ask classroom teachers about this paradox and why the
seems to be largely a single pedagogy, and they respond th
the conditions require it—elementary school teachers are r
sponsible for from twenty to forty children without a brea
during the day and secondary teachers may see between 15
and 250 different children during a day's five or more period
They assert either that "discovery" or "student-initiated
methods are unproven with "their" kinds of children or, whe
tried, require more time for preparation and more materia
and space than are available. They also suggest that "di

covery" and "non-directive" discipline rest necessarily on middle-class values that are relatively meaningless for their children, who come from other backgrounds.

What strikes one is the feeling of irrelevance. The distance between much of what the children are asked to learn and what they perceive as their needs is great. The formality of the school doesn't mesh with the informality out of school. School language isn't their language. School music, school stories, school expectations aren't theirs. This disjunction could cause rebellion (and does, in the form of "discipline problems" and dropping out), but it more often causes lassitude. School in its irrelevant way is to be endured. It is a necessary ritual, to the children meaning little more than that. It is no surprise that the children's test scores fall further and further behind the national average for every year they stay in school.

Though in the halls and classrooms one gets a feeling of order, an atmosphere of learning is virtually absent. The main worries of the teachers and the administrators are social worries: principally, control and regular attendance at school, less frequently troubles at home, inattentiveness and hostility, medical and dental problems. There are many children and few adults, considering the task, and the emphasis is on control. The front door bell interrupts teaching. The public address system interrupts. The principal, taking his visitors around, interrupts every class in turn. Interruption of learning is the rule; it suggests to all, teachers and students alike, that *learning is not the prime purpose of school.* The principal is not the principal teacher; he is the school's policeman and judge. The school's impossible teaching schedule clearly suggests that teachers need not really teach. The teachers claim that this is not anti-intellectualism, but that it is rather misplaced purpose. The school is in fact to control children, not to teach them. The locked door, the childish window cutouts made not by children but by teachers, the white line on glossy floors by walls ill cared for, the bitter and misunderstood teachers—all add to a feeling not so much of desperation as of confusion.

What is the school for? To move children quietly from class to class? To teach them a basic curriculum resting on a set of values and expectations irrelevant for many of the children? All suggest that simple conclusions—this city school is "bad," or understaffed, or ill staffed—are unwise. The problems here are complex and start with the question of purpose. This school appears not to reward imaginative learning. And there are noisier, more desperate schools in the city than this.

Ours is not the first period when the purposes and practices of schools, city schools among them, have been under scrutiny. Two other reform periods have occurred, both in conjunction with dislocating changes within the cities themselves. The first came in the 1840's and 1850's, led by a group of Whig reformers who saw schooling as a vehicle to maintain moral and political order. These men were Jeffersonian in their fear and hatred of urban life, and they sought to impose what can properly be called traditional agrarian ideals through schools. They failed, of course: the children they hoped to reach either remained employed at work, untouched by the saccharine injunctions of McGuffey and his imitators or, if at school, unmoved by their plea, irrespective of attendance. Legislators spoke in favor of schools—and then failed to appropriate money for their adequate support. And in only a limited sense did the families of those for whom the new city schools were primarily intended desire and support them.[2]

The second and far larger effort at reform occurred at the turn of the present century. The urban problems of the 1840's pale in comparison with the post-Civil War growth of cities. Industrialization, rapid foreign immigration, and agricultural failure combined to cause a rush to closely populated centers. With rapid growth came the inevitable range of problems—inadequate housing, rapidly shifting political patterns, the breakdown of traditional family structure, inadequate police and social welfare facilities—which in turn spawned a group of reformers whom Teddy Roosevelt promptly labeled muckrakers. Several of these focused in part on schools and children, most notably Joseph Mayer Rice, Jacob Riis, and

---

[2] See M. B. Katz, "The Irony of Urban School Reform," unpublished doctoral dissertation, Harvard University, 1966; and L. A. Cremin, *The American Common School* (New York, 1951).

Robert Hunter.[3] Where the reformers of the 1840's had been led by such middle-class "insiders" as there were at the time —men actively involved with schooling, Horace Mann, James Carter, Henry Barnard, and the rest—turn-of-the-century protest was led largely by journalists. The reforms they suggested were ameliorative: feed and clothe the poor and teach them to get jobs and to hold these as dignified workingmen. Their allies were drawn from a narrow group of academic politicians and progressives—Seth Low, Nicholas Murray Butler, Woodrow Wilson, John Dewey, Charles Eliot—and the middle- and upper-class readers of their journals. They had their successes, largely through private philanthropy—*noblesse oblige*—but their gains were small and briefly enjoyed. The particular success of the period was the absorption of the foreign and native immigrant, and the mushrooming public school system played a central part in this. The three R's, rote learning, and middle-class virtues were preached; those who learned well left the slum and entered the expanding middle-class mainstream of American life.

The schools in the twentieth century grew enormously in numbers and in the services they provided, but their essential purpose remained constant—to teach simple intellectual and social skills and the folkways of the dominant culture. By the 1920's they were staffed largely with the products of the system, those who had moved "up" in the world by means of their education. Their devotion to middle-class ideology was single-minded—no cultural pluralism here. Their leadership, both inside the system and among reformers, was middle and upper class and fundamentally afraid of the changes the new city dweller might bring. In a word, both schoolmen and their ideological leadership were essentially conservative, the

[3] For example, J. Riis, *Children of the Poor* (New York, 1892); J. M. Rice, *The Public-School Systems of the United States* (New York, 1893); R. Hunter, *Poverty* (New York, 1905), chap. 5. On the progressives in education generally, see L. A. Cremin, *The Transformation of the School* (New York, 1961); and S. Cohen, *Progressive Education and Urban School Reform* (New York, 1964).

label "progressive" notwithstanding.[4] They were devoted to social reform, but within an existing set of class and economic lines. Truly radical educational ideas that emerged in the 1930's had little effect. Concern for social adaptation and control were dominant.[5]

This background is important for two purposes—to explain the shape of today's city schools and to offer a contrast with the contemporary situation. Present community leadership is drawn from a far broader spectrum of society than previously and, most important, includes the concerned city dweller himself. Negro leadership, especially that of the civil rights movement, is centrally involved. The federal government's effort to give the "poor" a major stake in deciding programs for themselves through the local committees of community action programs is striking evidence of the change in American social reform. The potential political power of an alliance of liberal middle-class reformers in the older tradition and the poor is considerable, and the chance that lasting gains may be possible is substantially greater than ever before. (Racial and religious discord and extremism may shatter it yet, alas.) Schooling is important to this new alliance (though the purpose of that schooling is still unclear and a clash of traditional and radical positions inevitable). As it has political power, many increased resources will flow to it—as indeed they already have.

The strategy for reform demanded today is no different than heretofore: to decide what the schools should do and

---

[4] It is illuminating that most of the successful truly "progressive" educational experiment attempts before World War II took place in independent schools or their virtual equivalent within public school systems. Save in the extension of services, "progressivism" of a pedagogical sort reached neither city public nor parochial schools in any significant measure. See S. J. Clark, "Two Schools and Two Ideas: A Study of Progressivism in Boston, 1920–40," unpublished doctoral dissertation, Harvard University, 1965; and Cremin, *The Transformation of the School,* chap. 7.

[5] See, for an example of radical thought, George S. Counts, *Dare the Schools Build a New Social Order* (New York, 1932); and copies of *Social Frontier,* 1934–1939. See also R. Hofstadter, *Anti-Intellectualism in American Life* (New York, 1963), chap. 7.

then to harness the men with the money to see that those ends are met. According to the conventional wisdom, educational goals are set by "lay" boards of education. What really happens is that, like most policies, educational policy is largely shaped by clusters of interest groups and bureaucrats. Most boards of education and school committees react to ideas rather than create them.[6]

A new educational policy must meet certain constraints. First, the social, economic, and cultural problems of the city cannot be solved by schools alone, and school policy aimed at their alleviation must be closely locked into a plan that encompasses all social organizations. Evidence is overwhelming that schooling is but a minor influence on many children,[7] and though one might try to improve schools to alter this, at the same time one must take into account "nonschool" educational influences—the street corner, family, the union, church, job, television. The approach might be centered in the school department as in New Haven with its "community schools," or it might lead to a new kind of group such as New York's "human resource" agency launched by Mitchell Sviridoff. In sum, those educational ends best reached within schoolhouses should be worked toward in the schoolhouse; but, in turn, those that are better handled elsewhere—for example, some aspects of technical education or of civics—should be put elsewhere.[8]

Second, the ends of education (*not* the organization and control of the largest number of children at the least cost) should govern the shape of schoolhouses. This sounds so obvious as to be absurd, yet even the most casual visit to many schools (suburban as well as urban, it must be admitted) dem-

[6] See Neal Gross, *Who Runs Our Schools?* (New York, 1958), and R. A. Dahl, *Who Governs?* (New Haven, 1961), for two case studies.

[7] U.S. Office of Education, "Equality of Educational Opportunity" (Washington, 1966). This study, headed by James Coleman of Johns Hopkins University, raises a wide series of questions and is discussed below.

[8] The inclusion of civics may surprise some. Donald W. Oliver and Fred M. Newmann deal with this issue in a chapter in T. Sizer, ed., *Religion in Public Education* (Boston, 1967).

onstrates the irrelevance of much of what is going on. Such irrelevance is the *prime* blight on American education, far more grievous than understaffing, skimpy funding, and poor housing.

What policies are implied here? Clearly, some agency broader than present school departments (as they are now most usually constituted) must plan and direct educational programs, both those in schools and those out of school. More difficult, however, is the question of purpose. Insofar as is possible, I would like to argue, schooling should be deliberately pluralistic, primarily focused on teaching people alternatives and providing them the means to act upon them. One teaches not an American creed (as though there were only *one*) but the reasons for and the substances of the tensions that make American life viable (one studies Jefferson and Jackson less as presidents and more as representatives of different, important ideological positions). One tolerates a wide variety of views, and only insists on their rational justification. One teaches the skills children need to get ahead, not the skills tradition may impose. (This involves a list of priorities, for, as Benjamin Franklin observed on this topic over two hundred years ago, art is long and time is short. For example, one decreases the study of literary criticism in favor of more work in exposition; slights the study of plane geometry for work in the binary number system; cuts back on cabinet making and upholstery in favor of electronics.) One deliberately rewards a variety of forms of expression—visual, spoken, musical—not just that of the written language.

Though this argument for schools to teach "alternatives," for a deliberate educational pluralism, requires more discussion than can be made here, even in its simplest form it suggests a school of a clearly different character than that of the present. It would be a school where the child would move at his own pace and not necessarily be grouped by chronological age. The variety among teachers would be capitalized upon, and students would be exposed to and deal with many kinds of adults. The curriculum would not be "tracked," would be broad, and would accommodate itself to the progress of individual children. The vast resources of the city outside of the schoolrooms would be used.

This is hardly a radical conception. It has been suggested for sixty years or more and tried in a variety of guises. The Dalton Plan, briefly attempted in New York City among other places, is one partial experiment from the 1920's, and there are others. The Pittsburgh schools are experimenting along these lines today, and there is much talk there and elsewhere of "individualized instruction," "flexible scheduling," and "team teaching."[9] All seek to loosen up the controlled school and to let the needs of the children chart the shape of the curriculum, and in this sense they are at fundamental cross purposes with the traditional school, in the city and elsewhere.

If these be the elements of present reform, two facets are yet lacking. The issue of values has not been fully faced. Does the teacher accept the values of the child's parents or impose his own values? Does one acknowledge and encourage the rebellion of the children of aggrieved groups, like many of the Negroes, or does one try to discourage a rebellious nature? Until this issue is faced, and until school authorities recognize the contradiction between a scheme for truly educating individuals in a pluralistic setting and the present system, the experiments going forward will founder. The second element lacking is the resources for a vast experiment, one that goes beyond one "computerized classroom" or one "team teaching" school. A cluster of ideas needs to be tried out together, supported by a clear, if tentative, ideology, the kind that most educators tend to avoid. Boston's proposed "subsystem" (a portion of the public school system set aside for experiment) could be a forerunner here, as could similar plans in other cities, but it would require several hundred times the resources now available and an autonomy not now provided. Education is expensive and, though much of it in its present form is inefficient, any truly effective form will cost

[9] See J. T. Shaplin and H. Olds, eds., *Team Teaching* (New York, 1964); R. Bush and D. Allen, *A Design for High-School Education* (New York, 1964); J. Goodlad and R. H. Anderson, *The Nongraded Elementary School,* rev. ed. (New York, 1963); and various relevant articles in the special issue on computer technology of *Saturday Review,* July 23, 1966. In a somewhat different vein, see also Nat Hentoff, *Our Children Are Dying* (New York, 1966).

substantial sums. Efficiency should be one test of an experiment, but experiments, with their false starts and wrong assumptions, are inherently expensive. Resources for a major trial must be found.

Whatever the trial, whatever the purpose or purposes freshly identified for schooling (urban *and* suburban, it must be said), the need for a redefinition of this purpose is clear. Curiously, we tend to shy away from it, or we feel we can leave it to clichés or for philosophical fights in the academy. We miss the striking incongruity of the nonlearning of our learning institutions, of the anti-intellectualism or the non-intellectualism of our supposed cradles of rationalism and intellect. The professionals in education and concerned laymen must confront this.

While long-range restructuring of the system is clearly necessary, there is yet worth-while and badly needed intermediate-range work to be done. There is the central problem of people, the persons who staff the schools and those who, as "lay" representatives, serve supposedly as policy makers.

No large public service is so weakly staffed as education. Teaching is a form of personal service, and the staff Americans employ is enormous, over two million in public and private elementary and secondary schools in 1965–66. But the average educator, on several counts, leaves a good deal to be desired. First, he is drawn from the lower academic levels of the colleges and hardly at all from highly selective undergraduate institutions.[10] Second, he stays at the game of teaching (or counseling or administering) but a short time, around five years. This is a result in part, of course, of the fact of many young women in the teaching profession, and it makes continuity in many schools difficult, city schools among them. Third, his training has focused not on the profound ethical issues that educating implies (in spite of courses in "philosophy" of education), but rather on the tools of an unexamined

---

[10] According to norms computed for the Miller Analogies Test, the mean score of prospective teachers on that test is lower than that of any other academic or industrial group with a college degree. W. S. Miller, *Miller Analogies Test Manual, 1960 Revision.* The Graduate Record Examination corroborates this finding.

trade. And fourth, once on the job, he is largely cut off from contacts with the academic, political, and financial worlds by tradition and by the incredible time demand of his job.

What to do? Until professional leadership is strengthened, the situation in the schools will not be improved. First, the conditions of teaching must be improved—time demands, salaries, conditions of work, status. Considering the difficulty and subtlety of their tasks, teachers are grievously overworked. The average elementary school teacher has but a few minutes off a day from overseeing (much less seriously teaching) twenty-five or more pupils. The average secondary school teacher "teaches" over 150 different pupils a day, pupils he is supposed to understand and nurture as individuals. On top of their teaching, teachers have to keep up their subjects, prepare for future instruction, and correct and grade papers. Top this with the common practice of "moonlighting" —to earn extra money through odd jobs to help one's budget —and one sees the impossibility of the task. The psychic rewards of teaching clearly attract idealistic young people; if we can show them that in this job these rewards are fully attainable and that the teacher's self-respect and dignity are assured, the principal hurdle to recruiting will be overcome. Current public focus on big-city education makes these schools particularly attractive to many potential teachers. The conditions of employment—not the children, not the communities—presently give them pause. Perhaps the current militance among big-city teachers is a happy sign here. While the initial union—school board struggles were primarily over salaries, the raising for collective bargaining by some locals of the issue of conditions of work may spur school authorities to improve them. Militance often spurs self-respect, and though unionization (or its virtual carbon copy among certain large-city National Education Association "professional" groups) has brought problems, on the whole it has been a constructive movement. Teachers are looking after their own interests, and if these can be held in most respects consonant with their children's interests, much can be achieved.

Recruiting new teachers is, of course, far more difficult and time-consuming than making better use of those of high quality already in the schools. The top career people now in service must be the principal keys to school reform, and communities should work hard to find them. Some form of team teaching will be necessary both to use them more effectively and to defend paying the extra sums they deserve. Sometimes, the ablest teachers are not the pleasantest and certainly not the most docile—precisely those whom many school systems identify and reward the least. Lay groups can play a part here in spotting these persons and rewarding them in one way or another, with sabbatical grants, extra stipends, and so forth, even though (or perhaps because) it embarrasses the formal administration of the system.

Third, experienced persons from other professions will have to be lured into careers in the schools and local school and state licensing authorities persuaded to accept them. Many of the problems of operating a large school system are only partially educational and cut across many aspects of public administration and law. Persons from those fields should be recruited. (Why, for example, should a first-class teacher who has been promoted to a principalship arrange bus schedules, keep accounts, struggle with custodians, and deal extensively with local political concerns? Why can't he concentrate on instruction and have an appropriately trained colleague handle these other matters under his supervision? The present waste of most principals'—and in like measure, high school department chairmen's—time is scandalous.)

Part-time help for nonteaching tasks is also an obvious step, but one used far less than one might expect. Many teachers apparently are ill-at-ease and distrustful of other adults in "their" classrooms, and there has been surprisingly little call for such help from the professionals. However, one can see a triple virtue for schools hiring mothers from, for example, poor families in the community to work as aides: the women can well use the money, earned on a time schedule that will allow them to be at home when their children are at home; the jobs would provide them with experience and training in child care, the most appropriate concern for many of them; and the program would bring into the many classrooms that are staffed with middle-class teachers women familiar with the children's view of the world, their expectations, and their language.

In spite of teachers' and administrators' claim that a locally reared and trained staff is not unduly parochial, more varied personnel are undoubtedly needed in many systems, if for no other reason than to allow children to meet adults from highly different backgrounds. Many large cities recruit hard: Los Angeles, for example, has several teams on the road constantly. By contrast, until the last few years the New York City schools had but one man to handle their entire recruiting effort in a city with a staff of over 40,000. Fortunately, that community has changed its recruiting policies substantially. Many cities have special examinations, which are a nuisance for outsiders to take, and their administrative policies are hardly geared to lure strong personnel from other places. Salaries have improved in recent years, owing in part to pressure from organized teachers; beginning salaries for teachers with bachelor's degrees in the fifteen largest cities ranged from $4,590 to $6,120 with a median of $5,300 against a nationwide median of $5,000.[11] Top salaries are high, with that of Chicago's superintendent being one of the highest in the country.

These suggestions are neither novel nor radical; they just beg for resources and firm administration. Efforts at political reform, however, may be less obvious but perhaps more important. Where school board tenure is a rung on a ladder of political promotion, a position for party patronage, or a post of excessively short and impotent character, little progress is made. Education is a political matter because it touches on matters of great sensitivity and controversy. It *must* be a political matter, in the best sense: close to popular will and capable of change, not at popular whim but by a clear and studied popular mandate. Government must find devices to allow for this.

The fifteen Great City schools have a wide variety of gov-

---

[11] Research Council of the Great Cities Program for School Improvement, "Teachers' Salary Analysis of the Great Cities 1965–66" (Chicago, 1965); National Education Association, "Salary Schedules for Classroom Teachers, 1965–66" (Chicago, 1965).

erning bodies, from Boston's highly political, elected, and short-term committee to New York's long-term, Mayor-appointed board. The latter, by the operation of its nominating commission, has much to commend it, the former only that it stays close to what it detects as local majority opinion.

Much current opinion favors policies of "decentralization," of giving maximum feasible control to the particular communities the individual schools serve. This trend is more a reflection of the breakdown of adequate and responsive local politics than of a new educational ideology. Many newly articulate minority groups in the city are disaffected by their lack of power and control; they have seized upon the most visible local symbol of the political establishment, the public school. They want to govern it—and to try to make it relevant and powerful in a way they know it is not now. Most liberals support this trend, most notably those on the so-called Bundy task force that recommended a "community school system" for New York City.[12] Most organized teacher groups oppose it, as they see even greater and closer external pressure on their work, with proportionately less "teacher power." Most plans to date try to balance local power with central city power; the Bundy scheme calls for thirty to sixty autonomous units, each governed by an eleven-man community school board, six members of which are elected by parents and five appointed by the mayor from a list of nominees provided by the central school authorities. This balance of power is important if we are to avoid the errors of the past (seventy years ago Boston and New York, for example, had highly decentralized neighborhood control of schools). There must be provision for special schools, economical only in large units. There must be central control of pupil allocation and school construction sites, if racial and class integration is to survive as a goal. There must be countervailing pressures to neighborhood prejudices, whether these be in the hands of liberals, Birchites, Black Power advocates, or White Citizens Councils.

---

[12] "Reconnection for Learning: A Community School System for New York City," Report of the Mayor's Advisory Panel on Decentralization of the New York City Schools (New York, 1967).

The community-at-large needs a voice, as it will have to live with the products of the neighborhood.

All of this suggests that the "decentralization" fancy is an over-simplification. Schools must involve their neighborhoods, listen to and respond to parents, and become relevant in neighborhood terms, but they also must relate themselves more effectively than at present to a rapidly changing, highly mobile national community. The schools, then, must both broaden their views to respond to general social requirements and narrow them to respect neighborhood and parental needs. A balance between centralization beyond what we have now and decentralization beyond even the Bundy task force recommendations is needed. It will be difficult to achieve.

If sound purposes, able men, and effective control are crucial to reform, so is money. The cities spend vast sums of it, and education is often the largest item on their budgets, though not to the overwhelming extent it is in the majority of suburbs. (Welfare in a few cities takes first place at the public trough.) New York spends $737.45 per child per year, Los Angeles $512.85, Miami (Dade County) $410.54, and Cleveland $434.16. The national average per-pupil expenditure is about $500.[13] Why, then, are the cities so in "trouble"? For the obvious reason that it costs more to school the city's children, so many of whom are culturally "disadvantaged," and real estate and services come dear in congested settings. If one compares the number of citizens in elementary and secondary school—over fifty million in 1961, 26 percent of the total population—the country's investment in their future is niggardly. The percentage of America's gross national product devoted to education has not risen appreciably in the last fifty years; surely we can tolerate a rise without discomfort.[14] The largest single federal program for education,

[13] National Education Association, "Expenditures of Large Local School Systems" (Washington, 1966). It must be noted that inter-city comparisons indicate only a general tendency, and are misleading in detail.

[14] Charles S. Benson, *The Economics of Public Education* (Boston, 1961), p. 53. In 1958–59, total public school expenditures were a mere 3.09 percent of the gross national product.

Title I of the Elementary and Secondary Education Act of 1965, currently totals but one billion dollars a year, less than one month's expenditures on the war in Vietnam. It is worth repeating in this context the point that schools are inefficient and must be made less so; but this does not mean that improvements in efficiency will end in a cost to taxpayers the same or less. To do the minimal job of schooling that is clearly called for may cost more, and we should be prepared for it.

Where are these resources to come from? More and more, surprising to say, from private industry in the form of vastly improved teaching materials and devices, in-plant "vocational" training jointly sponsored with public authorities, and sponsored materials over the mass media. Industry's stake in the education market is growing and is best evidenced by the entrance into it of previously uninvolved companies such as IBM, Raytheon, and General Electric. Their most important single short-range impact may well be the pressure they put on public authorities, particularly the federal government, for the additional resources necessary for their wares to be purchased. They will be unaccustomed and powerful allies for the professional education lobby. The excellence of their wares will be a measure of their public responsibility.

Federal aid to the schools generally and to city schools in particular has been growing rapidly, but direct aid only accounted in 1965 for 1.3 percent of total elementary and secondary public school expenditure in the Great Cities (except Washington).[15] The proportion was substantially higher in some cities, however, because they contain large numbers of the poor toward whom many of the programs are directed. Federal funds will have to increase, as, in many areas, state and particularly local funds have been pushed to the limit.

Better men and more money: obvious remedies, and a part of the present rhetoric of urban education. The prior condition of a clearly stated purpose that is directly met by the schools is less obvious and, perhaps, more important in

[15] Research Council of the Great Cities Program for School Improvement, "Sources of Revenue for the Public Schools of the Great Cities" (Chicago, 1965).

the long run than the other two elements. Good men and vast sums are spent today controlling children and attempting to feed them a curriculum and a set of values that are in part irrelevant and, for some, insulting. The latent (or not so latent) hostility of many children to the so-called process of education is evidence not so much of a spirit to be broken as of the inadequate scope of schools.

It goes without saying that no particular issue is more pressing on many city school systems today than that of race. Staffing, housing, finances—all are important but big-city school boards and administrators are more disturbed by this issue than by any other. And for good reason. In a country that is 11.4 percent nonwhite, the fifteen Great Cities have total populations that are 21.1 percent nonwhite. The school-age population of these cities is 24.8 percent nonwhite, but the nonwhite public school population is even higher, as nonpublic schools are largely Caucasian and the nonwhite families in the cities tend to be larger than those of whites. In Philadelphia, which has a population that is 30 percent nonwhite, 57 percent of the public school enrollment is nonwhite. Seventeen percent of Boston's public schools had over 90 percent nonwhite pupils in a year (1960) when that city's nonwhite population was only 9.8 percent. Washington, D.C., has a nonwhite public school enrollment of over 90 percent, the highest in the nation. More striking is the fact that the percentage of nonwhites in most of these cities and especially in their public schools is steadily and rapidly rising. Owing to birth rates higher among Negroes than whites, the age cohort shortly to enter school will be between 15 percent and 17 percent Negro; given increasing white enrollments in private schools, the nation's elementary schools may be 25 percent Negro by 1985. These are national figures; and clearly the cores of the majority of our great metropolitan areas will shortly be predominantly Negro.[16]

[16] U.S. Bureau of the Census, *U.S. Census of Population and Housing: 1960 Housing Tracts* (Washington, 1962); Joseph M. Cronin, "Catholic Schools and Racial Balance," *Commonweal*, October 7, 1966; Commission on School Integration, National Association of Inter-group Relations Officials, "Public School Segre-

The issue here for schools—and it is a hotly contested issue—turns on the belief of many educators that children of different races must live and work together if they are going to learn to respect and tolerate one another. An open-minded attitude toward others, the argument goes, comes little from book learning or exhortation; it comes rather from real experience.[17] The best opportunity society now has to require the "mixing" of all persons is within the public schools. Accordingly, those who would teach the virtues of full integration preach the necessity of starting this social revolution in classrooms.

There are, of course, opponents to this view, both black and white. Some argue what seems a higher virtue, the neighborhood school. Children, this argument goes, should attend school with those with whom they live all the time and not with relative strangers from other parts of town. Others see the problem as not primarily a racial one, but an economic one, calling not for a deliberate mixing of races in classrooms but rather a massive "compensatory" education program that will allow all children eventually to compete in the economy as equals. Still others, both Negro and white, argue for racially segregated schools on theoretical grounds, not unlike the arguments of early immigrant groups who wished to preserve their traditions against swamping by a majority culture.

The debate on this issue received a fillip (rather than a conclusion) with the publication in July 1966 of a massive study by the United States Office of Education entitled, "Equal Educational Opportunity" (otherwise dubbed the "Coleman Report" after its senior author).[18] The study, required by the Civil Rights Act of 1964, was on the effects of segregated and integrated schooling on black children and their white

gation and Integration in the North" (Washington, 1963); (Pittsburgh) Board of Public Education, "The Quest for Racial Equality in the Pittsburgh Public Schools" (1965); and figures from a forthcoming volume on the Negro family by Daniel Patrick Moynihan.

[17] See, for example, Kenneth Clark, *Dark Ghetto* (New York, 1965), chap. 6.

[18] U.S.O.E., "Equality of Educational Opportunity." See especially chaps. 1–3.

colleagues. With all its imperfections, the massive study (over 600,000 children were tested, making the program the second largest social science survey in history) is highly suggestive. Social and economic class is found to be the overwhelming influence upon school learning (as defined by written achievement tests—and this is an admittedly narrow definition). Put more bluntly, your father and your mother control your educational opportunity much more than do your teachers; it is difficult indeed, it appears, to break out from one's birthright. By and large, newer school buildings, more teachers, more materials, libraries, special programs, and the rest did not now alter the central fact of socio-economic determinism. The school as the vehicle of upward social mobility did not seem to be operating in 1965–66.

These findings bear directly on the discrimination issue by suggesting that economic and social exclusion may be as powerful restraints on equal opportunity as is race. It is hard to overcome your ancestry whatever your color. The racial problem is compounded by this: black children from poor families tend not to achieve because they are poor—and their color clearly makes it difficult for their parents to become less poor.

Integrated schooling produces some gain, but it is small and uneven. When Negro children in the northeastern states went to integrated schools, their achievement increased by roughly one year (that is, their reading level, for example, was one grade ahead of comparable children in segregated schools) —and this finding is consistent even when social class is controlled. Findings for other parts of the country are less hopeful or are confused. All one can say is that integrated schooling in some areas of the country seems to make a small difference for Negro children. It is a comfort, but small comfort, for those who wish to use the present schools to increase Negro rights.

The report supports another hypothesis: schools are but part of the process of socialization and present schools are considerably less powerful influences than family and friends, perhaps because formal education is by its nature relatively impotent. But perhaps contemporary schools are a shadow of what they could be—irrelevant, shoddy, anti-intellectual. Perhaps powerful schools could make a difference. Cast within a large public effort to help children, they very well might be. We need a trial—and then another report.

Unfortunately, discussion of this issue has been clouded by extreme rhetoric. On one hand there are those who say that integration is the first order of business; on the other there are those who say we must get on with improving "ghetto" schools as they are presently constituted.[19] School integration is not and must not be an either-or proposition: we should integrate where and when we can, and use the full weight of the national government to do so; and where integration, because of recalcitrant politicians or demographic realities or both, cannot proceed quickly, we should intervene massively to help slum children as much and as imaginatively as we know how. There is no simple, single school policy unless that policy is one of extreme flexibility.

Though there are many school systems that, because of numbers and geography, are incapable of integration by race and class, there are many others that are—so long as local boundaries are redrawn to create large, metropolitan units.[20] This prospect scares most people. It spells the end, they fear, of local control, and of schools close to the people. It would require, they argue, a vast bureaucracy that would ignore the individual even more than present bureaucracies. It would encourage, some even feel, greater federal control.

These worries are misplaced. As I stated earlier, at the same time that one centralizes some functions one should also decentralize others. Curricular decisions, the choice of texts, the length of classes and sessions, the mix of teachers: these mat-

---

[19] For example, Joseph Alsop, "No More Nonsense about Ghetto Schools," *New Republic*, July 22, 1967, pp. 18–23; Robert Schwartz, Thomas Pettigrew, and Marshall Smith, "Fake Panaceas for Ghetto Education," *New Republic*, September 23, 1967, pp. 16–19; and Joseph Alsop, "Ghetto Schools," *New Republic*, November 18, 1967, pp. 18–23.

[20] This is not to suggest that other remedies—internal redistricting, educational "parks," busing, and the rest—will not serve well in some settings. For a metropolitan plan for racial balance purposes, see "Schools for Hartford," Center for Field Studies, Harvard Graduate School of Education (Cambridge, 1965).

ters should be delegated directly to the school principal who, with his teachers and the parents of his community, knows the children best. A broadening of school boundaries should be accompanied by a plan to decentralize many purely educational decisions and to involve the directly served community in the reaching of these. Even a casual look at, for example, the London County Council schools in England will show that it can be done. Thus, for reasons of integration as well as politics, we need to move in two directions at once: to centralize some functions and to decentralize others. The former alone will lead to a deadening bureaucracy, as many of our present large school systems already demonstrate. The latter alone will lead to missed opportunities and parochialism.

Metropolitan allocation of children, at least for some of their school life or for out-of-school programs, is a necessity if we are to have in communities any sort of racial or socioeconomic balance: this is obvious. But there are other virtues in metropolitanism, ones of possibly even greater long-term importance. New kinds of programs for children and adults may be possible. Certain economies may result from the elimination of small, duplicated offices. The wide area could easily support strong schools for special purposes, which could concentrate on the problems of groups such as the deaf, the retarded, the blind, and those otherwise handicapped. The region might also be able to support, perhaps in conjunction with the state, systems of collegiate and technical education that could be functionally related to lower schools. Of great importance is the possibility of far more diverse sources of local tax revenues, sufficient, perhaps, in many areas to maintain an independence of overwhelming state and federal aid.

Big-city schools have, since the turn of the century, provided millions of new and old Americans the means to move into the center of the economy and society. The schools' means for doing this were simple; today, with many persons in slum situations who will not be absorbed by the society, different and more flexible steps must be taken. Further, the inflexibility of traditional practice, with its control and order, stifles and warps. Schools, and all the other institutions that educate, should concern themselves first with learning in the broadest sense and with the learning most appropriate for each individual. Individual rights have become a cliché for educators; perhaps that is why they have never been fully respected. We must start with this respect, and reshape our institutions accordingly. What, then, is a sound public policy for urban schools?

To demand of educators a fundamental review and recasting of present schools to eliminate the irrelevant and shoddy, as a condition for massive new funding.

To launch comprehensive educational planning across all agencies that teach, schools and others together.

To redefine educational communities to capitalize upon the needs and strengths of entire metropolitan regions and, concurrently, to decentralize many educational matters to individual schools and to the particular communities which they serve.

POVERTY IN CITIES

Daniel P. Moynihan

Dr. J. H. Plumb of Christ's College, Cambridge, who is the most recent and with luck will be the most successful of those bold-hearted scholars who have undertaken to assemble a comprehensive record of man's experience, began his series with a proposition that will serve equally well to open a discussion of poverty in American cities. The theme of *The History of Human Society,* Plumb writes, is thus: "that the condition of man now is superior to what it was."[1]

Not to see that this is so with respect to the problem of poverty in the central cities is to risk a serious misinterpretation of the present concern over the issue. Things have not been getting worse. There are few groups in American cities who are not in fact considerably better off than they have been. In an entirely familiar pattern, however, the response to this situation has not been one of rising content but, for many individuals and groups, rising *dis*content. Many who suffered the worst deprivation in the past have begun to wonder why they need be deprived at all; many who have now attained a

[1] J. H. Plumb, introduction to C. R. Boxer, *The Dutch Seaborn Empire: 1600–1800* (New York: Alfred A. Knopf, 1965), p. xvi.

quite considerable standard of living find that this has only brought new sets of problems, further compounded by puzzlement as to what the others are causing such disturbances about. Hence a pattern of demand and resistance seems to be rising within American cities that threatens instability of a potentially serious and damaging variety. The fact is that for the first time since the late nineteenth century American cities are experiencing mass violence, brought on as an expression of discontent and fury by the poorest of the working classes. The fact that these masses are Negro seems somehow to have lessened the impact of the rioting: the events seem somehow more "natural," more an understandable response to a racially prejudiced society than evidence of any deep social imbalance. One wonders, for example, what might be the response within the business community if, instead of reporting Negro disturbances, the press were to inform the nation that the "workers" or the "proletariat" of Los Angeles had set fire to their quarter and had been suppressed only by the summoning of military force. Yet it is necessary to insist that these events take place in the context of steadily rising living standards and steadily improving public services.

It has always been the case that cities have been places of great extremes of wealth and poverty: some societies have rejoiced in the display and magnificence, others have been repelled by the degradation and inequality. American society has been ambivalent. Committed to the amassing of personal wealth (and endlessly adept at doing so), it has also had a persisting commitment to the ideal of social equality and a concern at the appearance of gross disparities between social classes—a concern commonly taken to the point of not wishing even to admit the fact of social stratification. Until very recently any discussion of the subject would be forced to depend heavily on impressions and measures made with fairly rudimentary instruments of uncertain coverage. However, income statistics have by now achieved a quality such that changes over time can be judged with increasing confidence. Moreover, since the enactment of the Economic Opportunity Act of 1964 a growing number of special surveys and studies have provided more new information on the subject than has ever before been available. We do not and likely never shall have as much or as good information as could be put to use, but the time has arrived when it is possible to state a number of general findings.

1. *Poverty in the United States is now largely an urban phenomenon.* This is a sharp break from the past, when the greatest proportion of poverty would invariably have been found in the countryside. As of 1965, however, only 6 percent of all poor households were located on farms. There is still a large amount of small-town poverty in the nation. Of some 32.5 million poor persons, 12.5 were living outside the 227 Standard Metropolitan Statistical Areas. But 17.2 million live within the SMSA's (where 66 percent of the population resides), including 10.6 million in the central cities of the metropolitan areas.

It must be kept in mind that the poverty population is neither static nor fixed. In a given year a fairly considerable number of persons appears to move in and out of poverty, part of a larger "at risk" population whose incomes rise and fall with changing employment conditions, personal circumstances such as health, family status, and so forth. To the extent that it is likely that this group would be proportionately larger in the more volatile urban setting, the relative preponderance of urban poverty becomes even greater.

2. *Urban poverty is concentrated among Negroes and other ethnic minorities.* Almost 13 million nonwhites live in central cities. About one third of this group lives below the poverty levels specified by the Social Security Administration, which are currently an income of $3,200 a year for a family of four, with adjustments for size up to a cutoff point of seven persons. This incidence of poverty is three times that of the white population living in central cities, and would be even higher if the Oriental population were excluded from the nonwhite totals. Negroes do not make up a majority of poor persons living in central cities. There are roughly 4.6 million nonwhites as against 5.9 million whites. But if the poor Puerto Ricans and Mexican Americans, classified by the Census as white, were added to the Negroes, it is almost certain that the combined total would make up a majority of the central city poor. (A further point is that among the aged poor whites greatly outnumber Negroes. For example, of the

1,061,000 elderly individuals living in central cities, that is to say persons not living in families, 909,000 are white and only 152,000 are Negro. Thus it may be said that Negroes and other minorities make up a large proportion of those growing up poor, or living in poverty during their most productive years.)

3. *Urban poverty is closely associated with large families and broken families.* Large families and to some degree broken families are commonly found among poor people. At the present time Negro Americans are the most conspicuous such group, but by no means the only group and in any event are merely the most recent in a long sequence of peasant migrants who have kept the slums of American cities in teeming disarray. (In addition to which, of course, there is a large and prospering Negro middle class, now frequently to be encountered in suburban areas.) The average size of the poor nonwhite family is 5.1 persons, nationwide, and 4.8 in central cities. The statistical probability that a large Negro family will also be poor is very high indeed. Thus in 1964 only *one quarter* of all nonwhite families with one child in the home lived in poverty, but *three quarters* of all such families with five or more children were poor. White families living in poverty are significantly smaller than nonwhite families in that circumstance: 3.7 persons for each poor urban white family as compared to 4.8 for each poor urban nonwhite family. This suggests that it is children as well as low income that is a cause of a certain proportion of Negro poverty. In central cities there are 2,395,000 nonwhite children under 16 years of age growing up in poverty. This contrasts with only 1,905,000 white children in that circumstance. Whereas children under 16 make up less than a third of the poor white population in central cities, they account for slightly more than half the nonwhite poor.

The contrast is most pronounced for children in female-headed families. In 1965 there were 1,209,000 nonwhite children under 16 living in central-city families headed by a woman under 65, as against 723,000 white children in that circumstance (many of whom, of course, would be drawn from other ethnic minorities). In the nation as a whole, almost two thirds of all nonwhite female-headed families live below the poverty line, as against less than one third of white female-headed units.

These conditions are unmistakably associated with population growth. During the six-year period between 1960 and 1966, the number of children under age 14 in metropolitan areas increased by 3.3 million. *Nonwhite children accounted for one third of the gain.* The average annual rate of increase of nonwhite children (2.4 percent) was three times the rate for white children. Ninety-five percent of the nonwhite increase was in the central cities, where the proportion of all children who are nonwhite rose from 23 percent in 1960 to 29 percent in 1966.[2]

As the heartbreaking decade of the 1960's came to an end, Census data began to reveal more clearly the *demographic* basis of much of the internal stress of the black urban population, as well as the degree to which that portion of the population living in poverty had become separated from the rest of the metropolis. Clearly a large proportion of the black city dwellers of the nation had been, and for a decade at least would be, living in a state of demographic siege, cut off by social and geographic barriers from their neighbors.

During this period the rate of increase of the Negro population was about three fourths greater than that of the white population. And in the same period the concentration of blacks in central cities became steadily more pronounced. Between 1960 and 1968 the American population increased about 11 percent, and that of metropolitan areas about 13 percent, but this latter growth was almost entirely suburban. Central cities grew by only about 1 percent, while the population of the suburban surrounds grew by 25 percent.

The over-all stability of the central city population conceals a pronounced change in the population mix. From 1960 to 1968 the number of whites declined 2.1 million and that of blacks increased 2.4 million. Negroes had by then become significantly more urbanized than whites, with 54 percent of

[2] U.S. Bureau of the Census, *Current Population Reports,* series P-20, no. 163, *Population of the United States by Metropolitan and Nonmetropolitan Residence: April 1966 and 1960,* March 27, 1967, p. 2.

the black population living in central cities, a proportion twice that of whites. It was over-all a younger population. In 1968 the median age of Negroes was 21.3 years, contrasted with 28.6 years for whites, and where it was poor and urban it tended to have a high incidence of disorganization. This exchange may be seen in Table 1. In the period 1960–1968 central cities lost three quarters of a million white male-headed families. They gained 172,000 black male-headed families. But the number of black female-headed families increased by 294,000. These are the data behind "the crisis in welfare," indeed behind much of the "urban crisis" generally.

Table 1. Change in number of families by sex of head, 1960–1968
(Numbers in thousands)

	White		Negro	
	Number	Percent	Number	Percent
Central cities:				
Male head	−757	−7	172	11
Female head	155	12	294	60

U.S. Bureau of the Census, *Current Population Reports,* Series P-23, No. 27, February 7, 1969, "Trends in Social and Economic Conditions in Metropolitan Areas."

The most that can be said about this process is that it can be traced but not explained. The 1960's were a period of great economic gains for black workers. Income data for 1967 revealed almost spectacular advances for Negroes during the decade.

Negro Money Income as a Percent of White

	Males, Ages 25–34	
1949	1959	1967
57.3	58.9	84.4

In particular, families headed by a black male, ages 25–34, earned 79 percent of the median income of their white counterparts in that year. However, the median income for all families in the young age group was considerably lower for blacks than for whites. Female-headed families brought the proportion down.* Between 1959 and 1967 the median income of male-headed Negro families in central cities rose 37 percent —twice the proportion for white families. In the latter year median earnings for such black families was $6,778. This was 78 percent of white earnings, and well above the median income of city dwellers anywhere else on earth. Simultaneously, the number of central city Negro families with earnings under $4,000 dropped from almost half (45 percent) in 1959 to a third (33 percent) in 1967.

Who was left behind in this surge of affluence? Fatherless children and abandoned or widowed women. In 1967 a full 95 percent of Negro children in families with incomes over $15,000 were living with both parents. For families with incomes under $4,000 the proportion was 24 percent.

In the long perspective of economic development the case can readily be argued that the United States is working its way out of poverty, and doing so at a steady and probably increasing rate. The actual number of persons living in poverty has been declining at about one million persons per year of late, and the proportion of persons in poverty has dropped even more rapidly as the size of the total population grows. It would apppear that the poverty population is made up of persons who are not "normal" but rather who suffer special disabilities. They are very old or very young, quite uneducated or else disabled, geographically or socially isolated, and most conspicuously of all, disabled by racial and ethnic practices that grievously diminish the life chances of millions of Negro Americans and numbers of other minority groups. A highly productive and increasingly well-managed national economy has offered exits from poverty to large numbers of persons who needed no more than that: an opportunity. Those unable to take advantage of national prosperity have become an increasingly large proportion of the poor. Thus, Herman P. Miller notes that "In 1947 only 16 percent of the families

* See Jane Newitt, "Young Negroes' Income as an Indicator of Progress Toward Equalization of Employment Opportunities." Hudson Institute, Inc., Mimeographed. May 23, 1969.

with incomes under $3,000 had a female head as compared
with 23 percent in 1960."[3]

Similarly, female-headed families accounted for about 18
percent of all families in the lowest fifth of income distribution in the period 1947–1949, but by 1950 they accounted for
23 percent. But even for persons in these situations, the
chances of being poor in a city are much less than elsewhere,
and for those who move to the city, the chances of remaining
poor would seem also to diminish quite sharply. Fifty-nine
percent of nonwhite, female-headed families in cities live in
poverty, but for those on farms the proportion is 79 percent
and in the small towns outside the metropolitan areas it is at
the three-quarters mark. Cities, in a word, continue to perform their ancient service of enhancing both the material as
well as the social and intellectual life of those who come to
and live in them.

At the same time it must be insisted that there *are* signs
that the problem of poverty in American cities is becoming
more difficult, that its steady diminishment can no longer
simply be assumed. There are signs that American society
lacks both the political will and the social inventiveness to
keep up the momentum and to prevent the formation of what
Gunnar Myrdal has graphically described as an "under
class."

Any number of indications might be cited, but it would
perhaps be most useful to take three quite disparate instances,
each in its different way arguing the hardening of the lines.

The first concerns the rising number of persons supported
by public welfare. There can be no question that the amount
and, within the groups most affected, the incidence of welfare
dependency is on the rise. The advent of Social Security—
each month one American in ten receives a Social Security
check—has reduced somewhat the number of older persons
dependent on public assistance. Thus in 1955 the proportion
of persons 65 and older receiving federal-state old-age assistance was 173 per 1,000. Ten years later this had declined to
119 per 1,000. But during the same decade, however, the

[3] Herman P. Miller, *Income Distribution in the United States*
(Washington, D.C.: U.S. Government Printing Office, 1966), p. 58

proportion of youth under age 18 receiving Aid to Families of Dependent Children (AFDC) rose from 30 to 49 per thousand, while the actual number of such children rose, in round numbers, from one and a half million to three and a half million.[4] The lifetime incidence rate also appears to be increasing. Estimates by Robert H. Mugge suggest that about one white youth in ten and six nonwhite youths in ten will be supported by AFDC payments at one point or another before reaching 18.[5] It does not at all follow that the incidence of persons eligible to receive welfare assistance is in fact growing: no one knows what a "true" eligibility rate would look like. But the number and amount of payments continue to rise. This situation has created genuine problems for large cities such as New York. Thus by June of 1964 the number of persons receiving public assistance in New York City reached 448,097, almost exactly the same point (449,105) reached in November 1941, the month before Pearl Harbor. But despite the continued and unexampled economic growth of the 1960's, which toward the end of the decade produced a national economy growing at better than a billion dollars a week, the number of families dependent on welfare grew in New York (and in the nation generally) at wholly inexplicable rates. By the end of 1966 there were 600,000 persons on the welfare rolls in New York City. A study by the research division of the Teamsters' Joint Council Number 16 of New York showed that where in 1956 the number of persons in the City receiving welfare assistance amounted to 8.9 percent of the nongovernment work force, by 1966 the proportion had risen to 17.9 percent. But still the increase in numbers continued. By the end of 1968 the million mark

[4] The Advisory Council on Public Welfare in its report of June 1966 estimated, however, that only 6.8 percent of the increase in the number of AFDC recipients from January 1961 to December 1965 could be classified as an "increase resulting from increase in rate of need for assistance among families in general population with female head and own children under 18 years of age." (p. 9.)

[5] Robert H. Mugge, "Demographic Analysis and Public Assistance," paper presented to the Population Association of America, New York, April 30, 1966 (mimeographed).

had been passed. At that point the rate of increase began to decline somewhat, but in the meantime the social structure of the city had sharply changed. The increase in the AFDC population in New York and in the nation could be partly attributed to rising rates of acceptance of applicants, to increased levels of payments which made more persons eligible to rising illegitimacy ratios, and to some changes in federal law. But *au fond* the matter remained a mystery: something had happened that no one understood.

A second indication of the seeming hardening of poverty lines within American cities can be had from the various special censuses that have been conducted in the aftermath of the rioting that swept many Negro slums during the summers of 1965 and 1966. These studies suggest most emphatically that despite steadily rising levels of income and general prosperity for the nation as a whole, the conditions of life in many slum areas of the great cities were becoming worse. Whatever might be the case for the population as a whole, the gap separating the lives lived in these areas from the rest of the city was widening.

Possibly the most dramatic evidence of the worsening trend emerges from the special census taken in South and East Los Angeles in November 1965, following the Watts riot of the previous summer. A mid-term census of this kind is rather unusual; the nation must normally wait from one decade to the next for such information. The survey showed that at a time of burgeoning national prosperity, when by many general economic indicators Negro families were making great progress, *things were getting worse in South Los Angeles*, an area of a quarter million Negroes. From 1959 to 1965 the typical nonwhite family's income rose 24 percent. But in South Los Angeles median family income *dropped* by 8 percent, from $5,122 in 1959 to $4,736 in 1965. In Watts median family income dropped from $3,879 to $3,803.

It will be recalled that 1960 was a recession year, but shortly thereafter the nation began the longest peacetime economic expansion in history in the course of which unemployment more or less steadily declined. By 1965 the rate for adult men had dropped to its lowest point since the Korean War years of 1953, and for Negroes the over-all rate dropped to the level of the prosperous 1957. But for male Negro workers in South Los Angeles the unemployment rate dropped only from 12.4 percent to 10.9 percent. In Watts it dropped only from 16.0 percent to 14.2 percent. Significantly, the labor force participation rate for Negro males dropped from 78.7 percent to 69.6 percent for the area as a whole, and in Watts from 70.0 percent to 58.5 percent. This contrasts with an over-all national labor force participation rate for males of 77.1 percent in November 1965. Inasmuch as persons not in the labor force are not classed as unemployed, it is at least possible that "true" male unemployment in the area went up during this period. During the five years the number of Negro males in the area declined slightly (by 998 persons), but the number of Negro males in the labor force dropped by 7,208. The number of Negro males holding jobs as craftsmen, foremen, and kindred workers increased during the period, but the number working as operatives and laborers decreased. Female unemployment rates were higher than male in both years, and the female labor force participation rate declined as well.

Inevitably, given these trends in employment and income, the proportion of Negroes living in poverty in South Los Angeles increased from 41 percent to 43 percent. Seemingly just as inevitably, this was accompanied by family break-up and a trend toward female-based households. The proportion of the poverty population (to use a less than fortunate term that has emerged from the Economic Opportunity Act of 1964) living in families with a female head rose from 45.5 percent in 1960 to 56.2 percent in 1965. The proportion of Negroes under 18 living with both parents dropped from 64.1 percent to 58.6 percent for the area as a whole, and from 55.5 percent to 44.4 percent in Watts. The average number of children in female-based households living below the poverty line increased from 2.54 to 2.93. (In 1966 the average number of children per household for the United States was 1.45.)

During this period the median age of nonwhite males in the area dropped from 24.8 years to 20.3—at which point it was a full four years below the median age of 24.5 for nonwhite females. In Watts the median age for nonwhite males in

1965 was a fantastic 13.5, both rates reflecting the disappearance of Negro males and the high birth rate of the Negro poor. During this period the total population of Watts declined somewhat, but again it was the males who vanished most. In 1960 there were 5,058 nonwhite males aged 20 to 64 in Watts, and 6,748 nonwhite females, a surplus of 1,690. By 1965 there were only 3,930 males for 5,810 females, a surplus of 1,880. The proportion of adult nonwhite males, twenty years and older, to infant and teenage population correspondingly declined.

A similar range of findings emerges from a recent Census study of poverty neighborhoods in Cleveland, including Hough, where a riot occurred. In 1960, 91 percent of Cleveland's Negro population, some 228,322 persons, lived in these areas. In the next five years the number of Negroes in Cleveland grew somewhat, but the proportion living outside the poverty neighborhoods grew to 15 percent, or 41,451 persons. During this period there was little change in the incidence of poverty among Negro families, which remained at about one quarter, but considerable change in the *concentration* of such families. For families living outside the poverty area the incidence of poverty dropped from 17.9 percent to 9.8 percent. Median family income rose $1,107 to a total of $7,285 in 1964. The number of female-headed families dropped from 13.9 percent in 1959 to 9.1 percent in 1964. The unemployment rate for males dropped to 8 percent, and the labor force participation to an impressive 82.2 percent, seven percentage points above the national average for the nonwhite males, and five points above the average for all males in the labor force. In a word, this 15 percent of the Negro population of Cleveland was made up overwhelmingly of hard-working, well-paid citizens on the way up in the world.

This made the contrast with the poverty areas all the greater. In these neighborhoods the incidence of poverty among Negro families *rose,* reaching 28.5 percent. Median family income (1959–1964) increased only $132, to a level of $5,085, while the proportion of female-headed households rose from 20 percent to 25 percent, and the male labor force participation rate dropped to 73.1 percent.

Even these over-all figures conceal the deterioration in some of the worst neighborhoods. In the Hough section, for example, median family income *declined* $776 to $3,966 in 1964, and in nearby West Central it dropped to $2,984. This decline in income was closely associated, as it almost invariably will be, with a rise in the proportion of female-headed families. From 1959 to 1964 the ratio in Hough rose from 22.5 percent to 32.6 percent, and in West Central from 2.6 percent to 35.1 percent. In Hough, the number of children living in poverty increased by one third.

These Census surveys indicated astonishingly high unemployment rates in such neighborhoods. In the West Central area, for example, the male unemployment rate rose to 20.4 percent in 1965, and the labor force participation rate dropped to 58.7 percent. These data have been dramatically confirmed by a survey conducted in November 1966 by the U.S. Department of Labor in a number of poverty neighborhoods throughout the nation. The unemployment rate was found to be 30 percent, or three times the national average. The Department of Labor found that "one out of every three residents in the slum has a serious employment problem," and, while pointing out that the number of persons concerned was small enough that the problem is still manageable, it concluded that "no conceivable increase in the gross national product would stir these backwaters."

This is the heart of the issue: Have we run into structural defects in the distribution of income and opportunity in the nation such that continued and growing prosperity will not necessarily bring about *widening* prosperity? It would be foolish to assume that this is the case, as it has never been the case in the past, at least for any length of time, but there are surely many indications that at the present time the system is working somewhat imperfectly, and also that it may be changing, and beginning to work on a somewhat different level. In particular there is evidence that the power of employment conditions to "control" matters such as welfare dependency and family integrity may be weakening. During the late 1940's and the 1950's, the correlation between the nonwhite male unemployment rate and the number of new

AFDC cases opened each month, or the number of nonwhit
married women separated from their husbands, was quit
close. The numbers rose and fell in what was sometimes al
most perfect accord. Thus, between 1948 and 1962 the correla
tion between the unemployment rate and the AFDC case rat
was a remarkable +.91. For the years 1953 to 1964 th
correlation between the unemployment rate for nonwhit
males aged 20 and over and the separation rate for nonwhit
married women at the interval of four months was a no les
remarkable +.73. However, with the onset of the 1960's thes
relations began to weaken, and by the mid-1960's disappeare
altogether.

The unemployment rates go down, but the rates of welfar
dependency and family instability do not. It must be en
phasized that here as elsewhere it is necessary to cite instance
drawn from nonwhite data only because the high concentra
tion of poverty among nonwhites makes it possible to get fror
over-all nonwhite statistics some indication as to what i
happening to groups living in poverty. There is as yet n
reason to suppose that the same phenomenon would not b
found in white slums if separate statistics were collected i
them, as hopefully they will be in the future.

A tradition going back at least as far as De Tocqueville
1839 report to the French Chamber of Deputies on the abol
tion of slavery in the French West Indies argues that famil
instability derives from forced servitude. W. E. B. DuBoi
and later E. Franklin Frazier, presented this case with clarit
and force. More recently, however, the researches of Herbe
G. Gutman have cast great doubt on the validity of this thesi
Employment patterns that developed in the late nineteent
century would appear, at least with respect to the Negr
American, to have had far more important consequence
and to be the true source of familial patterns so much to t
encountered in the slums of the present time. And yet by th
token, such patterns ought to have begun to respond to th
much improved employment opportunities open to blac
workers in the 1960's. And yet in the aggregate things g
worse, not better. It is likely that a decade or two hence even
will seem explicable enough—especially if what is involved i

essence is time lag—but for the moment there is no satisfactory explanation.[6]

A third and final indication that poverty lines may be hardening in the United States is the simple fact that the teeming, disorganized life of impoverished slums has all but disappeared among the North Atlantic democracies—save only the United States. It requires some intrepidness to *declare* this to be a fact, as no systematic inquiry has been made that would provide completely dependable comparisons, but it can be said with fair assurance that mass poverty and squalor, of the kind that may be encountered in almost any large American city, simply cannot be found in comparable cities in Europe, or Canada, or Japan. A quarter century of full and over-full employment, income supplements, health services, and social insurance has simply put an end to it. It may be that a matter of priorities is to be found here: vast numbers of French families do without a telephone, but none does without work. Higher education is sharply restricted in Britain and Germany, but teenage unemployment is practically unknown. Income taxes are heavily progressive everywhere, but there is not one such nation that does not automatically provide a monthly payment to every family with minor children to help with the costs of rearing them.[7]

[6] See Alexis de Tocqueville, *Report made to The Chamber of Deputies on The Abolition of Slavery in the French Colonies,* July 23, 1839 (Boston: James Munroe & Co., 1840); W. E. Burghardt DuDois, editor, *The Negro American Family* (Atlanta, Georgia: Atlanta University Press, 1908) [This edition is now out of print. It was reprinted by Negro Universities' Press in 1969 (New York), and a new edition, with a foreword by Daniel P. Moynihan, is to be published by The M.I.T. Press in 1970.]; E. Franklin Frazier, *The Negro Family in the United States* (Chicago, University of Chicago Press, 1939); Herbert G. Gutman and Laurence A. Glasco, "The Buffalo, New York Negro, 1855–1875: A Study of the Family Structure of Free Negroes and Some of Its Implications," prepared for delivery at the Wisconsin Conference on the History of American Political and Social Behavior, May 16–17, 1968.

[7] In some countries family allowances are not provided for an only child.

Whatever the reason, the fact does emerge with considerable clarity and force: the bleak industrial slums of Marxist lore have all but disappeared from the industrial democracies of Northern and Western Europe, but they continue to persist and even to worsen in the United States. Even were the United States among the weaker of these nations in economic terms, this matter would still have to be explained. But given the overwhelming American economic advantage, the persistence of mass poverty suggests that something more fundamental is amiss.

What? This is a far more troubled question than might at first be supposed, and accordingly as one chooses one answer or set of answers among the various options, program choices of quite different kinds will emerge. Walter B. Miller has noted that explanations of poverty tend to assign causative primacy to conditions the observer wishes to see changed, ranging from the innate sinfulness of the poor to the innate sinfulness of "the System." The most powerful hypothesis to emerge in the present age is Oscar Lewis' conception of "the culture of poverty," which he describes as "both an adaptation and a reaction of the poor to their marginal position in a class-stratified, highly individuated, capitalistic society."[8] The poverty Lewis describes is something considerably more tenacious than simply an absence of money. Indeed, poverty as such is almost an incidental aspect of the phenomenon, which is characterized principally by "the lack of effective participation and integration of the poor in the major institutions of the larger society"[9] and accompanied by the familiar patterns of unemployment, poor housing, disorganized family life, and strong feelings of helplessness and dependence. Lewis finds these traits in many parts of the Western world, but not at all, for example, among the lower castes in India, where despite the most relentless material poverty the integration of the individual into the caste system seems to produce a stable, well-organized personality. Lewis estimates the number of persons living in a culture of poverty in the United States at

[8] Oscar Lewis, *La Vida* (New York: Random House, 1966) p. xliv.
[9] *Ibid.*, p. xlv.

six to ten million people at most, but for them "the elimination of physical poverty *per se* may not be enough to eliminate the culture of poverty which is a whole way of life."[10]

It in no way detracts from the brilliance of Lewis' hypothesis to point out that it is as yet no more than that: the detailed study of life in American slums that his analysis requires has yet to be done. For the moment we must grope with a fairly limited understanding that nonetheless provides some guide to action. We know for the most part who the poor are; we know something about the "caste" lines by which they are kept apart from much of society; we know something of the effects of technology on the jobs the poor characteristically hold; and we are beginning to sense something of the surprisingly negative impact that portions of our welfare practices may be having.

In far the greatest number, the urban poor of the present time are made up of the urbanized agricultural proletariat. That is the overwhelming fact of life about Negro and Puerto Rican city dwellers of the present time: in bulk, they are the newcomers of this generation, and they bring with them all of the traditional burdens of refugees from a bankrupt, oppressive, and primitive agricultural society. There seems absolutely no question but that time and economic opportunity are the greatest elements in the transformation of such groups from displaced peasants into prospering city dwellers, a transformation that has already occurred many times in American history.

A second quality possessed by many of today's poor is that they are Negro. In contrast to the great success with which American cities have absorbed waves of Irish, Polish, and Italian peasants, to name but a few of the past migrations, American society has never yet been able to provide Negroes an equal place in social and economic arrangements, be they urban or rural. Negroes are seriously discriminated against on the basis of race, so that poor Negroes are almost locked in behind the double barriers of caste and class. The question of race is a new challenge; unless this issue is resolved, the question of poverty will inevitably remain.

10 *Ibid.*, p. lii.

A third quality of the present-day poor is that they ar
seeking employment in a job market that is becoming mor
and more difficult for them. It is not necessary to grov
apocalyptic about the disappearance of low-skilled jobs i
the American economy in order to admit that such jobs ar
relatively harder to find than they have been in the past an
moreover seem increasingly to be located in areas beyond th
suburban fringe, far from the homes of the central city poor
This question of providing guaranteed full employment i
surely the one that should be easiest for the United States t
solve, but unaccountably it has not been solved.

The fourth, and in ways the most frustrating, aspect of con
temporary poverty has to do with the nature of the America
social welfare system. The essence of this system is to assum
that no one needs help until he is in trouble, after which i
repeatedly emerges that no one in trouble can be helped. Thi
exaggerates the case, to be sure, but the case can nonetheles
be made. The most conspicuous quality of the poor is thei
relative lack of money, a quality which shows little change i
recent years. Wealth and income in the United States ar
most unevenly distributed and are showing no tendency t
become more equal. As Herman P. Miller writes, "For ex
ample, during 1947–1960, there was no change at all i
the distribution of income groups among urban families; th
top 5 percent and the top 20 percent received about the sam
share of the aggregate income in every year during th
decade."[11] At the other extreme, as Christopher Jencks an
David Riesman note, "The bottom 20 percent of all familie
have had between 4 and 5 percent of all income for as long a
we have had income statistics."[12] Recent federal fiscal policie
have if anything confirmed and even possibly accentuated thi
condition. The plain fact is that the United States needs
measure of income redistribution. Unfortunately, the Ameri
can social welfare system is wedded to the provision of *service*
to the poor rather than *income* and, as Lee Rainwater ha

[11] Miller, *Income Distribution*, pp. 20–22.
[12] Christopher Jencks and David Riesman, "The American Ne
gro College," *Harvard Educational Review*, vol. 37, no. 1, 1967
p. 11.

forcefully pointed out, the frequent result is neither the one nor the other.

Fortunately, the subject of income supports for the poor is being raised with increasing credibility. Proposals for some form of guaranteed minimum income are being put forward with increasing cogency and sophistication.[13] There is also a certain measure of interest in family allowances. The United States is one of the few industrial nations in the world that does not have a system of family allowances, which are small (or in countries such as France, not so small) monthly payments tendered to families with minor children. The particular attraction of family allowances is that they involve no means tests, go to all families so that there is no distinction made between the poor who receive the benefits and the remainder of society that pays for them, and not least, that they can be administered with a minimum of bureaucracy. Although family allowances have been shown in other nations to have no perceivable effect on birth rates, it is reasonable to assume that any such program in the United States should be accompanied by a genuinely adequate federal program to provide birth control services for all families desiring them.

In many important respects the United States would seem to be approaching a crossroads. The issue of poverty has been raised, and is now an open one. The fact confronts us that other nations with whom we would wish to be compared have themselves largely eliminated domestic poverty, at least in their cities. So also does the fact that the American nation is fully capable of eliminating the purely economic aspects of poverty by simple measures of full employment and income supplements, again of a kind familiar to most of the industrial democracies of the world. If in spite of these facts the conditions of impoverishment that are to be found in one American city after another should continue unchanged, the United States will be required to acknowledge that it is not what it has thought itself to be.

[13] See James Tobin, "On Improving the Economic Status of the Negro," *Daedalus* (Fall 1965).

URBAN PROBLEMS IN PERSPECTIVE

James Q. Wilson

It is only a slight exaggeration to say that the major urba
problem is the various and uncertain meanings attached t
the phrase, "urban problems." We are told by many seriou
and responsible people that urban problems are our "numbe
one" domestic issue; "the" urban problem has been mad
the subject of a special presidential message to the Congres
and of hearings conducted by a major Senate subcommittee
Mayors are almost unanimous in urging that a higher priorit
be given to the problems of the cities, and the theme is take
up at the national meetings of business, labor, civil rights, an
academic organizations. One would suppose that with suc
widespread and intense agreement, vigorous action would lon
since have been taken and the urban problem would cease t
be a problem.

In fact, a great deal of action has been taken; strangel
enough, very few people seem wholly pleased with the resul
and almost nobody believes the urban problem has bee
solved. On the contrary, most people seem to think it is gettin
worse.

The difficulty, of course, is that we have fallen into th

habit of using the phrase, "urban problems," to refer to a variety of often unrelated concerns, some of which are not, strictly speaking, urban at all and others of which are not even problems in any meaningful sense. The phrase conveys a false and misleading sense of specificity and concreteness and implies (to the politicians) an earnest but spurious consensus. We *think* we know what we are talking about—after all, everyone has a conventional mental picture of a city (usually, a drab, smoky downtown area with congested traffic, street-corner muggings, and stores having liquidation sales), everybody can think of a problem that is to be found in such a place, and we all would like things to be better than they are. The trouble with this mental picture is that it implies, wrongly, that every element in the picture is related to every other element—that there is an important connection between the smoke, the congestion, the mugging, the liquidation sale, the drab buildings—and that if we could discover and work on this connection, these unpleasant things would vanish. The obvious connection is that this is a picture of the downtown area of a city; therefore, there must be something about "city life" that creates problems.

We are also told that these problems will soon engulf us all, because we are becoming a "nation of cities." We are, but only in the trivial sense that the U.S. Census Bureau classifies every place with 2,500 population or more as "urban." While it is true that 70 percent of all Americans live in urban places, it is an empty truth (even though it is uttered by important people) when one realizes that for most of these people their "urban place" has less than 50,000 people living in it. Over 58 percent of our population lives in small-town America; less than 10 percent lives in the cities with over a million people that we often have in mind when we think of big-city America. And it is the small places, *not* the giant ones, that are growing. The percentage of people living in towns of less than 50,000 has increased by 50 percent since 1920; the percentage living in cities of over a million (or even of over 500,000) has scarcely increased at all.

There are, of course, problems in this country, but for the most part the adjective "urban" hinders rather than helps our understanding of them. It would be more accurate (though

not perfectly accurate) to make a list of all the ills to which
we object—poverty, crime, ugliness, pollution, discrimination,
congestion—and refer to them as "industrial problems" or
"social problems" or "human problems." More accurate, but
somehow less exciting. It is hard to imagine magazines
running special issues or Presidents delivering special
messages about "social problems." And if they did, we
would naturally ask, *"What* social problem do you mean?"
"Why do you lump them all together?" "What various
remedies do you propose for them?" We might even disagree
that everything on the list was a problem (one man's ugliness
is another man's home) or that they were all equally urgent
(if we end poverty, perhaps ugliness and even discrimination
will take care of themselves).

Naturally, many people who use the phrase "urban problems" know perfectly well that the problems they have in mind
are not to be found exclusively in big cities (or even in cities at
all) or that the problems are in every case caused, or made
worse, by the conditions of urban life. Why, then, do they
persist in using the phrase? I think there are several reasons.

One is that a political advantage can be gained from the intellectual confusion. A concern about "urban problems" can
be shared by Negroes anxious about civil rights, intellectuals
interested in poverty (or whatever), businessmen worried
about downtown retail trade, mayors threatened by high local
taxes, shoppers looking for a parking place, housewives fearful of purse-snatchers, and architects seeking beauty. And this
is not necessarily a bad thing. For almost any government
action to be taken, a political coalition must be formed out
of somewhat divergent interests. To the extent good things
have been accomplished by this coalition, it is not very important that it can be charged with intellectual inconsistency.

A second reason is that alluding to problems as "urban"
facilitates drawing attention to their concrete manifestations.
For most of us, it is easier to become concerned about ugly,
dilapidated houses than about poverty, which is their usual
cause. Blight is real, and affronts our senses; poverty is an
abstraction and engages (if anything) only our soul. Traffic
congestion is a nuisance; "something ought to be done about
it." The prosperity, freedom, and urban attractions that pro-

duce congestion are less obvious and, when one is stalled on the East Side Drive or the Santa Ana Freeway, hard to value properly. This reason for speaking of "urban" problems has real dangers, for it tends to the substitution of effect for cause and thus the misdirection of remedial action. If the house is ugly and dilapidated, tear it down; if skid row is unpleasant to stroll through, clear it out; if traffic congestion is unpleasant, ban the car. But slums and bums and cars are not the causes or problems, they are the symptoms, and if we tear them down or clear them out or ban them from one place, they will inevitably reappear somewhere else.

A third reason is that there are to be found within the very center of our biggest cities groups that have not wanted, or have not felt free, to move elsewhere. Lawyers, stock-brokers, garment manufacturers, and newspaper publishers have, with few exceptions, decided that the requirements of doing business, or the costs of an alternative location, make remaining in the city sound business, unpleasant though it may be for some of them. Intellectuals who like central city cultural and educational attractions regard the suburbs as "the sticks"—at least until they begin to have children. Negroes find it hard to move out because of both poverty and discrimination, but they also find it in many cases undesirable to move out—Harlem, as Ralph Ellison has pointed out, has excitement as well as problems, sufficient to make even accessible suburban locations rather dull by comparison. These groups—those who cannot leave, or do not wish to leave—speak the loudest about urban problems, by which they mean they want society to fix up the place where they have chosen, or are forced, to live. To the extent we force people to live in the big central cities against their will, or to the extent we leave behind in these cities important social institutions which we have a collective obligation to conserve, then perhaps we should fix up the place. The difficulty is that those who stay behind have very different ideas about how, and at whose expense, the place should be fixed up. Businessmen would like to get rid of slums (by which they must necessarily mean getting rid of Negroes); Negroes would like more and better space in which to live (which means less space for businesses and universities);

universities would like more space from the Negro and more money from the businessman.

There is a fourth sense in which the phrase "urban problems" is used; it has political and fiscal roots. The political center of gravity is now urban, however you use the term. The problems of big-city dwellers are going to get more attention than the problems of people who live elsewhere even if the small-city and rural people have more problems. In fact, a higher proportion of rural families than big-city families lives below the poverty line; a larger proportion of rural than urban housing is substandard. Once, the "Farm Bloc" in Congress made certain we all knew these things and did something about them; today, the Farm Bloc scarcely exists— the Urban Bloc has taken its place. And with some justification. The key element in the Urban Bloc—the big-city mayors —find themselves unable to raise the money to meet the expectations of the voters or the requirements imposed on them by state or federal standards. To get the money they turn to what appears to be the only available source—the federal treasury.

Answering the question "What is an urban problem?" is thus a good deal like answering the question "What is a Republican?" If one takes the label too seriously, one begins to suspect he is the victim of a gigantic hoax because the label is applied to such very different things—human poverty and architectural monuments in the case of urban problems, Jacob Javits and Barry Goldwater in the case of the Republicans. But perhaps both labels are valuable precisely because they are so misleading—getting something done about our many difficulties may be a bit easier if poverty fighters and monument builders believe that in their concern for "urban problems" they have something in common, just as running a successful two-party system may be easier if Javits and Goldwater think that it is barely possible to make common cause against the Democrats.

In deciding what subjects should be treated in this book, the editor began with the conviction that its purpose was to clarify a set of issues, not to sound a call to arms. To clarify, one must make distinctions; to clarify the term "urban problems," one must make distinctions among the various senses in which that word might be used. The authors of the various papers were told to assume that they were writing primarily about America's large central cities, not about cities generally. Even though over half of all urban renewal programs are in cities with less than 25,000 population, we do not believe that the scope of that program necessarily constitutes a proper definition of our subject matter; to assume otherwise is to believe that anything that goes wrong within the boundaries of a municipality is an urban problem.

An analytic approach does not encourage much synthesis, especially when the analysis is carried out by men from very different professional disciplines. There was another way in which this book could have been organized. There might have been a chapter on the development and structure of cities, another on the common patterns of action and social organization found in cities, a third on the irritations and malfunctions a city dweller (or city observer) might experience, two or three on alternative general plans for rearranging or improving the city, and finally a chapter on the "city of the future," with a special section on new towns. Such books have been written, and they are often stimulating and occasionally (but only occasionally) convincing. A book of that sort typically produces a sense of the whole rather than of the parts; emphasizes form and function, rather than substance or content; takes the point of view of the observer (and often the omnniscient observer) rather than that of the participant or citizen; and searches out and stresses interdependencies, co-ordination, mutuality, and pattern.

We have tried instead to examine the common concerns of the people who choose to live in large central cities—migrating to the city, forming and maintaining (or failing to maintain) a family, educating the young, finding a job and a home, coping with crime, moving about on the highways and buses, breathing the air and drinking the water, and last—but certainly not least—looking at the buildings and other artifacts of an urban culture. Though we have not succeeded in seeing these things as the average person does (frankly, we really don't know how most people experience these things), we have tried to concern ourselves with his concerns. Of necessity, the result is a set of partial and often conflicting accounts of big-city life. Just as the citizen must choose how he will spend his time and money, so an analytic account of urban life draws attention to conflicts and to the necessity of giving up something to get something else. Roger Revelle writes that one way to ease the problem of air pollution would be to tear down more buildings in order to speed up the flow of auto traffic through the city on express highways, thereby reducing the high rate of pollutants cars pump into the atmosphere when idling or driving at low speeds. John Burchard, concerned with urban beauty, would probably be aghast at the idea (for that matter, so in all likelihood would Revelle).

Though such a point of view is necessarily partial, it has the advantage not only of suggesting what choices must be made but of permitting a very careful study of at least some of the vital processes that shape cities. Cities, whatever else they may become, begin typically because people come together to exchange goods and services to their mutual benefit. Thus, three of the eleven papers in this volume are by economists.

The city is shaped by the location of jobs and industries. John Kain restates the obvious fact that, especially since World War II, there has been an enormous dispersal of economic activity—from the central city to suburban areas, and within the central city from the downtown business district to outlying sections of the city. But he goes on to show that there is no evidence at all that this dispersal is coming to an end or even slowing down; indeed, there is some evidence that the rate of dispersal is accelerating. There are some exceptions to this pattern. In some newer and smaller central cities, central locations are still attractive. And in almost all cities, central locations remain attractive for certain industries—those that rely heavily on face-to-face communication, require a large number of small suppliers near at hand, or have fixed installations (such as the cables running into a central telephone exchange) that would be very costly to move. But for most industries, outlying areas offer irresistible attractions—open tracts of land that permit modern, efficient plant layout, easy access to highways and airports, relatively low property taxes, and a freedom from central city violence (crime, riots, and demonstrations).

These are facts and, given the failure of most efforts to

alter them, perhaps immutable facts, at least in the foreseeable future. But do these facts add up to an "urban problem"? In one sense, the answer is surely "no." Locating industry at sites that permit their most efficient operation is a gain, not a loss, to society. At inefficient central city sites, prices to the consumer would be higher, or returns to invested capital would be lower, or both; if subsidies from the city (such as tax abatements) are made available to make efficient operation possible, then someone else must bear the cost of these subsidies in the form of higher taxes.

But the gains to society are not evenly distributed; they are affected by municipal boundaries, which determine who can be taxed for what services, and by the fact that some persons are employees of these industries, and not just consumers of their products. As employees, they must get to work, and locational decisions can make this harder. We normally assume that getting to work is now much harder for most of us; all of us have seen pictures of traffic jams on the expressways, and some of us have been in those pictures. John Meyer, however, shows that the pictures may be misleading; on the average—that is to say, for most of us—the time it takes to travel to work is *less* now than it was ten or fifteen years ago in most big cities (though not much less). Part of this improvement is the result of the opening of new, limited-access highways which *are* faster than the old roads, even though they are never as fast (at least at rush hour) as we would like (or as we are often led to believe before they are built). But part of the gain has been due to the movement of jobs and industry out of central locations, thereby reducing the number of people seeking to enter the downtown area. The dispersal of industry has lightened the peak-hour load, and as more industries and more households select outlying locations, that peak load in central areas will get even smaller.

In fact, the real transportation problem—one that is not simply the product of our natural but unrealistic desire to move instantly to any place at any time—is to be found among those people who have not been able to follow the jobs to the suburbs. Negroes in central city ghettos might substantially improve their economic position if they could take advantage of even the relatively menial jobs in outlying areas—as domestic servants, service workers, maintenance men, and the like. Unable to afford a car, they cannot drive there, and public transportation is badly arranged to take them there. (Decades ago, when most industry was in central city locations, low-income people walked to work or took a street-car.) And among those who have moved to the suburbs, "cross-commutation"—moving from one outlying area to another—is almost impossible except by car, unless one wants to take a bus into downtown and then another bus out again. And as the distribution of people and jobs over the metropolitan landscape becomes "flatter"—as John Kain predicts it will—the problem of providing an economical alternative to automobile transportation for those who cannot (or do not want to) use a car will become more significant and the possibility of doing so by any form of rail transit (which depends crucially on the existence of very high population densities) will become more unrealistic.

Some people hope that by developing high-speed mass transit, the dispersal of jobs and people can be halted or reversed. The evidence, in the judgment of John Meyer, does not support this hope. There is not much reason to believe that the availability of public transit greatly affects locational decisions, either for industry or for households. Some activities will concentrate along the transit corridor (there will always be some firms or households that prefer high-density locations), but new activities of this sort will not be called into being in large numbers.

All this is small comfort to the central city mayor who sees his tax base moving out and his problem population staying behind. It is understandable that he should want to lure industry into his city and hold on to what he has; under-standable but unrealistic. If anyone doubts it is unrealistic, let him perform the following mental experiment: what can a mayor do, with his limited powers over tax abatements, land-clearance projects, and transit-subsidy schemes, that will make a new factory owner or young couple with children believe it is to their advantage to locate in the midst of the area that has the highest rates of crime and delinquency, the worst schools, the most congestion, the greatest concentration of air pollutants, the most expensive land, and the least open space? Not much, obviously. The one thing he could do—clear out all low-income and "problem" people—is politically impossible, morally dubious, and in any case would simply transfer the problem from the mayor of one city to the mayor of another.

The fiscal problems of the central cities will have to be met by new fiscal strategies, not by vain efforts to preserve the traditional tax base. Dick Netzer outlines some of these strategies. One is to recognize the need for a metropolitan-wide tax base for at least certain purposes. To the extent central cities provide services that benefit the whole area, they should be paid for by the whole area. This has long been realized by states that provide equalization aid to local schools. The difficulty is that such formulas, as Netzer points out, assume that the cost of giving an equivalent education to a child is everywhere the same; in fact, the cost per pupil of central city education may be much higher (how much higher, no one knows, for it has thus far been very hard to show much relationship between how much we spend on education and how good that education is). If a metropolitan area wishes to upgrade the skills and capacities for citizenship of its central city poor (and such an objective is little more than enlightened self-interest), it will either have to do so out of its own resources or see the federal government play an increasingly important role in local education.

Some people find it easy to accept the idea of money being transferred into the central city but hard to accept the idea that the federal government should do it. Why, they ask, can't the states do it? In theory, they can and, to a limited degree, some do. But most do not and never will, because states are in a competitive position, one with the other, and must be wary of increasing taxes or redistributing income in a way that will enable neighboring states to attract away industry. Only the federal government is not in this competitive position. Thus, even though the money required for most central cities need only be shipped about ten miles (from suburbs to city), only the federal government is likely (however much we may regret it) to do the shipping.

There are, of course, ways in which we can minimize the cost—in terms of red tape, arbitrary standards, and unresponsiveness—of federal money transfers. One is by having the federal government make block grants (the so-called Heller Plan) to states and cities, leaving it (within broad limits) up to the states and cities to decide how to use it.

That a service should be financed on a metropolitan basis does not necessarily mean that it must be managed on such a basis. Schools can be locally run even if more broadly supported, at least up to a certain point. Other services, as Netzer argues, must be managed as well as financed on an area-wide basis—highway development, pollution control, public transportation, and the like.

More can be done than just shift the tax burden; indeed, if that were all that were done, little would be accomplished. From a political point of view, what makes the system work the way it does now is that those who must pay the bill are—in most older central cities—outnumbered by those who get the benefits. Property owners pay the bill, at a rate equivalent to about a 30 percent excise tax on the rental value of their property, while the demands for more services (and more expensive services) come from everyone—renters, organized groups of teachers, firemen, and policemen, and newspapers that insist that "something be done." No municipal service is in fact free, but often the costs are so well hidden or so unequally distributed that they appear free to the people voting for their expansion. The best evidence of this is the great resistance that meets anyone who suggests—however amply supported by scholarly opinion and practical experience—that the property tax should be replaced by one that is fairer in its incidence, easier (and more honest) in its administration, and more flexible in its capacity to respond to changing economic circumstances. Any conceivable change—to an income tax, a payroll tax, a sales tax—would mean that people not now paying, or now paying very little, would pay more, and in many older central cities these people are in the majority. And even where they are not in the majority, there is a widespread fear that any change in the taxing status quo would make everybody worse off and no one better off.

If the resistance to a new tax system is great, that to a system of user charges or "municipal prices" is even greater, though the justification is equally compelling. Not everything a city government does benefits everyone—on-street parking benefits the man who parks there, not necessarily the man whose taxes pay to maintain that street—and in such cases charging the user of those services a "price," as if the service were produced by a public utility rather than a government, would serve to reimburse the city for the actual cost of maintaining the facility and discourage its use by people who only want it if it is "free." Indeed, there are many aspects of almost all municipal services that could be rationed in this way. When the police patrol a street to deter crime and catch criminals, they provide a benefit for the whole community. But when they return a car stolen from an owner who had left his keys in the ignition, they are running an expensive lost-and-found department on behalf of people who have primarily their own negligence to blame for the loss. When the police make out a detailed auto accident report, they are providing a service for the insurance companies and the motorists involved (some report may be necessary to help the police plan accident-prevention programs, but rarely in much detail). When the police apprehend shoplifters and bad-check artists who were attracted to a store by lax security precautions and who then are released by the storeowners without prosecution, the police are running a rather tiresome collection agency. In all these cases, prices could be charged for the service.

Much the same sort of economic reasoning is applied by Roger Revelle to the problem of controlling pollution. Air pollution is the classic, textbook case of an "external diseconomy"—that is, a nuisance committed by one party on another for which no compensation is received. Governments exist in part to regulate such externalities, usually by raising the price to the offending party (through a tax, license fee, or fine) for committing the nuisance. The experience of the Ruhr Valley Administration in Germany shows that by a careful fee system, the amount of pollution dumped by industry and municipalities into rivers can be sharply reduced without much bureaucratic meddling in the affairs of the firm or the city. Each party decides for himself how much—and what kind—of pollution control system is appropriate given the "price" charged for the right to dump untreated pollutants into the water. Ultimately, of course, the cost of the system is charged to the consumer of the factory's product. This is fair; to allow him to buy, at a lower price, the products of a factory that pollutes a stream without charge is to allow him to buy a product at less than the full cost of producing it. By not controlling the pollution now, we are in effect subsidizing at public expense the manufacture of everything—beer, paint, soap—produced by a factory that discharges at no cost its noxious wastes into the air or the water.

The principal polluter of the atmosphere is, of course, the automobile. Steps are already being taken that will, in effect, increase the price of the cars in the interests of reducing exhaust and crankcase pollution. The available devices are far from perfect and their proper use apparently requires a level of maintenance not easy to achieve. It is no doubt possible to build better devices and enforce better maintenance; whether we do it depends on whether we are willing to pay the price. It is possible (one hopes not likely) that we will decide we like clean air but not well enough to buy it.

These problems that are to be found in and around big cities—fiscal imbalance, traffic congestion, air pollution, the movement of jobs away from minority groups—have certain things in common. They involve the relationships among people, not the psychic state of the people themselves; they are susceptible to rather precise formulation and study; alternative ways of coping with them can be conceived and evaluated with a certain rigor; the obstacles to remedial action are primarily political (and to a certain degree economic); and few of them have approached anything like a "crisis" state. We are not yet being poisoned by our own water supply, paralyzed by our traffic congestion, or bankrupted by our inadequate local tax system. Some of these crises may come to pass, but if they do, something will rather quickly be done and, what is most important, something *can* be done.

The other issues with which this volume treats are not of this kind. These concern the subjective as well as the objective conditions in which people find themselves. We are intensely aware of these conditions but find it exceptionally difficult to state precisely what is wrong or to measure the extent to which it is wrong; devising feasible courses of action seems to exceed the abilities of even our most ingenious statesmen;

and some of these issues have already produced crises of one sort or another, at least in some cities. These issues are poverty, crime, violence, inadequate education, family disorganization, discrimination, and rioting.

Not long ago, a book of this sort about cities would have lumped many, if not all, of these problems together under the heading "housing"—or perhaps "slum housing." For many years, the only federal agency with any large-scale urban program was the housing agency, and even at that it was more a suburban than an urban program. The U.S. Office of Education kept statistics and shuffled papers; the Department of Justice was unconcerned about local law enforcement (except for the FBI Academy); the problem of Negroes was addressed largely through sporadic efforts to eliminate the poll tax in the South. Parallel to this governmental pattern was an intellectual tradition that held bad housing—or slums generally —to be the "cause" of many of the difficulties one found in our central cities; fix up the housing, it was hoped, and you fixed up the people. It is not surprising that until rather recently, the "urban problem" was thought to be equivalent to whatever conditions the Housing and Home Finance Agency was trying to change—and since it was seeking mostly to change the quality of housing and the use of land, the urban problem was a housing and land-use problem. The principal organized groups that testified before Congress in favor of the urban renewal provisions of the 1949 housing act were the Urban Land Institute and the American Institute of Planners.

Perhaps the most significant change in domestic politics in the last twenty years has been not simply the intensification of federal concern for "the city," but the great broadening of the government's conception of what constitutes the problems of these cities. The Office of Education is spending billions; the Department of Justice has just presided over a major study of crime—primarily urban crime—that probably will result in tens of millions of dollars of federal money being spent on local law enforcement; the HHFA has become the Department of Housing and Urban Development and announced that its principal new policy will be a "Model Cities" program that emphasizes the attainment of social more than housing objectives and in the heart of the central cities rather than in the suburbs; a many-faceted (and necessarily uneven) anti-poverty program has enthusiasts, detractors, and money. When today testimony is heard on "urban programs," there are representatives from civil rights groups, universities, businesses, trade unions, the "New Left," police departments, and almost everyone else. It is becoming hard for a planner or housing specialist to get a word in edgewise.

The many new approaches to central city issues are reflected in the authorship of the eight papers in this volume on the social problems of cities: only one is by a planner, two are by sociologists and three by political scientists, and one each is by an educator and a humanist. The difficulty in writing about the subject is evidenced by the very different styles employed. Housing is measured with respect to quantity, quality (roughly), and occupancy, and thus Bernard Frieden is able to write a systematic and carefully documented account of the changes in the urban housing supply. Migration could be measured carefully, but it is not, and Charles Tilly must estimate (or just simply guess) at some of the crucial variables. We may think we measure crime, but Marvin Wolfgang shows we don't do it very successfully and that our best information comes from small studies—in one city, or part of one city—about which, of course, it is hard to generalize. We are just getting good data on hard-core Negro poverty and social disorganization in a few major cities, and Daniel Moynihan suggests what they reveal. With respect to beauty, systematic knowledge is naturally unavailable and it is hard to imagine how it could be made available; some things not only resist measurement, they would be destroyed by it. John Burchard relies instead on keen perception and an acute and lively taste.

The most important generalization that emerges from these eight papers is that we are not really sure whether or to what extent things are getting better or worse in all our central cities. That there should even be any uncertainty may surprise those who take it for granted that we face an "urban crisis." It is surely not the first time, however, that what appears to be true judging from newspaper headlines and television stories (and even from one's impressions while walking the treets downtown) is no longer so obvious or so simple when one studies systematically and with care the available facts.

Housing, about which we have the best data, is the most clear-cut case. Contrary to popular impression, our urban housing supply is not deteriorating, it is getting better; slums (if by slums one means dilapidated or substandard housing) are not spreading, they are contracting; blight is not a "cancerous growth" in our cities, it is a benign, though irritating and unfortunate, disfigurement. Of course, if by "slums" one means housing that does not appear attractive or is occupied by Negroes, then indeed the "slums" are spreading. But surely we can distinguish between low-income and Negro housing on the one hand and dilapidated or overcrowded housing on the other. There is an overlap, but they are not identical (after all, if you include the elderly poor, three fourths of all persons with incomes of less than $3,000 a year are white) and the worst *housing* problems are *outside* the metropolitan areas (60 percent of all families living in substandard housing in 1960 lived outside the 212 metropolitan areas). From 1950 to 1960, the numbers of substandard dwelling units declined sharply (by about 40 percent) almost everywhere (the number of overcrowded units also declined, but less dramatically), even in New York City, which many people regard as the archetypical "problem city." The gains are both absolute (the number of substandard units) and proportional (the percentage of such units).

Negroes shared in this gain, at least nationally. Within the larger metropolitan areas, however, their gains were only proportional. Apparently Negroes are still migrating to the big cities at such a rate that, though the percentage of them living in substandard housing is going down, the number living in such conditions is not.

This all sounds familiar. One assumes that "naturally" the problem will remain with us as long as uneducated, low-income Negroes with broken families continue to migrate from the rural South to the urban North. Here again, what everyone "knows" may no longer be true. Tilly shows that what evidence can be found indicates that the Negro who migrates to, say, New York City is today likely to be *better off* than the Negro already there. Most migration, he explains, is now from other urban areas and the migrants tend now (unlike in the past) to rank higher in education and occupational status than the Negroes already in the big city. And once in the city, these migrants are *less* likely to be criminals or delinquents and *less* likely to participate in a riot, such as that in Watts. The last point deserves emphasis. Watts was not set aflame by savage country folk who had not learned how to behave in a city or whose exaggerated expectations about the Promised Land were suddenly disappointed; it was set aflame by people who had lived in Watts most of their lives. Over half the juveniles arrested during the riot had been born in California; over three fourths had lived there for over five years.

Such findings—that housing is getting better, that the migrants are getting better—seem to leave us at a loss to explain what common sense tells us with absolute certainty: that things are not all right in Harlem, in Watts, in Detroit, in Newark, or on Chicago's South Side. There have been riots and demonstrations, the welfare rolls are growing, crime and delinquency and violence are commonplace. The rates of crime and delinquency are clearly higher in the big cities than in the small, and highest of all in the most central parts of the central cities. No one seriously doubts that Negro crime rates are higher than white crime rates, though there is much doubt and disagreement as to why this is true and the extent to which it is true. By the same token, it is far from clear exactly what crimes are in fact increasing in rate and what increasing only because we are reporting more or recording such reports more accurately. Wolfgang shows that the centers of our large cities have always had crime rates higher than the rest of the city, no matter who lived there, and that nationally, at least, the rates for the most serious crimes—murder, aggravated assault, and robbery—increased only slightly between 1960 and 1965, though crimes against property (burglary and theft) increased substantially. Finally, since the most common crimes—thefts—are crimes of youth, there is a question whether the higher rates of such crimes reflect a deterioration in moral standards or, what is just as likely, a great increase in the proportion of young people in our population, especially in our urban Negro population.

With all these qualifications, Wolfgang does not argue that big-city crime is a myth or that everything can be put down to "reporting errors." What he does show is that we know less about crime than we think we know; that violent crime occurs primarily among acquaintances and neighbors and among people of the same race and economic class; that most juvenile crime—even most juvenile "gang" crime—involves theft and not violence; that most delinquency cures itself as the boy grows older; and that although there may be some promising clues, nobody yet really has any sound, tested ideas about how to significantly reduce the amount of crime and delinquency. Wolfgang wrote this before the President's Commission on Law Enforcement and Administration of Justice issued its report, but that report, now available, confirms Wolfgang in most respects.

Urban crime seems to be an intractable and serious problem of unknown dimensions. Every central city businessman has had to cope with salesgirls who are assaulted, newspaper delivery boys who are robbed, property that is stolen or destroyed, windows that are smashed, and bad checks that are written. And now riots. Why, in the freest and most prosperous society in the world and in a city where housing is getting better, poverty declining, and migrants improving in quality, should all this be happening? Why can't something be done?

Good questions. Anybody who has read this book expecting to find the answers has already been disappointed. One possible explanation, and one for which we have suggestive but not conclusive evidence, is offered by Moynihan. In effect, he says, certain parts of our central cities have become human cesspools into which our worst human problems have flowed and in which, through some kind of bacterial action, a self-sustaining reaction has been created that is making matters worse despite the general improvement going on everywhere else. The better-off in-migrants avoid these places or get out as quickly as they can; anyone who manages to survive the social chaos of these places moves out; and people who have failed to make it elsewhere in the city move in. The lot of society is improving, the lot of Negroes generally is improving (and in opinion polls they believe it is improving), but in a few strategically located ghettos things are unaccountably going from bad to worse.

Moynihan argues, on the basis of evidence only recently available, that poverty is primarily a Negro (and Puerto Rican and Mexican) problem, that close to a majority of all poor people now live in our metropolitan areas (not so long ago, most poverty was rural), and that there is an unmistakable association between being poor and living in a large, broken family. In absolute terms, the poor are becoming less numerous —during the recent period of prosperity, millions of families have left the (arbitrarily defined) poverty category and, if the prosperity continues, many more will leave in the future. But in the most central portions of certain key cities—New York, Cleveland, Los Angeles, and others—things have become worse. The soaring gross national product, otherwise the best cure for poverty, has not reached the core of Harlem, Watts, or Hough.

Perhaps this situation does not represent a worsening of matters. Perhaps it is only a symptom of how fast things are getting better. The rates of unemployment and of female-headed households are going up and the median family income is going down in these places, one might conjecture, because the better-off Negroes are moving out at a fast clip, leaving behind those not so well off and thereby depressing the statistics. The *people* are not worse off, only the *area* is. Moynihan would no doubt concede that this accounts for part of it, but no one can say for certain that it accounts for all of it. And in any case, whether it is a people or an area that is deteriorating, the effect seems to be the same: the incidence of violence and the incidence of social disorganization are increasing simultaneously and in the same places. Those two facts may not be related, but it would take a brave man indeed to turn his back on the issue simply out of the *belief* that they are not associated.

The relationship between these trends and the recent wave of riots and rampages is perhaps the most puzzling problem of all. Not all the riots are the same; as Edward Banfield points out, some fundamental distinctions, based on motives, must be made among the many disorders we have lately experienced. Perhaps because these distinctions are rarely made, perhaps because a riot is a complex and dramatic event, such occurrences have become a kind of urban Rorschach test—people see in them primarily what they want to see and then proclaim as the "cause" whatever state of affairs is consistent with the observer's pet project. Advocates of jobs find unemployment to be the cause; proponents of increased police power find lawlessness and even conspiracies the cause; persons committed to residential integration find segregation and high-density ghetto living the cause; those who dislike the way political power is currently distributed find "alienation" and the need for self-determination to be the cause. Because riots have occurred in so many cities and will undoubtedly occur in more, it is almost impossible to test any of these explanations—for every riot that has erupted in a city with the conditions alleged to be the cause (high unemployment, "handcuffed" police departments, high-density ghettos, unresponsive local governments), another has occurred in a city with the opposite conditions (little unemployment, tough police, low-density populations, liberal and sympathetic governments).

Banfield suggests, as one answer to this paradox, the possibility that the immediate cause of tension and disorder may be less the objective conditions prevailing in the city than the subjective states to be found among both the rioters and those who predict, explain, or react to them. Except for those with clearly racial or political causes (though important, they are a minority of all recent disorders), most disturbances have been more "rampages" than riots—the excesses of (primarily) lower-class young males who are invariably rebellious, defiant, and desirous of immediate gratification whatever may be their color. Throughout history, large concentrations of such persons in the city have produced disorders; today, such persons happen to be Negro, but it is (in Banfield's view) their class more than their race that produces the rampages. But because the youth involved may assert their racial identity as a justification for such riots, and because observers may accept such assertions at face value, race may become the "cause" (or at least a contributing factor) whatever the initial impulse. Thinking it is so may make it so, at least up to a point. But such a "cause," if removed, would not produce a cure—if all

Negroes were turned white tomorrow, Banfield predicts, there would still be a large number of riots and rampages.

The culture of lower-class youth is not easily or quickly changed, especially if race complicates the matter. "Crash programs" are likely to be ineffective, or at worst to encourage persons to believe that violence is a useful way to get attention. The only institution by which society can deal over the long haul with the culture and morale of its citizens is the school system. Yet as Sizer points out, the U.S. Office of Education, in its massive study of educational opportunities (the so-called Coleman Report), found that most of the variation in a child's performance in the public schools is connected with his family background. In short, it is not necessary to decide whether the disorganized, impoverished family *directly* creates and sustains a "culture of poverty" or whether it does so only indirectly by adversely affecting the child's prospects for educational success; in one step or two, the condition of the family is strongly associated with a person's life chances and, by and large, the damage is done before the child ever gets into school.

This is a major challenge to public policy, if only because this country has been so careful to leave the family alone that it has avoided even thinking about it. The state shall not cross the threshold of even the humblest home; it may tear it down, but it may not interfere in its internal affairs. Furthermore, no one knows how to put a "good" family together by plan or how to keep a good one together that has been made so by happy accident. Our statesmen properly approach the subject with unease and uncertainty.

Moynihan suggests two initial steps that might help matters without interfering in things that are no concern of the government: family allowances to ease the financial burden of having large numbers of children without requiring that the father first desert the family; and widely available birth control assistance and information to reduce the number of families that have large numbers of children without intending to. These are not unprecedented steps; the allowances, at least, are a regular feature of the social services of most modern nations.

These are not the only ways of addressing even the low-income aspect of poverty. Other possibilities include rent supplements, discussed by Frieden (to make possible the renting of decent housing on the private market), as well as the negative income tax (that is, a guaranteed minimum annual income), and a public works program (to provide unskilled and semiskilled jobs in areas where no such jobs are available from private industry). Careful study will be necessary to select which method, or which combination of methods, is the best supplement to continued national prosperity—and the latter, of course, is the *sine qua non*.

But dealing with the shortage of money is not the only way of dealing with poverty. Traditionally, we have dealt with it by providing services to people who had somehow failed to earn enough. It is not likely that we can ever abandon such methods completely. But it is increasingly apparent that there is a very real limit to our ability to supply services and advice in a way that helps many people accomplish very much. Perhaps if we were endowed with limitless wisdom and infinite patience we could understand better what people need and persuade them to remedy those needs, but wisdom and patience are in short supply and meanwhile we are expected to "do something" right now. The schools are the institution through which our most important social service is dispensed, and as of now nobody has devised a sure-fire formula for making them significantly better. As the Coleman Report referred to by Sizer indicates, we can't even say now that one school is substantially better than another in terms of its output or, if it is, how it got that way. This does not mean that schools are of no value. If we had none at all we would be worse off, of that there can be little doubt. And if we changed radically the level of resources put into the schools—if pupil-teacher ratios were five-to-one instead of thirty-to-one, perhaps significant measurable differences would appear. A great deal of experimentation is necessary and none of it will be cheap. However education in central city slums can be improved, one can be absolutely certain that the methods will not cost less than present ones.

But besides the *income* strategy and the *services* strategy for dealing with poverty, there is still a third—the strategy of *dispersal*. Frieden alludes to this when he suggests that perhaps housing for low-income families is best provided in or near areas where the inhabitants are offered a wider range of living styles and given a guarantee that the political system will not deprive them of resources without depriving as well those who are advantaged. Scattering the sites for public housing, bussing ghetto children out to suburban schools, creating metropolitan-wide school systems, facilitating the movement of slum dwellers out to take jobs now being created on the periphery of the metropolitan area—these are all variants on the dispersal strategy. It is not a wholly new strategy—the government, through home insurance programs, has always helped empty out the central cities—but it is a radical strategy in that it seeks to achieve a social objective by deliberately arranging people around the landscape, not letting them decide entirely for themselves with whom they wish to live and go to school. It challenges squarely the concept of the modern suburb as a semi-private corporation with a state charter, which seeks to create and protect a distinctive way of life on behalf of its members, with little thought for the effects of that corporate behavior on non-members. Finally, dispersal seeks to meet the problem of low educational achievement by giving slum children the next best thing to a strong family of their own—acquaintanceship with other children who do have strong families and a keen desire to achieve.

If people object to pumping millions of dollars into the central cities, the alternative—unless we are to do nothing—is to draw the people out of the central slums and put them in new environments. Looked at another way, if we wish to maintain both our suburban life styles and our concern for the future of the central city, it is going to cost us a lot of money. Having your cake and eating it, too, is rarely accomplished but when accomplished, expensive. Those who oppose dispersal have a special need to think harder about incomes and services.

These papers have not been written so as to arrive at a conclusion among these three strategies—maintaining incomes, providing services, dispersing people. The authors themselves are not likely to agree even if they were asked. And frankly we know very little about the likely consequences of any of the three strategies. About one thing, however, I suspect all the authors are agreed: if one is going to talk about "urban problems," one must necessarily and primarily talk about the social issues to which these strategies are directed.

CONTRIBUTORS

Edward C. Banfield is Henry Lee Shattuck Professor of Urban Government at Harvard University. He teaches courses in public administration and political theory as well as urban government and affairs. Before coming to Harvard he was Associate Professor of Political Science at the University of Chicago, and previously had worked for the United States government with the Forest Service and the Farm Security Administration. His publications include *Government Project* (1955), *The Moral Basis of a Backward Society* (1958), *Political Influence* (1961), *Big City Politics* (1965), *Politics, Planning and the Public Interest* (with Martin Meyerson, 1955), *Government and Housing in Metropolitan Areas* (with Morton Grodzins, 1958), *City Politics* (with James Q. Wilson, 1963), and *Boston: The Job Ahead* (with Martin Meyerson, 1966); he edited *Urban Government* (1961 and 1968). He received his Ph.D. from the University of Chicago in 1952.

John E. Burchard, architect, urbanist, and historian, is Dean Emeritus of the School of Humanities and Social Sciences and Senior Lecturer at M.I.T. His publications include *The Evolving House* (with A. F. Bemis, 1932), *The Dilemmas of General Education* (1953), *The Urban Aesthetic* (1957), *The Architecture of America* (with A. Bush-Brown, 1961), and *The Voice of the Phoenix* (1966); he was the editor of *Mid-Century* (1949), and *The Historian and the City* (with Oscar Handlin, 1963).

Bernard J. Frieden is Professor of City Planning at M.I.T. and a member of the Joint Center for Urban Studies of M.I.T. and

Harvard. He has been a consultant to the Department of Housing and Urban Development and other federal agencies and was formerly editor of the *Journal of the American Institute of Planners.* He is the author of *The Future of Old Neighborhoods* (1964); *Metropolitan America: Challenge to Federalism* (a report of the Advisory Commission on Intergovernmental Relations, 1966); editor of *Urban Planning and Social Policy* (with Robert Morris, 1968); and of *Shaping an Urban Future: Essays in Memory of Catherine Bauer Wurster* (with William W. Nash, 1969). He received his Ph.D. in city planning from M.I.T. in 1962.

John F. Kain is Professor of Economics at Harvard University and a member of the Joint Center for Urban Studies. Previously he taught at the U.S. Air Force Academy, and from 1961 to 1962 worked as a research economist for the RAND Corporation. He is currently a part-time staff member of the National Bureau of Economic Research (NBER), a consultant to the Department of Housing and Urban Development and also to the RAND Corporation, and in the past has been a consultant to the White House Panel on Civil Technology, the Denver Research Institute, and the Commonwealth Bureau of Roads in Australia. His writings include *The Urban Transportation Problem* (with John R. Meyer and Martin Wohl, 1965), *Race and Poverty: The Economics of Discrimination* (1969), and many articles and papers. He received his Ph.D. in 1961 from the University of California.

John R. Meyer is Professor of Economics at Yale University. He is also currently President of the National Bureau of Economic Research and is and has been a consultant to several government and other organizations, among them the Council of Economic Advisers, the Department of Housing and Urban Development, the Agency for International Development on Housing and Urban Planning Problems in Latin America, and the Governments of Colombia and Israel. His publications include *The Investment Decision: An Empirical Inquiry* (with Edwin Kuh, 1957), *Economics of Competition in the Transportation Industry* (with M. J. Peck, C. Zwick, and J. Stenason, 1959), *Investment Decisions, Economic Forecasting and Public Policy* (with Robert Glauber, 1964), *The Economics of Slavery and Other Essays on the Quantitative Study of Economic History* (with A. Conrad, 1965), and *The Urban Transportation Problem* (with M. Wohl and J. Kain, 1965). He received his Ph.D. from Harvard University in 1955.

Daniel P. Moynihan is Assistant to the President for Urban Affairs. He is on leave as Professor of Education and Urban Politics at Harvard University and also a member of the Institute of Politics of the John F. Kennedy School of Government. He was formerly Director of the Joint Center for Urban Studies of M.I.T. and Harvard. From 1955 to 1958 he served in a variety of capacities under the Governor of New York State. In 1961 he joined the United States Department of Labor, becoming Assistant Secretary of Labor in 1963. He has been Chairman of the Secretary's Advisory Committee on Traffic Safety under the Department of Health, Education, and Welfare, Chairman of the American Academy of Arts and Sciences Seminar on Poverty, and is Vice-Chairman of the President's Temporary Commission on Pennsylvania Avenue. Immediately before coming to Harvard, he held a fellowship at the Center for Advanced Studies at Wesleyan University. He has also taught at Syracuse University, Cornell, and Russell Sage College. His publications include *Beyond the Melting Pot* (with Nathan Glazer, 1963), *Passenger Car Design and Highway Safety* (with James Goddard and others, 1962), *The Negro Challenge to the Business Community* (with Eli Ginzberg and others, 1964), *The Assault on Poverty* (with R. M. MacIver and others, 1965), *Poverty in America* (with Margaret S. Gordon and others, 1965); and *Maximum Feasible Misunderstanding* (1969); he is the editor of *The Defences of Freedom: The Public Papers of Arthur J. Goldberg* (1966), and of *On Understanding Poverty: Perspectives from the Social Sciences* (1969). He holds a Ph.D. from the Fletcher School of International Law and Diplomacy at Tufts University.

Dick Netzer is Dean of the Graduate School of Public Administration at New York University, where he was formerly Head of the All-University Department of Economics. From 1948 to 1960 he was with the Federal Reserve Bank of Chicago, of which he became assistant vice president, and since 1960 he has been an economic consultant to the Regional Plan Association of New York. He is the author of *Economics of the Property Tax* (1966), "Federal, State and Local Finance in a Metropolitan Context," in *Issues in Urban Economics* (1968), principal author of *Financing Government in New York City* (1966), and co-author of *Public Services in Older Cities* (1968) and *Economic Aspects of Suburban Development* (1969). He received his Ph.D. from Harvard University in 1952.

Roger Revelle is Richard Saltonstall Professor of Population Policy in the Harvard School of Public Health and Director of the Harvard Center for Population Studies. He was formerly Director of the Scripps Institution of Oceanography, and University Dean

f Research for the state-wide University of California. From 1961
• 1963 he was Science Adviser to the Secretary of the Interior.
lis recent articles include "Atmospheric Carbon Dioxide," an
ppendix to *Restoring the Quality of our Environment* (with
/. Broecker, H. Craig, C. D. Keeling, and J. Smagorinsky, 1965),
Can Man Domesticate Himself?" (1966), "Outdoor Recreation
ı a Hyper-Productive Society" (1967), and "Population and Food
upplies: The Edge of the Knife" (1966). He received his Ph.D.
om the University of California in 1936.

Theodore R. Sizer is Dean of the Faculty of Education at Har-
ard University. He has taught in secondary schools in both this
ountry and Australia, and since 1959 has been on the faculty of
ıe School of Education at Harvard. He is the author of *Secondary
chools at the Turn of the Century* (1964), *The Age of the Acad-
mies (1964), and the editor of *Religion and Public Education*
1967). He received his Ph.D. from Harvard University in 1961.

Charles Tilly is Professor of Sociology and History at the Uni-
ersity of Michigan. He has taught and held research positions at
ıe University of Delaware, Princeton, M.I.T., Harvard, the Uni-
ersity of Toronto and the Center for Advanced Study in the Be-
avioral Sciences. He is a member of the editorial board of *French
1istorical Studies* and of the Central Committee of the Behavioral
ıd Social Science Survey. His work deals mainly with the social
onsequences of urbanization. His publications include *The Vendée*
1964), *Migration to an American City* (1965), and *Race and Resi-
ence in Wilmington* (with Wagner Jackson and Barry Kay, 1965).
le received his Ph.D. from Harvard University in 1958.

Marvin E. Wolfgang is Professor and Chairman of the Depart-
ıent of Sociology at the University of Pennsylvania and is cur-
ently a Fellow of Churchill College and the Institute of Criminol-
gy, University of Cambridge and a member of the President's
Commission on Obscenity and Pornography, the Advisory Com-
ıittee on Reform of the Federal Criminal Law, and the Panel on
ocial Indicators, and is also Director of Research of the National
Commission on the Causes and Prevention of Violence and Asso-
iate Secretary General of the International Society of Criminology.
Ie was formerly President of the American Society of Criminology
ınd Associate Editor of the Annals of the American Academy of
Political and Social Science, and was also a consultant to the Presi-
lent's Commission on Law Enforcement and Administration of
ustice. His publications include *Patterns in Criminal Homicide*

(1958); *The Measurement of Delinquency* (with T. Sellin, 1964); *Crime and Race* (1964); *Studies in Homicide* (1967); and *The Subculture of Violence* (with F. Ferracuti, 1967). He received his Ph.D. in 1955 from the University of Pennsylvania.

INDEX